Nineteenth-Century Women at the Movies:
Adapting Classic Women's Fiction to Film

edited by

Barbara Tepa Lupack

Bowling Green State University Popular Press
Bowling Green, OH 43403

"Feminism in Brontë's *Jane Eyre* and Its Film Versions" originally appeared as "Feminism in Brontë's Novel and Its Film Versions" in *The English Novel and the Movies,* edited by Michael Klein and Gillian Parker (New York: Ungar, 1981), and is reprinted here by permission of the author, E. Ann Kaplan.

"Adapting Jane Austen's *Northanger Abbey:* Catherine Morland as Gothic Heroine" appeared in a slightly different version, as "Catherine Morland: Gothic Heroine After All?" in *Jane Austen Goes to the Movies,* a special issue of *Topic: A Journal of the Liberal Arts* 48 (1997): 22-30, and is reprinted here by permission of the author, Marilyn Roberts, and of the volume editor, Linda V. Troost.

"Filming the Nineteenth Century: *Little Women*" is a revised and expanded version of "Filming the Nineteenth Century: *The Secret Garden* and *Little Women,*" which originally appeared in *ATQ* N.S. 10:4 (Dec. 1996): 273-92. Reprinted by permission of The University of Rhode Island.

Portions of "Re-creating the Monster: Frankenstein and Film" first appeared as part of a longer work by Martin Tropp, *Mary Shelley's Monster: The Story of Frankenstein* (Boston: Houghton Mifflin Co., 1974). Permission to reprint is granted by the author and by Houghton Mifflin Company. All rights reserved.

Copyright 1999 © Bowling Green State University Popular Press
Library of Congress Cataloging-in-Publication Data
Nineteenth-century women at the movies : adapting classic women's fic
    tion to film / edited by Barbara Tepa Lupack.
        p.   cm.
    Includes bibliographical references and filmographies.
    ISBN 0-87972-805-1 (clothbound). -- ISBN 0-87972-806-X (pbk.)
    1. Film adaptations--History and criticism. 2. Motion pictures and
literature. 3. English fiction--Women authors Film and video adapata-
tions. 4. English fiction--19th century Film and video adaptations.
    5. American fiction--Women authors Film and video adaptations.
    6. American fiction--19th century Film and video adaptations.
    7. Lupack, Barbara Tepa.
PN1997.85.N56   1999
791.43'6--dc21   99-38681
                                                                       CIP

PN1997
.85
.N56
1999

Cover design by Dumm Art

For Al,

Who makes me believe in happy endings

CONTENTS

Acknowledgments   *ix*

Introduction   1
    Barbara Tepa Lupack

1   Re-creating the Monster: *Frankenstein* and Film   23
    Martin Tropp

2   The Importance of Being Married: Adapting *Pride
and Prejudice*   78
    Ronnie Jo Sokol

3   The Multiplex Heroine: Screen Adaptations of *Emma*   106
    Tom Hoberg

4   Adapting Jane Austen's *Northanger Abbey:*
Catherine Morland as Gothic Heroine   129
    Marilyn Roberts

5   Her First and Her Last: Austen's *Sense and Sensibility,
Persuasion,* and Their Screen Adaptations   140
    Tom Hoberg

6   Sympathy for the Devil: The Problem of Heathcliff
in Film Versions of *Wuthering Heights*   167
    Lin Haire-Sargeant

7   Feminism in Brontë's *Jane Eyre* and Its Film Versions
(with a new *Postscript* by E. Ann Kaplan)   192
    Kate Ellis and E. Ann Kaplan

8   *Uncle Tom* and American Popular Culture:
Adapting Stowe's Novel to Film   207
    Barbara Tepa Lupack

9   Filming the Nineteenth Century: *Little Women*   257
    Shirley Marchalonis

10   Love on the Algerian Sands: Reviving Cigarette
in *Under Two Flags*   275
    Victoria Szabo

11   George Eliot on the American Screen   299
    George V. Griffith

Contributors   319

ACKNOWLEDGMENTS

My thanks to all of the contributors in this volume, whose work afforded me new insights into familiar and favorite novels and films. I am especially grateful to E. Ann Kaplan, not only for allowing me to reprint her classic essay on feminism in *Jane Eyre* (co-written with Kate Ellis) but also for adding a *Postscript* that suggests interesting new approaches to Brontë's novel and its adaptations.

Several of the essays in this volume evolved from papers and discussions at the national meetings of the Popular Culture and American Culture Associations. Pat Browne and Ray B. Browne have been tireless in their efforts to foster the study of popular culture and to make the scholarly community aware of its scope and significance. Pat Browne, moreover, has been extremely supportive of the series on adapting fiction to film that I am editing and of which this volume is a part.

I would also like to thank a number of people who helped me with various aspects of this volume. Russell Peck kindly assisted me in the preparation of several stills. Linda V. Troost, author of a special issue of *Topic* titled *Jane Austen Goes to the Movies,* generously shared material on Austen adaptations and suggested an essay that is reprinted in this volume. Terry Geeskin, of the Museum of Modern Art Film Stills Archive, was gracious and expeditious in locating appropriate silent film stills. And Christy Schurmann, once again, offered her expertise and technical assistance.

The University of Rochester's Rush Rhees Library provided me with numerous materials and services. The George Eastman House/ International Museum of Photography and Film, particularly Becky Simmons, facilitated my research. At the Eastman House, Rachel Stuhlman, Ed Stratmann, Philip Carli, and Jackie Salerno also lent assistance.

Above all, I am grateful to Alan Lupack, whose insights are always keen and whose judgments, both personal and professional, I value beyond measure.

INTRODUCTION

Barbara Tepa Lupack

"Cinema began in wonder," notes Susan Sontag, "the wonder that reality can be transcribed with such immediacy" (60). And, since the beginnings of cinema, much of that wonder and that reality has come from the literature on which so many films are based.

The first to exploit the medium of film as a means of personal expression was revolutionary French film artist and magician Georges Méliès; he was also the first to adapt a work of literature to the screen. Méliès' *A Trip to the Moon* (1902), based on Jules Verne's *From the Earth to the Moon,* lampooned the scientific and mechanical interests of the new century by wittily depicting the lunar dream world of the professors and the futuristic hopes of some of the scientific societies (Jacobs 27). For years afterwards, Méliès continued to surprise moviegoers with similar "fantastic fantasies"; his best-known works included titles such as *Gulliver's Travels* (1902); *Robinson Crusoe* (1902); *The Damnation of Faust* (1903), based on Berlioz's celebrated song poem; *The Legend of Rip Van Winkle* (1905); and *Twenty Thousand Leagues Under the Sea* (1907).

Like Méliès and other French and Italian filmmakers who looked to literature (especially to the novels of Dickens, Balzac, Hugo, Bulwer-Lytton, and Sienkiewicz) for story material, Americans began turning routinely to novels as well as to poems, plays, and short stories. Edwin S. Porter, generally acknowledged today as the father of the story film and credited with the introduction of the principles of film editing, became a dominant figure in the industry with innovative works such as *The Life of an American Fireman* (1903); *The Great Train Robbery* (1903), which established Porter as the leading filmmaker of his day; and *Uncle Tom's Cabin* (1903), the largest and most expensive picture made until that time in America. (Produced for Edison, *Uncle Tom's Cabin* ran the extraordinary length of 1,100 feet and included fourteen scenes and a prologue and, according to its own advertisement, departed "from the methods of dissolving one scene into another by inserting announcements and brief descriptions" [Jacobs 42].) After leaving Edison, Porter pioneered with Adolph Zukor's Famous Players; directed the company's first motion picture, *The Count of Monte Cristo;* and went on to make other features, such as *The Prisoner of Zenda*—though his later work did not fully deliver on his early promise.

To meet the tremendous demand for stories, other moviemakers increasingly turned their attention to literature and the stage. One-reel screen presentations soon abounded, including, among many others, such titles as *Parsifal, The Lady or the Tiger, Ben Hur, As You Like It, Hiawatha, Evangeline, Dr. Jekyll and Mr. Hyde, The Merry Widow, Monsieur Beaucaire, The Scarlet Letter, The Last of the Mohicans, The Three Musketeers, Treasure Island, Martin Chuzzlewit, The Merchant of Venice, Alice's Adventures in Wonderland,* and *A Curious Dream.* The adaptation of fiction and plays was quickened by the censorship attacks that flared up in 1907-1908,[1] since producers believed that material taken from decorous literary works would ensure a kind of substantiveness and respectability that would discourage critics from attacking their productions.

The most influential film artist of his day and perhaps of all film history, D. W. Griffith also looked to literature, both high and low, to help forge the distinctive language of American film. Further refining the art of Méliès and Porter through his own techniques, a number of which were inspired by his "beloved Dickens,"[2] Griffith adapted works by writers such as Jack London, George Eliot, Shakespeare, Hood, Tolstoy, Poe, O. Henry, Maupassant, Stevenson, and Tennyson; in one year alone, the hundred or more pictures that he produced included *The Taming of the Shrew, The Song of the Shirt, Edgar Allan Poe, The Cricket on the Hearth, The Necklace,* and *The Lover's Tale.* These earliest pictures were followed by important films like *Pippa Passes; Ramona;* a remake of *Enoch Arden* (the first "two-reeler"); *Orphans of the Storm;* and, of course, his stunning *The Birth of a Nation,* based on Thomas Dixon's racist bestseller *The Clansman* and now hailed as the first film classic.

Griffith, in turn, was followed by other talented, if lesser known, men with a keen literary appreciation: Sidney Olcott, whose spectacular *Ben Hur* (1907) made a huge amount of money for its manufacturer (and, notably, forced the resolution of the copyright problem when the courts determined, in 1912, that literary rights existed in all filmed works); Frank Lloyd, renowned for his screen adaptations of literary classics (*The Gentleman from Indiana, A Tale of Two Cities, David Garrick*); John Stuart Robertson, brought to prominence with his *Dr. Jekyll and Mr. Hyde* (1920); James Cruze, remembered for satires like *Ruggles of Red Gap* (1923) and *Beggar on Horseback* (1923), adapted from a stage play by the same name; and the foreign invasion, particularly Sergei Eisenstein, the Soviet director whose brief tenure in Hollywood yielded an early script for *An American Tragedy,* and Sweden's Victor Seastrom, singled out in 1927 as one of Hollywood's top ten directors, largely because of the success of his adaptation the previous year of *The Scarlet Letter.*[3]

Early movies were met with praise not only for their innovation but also for the promise that they offered in educating their audiences. In fact, critic Stephen Bush, writing in *The Moving Picture World* in 1911, suggested that the very mission of the new medium of the motion picture might be to introduce literary classics to the masses:

It is the masterpiece of the ages that especially invites filming, and the reason for it is very plain. An epic that has pleased and charmed many generations is most likely to stand the test of cinematographic reproduction. . . . After all, the word "classic" has some meaning. It implies the approval of the best people in the most enlightened times. The merits of a classic subject are nonetheless certain because known and appreciated by comparatively few men. It is the business of the moving picture to make them known to all. (qtd. in Boyum 4)

Jack London likewise believed that motion pictures could batter down "the barriers of poverty and environment" and provide "universal education." "The greatest minds," he wrote in *Paramount Magazine* (1915), "have delivered their messages through the book or the play. The motion picture spreads it to the screen where all can read and understand—and enjoy."

Even after silent film gave way to sound, film adaptation remained popular—so much so, in fact, that in "The Evolution of the Language of Film," André Bazin observed with some overstatement that "the filmmaker [of the 1930s and 40s] . . . is, at last, the equal of the novelist" (40). But it reached some kind of zenith in 1939, when nearly every film competing for the Academy Awards was an adaptation—*Of Mice and Men; Goodbye, Mr. Chips; The Wizard of Oz; Wuthering Heights;* and *Gone with the Wind*—and when even the winner of the Oscar for best short subject was an adaptation, Walt Disney's version of Hans Christian Andersen's "The Ugly Duckling." In *Film & Literature* (1977), Morris Beja writes that, since the inception of the Academy Awards in 1927-28, "more than three-fourths of the awards for 'best picture' have gone to adaptations; and of those, about three-fourths were based on either novels or short stories." The figures would be roughly the same for the New York Film Critics Award for "'best motion picture,' which began in 1935" (78). Aljean Harmetz's count is comparable: "of the 56 movies [as of 1984] that have won Academy Awards as best picture of the year," she reports, "23 have been adapted from novels" (17). And George Bluestone, noting that no precise record has been adequately kept, estimated in his important study of *Novels into Film* (1957) that between 17 and 50 percent of total studio productions are "filmed novels" (3). Adaptation continues to be a lively art today, as even the most cursory glance at Hollywood and independent films demonstrates. *The Cider House Rules, Beloved, The Sweet Hereafter, The Ice Storm, L. A. Confidential, A Thousand Acres, Oscar and Lucinda, The Butcher Boy, The Horse Whisperer, Cousin Bette,* and *Snow Falling on Cedars* are but a few of the novels recently adapted for the screen.

Fiction by women in particular has provided some of the most interesting and some of the best sources for Hollywood's story ideas. From the once popular—and now largely forgotten—works of Elinor Glyn, Mary Roberts Rinehart, and Kathleen Winsor to the engaging, often quirky, tales of Francine Prose and Terry McMillan, fiction by women has afforded insights into society and character and given producers and directors a wealth of filmable material.[4] *The Good Earth* (1937; dir. Sidney Franklin), for instance, re-created in detail Pearl Buck's mammoth novel about the ways in which greed ruins the lives of a simple Chinese farming couple. The film, which won Oscars for actress Luise Rainer as the long-suffering wife (opposite Paul Muni) and for its screenplay, was—and still is—remarkable for its special effects.[5] *The Yearling* (1946; dir. Clarence Brown), based on Marjorie Kinnan Rawlings' sensitive tale of a boy attached to a young deer, was exquisitely filmed in Technicolor on location in Florida. Its excellent cast included Gregory Peck, Jane Wyman, Claude Jarman, Jr., Chill Wills, Forrest Tucker, and June Lockhart; and the film (remade less effectively in 1994 as a television movie by actress Jean Smart) won Oscars for Cinematography and Art Direction and a special Oscar for newcomer Jarman. *Gentleman's Agreement* (1947; dir. Elia Kazan), a triple Oscar winner based on Laura Z. Hobson's novel and starring Gregory Peck, was among the first attempts by Hollywood to address anti-Semitism as a social problem.[6] *Giant* (1956; dir. George Stevens), a near-legendary epic based on Edna Ferber's novel about two generations of Texans, starred Rock Hudson, Elizabeth Taylor, and James Dean in perhaps their best career performances and won an Oscar for director Stevens.[7] *To Kill a Mockingbird* (1962; dir. Robert Mulligan) focused on a Southern lawyer defending a black man accused of rape who tries to explain the proceedings to his children and their friends. An outstanding adaptation by Horton Foote of Harper Lee's novel, the film earned Oscars for both Foote and for actor Gregory Peck and is now considered a cinema classic. Katherine Ann Porter's *Ship of Fools* (1965; dir. Stanley Kramer), despite moments of soap opera, was a penetrating drama that won two

Academy Awards and included in its cast Vivien Leigh, in her last film role, as a disillusioned divorcée; Oskar Werner and Simone Signoret, as illicit lovers; and Lee Marvin, as a punchy baseball player.[8] *Looking for Mr. Goodbar* (1977; dir. Richard Brooks), a flawed adaptation of Judith Rossner's novel about female independence, featured a superb performance by Diane Keaton. While it shocked some viewers, the film nonetheless raised important questions about failed 1960s ideologies and about what E. Ann Kaplan called "the greater threat that the idea of female liberation still held for patriarchy in the mid-70s" (*Women and Film* 75). Triple-Oscar-winning *Coming Home* (1978; dir. Hal Ashby), based on Nancy Dowd's story "Buffalo Girls," depicted the effects of the Vietnam War on people at home; but the screenplay recast the central character Sally's political and feminist awakening by turning it into a conventional love story (and, in Dowd's words, "a male supremacist-film: men choose between ideas, and women choose between men"[9]). *Ordinary People* (1980; dir. Robert Redford), which won Oscars for best film and best director, illustrated the dynamics of a family in crisis, albeit by focusing on male perspectives and affording a shallow presentation of female characters, especially the villainized matriarch Beth Jarrett (Mary Tyler Moore). *The Color Purple* (1985; dir. Steven Spielberg), a controversial interpretation of Alice Walker's novel about an abused black woman who discovers her own identity, was characterized by numerous rich performances, including the film debut of Oprah Winfrey. *The Joy Luck Club* (1993; dir. Wayne Wang), which—reports Bernard Weinraub (7)—"frightened the movie studios" because "there simply was no precedent for a mainstream movie with an all-Asian cast," surrendered some of the authenticity of Amy Tan's novel by simplifying cultural issues, yet it proved to be a hit. *Interview with the Vampire* (1994; dir. Neil Jordan), a film that successfully traded on the tremendous cult following of Anne Rice and on the appeal of its male stars Tom Cruise and Brad Pitt, deflected the novel's pre-Oedipal search for the mother in favor of a male voyeurism—a surprising and disappointing twist, since Rice herself wrote the film's screenplay. *Waiting to Exhale* (1995; dir. Forest Whitaker), based on Terry McMillan's popular novel and panned by many critics for its shallow characters, particularly its stereotypical portrayal of men, focused on the friendships of four black women; but, like *The Joy Luck Club,* the film crossed ethnic (if not always gender) lines to become a commercial success.

And, of course, *Gone with the Wind* (1939; dir. Victor Fleming), based on Margaret Mitchell's beloved novel (1936) of the Old South, is considered by many to be the best Hollywood film of all time. A gamble in Hollywood terms—David O. Selznick paid Mitchell $50,000 for film rights, a tremendous sum for a first-time author, especially since Selznick International was a fledgling studio for whom the adaptation of Mitchell's work would be only its eighth production—*Gone with the Wind* went on to sweep the 1940 Academy Awards with a record ten Oscars.[10] Despite Mitchell's insistence that *Gone with the Wind* was about how some people "survived these turbulent times and some of them did not" (Molt 1) and that it was not meant to mirror the Depression or other topical events,[11] both the book and the film gripped the popular imagination of Americans who—in the aftermath of one world war and in the stirrings of another—felt the hard times and who admired the character of Scarlett, a survivor who triumphs over death, war, poverty, and the other tragedies that befall her.

Like Margaret Mitchell, who wondered why Selznick should want to adapt her "unfilmable" novel for the screen and who warned him that buying the rights would bring him "no end of headaches,"[12] other women writers of the early twentieth century had reservations about the process and the practice of adaptation.[13] Willa Cather, for instance, was so upset by the way that Hollywood had twice, in 1924 and 1934, mangled her novel *A Lost Lady* (1923) that she eschewed any further contact with the cinema while she lived.[14] Several memorable adaptations of other of her novels, however, have been made in recent years, including two television films of *O Pioneers!* (Hallmark Hall of Fame, with Jessica Lange in her television debut, and *American Playhouse,* with Mary McDonnell). And Cather's beloved classic *My Antonia* (dir. Joseph Sargent), filmed on location in Nebraska, premiered on the USA Channel in March, 1995. Scripted and produced by Victoria Riskin, it made the relationship between Jim Burden (Neil Patrick Harris) and Antonia Shimerda (Elina Löwensohn) more clearly a love story than a profound friendship and truncated the ending a bit, but—as Kay Mills observed—"the sense of the people, the era and the rich but unforgiving land" remained true to Cather's novel (42).

Virginia Woolf likewise distrusted the adaptation process. In "The Movies and Reality" (1926), she argued that alliance between cinema and literature was "unnatural" and "disastrous" to both forms. Books especially would be hurt, she believed, by becoming the "unfortunate victim" as the "parasite" movies preyed on them with "immense rapacity." "All this, which is accessible to words, and to words alone," she wrote, "the cinema must avoid." Yet Woolf's novels have survived the process adaptation surprisingly well. *Mrs. Dalloway* (1997; dir. Marleen Gorris), for example, beautifully played by Vanessa Redgrave in the title role, re-creates "the intensely female, hothouse climate of the novel" and establishes from the outset what the book achieves by indirection: "the suspicion that Mrs. Dalloway's exquisitely constructed world is an easily stormed edifice" (Merkin, "A Film of One's Own" 82). Even the lyricism of Woolf's language is preserved, as the filmic use of voice-over substitutes for the novel's interior monologue. And in *Orlando* (1992), an interpretation of a novel about history and sexuality, time and gender, androgyny and immortality, the director Sally Potter picks up on Woolf's notion of the work as an "escapade in writing" and successfully "conveys the spirit of fun, fantasy and caricature that Woolf applied to her subject" (Glaessner 14).[15]

Although in today's market blockbusters like *Titanic* or *Jurassic Park* have become the cinematic norm, there continues to be an interest in adaptations based on the works of writers of an earlier age, especially the novels of nineteenth-century women. That interest may in part be a reaction to what Sontag has called the "decay of cinema." The reduction of cinema "to assaultive images, and the unprincipled manipulation of images (faster and faster cutting) to make them more attention-grabbing," Sontag writes, "has produced a disincarnated, lightweight cinema that doesn't demand anyone's full attention." The sheer ubiquity of images, which "appear in any size and on a variety of surfaces: on a screen in a theater, on disco walls and on megascreens hanging above sports arenas," has—she concludes—"steadily undermined the standards people once had both for cinema as art and for cinema as popular entertainment" (60).

Dinitia Smith explains the interest in a similar way: "Numbed by brutal action movies aimed at teen-age boys, audiences are hungry for the classics. An aging, educated population wants to escape into the more universal themes of love and family, ambition and power." This educated audience, she continues, "is demanding more complex fare. Many of the new classical works [films based on Austen, James, and Hardy] . . . fill the void for adult entertainment, for women in particular." Smith suggests that the large audience of white middle-class women has been bereft of material for forty years, ever since the demise of Joan Crawford, Bette Davis, and Betty Grable; and that audience is drawn to the "new classics," which are often models of propriety and sumptuous feasts for the eye—"a return to period drama when every inch of skin is covered" and when sex becomes significant again because it is "seen against a society where social decorum rules" (4).

The hallmarks of the "new classic" appear to be not only its emphasis on interesting, well-developed characters, especially strong and surprisingly modern women, but also its solid and timeless plots, particularly love stories and intrigues (which in turn often involve love stories). While these qualities are common to good films of all ages, the new classic seems to combine them in compelling, dramatic, and memorable ways. This is true even of the male novelists who are enjoying renewed popularity. The world of Thomas Hardy, one of the most cinematic nineteenth-century novelists, for instance, is filled with female characters like Bathsheba Everdene and Sue Bridehead, who are assertive yet feminine and therefore unusually contemporary;[16] and Henry James's women, from Daisy Miller to Kate Croy, are also "fascinating bellwethers in the increasing struggle between individual rights and the traditional social order" (Swartley 22).[17]

If "the legacy of the nineteenth-century novel is the twentieth-century film" (Axelrod 204), as Neil Sinyard observed in his *Filming Literature: The Art of Screen Adaptation,* one of the most surprising cinematic trends in the late twentieth century is the fascination of filmmakers as well as audiences with adaptations of the nineteenth-century novel. Nowhere is this trend more evident than in the recent wave of Austen-mania. Jane Austen, quipped Martin Amis, "is hotter than Quentin Tarantino" (Amis 31). Yet, as novelist Fay Weldon, who wrote the screenplay for the 1985 BBC/Australian Broadcasting Company adaptation of Austen's *Pride and Prejudice,* observes, "Austen has little on the surface to recommend her. A spinster lady from the English shires, a vicar's daughter who never left home if she could help it, dead since 1817—no money, no title, no connections—what can she have to offer? Just *herself* and six novels, which in the 1990s have suddenly become the feverish obsession of film makers." Films based on Austen's fiction, however, seem to "have a guaranteed audience in a world increasingly bored by 'Pulp Fiction,' 'True Lies,' and special effects, an audience that would rather sit quietly and look at something nice that is not going to explode and shatter the nerves. Something that you can take the kids to, and hope to educate them just a bit. A little dose of English heritage as an antidote to CNN. See, child, the world isn't all Bosnia, O. J. and Bruce Willis. It's love as well, not to mention personal responsibility, long-term goals and delicacy of response, that kind of stuff" (Weldon H-15). Moreover, adds Weldon, from the filmmaker's perspective, Austen is "safe" because she "is not expensive to make. Small casts, location filming, no special effects, period detail so well mulled over by those who went before you that you hardly need a reference book. . . . [And] no one has to read the book" (Weldon H-15).[18]

There is, however, much more to Austen's popularity, especially the perennial appeal of her themes of "love, courtship and marriage" and her acute "sensitivity to social nuances," all of which resonate especially strongly with "youthful audiences today" (Takahama C6), as well as her exquisite use of language. "It's all about words," suggests Doug

McGrath, who directed one of the versions of *Emma*. "The power comes not from action but from these declarations—what [the characters] say and don't say to each other." Daphne Merkin also points to "the crispness of the dialogue and the essential exteriority of Austen's point of view—the sense that gesture is at least as revealing as intention—which yield to visual transposition" (Merkin, "The Escape Artist" 121).

Above all, though, is Austen's amazing ability to tell anew a very old story. Essentially, her novels are comedies about young couples—Elinor Dashwood and Edward Ferrars (and Marianne Dashwood and Colonel Brandon) in *Sense and Sensibility,* Elizabeth Bennet and Fitzwilliam Darcy in *Pride and Prejudice,* Fanny Price and Edmund Bertram in *Mansfield Park,* Emma Woodhouse and George Knightley in *Emma,* Catherine Morland and Henry Tilney in *Northanger Abbey,* Anne Elliot and Frederick Wentworth in *Persuasion*—finding their way toward a festive conclusion, namely marriage. Yet, as Tom Hoberg, Ronnie Jo Sokol, and Marilyn Roberts demonstrate in their essays in this volume, the appeal of this classic comedic situation makes Austen's work as accessible, as relevant, and as endearing to contemporary film audiences as it has been to generations of readers.

As good, however, as Austen may be, she "can't do everything." And so, according to Peter M. Nichols, filmmakers have also turned "to another estimable hand at the romantic epic, Charlotte Brontë" (77). Brontë's novel *Jane Eyre* is a classic love story, in which the affection between Jane and her former employer Rochester triumphs over circumstance, illness, and social barriers; but, as Kate Ellis and E. Ann Kaplan argue in their classic essay on feminism in *Jane Eyre* and its film versions, updated by Kaplan and reprinted in this volume, it is also a story of the inequalities of patriarchal structures and the ambivalence toward male domination, issues that speak as strongly to contemporary women as to women of Brontë's age.

Like her sister Charlotte, Emily Brontë sought to create a fictional tale of timeless passion; and, in the two-generational story of the Earnshaws and the Lintons, in which the second generation re-enacts and ultimately resolves their parents' drama, Emily succeeded. But, as Lin Haire-Sargeant demonstrates in "Sympathy for the Devil: The Problem of Heathcliff in Film Versions of *Wuthering Heights*" in this volume, Brontë's greatest triumph was the creation of the character of Heathcliff, the brooding and demonic lover whose passion for Cathy outlasts even death. The prototypical hero of Gothic romance, Heathcliff could be malicious and sadistic (he displaces his anger toward Cathy by starving a nest of the lapwings she admires); yet the allure of his evil is as integral to the power of the book as it is to the later film adaptations of it.

As did Austen and the Brontës (including Anne, whose novel *The Tenant of Wildfell Hall* was recently released to excellent critical reviews as a made-for-television movie), Harriet Beecher Stowe achieved a certain timelessness in her best fiction; and Stowe did it by focusing on the timeliest of issues: slavery. Stowe's *Uncle Tom's Cabin* quickly became a part of American popular culture (as a play in the nineteenth and early twentieth centuries, it was called "the world's greatest hit" for the frequency of its performances); but over the years, especially in silent and early film treatments, the novel's themes of the evils of slavery and of the inhumanity of man were downplayed and even lost entirely in the romantic depictions of a glorious South. Nevertheless, as Barbara Tepa Lupack suggests in her essay in this volume, the tremendous popularity of *Uncle Tom's Cabin* in its many productions, like its marked absence from the screen for more than half a century, reveals a great deal about the changing state of race relations and the emerging civil rights movements in the United States and throughout the world.

Similarly, the extant versions of *Little Women* (a 1918 American silent-film version and an earlier British one are now lost) demonstrate not only how Louisa May Alcott's classic story of American girlhood has endured but also how the period piece has been reshaped to reflect contemporary tastes and concerns. In her essay for this volume on Alcott and the filming of the nineteenth century, Shirley Marchalonis analyzes how the social and spiritual philosophies that informed the New England culture in the middle of the nineteenth century have been reinterpreted—and often largely misconstrued—by filmmakers for twentieth-century American audiences.

The many versions of Mary Shelley's classic *Frankenstein,* perhaps the most filmed story in literary history, also provide surprising insights into contemporary cultural concerns, particularly the fear of science and technology gone awry. Of the many forms Shelley's work has taken—translations, adaptations, comics, fumetti, verse, puppetry, musical tapes, stage plays, radio and television programs, parodies, and others—film is the most interesting because, as Martin Tropp suggests in his essay included in this volume on "Re-creating the Monster: *Frankenstein* and Film," it best sustains the myth and fulfills one of the book's own prophecies about the power to "mock the invisible world within its own shadows" (48). Moreover, each filmed version, whether serious, comic, or parodic, allows that myth to be redefined topically.

Like Shelley's *Frankenstein* and Stowe's *Uncle Tom's Cabin,* the works of another nineteenth-century novelist, George Eliot, proved to be especially popular among early filmmakers. Pious and full of picturesque images, Eliot's novels were considered safe entertainment by an emerging film industry still in search of respectability. Only in the past two decades, however, have filmmakers rediscovered Eliot's cinematic potential. But, as George V. Griffith demonstrates in his essay on "George Eliot on the American Screen" that concludes this volume, even recent versions continue to try to tame or ignore Eliot's realist ideology and to tell her stories without her own voice.

Whereas Eliot's realism posed some problems for American film audiences, fiction by "Ouida" (Louise de la Ramée) raised other concerns. The popularity of Ouida's novel, *Under Two Flags,* a hardy perennial of the stage and the basis for two silent films, led to a big budget Hollywood production in the mid 1930s; but that version, while offering a lot of spectacle, de-emphasized a number of the novel's most important themes. In her essay for this volume on "Love on the Algerian Sands: Reviving Cigarette in *Under Two Flags,*" Victoria Szabo discusses the film's downplaying of the central issues of gender identity and sexuality, and she examines the cinematic possibilities inherent in Ouida's work.

As all of the essays included in *Nineteenth-Century Women at the Movies* demonstrate, the nineteenth-century novel—from Austen to the Brontës, from Shelley to Ouida and Eliot, from Alcott to Stowe—continues to draw a wide audience of devoted readers and viewers; and it challenges filmmakers to eschew thin characters and broad violence in favor of fine language, "narratives that reflect the human heart without vulgarity or sentimentality," and "moral standards and manners now driven from our daily lives" (Fields 29). And ultimately, adaptations of nineteenth-century novels by women (to borrow phrases, respectively, from *Frankenstein* and *Jane Eyre*) not only endow those who view them "with perceptions and passions" but also offer an opportunity to revisit classic works with "an original, a vigorous, an expanded mind."

Notes

1. As far back as 1907, notes Lewis Jacobs, the *Chicago Tribune* condemned the nickelodeon for "ministering to the lower passion of children. . . . Proper to suppress them [nickelodeons] at once . . . influence wholly vicious. . . . They cannot be defended. They are hopelessly bad." Declaimed the *Christian Leader* that same year: "A set of revolutionists training for the overthrow of the government could find no surer means than these exhibitions [of early movies]" (63). The chief motive behind such attacks was economic, not ideological: "Movies had suddenly become a competitor of the church" (64). Although George Kleine of Kalem Pictures and other powerful men of early motion pictures fought back, regulation nevertheless became the norm: the first

National Board of Censorship of Motion Pictures (later renamed the National Board of Review) was formed in 1909.

At the heart of the moral and social uneasiness over early movies, writes Robert Sklar in *Movie-Made America* (18), was the fact that movies represented a working class pastime that had appeared without the control—or even the knowledge—of the middle-class guardians of culture. To lessen the uneasiness, according to Joel W. Finler in *The Hollywood Story,* "early film-makers turned to uplifting subjects. They adapted literary and stage works for the screen, and adopted the middle-class values of the period which stressed the sanctity of home and family, embraced Christian values, and were strongly anti-trade union and heavily patriotic" (10).

2. Among the most important of those devices was the close-up, which Griffith introduced in his adaptation of Tennyson's *Enoch Arden.* The device had been employed before, in passing, by Porter in *The Great Train Robbery.* Use of the close-up led to new concepts in the technique of editing, as did Griffith's use of cross-cutting. Another of Griffith's adapted films, *Ramona,* was the first to use "distant views," the model for all later panoramic shots. Joy Gould Boyum suggests that it was the work of Griffith's "beloved [Charles] Dickens" that is "generally credited with inspiring the innovations—the use of the close-up, parallel editing, montage, even the dissolve—which helped earn Griffith the epithet 'father of film techniques'" (3). For a brief discussion of Griffith's innovations, see Thomas and Vivian C. Sobchack's *An Introduction to Film* or Paul O'Dell's *Griffith and the Rise of Hollywood.* For a more complete discussion, see Tom Gunning's *D. W. Griffith and the Origins of American Narrative Film.*

3. Producers as well as directors left their special stamp on Hollywood's literary adaptations. Among them were Pandro S. Berman (*Of Human Bondage*); Samuel Goldwyn (*Dodsworth, Wuthering Heights*); Albert Lewin (*The Good Earth*); Kenneth Macgowan (*Little Women*); Hunt Stromberg (*The Thin Man*); and Darryl F. Zanuck (*Les Misérables*).

4. Among the many other popular or profitable films adapted from novels (or other works) by women are Vicki Baum's *Grand Hotel* (1932; dir. Edmund Goulding), winner of the Best Picture Oscar; Lillian Hellman's "The Children's Hour," released as *These Three* (1936; dir. William Wyler) and remade as *The Children's Hour* (1961; dir. William Wyler); Olive Higgins Prouty's *Stella Dallas* (1937; dir. King Vidor), remade as *Stella* (1990; dir. John Erman); Ellen Glasgow's *In This Our Life* (1942; dir. John Huston); Vera Caspary's *Laura* (1944; dir. Otto Preminger); Pearl Buck's *Dragon Seed* (1944; dir. Jack Conway); Betty Smith's *A Tree Grows in Brooklyn* (1945; dir. Elia Kazan); Mary Jane Ward's *The Snake Pit* (1948; dir. Anatole Litvak); Ayn Rand's *The Fountainhead* (1949; dir. King Vidor); Patricia Highsmith's *Strangers on a Train* (1951; dir. Alfred Hitchcock); Anita Loos' *Gentlemen Prefer Blondes*

(1953; dir. Howard Hawks) and *Gentlemen Marry Brunettes* (1955; dir. Richard Sale); Anya Seton's *Foxfire* (1955; dir. Joseph Pevney); Grace Metalious' *Peyton Place* (1957; dir. Mark Robson), later a hit TV series; Shirley Jackson's *The Bird's Nest,* adapted as *Lizzie* (1957; dir. Hugo Haas), and *The Haunting of Hill House,* adapted as *The Haunting* (1963; dir. Robert Wise); and again as *The Haunting* (1999; dir. Jan de Bont); Mary McCarthy's *The Group* (1966; dir. Sidney Lumet); Carson McCullers' *Reflections in a Golden Eye* (1967; dir. John Huston); Bel Kaufman's *Up the Down Staircase* (1967; dir. Robert Mulligan); Jacqueline Susann's *Valley of the Dolls* (1967; dir. Mark Robson), remade as a television movie (1981); Sue Kaufman's *Diary of a Mad Housewife* (1970; dir. Frank Perry); Joan Didion's *Play It As It Lays* (1972; dir. Frank Perry); Lois Gould's *Such Good Friends* (1972; dir. Otto Preminger); Hannah Green's (a.k.a. Joanne Greenberg) *I Never Promised You a Rose Garden* (1977; dir. Anthony Page); Lillian Hellman's *Pentimento,* released as *Julia* (1977; dir. Fred Zinneman), winner of Oscars for its stars Jason Robards and Vanessa Redgrave and for screenwriting; Alice Childress' *A Hero Ain't Nothing but a Sandwich* (1978; dir. Ralph Nelson); Katherine Mansfield's "Bliss," released as *Girlfriends* (1978; dir. Claudia Weill); Flannery O'Connor's *Wise Blood* (1979; dir. John Huston); Sylvia Plath's *The Bell Jar* (1979; dir. Larry Peerce); Maya Angelou's *I Know Why the Caged Bird Sings* (1979; dir. Fiedler Cook); Ann Beattie's *Chilly Scenes of Winter,* retitled *Head Over Heels* (1979; dir. Joan Micklin Silver); Tillie Olsen's *Tell Me a Riddle* (1980; dir. Lee Grant); Joyce Carol Oates' "Where Are You Going, Where Have You Been?," released as *Smooth Talk* (1985; dir. Joyce Chopra); Nora Ephron's *Heartburn* (1986; dir. Mike Nichols); Marilynne Robinson's *Housekeeping* (1987; dir. Bill Forsyth); Sue Miller's *The Good Mother* (1988; dir. Leonard Nimoy); Bobbie Ann Mason's *In Country* (1989; dir. Norman Jewison); Olive Ann Burns's *Cold Sassy Tree* (1989/made for cable; dir. Joan Tewkesbury); Gloria Naylor's *The Women of Brewster Place* (1989/made-for-television miniseries; dir. Donna Deitch), later, briefly, a television show based on the film; Whitney Otto's *How To Make an American Quilt* (1995; dir. Jocelyn Moorhouse); Jane Smiley's *A Thousand Acres* (1997; dir. Jocelyn Moorhouse); Dorothy West's *The Wedding* (1998/made for television; dir. Charles Burnett); Terry McMillan's *How Stella Got Her Groove Back* (1998; dir. Kevin Rodney Sullivan); Anna Quindlen's *One True Thing* (1998; dir. Carl Franklin); Toni Morrison's *Beloved* (1998; dir. Jonathan Demme); and Mona Simpson's *Anywhere But Here* (1999; dir. Wayne Wang).

Among foreign novels/films are *Out of Africa* (1985; dir. Sydney Pollack), a multiple Oscar winner (Best Picture, Director, Screenplay, Cinematography, and Music Score) and *Babette's Feast* (1987; dir. Gabriel Axel), based on the works and life of Karen Blixen (Isak Dinesen); Laura Esquivel's *Like Water for Chocolate* (1992; dir. Alfonso Arau); *The House of the Spirits* (1993; dir. Bille August); and Maeve Binchy's *Circle of Friends* (1996; dir. Pat O'Connor).

5. As Jerry Wald wrote in "Screen Adaptation," *Films in Review* (1954), "The film premier [*sic*] of *The Good Earth* boosted sales to 3,000 per week" (Bluestone 4). Similarly, Joy Gould Boyum noted that "in 1939, when the film version of *Wuthering Heights* was released, more copies of the novel were sold than in the previous near-century of its existence" (16). Today, of course, books and other products tied in to movies are a huge industry in themselves.

6. *Gentleman's Agreement* won Oscars for Elia Kazan as Best Director and for Celeste Holm as Supporting Actress. The screenplay was by Moss Hart. And while, as Leonard Maltin points out, the film now seems tame, in its day the approach to the subject matter was quite daring. See K. R. M. Short, "Hollywood Fights Anti-Semitism, 1945-1947," in Short's *Feature Films as History*, for a discussion of the film's positive and negative reception in Hollywood, throughout the United States, and overseas.

7. *Giant* was only one of several of Ferber's novels to be adapted. Others included *Showboat* (1929; dir. Harry Pollard), remade in 1936 (dir. James Whale) and again in 1951 (dir. George Sidney); *Cimarron* (1931; dir. Wesley Ruggles), Oscar winner for Best Picture and Best Screenplay, later remade by MGM (1960; dir. Anthony Mann); *So Big* (1932; dir. William A. Wellman), remade in 1953 (dir. Robert Wise); *Come and Get It* (1936; dir. Howard Hawks); *Saratoga Trunk* (1945; dir. Sam Wood); and *Ice Palace* (1960; dir. Vincent Sherman).

8. *Ship of Fools* was scripted by Abby Mann from Porter's novel. The film won Oscars for Cinematography (Ernest Laszlo) and Art Direction. Katherine Anne Porter herself had found early employment with the studios: around 1911, as a reporter for the *Chicago Tribune,* she was assigned to do a story on the Essanay Company, which was headquartered in Chicago. Mistaken for an extra, she was directed to a dressing room for make-up and clothing; that day, she appeared in a courtroom scene and received $5.00 for her work. After being fired from the paper, she returned to Essanay, where she remained for six months, until she refused to travel to the West Coast for an acting assignment. By 1920, though, she was working for the Arthur S. Kane Picture Corporation, which announced in *The Moving Picture World* (13 March 1920) that Porter, "a widely known magazine and newspaper writer . . . will be in charge of feature writing for the fan publications and newspapers." In later years, Porter had other Hollywood offers, most of which she rejected. During World War II, however, she accepted a fourteen-week contract with MGM and worked with producer Sidney Franklin on a projected film of Queen Elizabeth's early years. But, after disagreeing with Franklin's point of view—allegedly, he wanted to leave out all the historical material—she resigned, despite the $2,000 a week salary. "I was right to stay away [from Hollywood]," she concluded. "There wasn't one thing I saw there that was good for me" (Slide 65-67). That, however, was long before her best known novel was optioned by Hollywood. As James R. Messenger

writes, "For the dedicated novelist, there could be worse things than a bad adaptation [of his/her work]—like not having time to write, as Katherine Anne Porter complained on James Day's PBS interview program 'Day at Night.' The money for the screen rights to *Ship of Fools* finally gave Porter the freedom and independence to spend her primary efforts on her writing. Unfortunately, she was 72 years of age at the time. . ." (134).

9. Jane Fonda's IPC production company produced the film, and—according to Barbara Seidman in "'The Lady Doth Protest Too Much, Methinks': Jane Fonda, Feminism, and Hollywood"—Dowd was so upset by the rewrites by Waldo Salt on which Fonda insisted (e.g., the creation of a love story) that Dowd eventually "took Fonda to arbitration over the handling of her material" (208). Interestingly, *Coming Home* won an Oscar for Best Screenplay, which was awarded to Salt, Dowd, and Robert C. Jones. (The film's other two Oscars were awarded to Fonda and to her co-star Jon Voight, as Best Actress and Actor.)

10. Vivien Leigh won for Best Actress; Hattie McDaniel, the first black performer to win an Oscar, was named Best Supporting Actress. Victor Fleming (who took over from George Cukor after filming had begun and who later shared some of the directorial responsibilities with the unacknowledged Sam Wood) was named Best Director. Sidney Howard posthumously received an Oscar for Best Screenplay. Other Oscars were awarded to the film for cinematography, film editing, art direction, and special effects. William Cameron Menzies was given a special award for Outstanding Achievement in Use of Color. And David Selznick received the Irving Thalberg Memorial Award for Most Consistent High Level of Production Achievement by an Individual Producer, an award of particular significance to Selznick since he and the late Thalberg had been friends and colleagues for years. Clark Gable, however, lost out as Best Actor to Robert Donat in *Goodbye, Mr. Chips* (a film directed by Sam Wood); and Thomas Mitchell won for the Best Supporting Actor, not as Gerald O'Hara in *GWTW* but for his work in *Stagecoach* with John Wayne (Bridges and Boodman 238).

11. Herb Bridges and Terry C. Boodman, in *Gone with the Wind: The Definitive Illustrated History of the Book, the Movie, and the Legend* (7), write that "Margaret insisted she never had any intention of doing so [mirroring the Depression in her novel], and pointed out that when she began *GWTW*, the carefree, richly lived Jazz Age was at its peak. She had had no idea the Depression was on the horizon. She wrote about hard times, she said, because they were the stuff that was described to her throughout her childhood. They were the canvas on which her family's colorful heritage was painted."

12. Mitchell warned Selznick that buying the movie rights to her novel "would do him no good. She argued that the book was unfilmable and would cause him no end of headaches trying to make it a movie. But if he wanted the headache, he could have it." Selznick, however, was no novice when it came to

movie adaptations of famous books. He had already produced *David Copper-field, A Tale of Two Cities,* and *The Prisoner of Zenda.* "All had been popular and critical successes," write Bridges and Boodman. "David knew how to please an audience and was committed to remaining faithful to the original work—changing as little of the story as possible—and casting to type" (16).

13. Not all early twentieth-century novelists shared Mitchell's or Cather's reservations. Edith Wharton, for example, had attained significant literary recognition as well as some screen popularity in her own day: her novel *Glimpses of the Moon* was adapted for the screen by Famous Players, which later became Paramount, as a silent film in 1923 (the young F. Scott Fitzgerald, then on his first stint at the Hollywood studios, wrote the film's captions); *The Age of Innocence* won the 1921 Pulitzer Prize, sold 115,000 copies in two years, and earned its author $70,000, including $15,000 for the sale of film rights to Warner Brothers (the film was eventually made in 1934 by RKO [dir. Phillip Moeller]); *The Children* was adapted as *Marriage Playground* by Paramount (dir. Lothar Mendes) in 1929; and *The Old Maid* (dir. Edmund Golding), a soap opera par excellence adapted from Zoë Akins' Pulitzer-Prize-winning 1935 play based in turn on Wharton's novel, was filmed by Warner Brothers in 1939 with Bette Davis and Miriam Hopkins. But, as novelist Francine Prose notes, it has taken several generations for Hollywood to rediscover the real cinematic potential of Wharton's work. A film version of *Ethan Frome* was released in 1993; Martin Scorsese's acclaimed *The Age of Innocence* followed several months later. Wharton's last and unfinished novel, *The Buccaneers,* completed by Marion Mainwaring and published by Viking Penguin, was filmed as a joint BBC-TV/WGBH production (1995; dir. Philip Saville) and shown on *Masterpiece Theatre.* And reportedly the English playwright Christopher Hampton has written the screen adaptation of another novel, *The Custom of the Country,* for Michelle Pfeiffer, who owns the screen rights. Francine Prose points to Wharton's themes as the reason for her popularity with a new generation of readers and viewers. "The impossibility of following one's heart beyond the brick-wall barriers of social custom and class is central to much of [Wharton's] work," she writes, "and may strike a responsive chord in modern readers who have come to feel walled in by social conservatism—and by the ways that economic recession tends to limit one's options. Putting down the novel, leaving the film, we're newly sensitized to the tribal rituals beneath the social forms we'd taken for granted. And our vision of people and of the roles they play has been permanently altered" (29, 36, 37).

14. Apparently, Cather tried to dictate the control of her works even after her death. As Lacey Fosburgh writes, she provided in her will that after her death the executors should "not . . . release, license, or otherwise dispose of my literary properties for any dramatization whether for the purposes of the spoken stage or otherwise, motion picture, radio broadcasting, television (or any other)

mechanical reproduction whether by means now in existence or which may thereafter be discovered or perfected" (1). The 1924 version of *A Lost Lady,* a silent film, was made by Warner (dir. Harry Beaumont); the 1934 version was also by Warner (dir. Alfred E. Green).

15. Other adaptations/interpretations of Woolf's works include *Angel in the House* (1978; dir. Jane Jackson), based on a Woolf essay; *Sloane Square: A Room of One's Own* (1981; dir. Guy Ford and Derek Jarman), based on *A Room of One's Own; To the Lighthouse* (1982; BBC-TV); and *Golven [The Waves]* (1982; dir. Annette Apon).

16. There have been a number of adaptations of Hardy's works. *Masterpiece Theatre* alone has produced four: *Far from the Madding Crowd* (1998; dir. Nicholas Renton); *Jude the Obscure* (1996; dir. Michael Winterbottom); *The Day After the Fair* (1986; dir. Anthony Simmons); and *The Mayor of Casterbridge* (1978; dir. David Giles). Other memorable adaptations include *Far from the Madding Crowd* (1915; dir. Larry Trimble), remade by MGM (1967; dir. John Schlesinger); *The Mayor of Casterbridge* (1921; dir. Sidney Morgan); *Tess of the D'Urbervilles* (Famous Players, 1913; dir. J. Searle Dawley), remade by Metro-Goldwyn (1924; dir. Marshall Neilan), and again (as *Tess*) by Columbia (1981; dir. Roman Polanski) and as *Dulkan ek raat ki/Bride for a Night* (1967; dir. Dharm Dev Kashyap), an Indian version of *Tess; Under the Greenwood Tree* (1929; dir. Harry Lachman); *The Secret Cave* (1953; dir. John Durst), based on "Our Exploits at West Poley," remade as *Exploits at West Poley* (1985; dir. Diarmuid Lawrence); *Jude* (BBC, 1971; dir. Hugh David); *A Tragedy of Two Ambitions* (BBC-TV, 1973; dir. Michael Tuchner); *Return of the Native* (BBC-TV, 1994; dir. Jack Gold); and *The Woodlanders,* a 1997 British production (dir. Phil Agland).

17. Adaptations of Henry James's works include the following: *Berkeley Square* (1933; dir. Frank Lloyd), based on *The Sense of the Past,* later remade as *I'll Never Forget You* (1951; dir. Roy "Ward" Baker); *The Lost Moment,* based on *The Aspern Papers* (1947; dir. Martin Gabel), remade in 1981 (Connoisseur) as *Aspern* and also as a Spanish production, *Los Papeles de Aspern* (1991; dir. Jordi Cadena); *The Heiress,* based on Washington Square (1949; dir. William Wyler), remade as *Washington Square* (1997; dir. Agnieszka Holland); *The Turn of the Screw* (1959; dir. John Frankenheimer), a television adaptation, remade as *Otra Vuelta de Tuerca* (1985; dir. Eloy de la Iglesia); *The Innocents,* based on *The Turn of the Screw* (1961; dir. Jack Clayton), with a "prequel" made in 1972 and entitled *The Nightcomers* (dir. Michael Winner); *Daisy Miller* (1974; dir. Peter Bogdanovich); *De Grey* (1974; dir. Claude Chabrol), a television film; *Owen Wingrave* (1974; dir. Paul Seban), based on a James story; *Georginas Grunde* (1974, dir. Volker Schlendorff), a television production; *Un Recit Romanesque* (1976; dir. Paul Seban), a television film; *The Green Room* (1978; dir. Francois Truffaut), based on "The Altar of the Dead"; *The Europeans* (1979;

dir. James Ivory); *The Bostonians* (1984; dir. James Ivory); *The Portrait of a Lady* (1996; dir. Jane Campion); *The Wings of the Dove* (1997; dir. Iain Softley). Also based on work by James are the French production *The Pupil* (1996); *The Jolly Corner* (1977; dir. Arthur Barron); the very brief *The Real Thing* (1978; International Instructional Television Coop.); and a variety of television productions, including *The Spoils of Poynton,* a miniseries (1971); *The Golden Bowl* (1971); *The Ambassadors* (1977); and *The Haunting of Helen Walker* (1995), based on *The Turn of the Screw.*

18. Quoted in "Austen Anew," Lindsay Doran (producer of the 1995 Thompson adaptation of *Sense and Sensibility*) concurs with Weldon about the cost-effectiveness of adapting many classic novels of the nineteenth and early twentieth century. Doran notes that, after *"The Age of Innocence* actually got made . . . Everybody said, 'Wow! You can get that cast and that director for that?' So they all went to their favorite books. It's like everybody in Hollywood went back to school" (55).

Bibliography

Amis, Martin. "Jane's World." *New Yorker* 8 Jan. 1996: 31-35.

Anon. "Austen Anew." *New Yorker* 21 & 28 Aug. 1995: 55-56.

Armes, Roy. *French Cinema Since 1946.* 2 vols. London: Zwemmer, 1966.

Axelrod, Mark. "Once Upon a Time in Hollywood; or, The Commodification of Form in the Adaptation of Fictional Texts to the Hollywood Cinema." *Literature/Film Quarterly* 24.2 (1996): 201-08.

Basinger, Jeanine. *A Woman's View: How Hollywood Spoke to Women, 1930-1960.* New York: Knopf, 1995.

Bazin, André. "The Evolution of the Language of Cinema." *What Is Cinema?* 2 vols. Trans. Hugh Gray. Berkeley: U of California P, 1967.

Becker, Edith, Michelle Citron, July Lesage, and B. Ruby Rich. "Introduction: Lesbians and Film." *Jump Cut* 24-25 (March 1981): 17-21.

Beja, Morris. *Film & Literature: An Introduction.* New York: Longman, 1979.

Bluestone, George. *Novels Into Film.* Berkeley: U of California P, 1957.

Boyum, Joy Gould. *Double Exposure: Fiction into Film.* New York: Universe, 1985.

Bridges, Herb, and Terry C. Boodman. *Gone with the Wind: The Definitive Illustrated Story of the Book, the Movie, and the Legend.* New York: Simon and Schuster/Fireside, 1989.

Cagin, Seth, and Philip Dray. *Hollywood Films of the Seventies: Sex, Drugs, Violence, Rock'n'Roll & Politics.* New York: Harper, 1984.

Campbell, Edward D. C., Jr. *The Celluloid South: Hollywood and the Southern Myth.* Knoxville: U of Tennessee P, 1981.

Carson, Dianne, Linda Dittmar, and Janice Welsch, eds. *Multiple Voices in Feminist Film Criticism.* Minneapolis: U of Minnesota P, 1994.

Charbonneau, Claudette, and Lucy Winer. "Lesbians in 'Nice Films.'" *Jump Cut* 24-25 (March 1981): 25-26.

Coates, Paul. *Film at the Intersection of High and Mass Culture.* Cambridge: Cambridge UP, 1994.

Cripps, Thomas. *Making Films Black: The Hollywood Message Movie from World War II to the Civil Rights Era.* New York: Oxford UP, 1993.

——. *Slow Fade to Black.* New York: Oxford UP, 1977.

De Lauretis, Teresa. *Alice Doesn't: Feminism, Semiotics, Cinema.* Bloomington: Indiana UP, 1984.

Doane, Mary Ann. *The Desire to Desire: The Woman's Film of the 1940s.* Bloomington: Indiana UP, 1987.

Doane, Mary Ann, Patricia Mellencamp, and Linda Williams, eds. *Re-vision: Essays in Feminist Film Criticism.* Frederick, MD: American Film Institute/University Publications of America, 1984.

Ellis, Kate. "Life with Marmee: Three Versions." *The Classic American Novel and the Movies.* Ed. Gerald Peary and Roger Shatzkin. New York: Ungar, 1977. 62-77.

Erens, Patricia, ed. *Sexual Stratagems: The World of Women in Film.* New York: Horizon, 1979.

Finler, Joel W. *The Hollywood Story.* New York: Crown, 1998.

Fischer, Lucy. *Shot/Countershot: Film Tradition and Women's Cinema.* Princeton: Princeton UP, 1989.

Fishbein, Leslie. "The Snake Pit: The Sexist Nature of Sanity." *Hollywood as Historian: American Film in a Cultural Context.* Ed. Peter C. Rollins. Lexington: UP of Kentucky, 1983. 134-58.

Fosburgh, Lacey. "Why More Top Novelists Don't Go Hollywood." *New York Times* 21 Nov. 1976. Sect. 2: 1, 13-14.

Fuller, Graham. "That Unhappy Governess Yet Again." *New York Times* 7 Apr. 1996: H13, 21.

Geduld, Harry W., ed. *Authors on Film.* Bloomington: Indiana UP, 1972.

Gifford, Denis. *Books and Plays in Films, 1986-1915. Literary, Theatrical and Artistic Sources of the First Twenty Years of Motion Pictures.* London: Mansell, 1991.

Glaessner, Verina. "Fire and Ice." *Sight and Sound* 2.4 (Aug. 1992): 12-15.

Griffith, Mrs. D. W. (Linda Arvidson). *When the Movies Were Young.* New York: Dover, 1969.

Gunning, Tom. *D. W. Griffith and the Origins of American Narrative Film.* Urbana: U of Illinois P, 1991.

Hansen, Miriam. *Babel and Babylon: Spectatorship in American Silent Film.* Cambridge, MA: Harvard UP, 1991.

Harmetz, Aljean. "Lowry and Malamud Tested on Film." *New York Times* 14 June 1984: 17.

Haskell, Molly. *From Reverence to Rape: The Treatment of Women in the Movies*. London: New English Library, 1974.

Holden, Stephen. "By the Book but in the Here and Now." *New York Times* 7 Sept. 1997: H39.

Hollander, Anne. "Portraying 'Little Women' through the Ages." *New York Times* 15 Jan. 1995. Sect. 2: 11, 21.

Hollinger, Karen. "Theorizing Mainstream Female Spectatorship: The Case of the Popular Lesbian Film." *Cinema Journal* 37.2 (Winter 1998): 3-17.

Jacobs, Lewis. *The Rise of American Film: A Critical History*. 2nd ed. New York: Teachers College P, 1968.

James, Caryn. "Amy Had Golden Curls; Jo Had a Rat. Who Would You Rather Be?" *New York Times* Book Review 24 Dec. 1994: 3, 17.

——. "As Cameras Whir, The Brontë Novels Come into Focus." *New York Times* 24 Oct. 1997: E1, 28.

Kaplan, E. Ann. *Women and Film: Both Sides of the Camera*. New York: Methuen, 1983.

Kay, Karyn, and Gerald Peary, eds. *Women and the Cinema: A Critical Anthology*. New York: Dutton, 1977.

Klein, Michael, and Gillian Parker, eds. *The English Novel and the* Movies. New York: Ungar, 1981.

Kuhn, Annette. *Women's Pictures: Feminism and Cinema*. London: Routledge & Kegan Paul, 1982.

Kuhn, Annette, ed., with Susannah Radstone. *The Women's Companion to International Film*. Berkeley: U of California P, 1990.

Limbacher, James L. *Haven't I Seen You Somewhere Before? Remakes, Sequels and Series in Motion Pictures and Television, 1896-1978*. Ann Arbor, MI: Pierian P, 1979.

Linden, George W. *Reflections on the Screen*. Belmont, CA: Wadsworth, 1970.

London, Jack. "The Message of Motion Pictures." *Paramount Magazine* 1.2 (Feb. 1915).

Lupack, Barbara Tepa, ed. *Take Two: Adapting the Contemporary American Novel to Film*. Bowling Green, OH: Bowling Green State University Popular Press, 1994.

——. *Vision/Re-Vision: Adapting Contemporary American Fiction by Women to Film*. Bowling Green, OH: Bowling Green State University Popular Press, 1996.

Lyman, Rick. "James Follows Jane as Screen Writer of the Day." *New York Times* 7 Sept. 1997: H66.

Maltin, Leonard. *Leonard Maltin's Movie and Video Guide 1994*. New York: Penguin/Plume, 1993.

Mayne, Judith. *Cinema and Spectatorship*. London: Routledge, 1993.

——. *Woman at the Keyhole: Feminism and Women's Cinema*. Bloomington: Indiana UP, 1990.

McCreadie, Marsha. *Women on Film: The Critical Eye*. New York: Praeger, 1983.

McMurtry, Larry. *Film Flam: Essays on Hollywood*. New York: Simon and Schuster, 1987.

Merkin, Daphne. "The Escape Artist." (Rev. of *The Wings of the Dove*.) *New Yorker* 10 Nov. 1997: 121-22.

——. "A Film of One's Own." (Rev. of *Mrs. Dalloway*.) *New Yorker* 16 Feb. 1998: 82-83, 85.

Merritt, Russell, and J. B. Kaufman. *Disney in Wonderland: The Silent Films of Walt Disney*. La Giornate Del Cinema Muto; distributed by Johns Hopkins UP, 1993.

Messenger, James R. "I Think I Liked the Book Better: Nineteen Novelists Look at the Film Versions of Their Work." *Literature/Film Quarterly* 6.2 (Spring 1978): 125-34.

Mills, Kay. "Between the Action Thrillers and the Reruns, Willa Cather." *New York Times* 26 March 1995: H37, 42.

Nichols, Peter M. "Literary Cycle: Bookshelf, Broadcast, Video Store." *New York Times* 7 Sept. 1997: H77.

O'Dell, Paul. *Griffith and the Rise of Hollywood*. New York: Barnes, 1970.

Peary, Gerald, and Roger Shatzkin, eds. *The Classic American Novel and the Movies*. New York: Ungar, 1977.

——. *The Modern American Novel and the Movies*. New York: Ungar, 1978.

Penley, Constance, ed. *Feminism and Film Theory*. New York: Routledge, 1988.

Prose, Francine. "In 'Age of Innocence,' Eternal Questions." *New York Times* 12 Sept. 1993. Sect. 2: 29, 36, 37.

Rafferty, Terrence. "American Gothic." (Rev. of 1994 version of *Little Women*.) *New Yorker* 9 Jan. 1995: 83-84.

Rich, B. Ruby. "In the Name of Feminist Film Criticism." *Multiple Voices in Feminist Film Criticism*. Ed. Diane Carson, Linda Dittmar, and Janice Welsch. Minneapolis: U of Minnesota P, 1994. 27-47.

Richardson, Robert. *Literature and Film*. Bloomington: Indiana UP, 1969.

Rosen, Marjorie. *Popcorn Venus: Women, Movies and the American Dream*. New York: Coward, McCann, 1973.

Russo, Vito. *The Celluloid Closet: Homosexuality in the Movies*. New York: Harper, 1981.

Shelley, Mary. *Frankenstein*. Ed. M. K. Joseph. London: Oxford, 1969.

Silverman, Kaja. *The Acoustic Mirror: The Female Voice in Psychoanalysis*. Bloomington: Indiana UP, 1988.

Sklar, Robert. *Movie-Made America: A Social History of American Movies.* New York: Random House, 1975.

Slide, Anthony. *Aspects of American Film History Prior to 1920.* Metuchen, NJ: Scarecrow P, 1978.

Smith, Dinitia. "Isn't It Romantic? Hollywood Adopts the Canon." *New York Times* 10 Nov. 1996. Sect. 4: 4.

Sobchack, Thomas, and Vivian C. *An Introduction to Film.* Boston: Little, Brown, 1980.

Sontag, Susan. "The Decay of Cinema." *New York Times Magazine* 25 Feb. 1996: 60-61.

Spiegel, Alan. *Fiction and the Camera Eye: Visual Consciousness in Film and the Modern Novel.* Charlottesville: U of Virginia P, 1976.

Swartley, Ariel. "Once More to the Well of Hardy's Rural England." *New York Times* 3 May 1998. Arts Section: 22-23.

Takahama, Valerie. "Jane's Reign, Again and Again." [Rochester] *Democrat and Chronicle* 20 Oct. 1996: 6C.

Todd, Janet, ed. *Women and Film.* New York: Holmes & Meier, 1988.

Trinh, T. Minh-Ha. *When the Moon Waxes Red: Representation, Gender and Cultural Politics.* Metuchen, NJ: Scarecrow P, 1978.

Wagner, Geoffrey. *The Novel and the Cinema.* Rutherford, NJ: Farleigh Dickinson UP, 1975.

Weldon, Fay. "Jane Austen and the Pride of the Purists." *New York Times* 8 Oct. 1995: H15.

Weinraub, Bernard. " 'I Didn't Want to Do Another Chinese Movie.' " *New York Times* 5 Sept. 1993: H7, 15.

Welch, Jeffrey Egan. *Literature and Film: An Annotated Bibliography, 1909-1972.* New York: Garland, 1981.

Williams. Linda, ed. *Viewing Positions: Ways of Seeing Film.* New Brunswick, NJ: Rutgers UP, 1995.

Winfrey, Lee. "Eerie Romance at Thornfield." *Philadelphia Inquirer TV Week* 19 Oct. 1997: 4-5.

1

RE-CREATING THE MONSTER:
FRANKENSTEIN AND FILM

Martin Tropp

"The brain you stole, Fritz. Think of it! The brain of a dead man waiting to live again in a body I made with my own hands!"
—*Frankenstein* (1931)

"Alone you have created a man. Now, together, we will create his mate."
"You mean . . ."
"Yes! A woman! That should be really interesting!"
—*The Bride of Frankenstein* (1935)

Even before the moment Mary Shelley, in the words of her 1831 introduction to the second edition of *Frankenstein,* "bid [her] hideous progeny go forth and prosper" (10), her scientist and her Monster had begun to take on the protean forms that popular culture imposed upon them. The author herself had attended the first production, Richard Brinsley Peake's *Presumption, or the Fate of Frankenstein,* at the English Opera House in 1823.[1] In this play (which alternated a few spectacular scenes from the novel with irrelevant songs, unintentionally creating the first musical comedy version), as in the many incarnations that followed, a pattern was set that would be duplicated on film throughout the twentieth century and unbroken until just a few years ago.

The first theatrical Monsters, Thomas Potter Cooke (see Figure 1) and Richard John ("O.") Smith, performed the role in play after play. Unlike the articulate creature of Mary Shelley's imagination but like the film Monsters who followed them, they were mute, given to crashing through doors and otherwise displaying brute power. Much of the action, including the creation scene, soon became stylized, though each production tried to outdo the last in staging the Monster's death. It jumped into the smoking crater of a volcano, froze in an Arctic storm, was buried in an avalanche, and burned to death in a church. Finally, in a theatrical

23

M:T.P.COOKE,
Of the Theatre Royal Covent Garden
In the Character of the Monster in the Dramatic Romance of Frankenstien.

Figure 1. Thomas Potter Cooke became the "Boris Karloff" of the nineteenth century, portraying the Monster in numerous melodramatic versions of the story. (All *Frankenstein* film stills and images from the collection of Martin Tropp.)

foreshadowing of the Abbott and Costello Frankenstein films, excess gave way to parody when a series of short-lived burlesques aped the Frankenstein stage tradition. As the intricacies of the novel were quickly left behind, the story became a commentary on the myth the novel engendered and a vehicle for the possibilities of the nineteenth-century stage, which thrived on spectacle and melodrama.

This same formula became familiar to a new audience when *Frankenstein* was retold in the twentieth century through the motion picture, a technological medium perfect for sustaining myth. Each moviegoer is isolated in the darkness, seeing his fantasies projected before him, while at the same time he is bound to those around him by the similarities in culture that produce popular film. Film is itself evidence of Mary Shelley's prophecy come true—what Professor Waldman in the novel called the power to "mock the invisible world with its own shadows" (48). Alone together at the movies, we experience the fusion of self, society, and technology that is the domain of the myth of Frankenstein.

The story first came to the screen in two silents, the Edison Company *Frankenstein* (1910) and *Life Without Soul* (1915). The Edison version, starring Charles Ogle as a barrel-chested, Brillo-haired Monster (see Figure 2), was only one reel long and consisted of twenty-five hand-tinted scenes of the Monster's creation and destruction. A transitional piece, it retained the structure of the melodramas while demonstrating the additional effects possible with film. Of chief interest is its conclusion: in a bow to the Doppelgänger tradition and a demonstration of the power of cinema, the Monster fades away before a mirror, leaving its reflection behind. As Frankenstein embraces his bride, the reflection disappears, showing the relationship between what Mary Shelley called "domestic affections" (56) of the scientist and the existence of the creature—a recurring theme. *Life Without Soul,* four reels longer, is notable for its far-flung locales, its un-made-up Monster, and the sympathy Percy Darrell Standing evoked in his role as "The Creation."

But both these silents are minor fragments. Mary Shelley's Monster got its definitive incarnation in two films directed by James Whale and starring Colin Clive as the scientist and Boris Karloff as the Monster. Not only are they the most famous (and perhaps the best) films of their type ever made, but each engendered its own progeny, taking the myth of Frankenstein on two very different paths that set the pattern for Frankenstein films for the next fifty years.

What Whale realized was that the myth had to connect with contemporary fears rather than remain faithful to the events that gave Mary Shelley her famous dream during the summer of 1816. As the myth went on to be filmed more times than any other novel,[2] it remained true, not to its historical origins in a discussion between Lord Byron and Percy Shelley on "the nature of the principle of life" (8), but to its underlying impulses—the Monster as a dangerous and neglected child, the populace

SCENE FROM
FRANKENSTEIN
FILM No. 6604

EDISON FILMS TO BE RELEASED
FROM MAY 11 TO 18 INCLUSIVE

Figure 2. Charles Ogle as the Monster, in an advertisement for the first film version of *Frankenstein* (Edison Company, 1910).

as blighted by ignorance and hatred, and science as Promethean over-reaching, the reflection of ego gone mad.

Frankenstein was originally envisioned as a companion piece to Universal's *Dracula* (1931). That film ends with Edward Van Sloan coming from behind a curtain to argue the existence of vampires; he returns before the opening credits of *Frankenstein* to warn us of the ensuing threat to our nerves. He and Dwight Frye[3] play similar roles in both films. His Professor Waldman is really another Professor Van Helsing (Dracula's nemesis), who tries, but fails, to destroy the Monster, while the words Frye made famous as Dracula's mad disciple Renfield— a whispered "Yes, Master"—have become part of the vocabulary of laboratory assistants, though they are never spoken in the film *Frankenstein.*

Both films have, as their immediate inspiration, stage plays and not the novels. This source proves almost fatal for *Dracula,* which too often bogs down in talkiness. The theatrical roots of *Frankenstein* (primarily a play by Peggy Webling, adapted by William Hurlbut and John Balderston) are responsible for some of the more static moments in that film, as well as for the name changes (Victor becomes Henry, Henry Clerval becomes Victor Moritz) and the famous scene at the water between the Monster and the little girl. Robert Florey, who was first slated to direct the film, contributed its most absurd and unnecessary sequence, when Frankenstein's assistant mistakenly steals a pickled criminal brain (prominently labeled "ABNORMAL BRAIN," "DISFUNCTIO CEREBRI") from Goldstadt Medical College.

Florey, however, may have had something to do with the marvelous sets, designed by Charles D. Hall and Herman Rosse, which brought German expressionism to the American film. Frankenstein's watchtower-laboratory is a jumbled collection of massive, off-plumb walls, crazily tilted beams, and oddly cut windows—there seems not to be one right angle in the place. The inspiration is no doubt films like Robert Weine's classic *The Cabinet of Dr. Caligari* (1919) and Paul Wegener's *The Golem* (1920). *Caligari* is a relevant Gothic parable of an authoritarian doctor's power over a young man who is both his instrument and victim—the somnambulist Cesare. The setting is a surreal landscape that gives the scenes the fragile and threatening perspective of nightmare. *The Golem* uses the same methods in a more muted fashion, retelling the medieval monster legend in a gnarled Prague ghetto that seems about to collapse at any moment. Florey's original conception of the Monster was clearly modeled closely on Wegener's most famous role. Some test scenes were even shot with Bela Lugosi stomping around the set of Dracula's castle in Golem make-up.

The convoluted genesis of the film could well have destroyed it. But Robert Florey was relieved of his directorial duties and replaced by James Whale, who asked to direct the film. Whale was responsible for casting Colin Clive as Frankenstein and, when Lugosi rejected the Monster role, recruiting an obscure actor, William Henry Pratt, who in 1910 had taken the stage name Boris Karloff. He also brought to the production a distinctive style and organizing vision. Retaining an expressionist feel for light and shape, he expanded the dimensions of space and movement, giving *Frankenstein* a feeling of openness that *Dracula* lacks. Whale explored the conflicts at the core of the myth while contributing his own interest in the humanity of monsters and the inhumanity of man. The result is a *Frankenstein* with new relevance for a world recovering from the Great War, in the depths of the Depression, and threatened with a more terrifying conflict in the future.

The time of the film is indefinite but appears to be contemporary; the place has moved from the Swiss cities of Geneva and Ingolstadt to a remote village somewhere in central Europe. Victor Frankenstein created his Monster in the bare attic room of a boarding house in the midst of a thriving city; his curse as the novel progresses is his gradual estrangement from humanity. Henry Frankenstein chooses to isolate himself in an old watchtower in a blasted, empty landscape, far from humanity and its needs.

James Whale was British, served on the Western Front in World War I, and grew thin during fifteen months in the German prison camp at Holsminden (Curtis 3). He made his reputation directing R. C. Sherriff's bitter war drama *Journey's End* on stage and as a film (which also starred Colin Clive in a psychologically similar role, as the mad Captain Stanhope). Sherriff's story is set in the trenches, and Whale's film of *Frankenstein* also has the distinct atmosphere of No Man's Land—intensified by the opening scenes of graveyards, gibbets, and corpses. When the Great War began, it was fought by cavalry on horseback; it ended four years later with millions dead by tanks, poison gas, airplanes, machine guns, and high explosives. Mary Shelley's fear of science finding "the principle of life" became the reality of science dedicated to the new technology of death. The creation of the Monster is, then, seen in the light of what science created and mankind suffered in the horror of the Great War. Whale retells the myth after disaster has come; the nameless forces that brought about the war and Depression are, in his film, tinkering among the ruins with new and greater powers, threatening to unleash an even more spectacular disaster.

The laboratory in the ruined watchtower, the most famous set in all Frankenstein films, evokes the attraction and repulsion science holds for the layman. The central structure is a glittering gadget (designed by Kenneth Strickfaden) that hauls the Monster through a skylight into the midst of an electrical storm, where it receives the mysterious spark of life from "the great ray that first brought life into the world." The crescendo of effects that brings the Monster to life is the scene we all remember first from the film—a controlled catastrophe combining our fascination for electronic wizardry with the horror of its product. The capture of nature's lightning inside the tower suggests, as it does in the novel, the Promethean travesty of cosmic power put in mortal hands. As the fingers of the creature move, Frankenstein maniacally shouts over and over, "IT'S ALIVE!" until he has to be restrained.

When his friend Victor Moritz admonishes, "Henry, in the name of God!" he replies, "Oh—in the name of God. Now I know what it feels like to *be* God!" Although this bit of megalomania was cut from some later prints of the film, the madness of the whole project is quite evident. In Mary Shelley's novel, the interplay between the characters takes place in the external world and within one mind. The failure of Frankenstein's experiment is due to his ignorance of the contradictory possibilities within his own personality. In much the same way, the laboratory scenes in the film both caricature modern technology, laboring in electrical splendor to bring forth a monstrosity, and define the relationship between the Monster and the mind of Henry Frankenstein.

This aspect of the laboratory becomes clearer when we look at a character derived from the plays but given his own prominence in the film. Frankenstein's hunchback assistant, Fritz, played with demonic glee by Dwight Frye (see Figure 3), joins Frankenstein on his midnight rambles to the gibbet and graveyard and guards the door of the watch-tower. He is responsible for the "criminal brain" (a cumbersome attempt at establishing motivation) and amuses himself by torturing the newly resurrected Monster with whips, chains, and torches until it responds by hanging him.

Nowhere in Shelley's novel, Fritz is undoubtedly descended from the imps and demons who accompanied medieval sorcerers as well as the stock comic assistant of melodrama (the servant in *Presumption,* the first *Frankenstein* play, is even named Fritz), with a cinematic bow to *Dracula's* Renfield and Lon Chaney's Quasimodo from the 1923 version of *The Hunchback of Notre Dame.* But Whale gives him a personality all his own. Fritz is afraid of the electrical storm and the unawakened Monster. In one memorable scene, like the porter in *Macbeth*,[4] he answers the door, mumbling about "people messing about at this time of night," then stops to straighten his sock; in another, his twisted body clashes, physically and symbolically, with a hanging skeleton. Whale and Frye make Fritz an endearing, somewhat comic character. But he cannot be seen apart from his master; he may be the most grotesque incarnation of a standard American figure—the sidekick. Like Cooper's Hawkeye and Chingachgook or Twain's Huck Finn and Jim, Whale's Frankenstein and Fritz face the future together, partners on a scientific frontier.

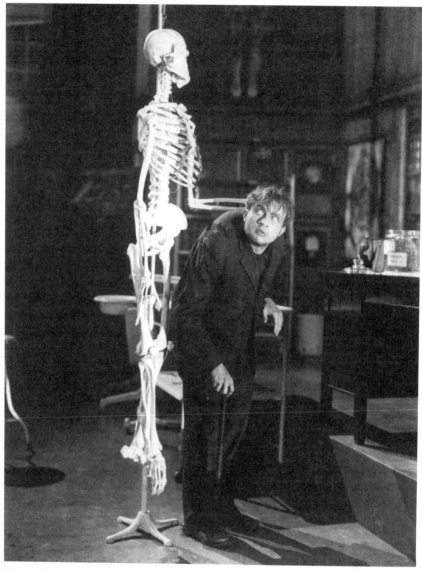

Figure 3. Dwight Frye as Fritz in *Frankenstein* (1931), the first in a long line of cinematic sidekicks in Frankenstein films.

At the same time, since Fritz is so intimately involved with giving the Monster its destructive personality (via both heredity and environment—the wrong brain and the wrong treatment), it is more than possible that he is a projection of the demon hidden in the mind of Henry Frankenstein—an embodiment of his twisted emotions. Fritz is first seen peering through a graveyard fence; the opening line in the film is Frankenstein hissing "Down . . . down, you fool!" Later we see Fritz looking through the window at the Medical College and the grated door of the watchtower. He is the part of Frankenstein that must constantly be kept in check but always threatens to break out. The tower they share is itself symbolic of the mind. Isolated, rickety, yet topped by a gleaming laboratory, it embodies the aloofness, instability, and brilliance of its most famous tenant.

But Fritz lives there too. He helps build the Monster and adjust the equipment, although his fears and sadistic pleasures imperil the experiment and ultimately sabotage it. While Fritz is tormenting the Monster with a torch, Frankenstein enters and ineffectually pleads, "Oh, come away, Fritz. Just leave it alone. Leave it alone." Even though Frankenstein has defied God, Fritz defies him. When the Monster finally hangs the hunchback, Frankenstein collapses on the stairs. Waldman must bring him to his senses with the telling line, "Come, come, pull yourself together!" He weakly replies, "What can we do?" and agrees to destroy the Monster. Soon after, Frankenstein collapses again, moaning over and over, "Oh, my poor Fritz," then follows Waldman's suggestion to "Leave it all to me." The loss of Fritz and his replacement by Waldman suggest Frankenstein's change in moral direction. Throughout the experiment, he never seemed to realize that the Monster was a product of both himself and the hunchback—cold rationality served by demented feelings.

The Monster itself is both a pathetic creature—wandering, friendless, misunderstood—and a destructive menace. Boris Karloff's masterful portrayal, aided by Jack Pierce's equally masterful make-up job, created a Monster that was both abominable and sympathetic. (See Figure 4.) Machinelike attributes (primarily a lurching walk and stiff movements) contrasted with childlike innocence and a superhuman rage and power. Whale made the Monster's first appearance a study in its contradictions. We do not see it rise from the table. Instead, a few days after its creation, Waldman and Frankenstein, sitting in a room in the tower, hear the Monster's heavy footsteps on the stairs. The first shot of the Monster as it enters the darkened room is from the back. It slowly turns and, in a series of quick cuts, Whale moves in to the face. Familiarity had not yet dimmed the shock of Karloff's cadaverous skull, circled by scars and pierced by clips and electrodes. It remains one of the most frightening moments in the history of film.

This effective bit of horror is immediately followed by the opening of a shutter that allows light into the room. Like a child, the Monster raises its great hands, trying to catch the sunlight, while making an almost infantile mewling. (See Figure 5.) We are left unsure what to feel, caught between the horror of its appearance and the appeal of its innocence. Its very innocence, in fact, proves to be dangerous. It drowns a little girl by

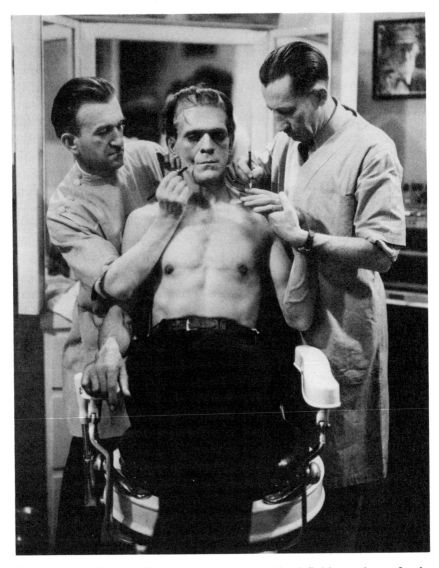

Figure 4. Jack Pierce (left) and assistant creating the definitive make-up for the Monster.

trying to make her float like the flowers the two have been throwing in the water. (The crucial moment in this scene was cut in American prints at the insistence of Karloff, who later said that Whale had him throwing the girl in the water with too much violence, spoiling the sensitivity of the moment. As shown, we see the Monster reach for the girl, then cut to the girl's father carrying her corpse through the village. Unfortunately, what is implied is much worse than what Karloff feared.)

Figure 5. The Monster reaches for the sunlight in Whale's *Frankenstein* (1931).

The Monster's only other murders are motivated by self-preservation. It strangles Waldman as the doctor is about to dissect it and hangs Fritz to end his torments. The shorthand of cinema precludes the philosophical complexities of Mrs. Shelley's Monster, but Karloff's creature draws its power from the same source—a carefully maintained balance between sympathy and horror.

The Monster as outcast also has contemporary political overtones. In one sense, it is a creature of the Thirties, shaped by shadowy forces beyond its control, wandering the countryside like some disfigured veteran or hideous tramp. The special pathos of the Monster, never really recaptured in most of the later films, is due in part to its affinities with the refugees from political and economic disaster cast out from a society that can find no place for them. In many ways, the 1931 *Frankenstein* plays upon the particular collection of fears that haunted the Thirties. The scientist and hunchback personify the forces of mad authority and sadistic servitude that brought disaster to the world and, perhaps, were plotting new horrors for the future. Their "science" is both technological and political; the Monster is weapon and victim, a mechanical engine of destruction and a collection of misused human beings. Its rage and rejection threaten all of society. At the same time, the film plays upon the seduction of gadgetry (our affinities with the scientist) and our identification with the isolation and sexual force of the Monster.

Whale's *Frankenstein* has its shortcomings; most are relics of its checkered origins. Colin Clive overacts badly in spots and, for some reason, plays the last scenes in riding boots. The romantic interludes are pedestrian, while the comic old Baron seems dragged in for no purpose whatsoever. Whale used the most conventional methods for sequences that we may assume held no interest for him. He is best at "building" shots with careful framing, dramatic lighting, and a camera tilted slightly upward to suggest the monumentality of the figures. Whale's distinctive style comes, as well, from the inventive touches he added to what could have become stock situations. His grotesques (Fritz and the Monster) are deeply detailed, while the stock characters of melodrama (Elizabeth, the Baron, and Victor Moritz) are cut from thin cardboard.

Although strongly influenced by expressionist cinematic techniques and led by his own taste for the unusual, Whale was familiar with Mary Shelley's novel. He carefully re-created the moment that Frankenstein finds Elizabeth's body sprawled on the bed with the Monster peering through the window, although in this case she has only fainted. He also blended a pattern from the novel with his own ironic symbolism, creating two threads that wind through the film and come together in the last scenes. In the first minute of the film, a gravedigger pauses from his work to light his pipe. Whale thereby introduces the image of fire, which becomes, as it did in the novel, a metaphor for knowledge, power, and destruction.

As Fritz and Frankenstein enter the graveyard to dig up the body, the second motif becomes evident. It is surely no accident that they work in the shadow of two statues not often found in country graveyards. We see them enter from behind a statue of Death and then take their places in a tableau of the Crucifixion. (See Figure 6.) The scene is lit by the evening sky, the three crosses are carefully askew, and the echo unmistakable. They put their clothes on a stick; Frankenstein pulls out a stake from the grave and casually plants it to form another cross. As they haul up the casket in front of a statue of Christ crucified, the empty black clothes between the cross and the figure of Death form another, ominous Calvary. That Whale built the scene is made clear by the hat on the stake, which neither character is wearing when he enters. Victor's line as he holds the casket is significant: "He is just resting, waiting for a new life to come." The scene is a perverse Resurrection, and the Monster destined to parody Christ.

The next scene carries forth both images as Frankenstein and Fritz climb a jagged studio mountain to cut down a hanged man for their collection of raw materials. Fritz scales the gibbet while Frankenstein holds a lantern, which is given some prominence. Like the figure of Death

Figure 6. Christian imagery from the opening shot of *Frankenstein* (1931).

brooding over the graveyard, the lantern is prophetic. Fire comes to represent the power Frankenstein will hold in his hands and the destruction it will cause. Fritz carries the lantern down the steps of the tower when he lets in Waldman, Victor Moritz, and Elizabeth, while the sparking equipment illuminates the creation scene they witness. For a moment, Frankenstein controls the explosive power of the lightning bolt and uses it to give the Monster life; everyone else cringes in fear for his own life.

The "education" of the Monster is also presented through images of light. When it lifts its hands to the skylight, only to see it shut, we realize that one possibility has been closed off forever. Heavenly light is replaced by hellfire; a burning torch is used to scourge the Monster and goad it to violence. The contrast is pointed up in another marvelous scene. In a weirdly off-center stone dungeon, Fritz jabs the torch at the Monster, shouting "Ha! Here's fire for you!" In the background, rays of sunlight struggle through a small barred window. Sunlight will bathe the creature for only one moment—when it almost finds happiness floating flowers with the little girl.

The conclusion of the film returns to the actual and symbolic locale of its opening. The villagers, armed with torches, split up into two groups. Frankenstein leads one contingent through the barren countryside. Before his "conversion," Frankenstein gave a misshapen being unnatural life; now he drives a mob to destroy what it cannot accept. Cut off from his followers, he confronts the Monster on the same spot where the gibbet of the hanged murderer once stood. Whale cuts back and forth between them, uniting them. The action stops for a moment, and we realize that the Monster has come to a new level of awareness. It strides to its maker and brushes aside his torch. Losing his symbol of power and control, Frankenstein suddenly screams for help.

For a brief moment, the Monster is in command and carries its maker off to an old windmill. The structure reminds us of the tower and, in fact, one draft of the script had set the laboratory in the mill. In any case, the meaning is clear: scientist and Monster are tied together in creation and destruction. The trip to the old mill is a cinematic equivalent of the long journey in Mary Shelley's novel from Geneva to the frozen expanse near the Arctic Circle. On that journey, Frankenstein became aware that he and the Monster were doubles; the same realization touches Whale's *Frankenstein*. Karloff and Clive face each other through a revolving mill wheel. A flickering shot between the spokes reminds us of film itself, while Whale, rapidly cutting between the images of both faces, dramatically makes them one—they wear exactly the same expression. (See Figures 7 and 8.)

After the Monster throws Frankenstein to the mob, they call for its death and use their torches to set fire to the mill, thus bringing a fitting conclusion to the images of fire and a perverse Christianity. As Frankenstein falls, he hangs for a moment on the blades of the windmill. These same blades form, in the final fadeout, a gigantic cross on top of a bleak hill. The Monster, trapped under the weight of a great beam, is finally returned to Calvary. The mob, given the thief who stole life from God, destroys the being forsaken by its creator. Although the movie should have ended here, a Hollywood epilogue was added only a few days before the film was finished and after the initial previews. We see Frankenstein recuperating, while the Baron and maids toast the future. The ending is so obviously tacked on that it fails to destroy the impact of the double death at the windmill.

Whale's Christian imagery there and throughout the film was in large part meant to be seen sardonically—the same impulse dubbed eighteenth-century graverobbers "resurrectionists." In equating the Monster with Christ and not Satan, however, Whale made clear his differences with Mrs. Shelley. In a sense, he kills off the Monster when, in the novel, it still is "innocent"—before it vows destruction on all that Frankenstein loves. At that point, the guilt clearly rests on the Monster's creator and on an unfeeling world. The image of the burning cross, which must have had strong associations in the Thirties when the Klan was at its height, points up the mob mindlessness that does the Monster

Figure 7. Maker and Monster seen as doubles through the flickering mill wheel in *Frankenstein* (1931).

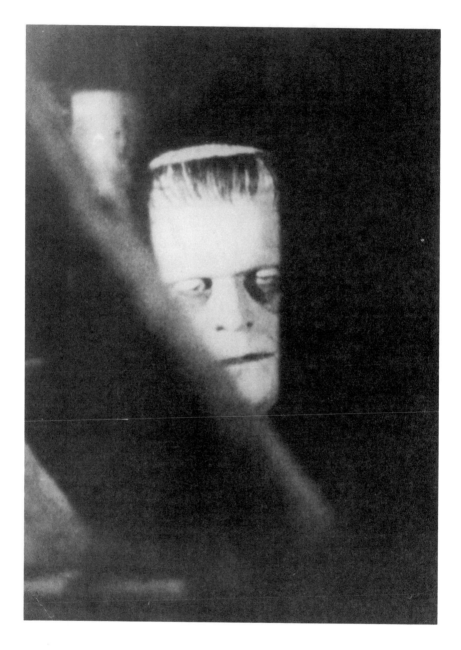

Figure 8. Maker and Monster seen as doubles through the flickering mill wheel in *Frankenstein* (1931).

in. The final fire is only an extension of the torch wielded by Fritz to torment what he feared and therefore hated.

Mordaunt Hall, reviewing *Frankenstein* in the December 5, 1931, issue of the *New York Times,* recognized the "disturbing nature" of this "artistically conceived work" when he described the soundtrack of the Monster's death: "From the screen comes the sound of the crackling of the blazing woodwork, the hue and cry of the frightened populace, and the queer sounds of the dying monster" (A-21). We are far from the Arctic conclusion of Mary Shelley's novel and closer to the vision of James Whale, a man who saw death and disfigurement close up and who recognized what can happen when mobs of men are led to slaughter the innocent.

The phenomenal commercial success of *Frankenstein* inspired, four years later, its first and best sequel. James Whale's *The Bride of Frankenstein* again starred Colin Clive, Karloff (temporarily shorn of his first name), Valerie Hobson as a new Elizabeth, and Elsa Lanchester in a dual role as "The Mate" and Mary Shelley herself. The film opens with an "historical" prologue. Byron, Shelley, and Mary, gathered around a baronial fireplace with four huge Russian wolfhounds as an electrical storm rages outside, discuss the implications of her story of "the punishments that befell a mortal man who dared to emulate God." That the story to which they refer is the 1931 screenplay and not the novel becomes evident when Mary Shelley reveals to the breathless pair that "the Monster didn't die in the fire at the burning mill." This clumsy attempt at authenticity, while cinematically unnecessary, makes explicit what has been true throughout the history of *Frankenstein*—theater and film have supplanted the novel as a source of myth. Mary Shelley, like her characters, has been re-created in the crucible of popular culture to suit the needs of a modern mass audience and a new medium.

The film takes up what Whale calls Mary Shelley's story with no lapse of time, beginning exactly where and when the last film left off. The two can almost be seen as one. Although *The Bride of Frankenstein* is a more elaborate, more bizarre, more darkly comic production, it continues retelling the myth after the Monster has lost its innocence and science has gained knowledge of the secrets of life.

Whale's desire to tie the two films together as closely as possible extended even to Karloff's make-up, which was altered to account for the Monster's (offscreen) fall from the burning mill into a watery cistern underneath. Most of its hair is singed away, part of its face is burned, and its one black suit is torn and stained. More importantly, its ignorance and innocence are gone. Whale points this up through the ironies of the opening sequence. The parents of little Maria, whom the Monster accidentally drowned in the first film, wait by the wreckage of the still smoldering mill to be sure the Monster is dead. The father enters the ruin to investigate, falls through the floor, and is promptly strangled and drowned by the Monster, who climbs out and does the same to his wife. As it rises reborn from the pool of water (a nice Freudian touch), we realize that this second resurrection will be even more deadly than the first. Full of hatred, the Monster wanders off into the world.

Meanwhile, back at the castle, Frankenstein's anguished recovery is interrupted by a booming knock at the door. When his comic servant, Minnie (a new character), answers with a great bustling and with the words, "All right, don't knock the castle over, we're not all dead yet!" the tone of the film is set. The door opens, and in stalks the maddest of all mad scientists, the notorious Dr. Pretorious (played with manic effectiveness by skeletal Ernest Thesiger). His name is significant (obviously so, since Minnie hollers out "Pretorious" at least five times). It combines the Latin for "causing to be known" and "of the ruling class"; like Frankenstein, he is obsessed with creating life, but not to aid mankind or even solely to glorify himself. He wishes simply to rule the rest of humanity, whom he regards with contempt as inferiors.

His handiwork, which he takes out of a casket-shaped case to show Frankenstein, consists of a grotesque collection of homunculi sealed in glass jars and dressed as mermaid, devil, ballerina, bishop, king, and queen. Pretorious' black costume, his medieval skullcap, and the archaic wax-sealed ribbons on his jars clearly make him another alchemist like Cornelius Agrippa or Paracelsus, who inspired Victor in the novel to seek the secrets of life and death. This medieval relic needs the modern technological know-how of Frankenstein to turn his own small madness into a method for ruling the world. Dr. Pretorious has a glass of gin ("It's my only weakness") with Frankenstein, and proposes a toast "To a new world of gods and monsters!" Gone is the desire to create a perfect being—the goal now will become a perfect weapon. The character of Pretorious surely owes something to the rise of Hitler in the four years since the 1931 film. The altruistic (if insane) Frankenstein is to be used by the fascistic and somewhat perverse Pretorious. Hitler's "New Order" and Pretorious' "New World" spell the same disaster for the human race.

Humanity doesn't come off much better in this film than the scientists. While Pretorious is plotting the future, the Monster saves a drowning shepherdess, only to be shot by misunderstanding hunters. The scene comes straight from the novel; in both *Frankenstein*s it occurs soon after, as Mary Shelley's Monster puts it, "the mildness of my nature had fled, and all within me was turned to gall and bitterness" (140). In novel and film, the act seems somewhat out of character. Mrs. Shelley probably added the episode as a Romantic set piece—"rustics" and shepherdesses were a part of nearly every literary landscape at the time. In the film, it may suggest that, although the Monster is no longer innocent, it is still capable of acts of kindness and able to be redeemed by human love.

This interpretation is strengthened by the famous next scene, which faintly recalls the De Lacey episode in the novel but gives it a different twist. The Monster wanders into an isolated hut where a blind hermit gives it refuge. In an episode that straddles the thin line between the pathetic and the ludicrous, the Monster finds a friend. It learns to talk, drink, and smoke; puffing on an after-dinner cigar, it listens to the hermit play "Ave Maria" on his violin. The irony is that the Monster can only find its brief happiness with another outcast, and a blind one at that. As soon as another hunter shows up to ask directions, the Monster is doomed. In fact, they are both doomed. In the confusion of discovery, a fire burns down the cottage, the hermit is led off, and the Monster escapes, calling for its only friend.

Whale's use of misty "romantic" close-ups and a syrupy soundtrack in this sequence is more evidence of his ironic viewpoint and another cinematic joke—the love scene at its least lovely. But it also points up the absurdity of the Monster's ever living a domestic existence while introducing another spate of Whale's weird Christian symbolism. The hermit wears a monk's robe; his choice of music and sustenance—he feeds the Monster bread and wine—make this the Monster's last and only supper. After this brief communion, it escapes to a surrealistic forest of bare tree trunks and is captured by a mob of villagers. They truss it to a stake and hoist it in the air; for one short moment it hangs suspended, a grotesque Christ, before it falls into a hay wagon and is hauled into the village. There the mob chains it to a great throne in a dungeon and torments it some more. It easily escapes, pulling off its chains and ripping off the cell door. The scene owes more to *King Kong* (1933) than to the Gospel, and the effect is the same—our sympathy goes to the powerful humanoid prisoner, who has superhuman power and a strange nobility.

Pursued by the howling mob once again, the Monster heads for a graveyard where, in sight of the same figure of Death that brooded over the opening sequences of Whale's first *Frankenstein,* it overturns the statue of a bishop and invades the tomb. The overall religious imagery is more playful here than in the last film, but it does accentuate the uniqueness of the Monster and returns the mythic relationships of *Frankenstein* to their most perplexing level. Man may be guilty of rejecting Christ, but what responsibility does it have for the Monster? If Frankenstein and Pretorious are would-be gods, then the Monster is their forsaken and misshapen Son. But it is a perverse Christ; rather than harrowing Hell, the Monster finds a home in the world of the dead.

In the crypt it runs into Pretorious, who is enjoying a slabside picnic after a bit of grave robbing. The two necrophiles strike up a friendship, especially after he promises to build a mate for the Monster. Pretorious and the Monster become the prime movers in the final creation scene; in a sequence probably inspired in part by gangster films, Pretorious and his inhuman henchman strong-arm Frankenstein into helping out by kidnapping his own bride and hiding her in a cave. Her life depends upon Frankenstein's giving life to the Monster's bride. Reluctantly, he sets to work, back in the tower, spurred on by Pretorious' frenetic enthusiasm and the Monster's timely growls. The Mate's brain has been grown artificially by Pretorious (no formaldehyde-soaked criminal brain this time around) so that it will truly be a blank slate. Its heart has been supplied by Dwight Frye, playing another assistant, with a new name, Karl, and a hump reduced to a limp. In the original script, he was sent to get a heart at the morgue but extracted Elizabeth's instead. In the mellower final version, he kills a villager to get it, then comments too rashly to Frankenstein, "It's a very fresh one!" Finally, wrapped in bandages, and of a considerably better lineage than the Karloff Monster, the bride-to-be awaits the spark of life.

The creation scene is more extravagant than ever. (See Figure 9.) The tower has had some renovations; it is taller, with more elaborate (and appropriately phallic) equipment, while lightning is attracted by giant kites that Karl releases from the roof. Whale's techniques are similarly less restrained. He cuts madly from dials to hands, to a heart, to sparking equipment, to optically prolonged shots of lightning, keeping up a mad staccato rhythm, building to an inevitable climax. In his first *Frankenstein,* the angled expressionist sets suggested a surreal mood; here, the camera itself is often tilted sharply—a device copied later in the *Batman* television series to serve much the same satirical purpose.[5] At the moment of birth, Karl falls to his death—a life for a life—and the slab is lowered from the roof. For the second time (and the second Monster) Frankenstein shouts, with only a minor change of gender, "She's alive! ALIVE!" The table is tilted up (this piece of equipment became a stock cinematic laboratory prop) and the Mate's eyes open, while her hands jerk forward. In the next shot, the bandages are gone from her face.

The final scenes comprise a series of comic commentaries on the curious marriage. We see the effeminate Pretorious and Frankenstein standing on either side, the symbolic parents of the Mate. (One may well argue that Whale, homosexual himself, suggested here, and in the scene

Figure 9. The phallic imagery is evident on the set of the creation scene in *The Bride of Frankenstein* (1935).

in the hermit's cottage, a gay subtext.) They have dressed the Bride in a white wedding garment that doubles as a shroud. The fact that she is the same actress, Elsa Lanchester, who appeared in the prologue as Mary Shelley adds another twist (as did the original plan to give her the heart of Frankenstein's bride-to-be Elizabeth). A series of close-ups of the face reveals a Nefertiti hairdo streaked by a lightning bolt of silver hair, lips smeared with color, and skin mapped with scars. (See Figure 10.) It is, all in all, a much neater job than the first Monster. In a final bit of impish humor, the soundtrack fills with church bells as Pretorious shouts, "The

Figure 10. On the set of *The Bride of Frankenstein* (1935), Elsa Lanchester checks her famous fright wig.

Bride of Frankenstein!" Despite the four-star wedding, the marriage is short-lived. Although her body is a corpse, the bride's brain has never been dead; her natural reaction to the Monster is disgust and horror. She recoils from its clumsy advances with a resounding hiss. Announcing "We belong dead!" the Monster finds the convenient destruct lever and blows the tower to atoms, and Pretorious' new world of gods and monsters dies at the altar.

Of course, this scene is first and foremost the final explosion that audiences demand and films like this deliver. But it is also an attempt to use the formula to examine the new science, its monsters, and mankind. The novel's Victor Frankenstein, in a passage that inspired the conclusion of the film, wondered about the implications of creating a mate for the Monster: "They might even hate each other . . . She might also turn with disgust from him . . . Even if they were to leave Europe . . . one of the first results of those sympathies for which the daemon thirsted would be children, and a race of devils would be propagated upon the earth, who might make the very existence of the species of man a condition precarious and full of terror" (165). It is obvious that the "science" of creating life in both Frankenstein films is not taken seriously. The early nineteenth-century belief in the imminent discovery of the secret of life through the power of electricity had, by the nineteen-thirties, become quite dated. But the possibility of a "race of devils" and the science to create them were real fears.

Early in the film, we learn that Pretorious' own technique was to grow people "as nature does, from seed." At one point, he prevents his miniature King Henry VIII from getting at his tiny ballerina. He is, then, more interested in controlling the natural breeding of his creatures to obtain his "gods and monsters" than in building them out of corpses. He enlists Frankenstein's help only to obtain the female he needs to continue his own genetic experiments on a grander scale. The mad dream he carries around in his little jars and hopes to impose upon the world was a contemporary one; the science is eugenics. Extremely popular in the Thirties, eugenic theory promised a race of men like gods, created through selective breeding and sterilization of the defective and inferior. The abortive marriage of Monster and bride that ends the film is a grotesque parody of the process, short-circuited by the revolt of the experimental subjects. Eugenics fell out of favor when the Nazis used it ruthlessly to attempt to create a master race. Through Pretorious, Whale shows us the true nature of the eugenic dream—the "gods" are indistinguishable from the monsters.

Pretorious' passion to breed a new race and new life compensates for his own apparent homosexuality and perverse love of death. He keeps his jars in a casket and eats lunch on a tombstone. Whale makes clear that if Pretorious were ever to succeed, he would make the world a cemetery. Frankenstein turns out to be little better. He first cooperates with Pretorious reluctantly in order to save Elizabeth but soon gets swept up in the glory of his achievement. At the creation of the would-be bride of the Monster, he is as triumphant as Pretorious, and equally responsible. It is up to the manipulated victims to assert the proper priorities. The

Mate rejects the future selected for it, and the Monster recognizes that there can be no place in the land of the living for creatures of death. It tells Elizabeth and Frankenstein to go and includes Pretorious among those who "belong dead."

The survival of Frankenstein recalls the escape of Walton in the novel while suggesting, as the presence of Dr. Waldman did in the first film, that there is a "good" science needed to combat the black arts of the new alchemy. But this conclusion was stitched in only at the last moment. A close look at the final holocaust reveals that Frankenstein is present. In the shooting script, however, he was slated to perish along with the rest. When it was decided at the last moment to spare him (for the second time), probably as a concession to the standard Hollywood ending and a hint that someone may well have been thinking of yet another sequel, the laboratory explosion had already been filmed. It was hoped, rightly, that the audience would focus its attention on the exploding equipment and ignore the extra victim.

The black comedy of *The Bride of Frankenstein* only darkens the bleak vision of the earlier film. Men are either hunters or a tormenting mob; their future is determined by a group of bizarre misfits playing God in a lonely tower, isolated from the people they affect and numb to the pain of the victims they create, acting out fantasies of power and destruction. The Monster must decide where they all belong and become, finally, the unlikely savior of humanity. The blend of fascist lunacy, religious allegory, and gallows humor in *The Bride of Frankenstein* has a feeling about it of helplessness before a future that was becoming clearer and more terrifying all the time. Mussolini, already in power for many years, was about to invade Ethiopia; Hitler, whose New Order was two years old in 1935, was giving life to a huge disciplined war machine and preaching the myth of Aryan superiority. The cataclysmic ending of Whale's last *Frankenstein* film is, like the ending of the novel, safely remote from the rest of humanity, but the tone of the film and the ambiguity of its conclusion hold out little hope for a future free of madmen or monsters.

II

"Mr. Karloff's best make-up should not be permitted to pass from the screen. The Monster should become an institution, like Charlie Chan . . ."

—Review of *The Bride of Frankenstein,*
New York Times, May 11, 1935

The *New York Times* movie critic, Frank S. Nugent, need not have worried. The Karloff Monster (with and without Boris himself) developed a catlike ability to escape even the most obliterating catastrophes more or less intact. In the ten years after *The Bride of Frankenstein,* it returned in *Son of Frankenstein, The Ghost of Frankenstein, Frankenstein Meets the Wolf Man, House of Frankenstein,* and *House of Dracula* played, in order, by Boris Karloff, Lon Chaney, Jr., Bela Lugosi, Glenn Strange, and Glenn Strange again, with occasional stand-ins by stuntmen Bud Wolfe and Edwin Parker. Aside from minor changes to accommodate the different physiognomies of the actors under the gashes and greasepaint, the Monster returned to the contours and muteness of Whale's first film.

In fact, Whale's two films each inspired its own branch of the Frankenstein tradition. Part One, with its silent Monster and well-meaning but misdirected scientist, became the basis of Universal Studio's many sequels, which in turn firmly established a pattern that would influence science fiction and horror films through the Fifties and Sixties. *The Bride of Frankenstein,* with its articulate Monster and cold, perverse "Pretorian" scientist, was, for the time being, forgotten. Late in the Fifties, these characters returned to inspire a whole new Frankenstein cycle. But as the concerns of the Forties prevailed, Frankenstein, symbolically at least, joined a world at war.

Of course, the reasons for the appeal of horror lie deep in the realm of nightmare. Like bad dreams themselves, the films project images that portray the monstrous impulses within each of us. Walter Evans argues quite cleverly that the wolf men whose palms turn hairy by the light of the full moon, the monsters with ungainly bodies and misdirected libidos, and the scientists who abandon their fiancées to create life in secret laboratories are related to adolescent anxieties about sex (Evans 353-65). But the timing of the cycle suggests that the traditional appeal was given a new impetus—the real horrors of the Second World War.

The Forties cycle of horror movies was, of course, not confined to Frankenstein remakes. The Hollywood monster factories were going at full scream. Other Thirties creatures like the Mummy, the Invisible Man, and Dracula returned; the Wolf Man, Invisible Woman, Leopard Man, Ape Woman, Cat People, and assorted zombies and gorillas joined the war effort, while Dracula enlisted a son. At Universal, monsters made guest appearances on each other's turf, dragging along perennial favorites like Gypsy woman Maria Ouspenskaya and hunchback-turned-villager Dwight Frye.

Some horror films dealt directly with the conflict. In *The Return of the Vampire* (1944), Dracula is revived in the Blitz and terrorizes London. The Invisible Man was recruited in 1942 and became *The Invis-*

ible Agent. More often, though, the Europe of horror films has no Nazis and, indeed, no direct references to the war at all. Of course, fantastic films exist in the nonspecific world of the imagination; too close a fidelity to outside realities would spoil the suspension of disbelief that keeps the monsters alive. But within the horror conventions, political fears took hold. In the Universal films, werewolves, vampires, hunchbacks, and mad scientists wander the back roads of the Old World, refugees looking for an elusive cure, or more often, an opportunity to stir up more mayhem. It is taken for granted by moviegoer and monster alike that the destruction of each creature can only be temporary. Even films set in America, like *Son of Dracula* (1943), deal with the infection of a new land by an old European disease.

The war years meant an indefinite suspension of the happy ending that, in Hollywood, resolves the conflicts of youth. Those waiting at home were aware that when the "boys" returned, they would be boys no longer. All of these feelings could be, and were, incorporated into the horror film. For the lineage of Frankenstein, war meant the power of technology wedded to fascism, translated into an undying Monster used for destructive purposes by a new and dangerous master. The Frankenstein cycle degenerated quickly after *The Bride of Frankenstein,* but the series is still of interest. It evolved into a cinematic tradition of characters and motivation that owed little to Mary Shelley's novel but helped keep her fears contemporary, until it spawned even greater monsters in the postwar decades.

Son of Frankenstein (1939) sported a big budget, a good cast that included Basil Rathbone, Boris Karloff, Bela Lugosi, and Lionel Atwill, stylish sets, and a literate script by Willis Cooper. Still, marred by director Rowland Lee's slow pacing and Rathbone's histrionics, it pales by comparison to its predecessors. The best moments are provided by Lugosi's excellent characterization of Ygor, the Monster's demented keeper. The deformities of Fritz and Karl are recalled by Ygor's broken neck, the result of an unsuccessful execution for grave robbing. Ygor (the name has become almost a generic term for deformed assistants) has many talents; he not only plays eerie recorder tunes in the ruins of the old laboratory but also sews his monstrous friend a new sheepskin vest to replace, for this film at least, its basic black suit. Despite his domesticity, Ygor is a much more menacing figure than either of his two cinematic ancestors, since he has absolute control of the Monster and murderous plans. The Monster has little to do in much of the film but lie unconscious on a slab. A new convention is established; the Monster "cannot die" but is perpetually sick and will need the help of an unending series of doctors to make it well again.

The first of these is Wolf Frankenstein (Basil Rathbone in his pre-Sherlock Holmes days), who has returned to the homestead twenty-five years after his father's death. Ygor brings him to the Monster and asks him to cure his "friend"; after some initial hesitation, Wolf sets up the old lab equipment and gives the Monster a revivifying jolt. Though at first it does not seem to work, the Monster soon takes to walking the halls of the castle and visiting Wolf's young son, Peter, who enjoys playing with the "giant."

We learn of this incident secondhand. Only slightly more emphasis is given to the fact that Ygor has been using the Monster as a kind of "smart bomb," sending it out to kill the members of the jury who sent him to the gallows. The deficiencies of *Son of Frankenstein* as a film are suggested by these two missed opportunities. Karloff is given only a few moments to let the Monster show a glimmer of its former complexity. Its howling response to Ygor's death and kindness towards Peter do little to offset the general impression that the Monster is no more than a weapon. In a raucous climax, it engages Police Inspector Krogh and Wolf in a wild battle that ends when Frankenstein manages, Tarzan-style, to knock it over a ledge into a convenient pool of molten sulfur. Victim to the end, the Monster is revived only to be used and abused, sent out to kill, and then be destroyed.

Whether or not the menacing prewar atmosphere had something to do with altering the image of the Monster from isolated outcast to controlled weapon and transforming its caretaker and "friend" from scientist to criminal, it certainly contributed a new member to the Frankenstein troupe. The bumbling Baron and burgomaster of the earlier movies are replaced in *Son of Frankenstein* with the crisply authoritarian Krogh, played by Lionel Atwill. Except for a mad doctor stint in *The Ghost of Frankenstein* (1942), Atwill plays an identical role in all of the films in this series, always dressed in a shiny comic opera costume that looks like a Hollywood parody of German officialdom. As Krogh, he has both a monocle and a wooden arm to hold it, his own arm having been torn off in childhood by the Monster. When he swivels his arm up with an audible screech, viewers in 1939 could not help but be reminded of the hordes of German soldiers and civilians giving the mindless, stiff-armed Nazi salute. At the end of *Son of Frankenstein,* the Monster rips off the wooden arm and swings it around its head, in a momentary triumph of victim against authority and a nice bit of macabre filmmaking.

Wolf Frankenstein is the first of the mad doctors who largely replace mad scientists like Pretorious and Henry Frankenstein. Like his brother Ludwig in *The Ghost of Frankenstein,* Dr. Mannering in *Frankenstein Meets the Wolf Man,* and Dr. Edelmann in *House of Drac-*

ula, Wolf is a medical man, who first examines the Monster reluctantly and then is obsessed with the idea of seeing it "restored to full strength." None of them is a researcher after the secrets of life and death, and two are psychiatrists. Most of their Monster-making knowledge comes from the "old Frankenstein records," which Colin Clive entrusted to Dr. Waldman in the 1931 film. Like the Monster itself, they have a way of showing up with astonishing ease.

In purely political terms, the change from scientist to doctor is logical; the "Monster" contemplated in earlier films is here and seems immortal—it is up to the doctors of body and mind to repair a world that has grown monstrous and gone mad. In at least two films, they have to contend with the brain of Ygor, who wants the Monster for his criminal schemes of death and power. His simple-minded viciousness replaces the refinements of Pretorious and is more suited to the straightforward savagery of war. All of the doctors set out to destroy or cure the Monster, but, by allowing their egotism to awaken the sleeping giant, only give Ygor a tool for magnifying his own destructiveness. Their ineffectual attempts to fix things and the ease with which Ygor uses them underline the danger that is loose in the world.

Each film, from *Son of Frankenstein* on, ends in momentary victory for mankind, with the almost certain assurance that the Monster will rise again. Curiously, the films can be seen as installments in one long movie serial; each attempts to account for the seeming death of the Monster in the last, and all refer to each other and other Universal creatures, who meet in nearly every film. More monsters do not make better movies, as this series proves; however, the fact that the sets, creatures, and plotlines are so similar creates an odd and comforting familiarity. This is a neighborhood in which the doctor is apt to be mad, assistants are invariably deformed, and the strangers are more than likely to be half wolf or previously dead.

The Ghost of Frankenstein (1942) resurrects both Lugosi's Ygor and the Monster, played this time in stodgy fashion by Lon Chaney, Jr. Lionel Atwill is back, accompanied by Sir Cedric Hardwicke as Ludwig Frankenstein, Doctor of the Mind, and an hilariously miscast Ralph Bellamy dashing about in a white suit and riding boots as public prosecutor Eric Ernst. Dwight Frye even appears for a moment leading the inevitable mob of villagers, but the spirit of the original *Frankenstein* is indeed only a ghost. The one memorable scene is with a little girl the Monster befriends.

In all of the Frankenstein films, and as far back as Wegener's 1920 film *The Golem,* the Monster had been linked to children, the only people who do not run from it in horror. Their reaction contrasts sharply with that of Victor Frankenstein's son, William, in the novel; he responds with an instinctive loathing that emphasizes the unnaturalness of Mary Shelley's Monster. The movie Monster is seen almost as another child, an orphan raised to do evil by wicked, uncaring adults. In *The Ghost of Frankenstein,* the Monster helps the girl retrieve her toy, a large ball on a string. Of course, the townspeople believe it will hurt her, so they coax it down and attack it, causing it to kill one of them. After a bit more adult duplicity, they manage to capture it for a while. Later, the Monster kidnaps the girl and goes back to get the ball. As the lumbering Monster carries her off, dragging the ball by the string, we glimpse the spark of innocence still smoldering inside the much-tortured human junk heap that the Monster has become.

The Ghost of Frankenstein introduces one of the most popular operations in horror movies to the *Frankenstein* saga—the brain transplant. Everyone has a candidate for the Monster's new brain, depending upon his own hopes for the future. Ludwig, wanting to correct the mistakes of his illustrious ancestor, chooses kindly Dr. Kettering, murdered by the Monster. The Monster itself chooses innocence, kidnapping the little girl in order to borrow her brain. Atwill, as the evil Dr. Bohmer, manages to slip Ygor's brain into the body of the Monster after he is promised a place in Ygor's projected dictatorship. Ygor's literally twisted mind has hatched a political plot. The Monster will be a one-man army, giving him "the strength of a hundred men" and the means to "rule the country." The joining of deformity and brute power brings together the elements of the myth that reflect the political realities of 1942. The Monster awakens from the operation and announces, "I, Ygor, will live forever!" Frankenstein cries, "The crime of my father is now mine, but a thousandfold!" Fortunately, Ygor's blood and the Monster's do not mix; instead of eternal life, or even a rule that will last a thousand years, all Ygor gets is blindness and a losing bout with the inevitable conflagration.

Frankenstein Meets the Wolf Man (1943) is best passed over quickly. Aside from a nicely chilling opening sequence in a cemetery, the movie is notable for Bela Lugosi's execrable stint as the Monster and the incomprehensible gaps in the plot. Both were partly the fault of a last-minute editing job. Originally, the Monster was to be blind and speak with Ygor's voice, continuing from *The Ghost of Frankenstein.* In the final release print, all scenes with the Monster talking and any references to its blindness were cut. As a result, the Monster's stiff-armed groping is never explained, though ironically it contributed to the transition of the Monster's public image from a feeling being to a mindless robot. The plot is simple and predictable. Dr. Mannering, like Ludwig

Frankenstein, starts his operation intending to kill the Monster but decides, like any boy with a new technological toy, that he has to power it up. The seduction of power backfires; Wolf Man and Monster clash in a violent battle until the villagers (among them we can glimpse the immortal Dwight Frye) explode a convenient dam, washing them both to the next film. The "battle of the monsters" is clearly the only reason for the movie; although it fits the mood of wartime, *Frankenstein Meets the Wolf Man* is really a mindless exercise, reducing the subtleties of the tradition to little more than the Monster's blind violence.

Mindlessness is certainly a theme in *House of Frankenstein* (1944); in this case it is interpreted quite literally in an obsession with brain transplants. After leaving the *Frankenstein* series at Universal, Boris Karloff went over to Columbia, where he made a series of quickie "mad doctor" films. His experiments all backfired, though the movies did not—they managed to make respectable amounts of money. As a result, Karloff came back in *House of Frankenstein* as Dr. Gustav Niemann, the only certified mad doctor in the series, having been locked in an insane asylum for trying to fit a man's brain into a dog's head. After escaping with Daniel, his hunchback (of course) assistant, he manages to revive Dracula and thaw out the Wolf Man and Frankenstein Monster, who have been neatly frozen in the ruins of the dam. Like Ygor in *Son of Frankenstein,* he uses the monsters to avenge himself against those who had him imprisoned.

This generally awful movie has a few unintentionally funny moments. The best is when Niemann plans a marathon brain switch involving the Monster, the Wolf Man, and two of his enemies. When Daniel is left odd brain out, he begins the general catastrophe that ends the picture. The Monster is barely given time to rise from the operating table and grunt (it is sick again) before it is driven into quicksand with Niemann. *House of Frankenstein* is really a Gothic vaudeville show where each monster gets to do its act, then is disposed of just in time for the next one to growl center-stage. Even the subplot, between Daniel and a Gypsy girl, is clearly taken from the Quasimodo-Esmeralda relationship of the latest Charles Laughton version of *The Hunchback of Notre Dame* (1939). Originality was flagging, along with audience interest— the Universal *Frankenstein* series was obviously dying out.

Yet before Abbott and Costello met Frankenstein in 1948 and delivered the *coup de grace,* one more film intervened. Erle Kenton's *House of Dracula* (1945) contained many of the familiar elements, including all three monsters and a Jekyll/Hyde Dr. Edelmann, modeled on the Spencer Tracy portrayal four years previously. Despite the staleness of the formula, this film is in many ways delightful, marked by touches of offbeat humor and parody as well as some optimistic twists that show a fond familiarity with the traditional elements of the genre. Dr. Edelmann's assistant, for example, is first shown in a soft focus close-up. She is a beautiful woman and, we expect, destined to be the standard vapid heroine. Slowly the camera moves back and we discover that she is a whiteclad hunchback who turns out not to be a demented dwarf but the doctor's assistant (of course) and, surprisingly, the moral force in the film.

Edelmann is, at least at first, a kind and quite sane psychiatrist who sets out to cure both Dracula and the Wolf Man. In an early scene, while the Wolf Man waits in the outer office, Edelmann gives Dracula one of his "treatments," commenting, "Your next appointment will be Thursday evening, same time." A bit later, he reassures Lawrence (Wolf Man) Talbot (played by Lon Chaney, Jr.), who has locked himself up in Lionel Atwill's jail cell, that "there is no such thing as a werewolf, it's all in your mind!" Unfortunately, Talbot begins to sprout hair at that moment, forcing Edelmann to change his diagnosis to a combination of "pressure on the brain" and "abnormal hormones." All of this absurdity is pointed up by a weird character (played by Skelton Knaggs), who appears periodically to whisper lines like, "Strange business, if you ask me."

It is possible to see the obsession with brain transplants in the earlier films as influenced, in part, by a contemporary fear of psychoanalysts, who seemed to many to have mysterious, almost supernatural power, suggested by the popular title of "head shrinker." At the same time, it was another manifestation of wartime concerns. Fear of the power of propaganda and fascist control of the mass showed up in many war films; even the zombie movies made at the time gained their horror from the idea that human beings could be made into mindless slaves. In the Frankenstein films, the brain transplant symbolized the power of science to change and control the personality. Edelmann is refreshingly different. He uses his ability at instant diagnosis and a secret "skull-softening" technique literally to expand the Wolf Man's head, relieving the "pressure on the brain" and curing Larry (Wolf Man) Talbot of his horrid hirsuteness.

After Edelmann, near the end of the picture, finds the Monster conveniently washed into a cave near his hospital, he falls into the now familiar pattern of renovating his laboratory and attempting to revive it. Edelmann's motives are, however, purely humanitarian. He must try to cure the Monster because of his responsibility to aid the sick, whether they be men or monsters. The expected disaster is literally short-circuited after the following somewhat stilted conversation with Nina, his assistant:

Edelmann: Can man sit in judgment over life and death?
Nina: What man creates he can also destroy.
Edelmann: That would be murder! My responsibility is to this help-
less body.
Nina: Man's responsibility is to his fellow man.
Edelmann: Perhaps you're right, Nina. Frankenstein's Monster must
never wreak havoc again.

He turns off the equipment, scoring a victory for humanity and restoring the good name of doctors everywhere. This outcome, which may owe something to the optimism that accompanied the end of the war, is unfortunately short-lived. Edelmann is infected with vampire blood and goes quite mad. He returns to his laboratory and, in some great atmospheric shots projecting his enormous shadow against a giant door, stalks around preparing to learn "the secret of immortality" by animating the Monster. In a last bit of humor, just as the machinery reaches a crescendo, it blows a tube and goes dead. Edelmann finally manages to revive the Monster for about ten seconds. It blunders into its third fire (second actually—the footage was scissored out of *The Ghost of Frankenstein*) and falls to a final confrontation with Abbott and Costello.

This new film, aptly named *Abbott and Costello Meet Frankenstein,* has been variously described as a travesty of the classic films and a faithful piece of satire. It is, in either case, pretty thin stuff, marked by the contrast between the idiocies of Lou Costello and the pathetic earnestness of Lon Chaney, Jr., and Bela Lugosi taking their famous Monsters out for a last airing. As a faithful, witty, and coherent conclusion to the Universal series, *House of Dracula* stands up much better.

The legacy of the post-Whale Frankenstein cycle included an emphasis upon the Monster as an eternal nuisance and potential weapon and the scientist as a well-meaning doctor who allows his own vanity and scientific curiosity to get the better of him. Instead of the inevitable band of villagers as an ignorant mob, they are needed to burn the house, blow up the dam, chase the Monster into a swamp, or otherwise take destiny into their own hands. The ambiguity of the Whale films and the complexity of Karloff's creature are largely gone, while Mrs. Shelley's novel is almost totally forgotten. The ritual energizing of the dormant creature and its casting out by the villagers do, however, dimly reflect the opposition of science and society that Mrs. Shelley found inherent in Frankenstein's experiments. In the Fifties, when the Universal Monster seemed finally consigned to oblivion, this same pattern returned on a grander scale to give form to the greater dangers of the post-Hiroshima age.

From the flying saucer scare that started in the late Forties came *The Thing* (1951), directed by Christian Nyby, reportedly with the help of Howard Hawks. The isolated village of the Frankenstein series is here transferred to an Air Force station in the Arctic—the place where we met Mary Shelley's Frankenstein and Monster. Despite the setting, the plot follows the pattern of the earlier films, not the novel. After the discovery of an alien vegetable man (played by James Arness) frozen in the familiar block of ice, we need wait only a few minutes for the expected thaw. Again, we have a well-meaning scientist who tries to understand the creature and even takes to growing its seeds and nourishing them on human blood. But, as in the post-Whale Frankenstein cycle, the film is solidly on the side of the villagers. They destroy the multiplying alien seedlings just in time, then "cook" the vegetable man with the scientific torch of electricity. When we finally glimpse the alien, we are not surprised that it looks like a bald Karloffian Monster.

The Thing is a transition piece; two years later, atomic experiments in the Arctic released *The Beast from 20,000 Fathoms* (1953) featuring the first of a host of gigantic creatures which, as the Japanese can best attest, continually emerged to test man's defenses. In each of these films, a creature comes from the waste places of the world—either the desert, the ocean floor, or (in this case and in *The Thing*) the Arctic, where, of course, Mary Shelley's Monster disappeared—to threaten all of mankind. It is often awakened from a long hibernation by atomic tests or some other ill-conceived experiment; after a few isolated attacks on outlying human settlements, it heads for the centers of civilization. Penetrating the elaborate defenses of the military, it enters the heart of a major city (New York, Tokyo, and Washington are prime targets) and proceeds to tear it apart. The Monster is finally destroyed by some last-ditch stratagem or exotic scientific device, but everyone concerned knows that mankind has only been reprieved. The films invariably end with a warning: either, as in *The Thing,* we are told to "Keep watching the skies!" or, more commonly, we hear a variation of the ritual phrase "There are things man is not meant to know." It is taken for granted that science will revive more monsters and mankind will need to keep casting them out.

The monsters of the Fifties films are not of the same species as the first Monster, though they have much the same function and share a common ancestor. On the cultural level, monsters visualize and exorcise group anxieties. Mary Shelley's Monster was in part a manifestation of the fear, engendered by galvanic experiments, that the secret of life was about to be discovered. The Forties monsters were linked to the relatively tame horrors of World War Two; with the growth of our technology's potential for destruction, the monsters grew in size and destructiveness. The popularity of giant monsters in the mid-Fifties in America, and from then until now in Japan, visualizes and exorcises our fear of the atomic bomb and Japan's experience with it.[6]

The bomb shelter craze and the Monster craze complemented each other; one madly prepared for an indescribable fear, the other attempted to confront that fear in some tangible form. At the same time, the popularity of all monsters owes something to what Freud called the "inclination to aggression . . . the cause of hostility against which all civilizations have to struggle" (Freud 69, 44). Like the monsters of myth, these creatures, whether reptilian or near-human, are a modern expression of the spontaneous, natural, irrational, and primitive emotions that delight in destruction. The Frankenstein Monster is often equated with a child because its hatred for the adult world that casts it out is childlike in its rage and simplicity. The giant dinosaurs, insects, and crustaceans are all relics of a past age, literally primitive remnants of the childhood of earth, returned to battle with a grown-up world. The conflict that ensues in all these films is the struggle between order and disorder, suppression and aggression, that is as old as society itself.

In the decade following 1948, Mary Shelley's Monster lay dormant, making its presence felt indirectly. To find direct connections with the myth, it is necessary to look in a most unlikely place. Makers of "serious" science fiction films often try to dissociate themselves from mad scientists and monsters, yet the myth still influences them. It shows up through the Sixties, in films like *Dr. Strangelove* (1964), *2001: A Space Odyssey* (1968), or *Colossus: The Forbin Project* (1970), where the survival of humanity is threatened by a conflict between "mad" or at least misdirected science and machinery designed to be near perfect and almost human, which turns rebellious and monstrous. In 1956, *Forbidden Planet,* the most elaborate science fiction film made until that time, used dazzling special effects to project viewers across time and space, examining the future of technology in terms familiar to anyone who has gone no further than Mrs. Shelley's novel or a Frankenstein movie.

Forbidden Planet is set in the year 2200 A.D. Commander Adams (played by Leslie Nielson when he was a romantic lead) and the crew of starship C57D have traveled to the planet Altair 4 to search for the survivors of a ship that crashed twenty years before. What they find is Dr. Morbius, his beautiful daughter, Altaira, and a comic robot servant named Robby. (The screenplay, by Cyril Hume, is in part modeled on Shakespeare's *The Tempest*—Morbius is Prospero, Robby Ariel, and Altaira Miranda.) Morbius has discovered the remains of an extinct civilization, the Krell, which had carried technology to its limit. The interior of the planet is one vast machine the purpose of which, Morbius learns, is to materialize one's desires instantaneously. This machine, resembling Frankenstein's laboratory blown up to immense proportions, clearly symbolizes the end to which technology itself strives—the granting of limitless power to man. Morbius plans to keep that power for himself, dispensing bits of the Krell knowledge to humanity when he deems us ready. In order to boost his already elevated IQ, he hooks himself up to the machine. Too late, he finds out why the Krell vanished in a single night. In giving their conscious minds infinite power, the Krell had forgotten about their subconscious hatreds—the machine gave birth to a planet of invisible monsters. Morbius' own Caliban, his "Monster from the Id" empowered by the machine, now roams the planet, threatening Commander Adams' crew and even his own daughter, who has defied his wishes.

At the end of the film, Morbius barricades himself behind massive steel doors with the spaceship crew and watches his monster slowly tear its way through his elaborate technological defenses. Shouting "My evil self is at the door and I have no way to stop it!" he allows the crew to escape, finds the familiar destruct lever, and annihilates the entire planet. The last scenes of the film show the exploding planet as a brief burst of light, soon lost in the surrounding infinity of stars. Like Walton and his shipmates in *Frankenstein,* Adams and his crew watch the mutual destruction of scientist and Monster, two sides of the same self, then head back from the limits of the known world to civilization. In both cases, they bring with them awareness of what awaits a culture that lets its technology grant limitless power without self-knowledge. Perhaps the name Adams and his imminent marriage to Morbius' daughter, Altaira (cut from the final print), suggest that with this awareness, mankind can begin again.

The film ends as uncertainly as Mary Shelley's novel or any of the Universal movies. Though *Forbidden Planet* seems far from the Romantic origins of Mary Shelley's novel or the dark, relatively compact landscape of James Whale and the numerous directors of the Universal series, it explores the same relationship between science, self, and society. From the films comes the elitist though well-intentioned doctor, his less-than-perfect assistant (in this case a robot), the self-destructible and fantastic laboratory, and the idea of the Monster as a weapon, awakened from its sleep by the scientist's tinkering. At the same time, *Forbidden Planet* enters the psychological realm of the novel, suggesting, as the original *Frankenstein* did, that what a scientist creates in isolation from humanity can fail to meet its creator's high expectations, and instead magnify his worst subconscious impulses. The result is a film that follows elements of the Frankenstein myth in order to see where our technology is taking us. It is a grim vision, foreshadowed in the mutual destruction of Frankenstein and his Monster on Walton's ship and in the windmill and laboratory of Whale's cinematic landscape. But, as in Fifties monster movies generally, the awareness of thermonuclear power has intervened to make the scale and potential for destruction immense and cataclysmic.

III

"... it is of the essence of the scientific spirit to be mercilessly ascetic, to eliminate human enjoyment from our relationship to nature, to eliminate the human senses, and finally to eliminate the human brain. ... Pure intelligence is thus a product of dying, or at least of becoming mentally insensitive, and therefore is in principle madness."

—Norman O. Brown, *Life Against Death*

When fantasy and science fiction films carried on the Frankenstein tradition in the Fifties, they emphasized the arrogant Promethean scientist or doctor who discovers his limitations through inability to control the Monster he revives. His failure is accompanied by remorse and recognition of his own human frailty, of the danger of trying to become, in Mary Shelley's words, "greater than his nature will allow" (53). The message of *Forbidden Planet,* delivered by Commander Adams after Dr. Morbius has met his Monster from the Id, is that "men are not gods"; the line could stand as an epitaph to the House of Frankenstein, from Victor and Pretorious to their many high-strung, neurotic, and usually guilt-ridden cinematic descendants.

One other theme in the Frankenstein tradition tended to be downplayed. Mary Shelley uses language in the novel to suggest that, for Victor Frankenstein, creating the Monster is a kind of substitute sexuality. Closed off from family, friends, and fiancée, apart from human love and natural beauty, he goes about his nights of "secret toil" with "unremitting ardor" (54) and an "eagerness which perpetually increased" (55) until, one night, with "an anxiety that almost amounted to agony" (57), he infuses the spark of life into his "child" (54). The physical effects of his nighttime activities—pale cheek and emaciated body (54)—and his mental state ("I shunned my fellow-creatures as if I had been guilty of a crime" [56]) hint at the ambiguous nature of his solitary pleasures. So do Frankenstein's own reflections: "I then thought that my father would be unjust if he ascribed my neglect to vice ... but I am now convinced that he was justified in conceiving that I should not be altogether free from blame" (55).

In the 1931 film, Henry Frankenstein ignores his upcoming wedding and carries his experiment to an explosive climax while locked in his private tower—the life-giving machine, like the tower itself, is unmistakably phallic. The old Baron in the film hints at this aspect of Frankenstein's activities when he suspects that the "work" that keeps him shut away is really another woman. But both Victor and Henry come to regret their actions as perverse and try to reconnect themselves to the world of human feeling around them. The character who carries out his Monster-breeding with no remorse, no scruples, no interest in the natural world, and with obvious sexual excitement is Dr. Pretorious, who appears only in the 1935 film. Not until the British Hammer film series of the late Fifties and Sixties did Pretorian science return in full force, with a Baron Frankenstein who combined cold detachment with a perversity that turned his Monsters into substitute children and sexual playthings.

Two perfectly awful American films released in 1957 and 1958 stood outside both the Universal and Hammer cycles, though they pointed toward the conception of the scientist that took hold in the Hammer films of the next decade. *I Was a Teenage Frankenstein* (1957) suffers from the bargain-basement look of the early American-International productions, with a wretched laboratory, cardboard sets, and a Monster wearing a T-shirt and Ivy League slacks. Yet the film grossed over two million dollars, following the formula of the even more lucrative *I Was a Teenage Werewolf.* The new audience for horror was largely adolescent; the old Universal films had, at this time, been released to television and started a teen-age fad. The makers of *I Was a Teenage Frankenstein* simply geared the story to the paying customers. Since American-International films were intended primarily for the drive-in crowd, the Monster is assembled from the corpses of dead hot-rodders. As the title implies,[7] it is itself a teen-ager, given to cruising lovers' lane and ogling young girls.

The gruesome detail, tongue-in-cheek humor, and few minutes of color the budget would allow enliven the proceedings somewhat, but the focus of the film is clearly on the father-son relationship of scientist and Monster. In the novel, Victor Frankenstein imagines the reaction of his prospective race of creatures: "No father could claim the gratitude of his child so completely as I should deserve theirs" (54). In *I Was a Teenage Frankenstein,* Dr. Frankenstein (played by Whit Bissell) sees the father-son relationship in more modern terms; he gets to mouth such lines as "Answer me! You have a civil tongue in your head. I know; I sewed it in there!" His Dr. Frankenstein, head-hunting with his creature through lovers' lane, displays the sexual jealousy the young attribute to the old. When, at the end of the film, he tries to dismantle the Monster to take it back to Europe, the creature rebels. Preferring the new world of Southern California to the old world of Upper Transylvania, it kills its maker but accidentally electrocutes itself, as the screen goes from black and white to color.

Frankenstein 1970 (1958) (the title is a flimsy attempt to suggest the film is futuristic) is, despite the services of Boris Karloff in his only role as a Frankenstein, an even more shoddy exercise, memorable for only the last shot—the face of the dead Monster. Its features are those of a young Frankenstein. The new Monster-maker seeks, through his creation, to renew his sexual vitality and live again.

Both of these elaborations of the myth appeared in the Hammer Frankenstein series, which began in 1957 with *The Curse of Frankenstein*. Directed by Terence Fisher and starring Peter Cushing and Christopher Lee as maker and Monster, this film was phenomenally successful and set the pattern for the series that followed. For the next fifteen years, Hammer Studios mined the Frankenstein ore and discovered it turned up gold. Besides Cushing, the series has as its continuing elements ornate period sets, voluptuous women, and various internal organs, all projected on widescreen and bathed in color. The Hammer films have a very different texture than the Universal films or their wretched imitators, though they borrow some of the familiar elements, such as hunchback Germanic assistants, brain transplants, and elaborate laboratories.

The impact of the Hammer films depends, most of all, upon their most striking original feature—the new interpretation of Baron Frankenstein. Peter Cushing establishes the character as a classic Gothic villain. It is no coincidence that he resembles Count Dracula; director Fisher and scriptwriter Jimmy Sangster were, at the time, working on Hammer's equally successful Dracula series. Both Frankenstein and Dracula are aristocrats with refined manners and eccentric private tastes who travel from drawing room to torture chamber with little change in demeanor. The conception contrasts strongly with the agonized Frankenstein of the Universal epics, though in some ways it reminds us of Dr. Pretorious. There is something slightly effeminate about Cushing's dandified Baron. He creates his Monsters in tanks of water—a "feminine" method foreshadowed by the homunculi in Pretorious' little bottles. Both enjoy dabbling in what Victor Frankenstein called the "unhallowed damps of the grave" (54); like him, their "attention was fixed upon every object the most insupportable to the delicacy of human feelings" (52). And Cushing's Baron believes, like Shelley's Victor Frankenstein and Whale's Dr.

Pretorious, that he can artificially create his own children. What is more, the Baron displays a strong masculine drive violently directed, more than once, at the young women around him.

Pretorious' fascist intentions are undercut by his comic and excitable nature; Cushing's Frankenstein is, above all, serious and restrained. If momentary success excites him, he never exults; if he is beset by doubts, he never shows them. His single-minded devotion to his work, no matter how many times he fails or how far his results are from his intentions, is the source of his strength and his horror. Reversing the pattern of the Universal films, in each film of the Hammer series the Monster is irrevocably destroyed. But the scientist keeps coming back, sometimes disguised as Dr. Frank, sometimes as Dr. Stein, working quietly in some gaslit laboratory, undeterred by the "little miscalculations" that invariably botch things up.

The assorted Monsters are of secondary significance in these films. None of them comes close to possessing the individuality and power of Karloff's creature; the filmmakers wisely avoided trying to emulate his portrayal. Christopher Lee played "The Creature" only once, in *The Curse of Frankenstein,* emphasizing its defective brain and brutal power. In that film, Cushing has obtained a brain by murdering a scientist, though it is damaged inadvertently by his assistant, Paul Krempe. The Monster is animated one night when a lightning bolt starts the equipment; Frankenstein is thus spared the necessity of his presence at the creation and any accompanying emotional display. As Frankenstein enters the room, the creature staggers to its feet, tears the bandages from its face, and immediately tries to strangle its creator. There is no attempt to create pathos or deepen the characterization. During its few brief appearances, the Monster is little more than a destructive menace. After Krempe rescues Frankenstein, the Monster escapes to a forest where it kills a blind man. This dim echo of the novel destroys any sympathy for the Monster, contrasting the sylvan setting with the abominable thing that violates it.

When Krempe shoots it through the head and Frankenstein promises to bury it, the audience feels little pity. Frankenstein, of course, soon revives the Monster, though its brain is more useless than ever. In one of the best sequences of the film, he proudly demonstrates to his assistant its ability to follow his simple commands like a badly strung marionette. The Baron then uses it to murder a young servant girl he has impregnated. Finally, the Monster is set ablaze and dissolved in acid, decisively ending any chance for a comeback. The film ends with Frankenstein facing a just punishment as a murderer and sexual predator—his own mutilation by guillotine.

The next in the series, *The Revenge of Frankenstein* (1958), explains his unlikely escape: a deformed prison guard shoves the priest under the guillotine in return for the promise of a new body. Despite the improbable opening, this film in some ways surpasses its predecessor, adding to Cushing's characterization and introducing a genuine note of pathos. The hunchback's new self seems perfect; we see him gleefully burning his old, twisted body after the operation. But he is brutally beaten a few minutes later by a night watchman. As he reverts to his old form, there is a suggestion of a divine and terrible fate that cannot be negated. He is what he must be; Frankenstein's revolt against God's errors of creation, though possibly in this case justified, is doomed to failure. When the Monster bursts through the window of a fashionable home and confronts Dr. "Stein" crying, "Frankenstein, help me!" we are presented, for the first time since *The Bride of Frankenstein,* with an articulate, pathetic Monster who, like the Monster of the novel, asks its creator to take responsibility for it. (Typically, the sequence is mixed in with some awful business about a chimpanzee that has become a cannibal through brain transplants; in addition to its physical problems, the Monster develops a wholly unnecessary taste for human flesh. Restraint is not one of the virtues of the Hammer series.)

In this film, Frankenstein himself is a somewhat enigmatic figure; he works in a hospital for the poor, if only to secure a supply of human parts. Although he has his selfish motives, he does try to help his assistant by giving him a new body. When the patients at the hospital discover the Baron's true identity, they beat him to death. He has, in a sense, taken the philosophical place of the Monster; we are unsure whether his destruction is inevitable and necessary, or if he and his work should be accepted by the world. This transference of the film's center from monster to creator is made explicit in the last scene. After he dies, his assistant puts his brain in a new body. We see Dr. "Frank" opening another office, succeeding where Ygor failed, literally becoming his own Monster.

Later Hammer films make no attempt at maintaining continuity. Peter Cushing shows up and, after some preliminary scrounging for parts, rolls up his sleeves and gets to work. Despite the lavish trappings that drape the films, none has the individual style and impact of James Whale's classics. Their greatest significance is collective; memories linger of Cushing's cultured accents and diabolical designs, the inevitable laboratory gore and gizmos, well-endowed servant girls parading through the scenes, and disasters that occur like clockwork. As the series progressed, elements that endeared it to its young audience came to the fore. Frankenstein grew older and more undeniably depraved; the Monsters became younger and more appealing.

In *Frankenstein Created Woman* (1967), the "Monster" is an ex-*Playboy* centerfold, Susan Denberg, re-brained and (at least in publicity photos) seemingly raped on the operating table by the dastardly Cushing. In *Frankenstein Must Be Destroyed* (1969), the bumbling Baron casually slices off the head of a passer-by and then gets involved with a pair of young nineteenth-century drug dealers. Male chauvinist that he is, he uses the man for his assistant and keeps the woman around, as he says, to "make coffee." In the British version, he rapes her to assert his dominance. It is to Terence Fisher's credit that he can, at times, transcend the numbing sameness of the Hammer formula. His importance to the series is shown by the unremitting sleaziness of the films he did not direct, such as *The Evil of Frankenstein* (1964), which combines an unconvincing Monster with an absurd plot revolving around a hypnotist called the Great Zoltan, reminiscent of the Universal series at its worst.

Fisher's style avoids the expressionist idiom of James Whale and relies on straightforward medium shots, a measured pace, and an uncluttered story line. He returns the myth to the Gothic atmosphere that spawned Mary Shelley's nightmare, using the familiar Hammer period sets, the evil Baron, and an undercurrent of sexuality to maintain a Romantic mood of depravity and horror. Hammer films have been criticized for their attention to gruesome detail, yet anatomical shock is a traditional surprise in the Gothic bag of tricks. The heroines of the demure Mrs. Radcliffe's novels were, for example, forever pulling aside veils and discovering the most loathsome things, while Matthew Lewis's *The Monk* ends in an orgy of torture that makes the Hammer films themselves seem demure by comparison.

At their best, the Hammer films are polished and entertaining, playing with the emotions hidden behind the scientific culture, just as the Gothic movement explored the morbid nightmarish side of Romanticism. No longer is the creation of a monster the core of the film. It is accepted that such things can be done with little trouble. More important is the attitude of the creator and the motivation that keeps him at it after all of his experiments have such disastrous consequences. Fisher focuses on the Baron's obsession with the literal separation of body and mind and with the sexuality behind it. The metaphor for the divorce of thought and feeling is the brain transplant, an operation that shows up in all of the Fisher films, always tied to an exploration of the dimensions of the human personality.

Despite his occasional attempts at benevolent surgery, Baron Frankenstein is clearly dangerous and insane. He believes the mind is equal to the self; the result is a compulsion to transplant brains, thus reducing the organs of feeling to interchangeable husks. His detachment from his own body makes it possible for him to rape and murder with equal nonchalance and to have his brain moved from Dr. Stein to Dr. Frank with no complications. Such brain switches never work on anyone else. When he murders a famous scientist in *The Curse of Frankenstein* in order to steal his brain, the Baron believes it is not really murder, since his mind will live again in the Monster's body. Of course, the brain is damaged and his plan is thwarted. As we have seen, he does little better with his assistant in *The Revenge of Frankenstein,* whose new body reverts to the form of his old self. In *Frankenstein Created Woman,* the Baron calls his operation a "soul transplant," but it still fails. Christina, his pin-up monster, is given the soul of her dead lover. Instead of the perfect union he anticipates, she is driven to murder and suicide. Finally, in *Frankenstein Must Be Destroyed,* he does his best job to date. The Monster is barely disfigured, with a line of neat stitches around its skull. Again, the Baron's motives seem admirable; he has saved the life of a fellow doctor by transplanting his brain into a new body, curing him of insanity in the process. (Typically, our reactions to his cure are mixed, since he caused the doctor's death.) The Monster visits what was once his wife and tries to convince her that the figure before her is really her husband with a new body. Her uncomprehending revulsion points up the hopelessness of Frankenstein's dreams; she will not accept the idea that he is no more than his brain.

Frankenstein's denial of the part the body plays in making up the self is, first of all, a denial of death. If the brain can outlive the body then, in the Baron's mind, the self is immortal. But in the process, he must deny feeling and life. He sees man as only matter, reducing existence to "a dull affair, soundless, scentless, colourless, merely the hurrying of material endlessly, meaninglessly" (Brown 316). In trying to move personalities from one body to another, he displays the scientific aspect of his generally fascist attitude; control of the body means, on the largest scale, domination of nature and the external world. Frankenstein's insensitivity to the importance of the senses, the totality of the self, the universe of the body, both makes him the Monster and dooms his operations to failure.

The Baron's scientific attitudes are reflected in his aberrant sexuality. He lives at some distance from his own body, in a world of nonbeing and non-feeling, where intellect is all; that explains his personal coldness and matter-of-fact mutilations. His desire for dominance over the world of the body comes out in his violent rapes and murders. His actions suggest that underneath his calm exterior, he hates the body for its frailty and mortality. Therefore, as he gets older he becomes more brutal toward his young assistants and creations; like the Gothic villains, or even the scientist in *I Was a Teenage Frankenstein,* he becomes the evil father, seeking sexual domination and new life through control of the next generation. The Baron's sadistic madness is conveyed most subtly through the pornographic display of internal organs that fills the laboratory scene in each film. His compulsion to sexually violate his young victims is suggested by his secret, loving manipulation of their most private parts, as he quietly sings a tune.

IV

Mythical thought for its part is imprisoned in the events and experiences which it never tires of ordering and re-ordering in its search to find them a meaning.

—Claude Levi-Strauss

Myth is a sentence in a circular discourse, a discourse that is constantly changing its meaning: repetition and variation.

—Octavio Paz

The success of the Hammer films meant that the cinematic House of Frankenstein now had two distinct lineages. Although they both derived characters and sensibility from Mary Shelley's novel, fusing personal madness with the cultural insanity of misused technology, their styles and messages differed. The Universal films, spare, monochromatic, mixing offbeat humor with the off-center visuals derived from German expressionism, contrast with the opulence and excess of the Hammer films. In the former, the Monster can never die; in the latter the scientist is immortal and becomes the Monster. Each branch of the myth evolved into many lesser descendants, carrying the traditions to television, low budget films, and other media from popular music to mass advertising. More distant relatives include such films as *Robocop* (1988), *Edward Scissorhands* (1992), and even *Jurassic Park* (1995).

In the Seventies there were a number of attempts to retell the myth in new ways, or even to purport to return it to its origins in Mary Shelley's novel. Most such versions, including *Frankenstein: The True Story* (1973), which was anything but, and the gory but otherwise undistinguished Andy Warhol's *Frankenstein* (1974), were quite forgettable. *The Rocky Horror Picture Show* (1975) certainly wasn't. It turned the legend into a camp classic still going strong after a quarter century, the unlikely staple of late-night weekends for a legion of young cult followers. But its connections to the myth (and the novel) are pretty tenuous. The real masterpiece of the period was Mel Brooks' *Young Frankenstein* (1974) because it tried, and mostly succeeded in, evoking the atmosphere and mood of the Universal series and, incredibly, in finally concluding that branch of the myth with creator and creature each married and settled into happy domesticity.

Mel Brooks claims to have read Mary Shelley's *Frankenstein* carefully and taken it seriously; Peter Boyle, who played the Monster, wrote to me that he saw the part as more than an opportunity for humor but as a way to make a statement about science and society. Both obviously had an intimate feeling for the great Universal films of the Thirties. Shot in nostalgic black and white, *Young Frankenstein* is replete with archaic devices such as iris and wipe shots that mark the transition between scenes as well as little touches familiar to lovers of the old Frankenstein movies. Ygor's truncated walking stick, Inspector Kemp's wooden arm, the Caligariesque village, and the cobwebbed castle are only a few of the details that make the film a visual retrospective. The principals even act in the grand manner. Gene Wilder does a splendid imitation of Colin Clive, Basil Rathbone, et al., at their most frenetic, while Peter Boyle's sensitive interpretation of the Monster, in Karloffian make-up by William Tuttle, rivals that of the great Boris himself. (See Figure 11.) At the same time, the characters pay homage to Mary Shelley, actually quoting directly from her novel, here called *How I Did It,* by Victor Frankenstein.

But Brooks does not borrow from the past merely to mock it. Although a satire, the film sets out quite deliberately to remake the entire myth and bring it to a comic conclusion. Brooks' film is diametrically opposed to the sardonic sadism of the Hammer films; infused by a genuine love for the old Monsters and faith in human nature, Mel Brooks tries, once and for all, to transform the horror tale into a fairy tale and let maker and monster live happily ever after.

The title suggests his approach. *Young Frankenstein* is a cinematic Bildungsroman; Frederick Frankenstein, grandson of Victor, comes to maturity by coming to terms with his own past. At the beginning of the film we see him lecturing on the dissection of the brain at Baltimore General Hospital. He parodies the detachment of the scientist when he uses an old man to demonstrate the action of the central nervous system. After Frankenstein kicks him in the groin while cursing in his ear, the patient is wheeled out, doubled over in pain, as the good doctor tells his assistant, "Give him an extra dollar." When a student asks about his grandfather, Frankenstein explodes into an hysterical denial of any but an "accidental relationship to a famous cuckoo." He even denies his family name, insisting it be pronounced "Fronk-en-steen." His actual psychological bonds with his ancestors are exposed when, with manic

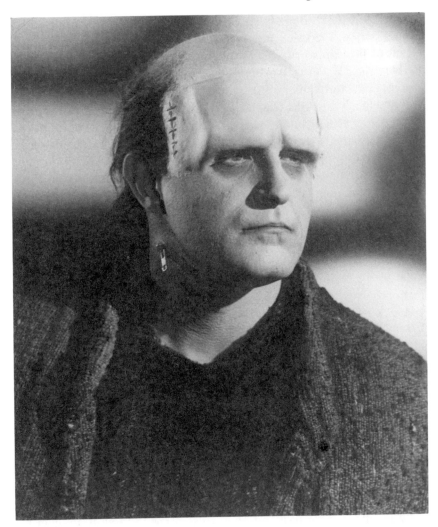

Figure 11. Peter Boyle in *Young Frankenstein* (1974). Despite the zipper, Boyle did what may be the best job next to the great Boris Karloff himself in portraying the Monster.

vehemence, he emphasizes his rejection of the past by driving a scalpel into his leg. In a way, Frankenstein's personal reaction to his lineage parallels the suppression by modern science of the questions raised in the Frankenstein myth. Frederick insists that since the central premise that Mary Shelley feared was imminent—the creation of life—is impossible, the story itself has no significance.

When, after his lecture, he is presented with his great-grandfather's legacy, he is forced to travel to Transylvania and there relive his past and face the Monster. The pre-creation scenes are handled brilliantly. At the railroad station, Frederick meets his beautiful laboratory assistant, Inga, and Ygor's grandson (who pronounces his own name "Eye-gor"). Together they travel to the family castle, a Gothic pile complete with scurrying rats, forbidding stone staircases, and a stone-faced housekeeper, Frau Blucher. That night, Frankenstein awakens from a nightmare, chanting, "Destiny, destiny, no escaping that for me!" Drawn by violin music to his grandfather's secret library, he reads Mary Shelley's creation scene from Victor's book and immediately decides, "It Could Work!"

Borrowing a body from the gallows, he adds a brain stolen by Ygor from the "brain depository." (Of course, as Ygor later admits, "It's from someone named 'A. B. Normal.'") The James Whale creation scene is staged using the original Strickfaden apparatus from his 1931 film. As maker and Monster ascend to the roof together, Frankenstein extends his arms in a crucifixion pose that casts a huge shadow on the wall and exults in the resurrection of his grandfather's madness. Soon after the creation comes to life, it escapes and, like his predecessor in the novel, Frederick awakens from his madness, voicing the familiar lament: "Oh God in Heaven, what have I done?" He manages with considerable difficulty to subdue the Monster with a sedative and (as in Whale's *Frankenstein*) lock it in a small stone room. But here *Young Frankenstein* and its sources diverge.

Rather than abandon the Monster, Frederick decides to enter alone and win it over. He tells the others to ignore his pleas to be let out, adding, "Love is the only thing that can save this poor creature, and I am going to convince him that he is loved, even at the cost of my own life." At first, of course, he screams to be released, pleading, "I was joking! Don't you know a joke when you hear one?" Then he calls for "Mommy!" The scene is the most important in the film; Frederick is really facing his own past and his own self, trying to work through his fear to love. When he realizes he cannot escape, he turns from the door to tell the Monster, "You are not evil; you are good." As it starts to sob, he hugs it and continues, "This is a nice boy, this is a good boy, this is a mother's angel . . . I want the world to know once and for all and without any shame that we love him!" By conquering his own creation with love, he can accept his own self and undo the curse that hangs over the House of Frankenstein, fulfilling the hope of Shelley's Frankenstein to become loving father to a grateful child. His new understanding is shown when Inga asks, through the door, "Dr. Fronk-en-steen, are you all right?" He screams back triumphantly, "MY NAME IS FRANKENSTEIN!"

The suggestion that the Monster is linked to its maker is underscored in the next scene when both appear identically dressed in top hat and tails to perform "Puttin' on the Ritz." The Monster's debut before a paying audience stirs memories of King Kong and results in a similar debacle. Frederick Frankenstein has done better than any of his prede-cessors in taming the Monster, but he still thinks like Carl Denham, who presented Kong as "The Eighth Wonder of the World" and a means to indulge his own ego. While locked in the room, Frederick told the Mon-ster that together, they "would make the greatest single contribution to science since the creation of fire," and here, before the performance, he treats it like the old man in the lecture room, showing off the refine-ments of its nervous system and its ability to obey simple commands while rewarding it like a trained seal. In *King Kong,* the monster is frightened by popping flash bulbs; in *Young Frankenstein,* an exploding footlight accomplishes the same thing. When they are unable to pick up the tempo for the final chorus, Frederick cries, "For God's sake, come on! Are you trying to make me look like a fool! I will not let you destroy my work . . . as your creator I command you to come back!" The Mon-ster lurches off into the night, leaving its creator unable to control what he has made.

The answer had been before him all along. Throughout the film, the two emotions of fear and love presented to the Monster are symbolized by fire and music. The first time the Monster escapes, it wanders into a series of parodies of famous scenes from the Whale films. It meets the little girl and has soup and a cigar with the blind hermit (played by Gene Hackman) but leaves them both unharmed, killing only a sadistic guard who torments it with fire (as Fritz did to Karloff's Monster). When the burning footlights, the villagers' fear, and Frankenstein's megalomania-cal commands frighten off the Monster again, it is drawn back to the castle, as always, by violin music.

Frau Blucher had first used the violin to lure Frederick into repeat-ing his grandfather's experiment. After the creation, she releases the Monster while Frederick and Ygor cringe in terror. She shows them the power music has "to reach the soul when words are useless"; as she plays the violin, the creature Frankenstein called a "seven-and-a-half-foot long, fifty-four-inch-wide gorilla" pathetically tries to grasp the notes from the air. At the same time, she reveals that Victor Frankenstein was once her "boyfriend." Frau Blucher's awareness of the power of love teaches her how to tame the Monster and reform Frederick Frankenstein. When he locks himself in the room with his creation, Frau Blucher is the only one who helps him, by preventing the others from letting him out too soon. Her violin theme, heard from the opening moments of the film to its final fade-out, is a continual reminder of the redeeming power of love.

The "power of love" has other, more direct, manifestations. The sexual prowess of the Monster, used for a lot of laughs, is also one clue to the meaning Victor's creation holds for its creator. Frederick is sexually frustrated; his fiancée, Elizabeth, who joins him at the castle near the end of the film, rarely lets him touch her and is careful to warn, "No tongues!" before they kiss. Monster-making is, again, substitute sexuality; he makes love with Inga on the operating table, describes the creation itself as an attempt to "penetrate the very womb of impervious Nature," and emphasizes that his creature will have what she calls "an enormous schvannschtuker."

After Elizabeth has sent a grunting Frederick off to bed in his own room, the grunting Monster breaks in and does what Frankenstein is obviously fantasizing—it carries her off and rapes her. We discover its sexual powers are magical; as Elizabeth is raped, she begins singing, "Ah, sweet mystery of life, at last I've found you!" But love is the stronger charm; the Monster is called away from the now-compliant Elizabeth by the music. Frankenstein entices it back to the castle in order finally to make it "as right as rain." The second time he risks his life, this time with his motives untarnished by hopes of scientific glory, he succeeds. Frankenstein transfers part of his brain to the Monster and receives its most prominent part in return.

The exchange makes clear what Frankenstein has discovered by reliving the myth. He and the Monster become one, while each gets what he needs to complete himself. Frankenstein learns that intellect without love means failure; the Monster gives up some of its sexual power in order to gain, in its own words, "a calmer brain and a somewhat more sophisticated way of expressing myself." The Monster is, on one level, the shadow of Frederick Frankenstein, the side he feared and repressed. By learning to love that part of himself, he gains its magic, accepts his own past, and changes the future. The Monster receives the wisdom, direction, and love necessary to make it human.

This same recognition of our affinities with the Monster is pointed up when Inspector Kemp bursts in with the familiar band of torch-bearing villagers just as the cure is nearing completion. After the Monster rises from the table and startles everyone by telling them of its rehabilitation, Kemp replies, "This is, of course, an entirely different situation. As the leader of this community, may I be the first to offer my hand in friendship." Since Kemp, like Inspector Krogh in *Son of Frankenstein*, has a wooden arm, the Monster takes him at his word and tears it off. We remember that Kemp, like the Monster, has trouble being understood when he speaks and is partly artificial. The scene shows everyone accepting the Monster among them and within them. The villagers, who have been "threatened five times before," will finally have nothing to worry about from the House of Frankenstein.

Mel Brooks leaves the Monster in bed reading the *Wall Street Journal*. It has married Elizabeth, who has miraculously sprouted Elsa Lanchester's hairdo from *The Bride of Frankenstein* and now slinks to bed, hissing merrily at her "old zipper neck." Frankenstein has married Inga and waits, grunting eagerly, to unveil to his bride what the Monster has given him. As is often the case in the traditional Bildungsroman, marriage concludes the adventure and shows us that the hero has finally reached sexual and emotional maturity. The ending fulfills the expectations of all of us who have always had a place in our hearts for the Karloff Monster and hoped, in one film at least, that it could find peace.

At the same time, *Young Frankenstein* portrays an end to the conflict between science, technology, and society. Earlier, while preparing to make Frederick "curse the day he was born a Frankenstein," the villagers curse scientists in general, who "say they're working for us, when what they really want is to rule the world!" The film argues that, through an understanding of the Frankenstein myth, such fears can be eliminated. Frederick learns, as Mary Shelley indicated, that our technology reflects ourselves and our motives. If we replace repression, fear, arrogance, and the desire for control with acceptance, love, humility, and the capacity for understanding, our machines can become a well-adjusted part of our culture. In seeking to coexist with our technological Monster, we must remember that its grip on life is tenacious, its arguments for acceptance compelling, and its potential for destruction boundless. It is a magnified image of ourselves.

V

After Mel Brooks brought at least one branch of the cinematic lineage of Frankenstein to a satisfying conclusion, little happened in the next two decades. Aside from the low budget film and television reworkings of the story (for example, *Doctor Frank* [1980], which set the story in New York City), the latest innovation in the genre was to return to the Romantic lushness and Gothic excess of the Hammer versions. This time, however, there was at least an attempt also to return to Mary Shelley's novel and even, in the case of Ken Russell's *Haunted Summer* (1988), to the occasion that gave birth to *Frankenstein*.

In 1993, Turner Television produced a version of *Frankenstein,* directed by David Wickes, starring Patrick Bergin and Randy Quaid as maker and Monster, which returned to the time and places in the novel and even included many of its elements, from Walton in the Arctic to the

De Lacey episode. The most interesting innovation was to link the Monster to its maker psychologically, adapting the creation scene to make the Monster literally a projection of Frankenstein. However, the film was quickly forgotten, probably because all the period trappings could not disguise a plodding story and lackluster performances. In particular, Randy Quaid's Monster was neither horrific, powerful, nor articulate—an endearing goofiness was the best he could muster.

A number of specific details of that film, however, showed up a year later as elements in what was perhaps the most heralded (and commercially the most disappointing) attempt to return to the novel. Kenneth Branagh had made his reputation with the help of William Shakespeare. After starring as Hamlet in the Renaissance Theater Company (which he co-founded), he had directed and starred in a film version of *Henry V* at the age of twenty-nine and repeated his triumph with *Much Ado About Nothing* in 1993 (as writer, producer, director, and performer). Then, perhaps inspired by Francis Ford Coppola's 1992 film, *Bram Stoker's Dracula,* he took on *Mary Shelley's Frankenstein* (1994).

Like Coppola's film (as in the Hammer productions, Dracula and Frankenstein seemed to merge into one visual style), Branagh had big stars (including himself as Victor, Robert De Niro as the Monster, and a stable of dependable period actors like Helena Bonham Carter, Ian Holm, Robert Hardy, and even John Cleese as Dr. Waldman). He also had the budget to engage in Gothic excess and re-create the world-spanning settings of the novel. In fact, Branagh stays reasonably close to Shelley's story, complete with the frame of Robert Walton in the Arctic, the complicated family dynamics of Frankenstein's household, and even familiar episodes like the scenes in the De Lacey cottage. Yet, like Victor's experiment itself, it all goes horribly wrong.

The fault is not with the intentions. The changes made to the novel are usually benign. Although Frankenstein's creation dream ("I thought that I held the corpse of my dead mother in my arms" [58]) is missing, her death is clearly the impetus for his Monster-making—when she dies giving birth, Victor repeats "Please bring her back!" She even bequeaths him the journal in which he will record his experiments, while the address she wrote on the first page enables the Monster to find his creator after being abandoned. Victor's experiments in the charnel house and his attraction to Professor Waldman's promises of power are vividly rendered, although in this case (as in so many films) Waldman becomes an unwilling brain donor when he is stabbed to death by what will become the chief source of body parts. De Niro's Monster is closer to what we imagine was Mary Shelley's conception; it is mapped with scars, yet articulate and capable of kindness—driven, as the original

Monster was, to revenge and murder by the hatred shown it by everyone it meets. So what happened?

The scene when Justine Moritz dies for the murder of Frankenstein's little brother provides a clue. It echoes the plot of the novel, but in this case she is lynched by a mob right out of the Universal films. Someone even cries "The townspeople have gone mad!" though no torches are in evidence. That scene, like so many others, points up the fatal flaw in *Mary Shelley's Frankenstein*. The problem is both with how it is acted and directed and with how the two elements of novel and film tradition are blended.

No one and nothing (including the camera) is at rest for more than a few seconds. Everyone, happy or sad, tormented or content, acts at fever pitch, and lurches about the ornate sets in constant motion. The camera spins, zooms, tracks, and pans constantly. Helena Bonham Carter, who has seemingly perfected the art of acting in period films, in this case wears what reminds the viewer of a brunette version of Elsa Lanchester's wig from *The Bride of Frankenstein* and seems demented from the start, staring and shouting at every opportunity. Branagh, as both the star and director, puts himself in the center of nearly every shot, galloping through the sets or running around his laboratory at a fever pitch. He cannot even just abandon his creation; he has to engage in a semi-nude wrestling match with it in a pool of spilled fluid, then somehow accidentally string it up in chains. Early on, we know we are in trouble when the Frankenstein home turns out to be an enormous pile with very little furniture and a huge curving staircase without a banister (right out of the original 1931 *Dracula*). In this case, instead of the Count descending slowly to confront Renfield, *Frankenstein* races up it, and his bare-chested father, covered in blood, collapses on it after his mother dies in childbirth. Throughout *Mary Shelley's Frankenstein,* we are reminded of the films and not the novel; what is more, we are reminded of how the films did it better.

In fact, the most interesting elements are those that do not recall the novel but which we recognize from both the Universal and Hammer traditions. Like Colin Clive in 1931, Branagh's Frankenstein repeats "It's Alive!" as sparks fly at the crucial moment, although in this case the power of electricity is harnessed in a different way and with new ingredients. In the novel, the "astonishing secret" of life (52) Victor Frankenstein discovers is never explained. Clive's Frankenstein finds it by harnessing lightening, which in *Mary Shelley's Frankenstein* is used only for a Franklinesque (and highly unlikely) experiment to amuse the ladies.

Branagh's version of the creation recalls the methods in the Hammer films taken to wretched excess—he uses electric eels (with a bit of acupuncture thrown in) to animate his creature in a tub of amniotic fluid harvested from women giving birth. (This substitute sexuality and procreation is, as in the novel, accompanied by the abandonment of fiancée Elizabeth before the act and a post-coital disgust with what he has done when it is over.) Like the Dr. Frankenstein created by Peter Cushing in the Hammer films, he sees human bodies as "materials, nothing more." Unlike Cushing's Frankenstein, however, but like his namesake in the novel, Branagh's Victor Frankenstein will pay with the lives of his family for his denial of the body. In fact, when he refuses to build the Monster a mate in the film, it is because the body is of the lynched Justine, and he realizes that he cannot see it as merely raw material or condemn her body to a lifetime with the Monster. It is a good and original moment, but such moments are all too rare in this film.

In short, the disappointment of *Mary Shelley's Frankenstein* tells us something about what happened to the myth in the nearly two centuries since Mary Shelley created it. The popular audience knows the story from the popular media. In his film, Branagh must account for the tradition of Frankenstein films that preceded it, which affects the way we compare what we see with what we have seen. But it also means that a similar style of acting (or overacting) determines whether we will react to the story in the way Branagh may have intended. He wants, most probably, to return to the novel in order to examine the issues of love, life, and death—the philosophical complexities it contains. De Niro's speeches, Carter's anguish, and Branagh's rantings on life and death, however, are the weakest parts of the film.

Branagh also wants to draw on the Gothic imagery of creation and the horror of what was created, but he cannot do that without evoking his cinematic predecessors. His bag of writhing electric eels, amniotic fluid, and acupuncture are clearly an attempt to top Whale's creation scene, while, rather than redefining the role of the Monster created by Boris Karloff, Robert De Niro's soft-spoken portrayal of the Monster never evokes the power Karloff gave it. A scene Branagh added to the novel, when Victor reanimates Elizabeth after the Monster has ripped out her heart, reminds us of the conclusion to *The Bride of Frankenstein,* complete with her rejection of the Monster as a mate and with a subsequent conflagration. In order to render Shelley's story cinematic, Branagh restages the elements of the cinematic tradition of *Frankenstein,* undercutting its pretensions to be something more than another such film.

Can Mary Shelley's vision be both faithfully and effectively rendered on film? Perhaps not. Perhaps the myth that has supplanted it and that will continue to infuse popular culture is the only way it can be rendered in a visual medium. As *Mary Shelley's Frankenstein* opens, we hear her words from the preface to the 1831 edition of her novel: "I busied myself *to think of a story*. . . . one which would speak to the mysterious fears of our nature, and awaken thrilling horror" (8). Transformed by theater and film, *Frankenstein* has become so much a part of our culture that, paradoxically, her original story may not translate to film without losing its power. *Frankenstein*'s philosophical complexities and the fact that it depends upon what we do not see directly (the novel is a series of stories within stories) suggest it is made to be read. When Walton (who stands between the events of the novel and the reader) actually glimpses the Monster, he calls it "a form which I cannot find words to describe" (218). To actually visualize a Monster who is both terrifying and articulate may, in fact, be impossible. Once the electrical equipment is turned off and Robert De Niro's Monster speaks, we no longer find him horrific, and *Mary Shelley's Frankenstein* runs out of juice.

The cinematic tradition that translated Mary Shelley's vision to a new visual medium by necessity simplified the story and redefined it to fit the concerns of a popular audience at the time. Whale's films and the Universal series that followed are clearly influenced by two world wars; the Hammer films (like the subspecies of Frankenstein-inspired Monster movies) evoke the fear of science and scientists in a post-nuclear age. Films that return to the period and treat Mary Shelley like Jane Austen simply do not work. Both the elements that give the specific power of her novel as well as the genre in which she wrote preclude turning *Frankenstein* into a faithful Hollywood costume drama. Instead, the creator and her creation must be appreciated for the great and unique triumph that it was. At the age of eighteen, struggling to *"think of a story"* (8), Mary Shelley created a myth.

Notes

1. Much of the factual information on the theatrical productions comes from Elizabeth Nitchie, "The Stage History of *Frankenstein*," *South Atlantic Quarterly* 41 (1942): 384-98.

2. Donald F. Glut, in *The Frankenstein Catalog,* manages to fill almost 450 pages with a comprehensive listing of almost every appearance of Frankenstein's Monster in popular culture from film to sheet music. Although film is only one part of this Herculean achievement, the sheer volume of references makes Mary Shelley's novel the likely winner of most filmed story in literary history. There are also many film histories of *Frankenstein,* among them "The Stage and Film History of *Frankenstein:* A Survey" by Albert J. Lavalley in George Levine and U. C. Knoepflmacher, eds., *The Endurance of Frankenstein*

(Berkeley: U of California P, 1979) and "*Frankenstein* at the Cinema: Franken-stein in Films from the Silents to Hammer."

3. Frye, who has become something of a minor cult figure, was once voted one of the ten best legitimate actors on Broadway, appearing in plays as diverse as *La La Lucille* and *Six Characters in Search of an Author*. His first film success was in *Dracula* (1931), where his cackling performance as Renfield earned him the reputation as the actor who went insane better than anyone else in pictures. Frye went on to appear in every film in the Frankenstein cycle through *Frankenstein Meets the Wolf Man* (1943) as either a featured performer or bit player until, on November 11, 1943, he died of a heart attack at age forty-four.

4. William Shakespeare, *Macbeth*, Act II, scene iii, lines 1-21. The situation is parallel. Fritz answers the door in the midst of Frankenstein's criminal experiments and lets in three people who will attempt to undo his blasphemy; the porter in *Macbeth* admits Macduff and Lennox soon after the murder of the king—also a crime against the natural order, committed late at night in a castle. In both cases, the interlude provides contrast and comic relief and, as Thomas De Quincey said of Shakespeare in his famous essay "On the Knocking at the Gate in *Macbeth*" (1823), makes us more aware of the unnaturalness of the crime by re-establishing the normal occurrences and rhythms of life.

5. An observation made by Roy Huss in "Almost Eve: The Creation Scene in *The Bride of Frankenstein*," *Focus on the Horror Film*, ed. Roy Huss and T. J. Ross, 77. I am indebted to the entire article for a shot-by-shot analysis of the laboratory creation scene.

6. This aspect of monster films has been commented on before. Carlos Clarens, in *An Illustrated History of the Horror Film*, 131, writes, "The monsters of the nuclear age are all creatures of the Bomb," while John Baxter, in *Science Fiction in the Cinema*, 136, states that "In all of these films it is possible to see the characteristic American ambiguity about technology . . . To American audiences the havoc wreaked on their homes by various dinosaurs is as welcome as the lash to a flagellant. . . ."

7. Erroneously, of course. "Frankenstein" here is a synonym for Monster. This may have begun with Whale's *The Bride of Frankenstein*, though in that film both scientist and Monster are, after a fashion, married. *The Ghost of Frankenstein* contains an apparition of Henry Frankenstein as well as a ghostly Monster covered in dried sulfur, while in the next film the Wolf Man meets both Frankenstein's Monster and Baroness Elsa Frankenstein, making the title, *Frankenstein Meets the Wolf Man*, equally ambiguous. With *I Was a Teenage Frankenstein*, such subtleties are gone; Whit Bissell's scientist could hardly pass for a teenager, while Gary Conway's Monster is decidedly at that awkward adolescent age.

Works Cited

Baxter, John. *Science Fiction in the Cinema*. New York: Paperback Library, 1971.

Brown, Norman O. *Life Against Death*. New York: Vintage, 1959.

Clarens, Carlos. *An Illustrated History of the Horror Film*. New York: Capricorn, 1968.

Curtis, James. *James Whale*. Filmmakers, No. 1. Metuchen, NJ: Scarecrow P, 1982.

Evans, Walter. "Monster Movies: A Sexual Theory." *Journal of Popular Film* 2 (1963): 353-65.

"*Frankenstein* at the Cinema: Frankenstein in Films from the Silents to Hammer." http://www.scottiedog.co.uk/cinema.html, 1997.

Freud, Sigmund. *Civilization and Its Discontents*. Ed. James Strachey. New York: Norton, 1962.

Glut, Donald F. *The Frankenstein Catalog*. Jefferson, NC: McFarland, 1984.

Huss, Roy. "Almost Eve: The Creation Scene in *The Bride of Frankenstein*." *Focus on the Horror Film*. Ed. Roy Huss and T. J. Ross. Englewood Cliffs, NJ: Prentice Hall, 1972. 74-82.

Lavalley, Albert J. "The Stage and Film History of *Frankenstein:* A Survey." *The Endurance of Frankenstein*. Ed. George Levine and U. C. Knoepflmacher. Berkeley: U of California P, 1979.

Nitchie, Elizabeth. "The Stage History of *Frankenstein*." *South Atlantic Quarterly* 41 (1942): 384-98.

Shelley, Mary. *Frankenstein*. Ed M. K. Joseph. London: Oxford, 1969.

2

THE IMPORTANCE OF BEING MARRIED:
ADAPTING *PRIDE AND PREJUDICE*

Ronnie Jo Sokol

In the fall of 1995, 11,000,000 British stayed home on six consecutive Sunday evenings to view a six-part miniseries devoid of sex, violence, and drugs and adapted from a popular literary work (Jacobs 76, Amis 32). The following January, this phenomenon was repeated by 3.7 million Americans, who spent three consecutive weeknights watching the six-hour program (Thomas 61). The late author of the novel on which the series was based had just been declared a "hot Hollywood property" (Morell C1), with two movies inspired by her writings tying for *Time* magazine's best movie of 1995 (Barton 1, 23). She herself had recently been named one of both *People* magazine's "Twenty-Four Most Intriguing People of 1995" and *Entertainment Weekly*'s top ten entertainers of the year. Long under-appreciated actor Colin Firth, the male lead of the 1995 adaptation, caused "a sexual upheaval of volcanic intensity" (Koenig 494), and Jennifer Ehle, the female lead, won a BAFTA, the British equivalent of an Emmy. The video of the series immediately sold out; sales of the novel in England alone were boosted to 35,000 copies a week (Rothstein 14); and new interest was shown in screen adaptations of the author's other works. A literary society based on the author boasted hundreds of new members; scholars of the genre in which she wrote became honored guests at parties; and fans developed the affectation of speaking in her style (Gold B3, Amis 34). Tourists flocked to the English countryside to tour the spots described in the novel. What caused all the fuss? A 182-year-old comedy of manners, Jane Austen's *Pride and Prejudice*.

The immensely popular 1995 adaptation of *Pride and Prejudice* was not, however, the first filmed version of Austen's novel. For years, the standard had been the 1940 film starring Laurence Olivier and Greer Garson, directed by Robert Z. Leonard. While much admired, that version contained numerous inaccuracies and deviations from the novel, some of which would surely rankle audiences were the film released today. Several BBC (British Broadcasting Company) television adaptations of *Pride and Prejudice* followed over the next two decades—a six-part dramatization by Cedric Wallis, produced by Campbell Logan in 1952; a six-part black and white dramatization, also by Cedric Wallis, produced by Barbara Burnham in 1958; and a 1967 dramatization by Nemone Lethbridge, directed by Joan Craft and produced by Campbell Logan. But few viewers outside the United Kingdom saw these versions. A more memorable and widely-viewed adaptation, directed by Cyril Coke and starring David Rintoul and Elizabeth Garvie, was produced in England in 1979. Shown on *Masterpiece Theatre* in America in October, 1980, it delighted purists with its faithful rendering of Austen's dialogue and the subtleties of her text. Yet it was not until the 1995 adaptation featuring Colin Firth and Jennifer Ehle that the moviegoing public became completely smitten with Elizabeth and Darcy. Austen admirers, their cinematic appetites whetted by the recent successes of *Clueless, Persuasion,* and *Sense and Sensibility,* looked forward to an innovative and authentic entertainment in the latest version of *Pride and Prejudice;* and they certainly were not disappointed. Austen-mania appeared to be at its height.

Upon the release of *Pride and Prejudice* (1813), her second published book, Jane Austen sent a letter dated January 29 to her sister Cassandra. Referring to the first three-volume edition of the book, Jane wrote, "I have got my own darling Child from London." She related to Cassandra how, on the very day of the book's coming out, their brother Henry had read the story to his dinner guest, Miss Benn, who apparently enjoyed it very much. "She really does seem to admire Elizabeth," Jane confided. "I must confess that I think her [Elizabeth] as delightful a creature as ever appeared in print, and how I shall be able to tolerate those who do not like *her* at least, I do not know" (Le Faye 201).

Austen had little reason to worry about the critical or popular reception Elizabeth—and all of the other Bennets—would receive: the response to her novel was overwhelmingly favorable. The *British Critic* for February stated that "the story is well told, the characters remarkably well drawn and supported, and written with great spirit as well as vigour. . . . we have perused these volumes with much satisfaction and amusement and entertain very little doubt that their successful circulation will induce the author to similar exertions" (Harris 30). The *Critical Review* for March summarized the plot and praised the "domestic scenes" as superior; all the characters were integrated into the tale, and none "appears flat, or obtrudes itself upon the notice of the reader with troublesome impertinence" (Nokes 402). The *New Review* for April also gave an admiring synopsis with quotations (Myer 185). The hit novel of 1813, *Pride and Prejudice* was the topic of discussion among readers and intellectuals like Richard Brinsley Sheridan and Annabella Milbanke, the future Lady Byron, who praised the cleverness of the book and pondered the author's identity. *Pride and Prejudice,* moreover, was appreciated as much by royalty as by circulating library subscribers. The Prince Regent, it is reported, kept a copy of *Pride and Prejudice,* along with Austen's other works, in each of his residences (Myer 214).

Austen had begun writing *Pride and Prejudice,* then titled *First Impressions,* in 1796. That same year, her father tried unsuccessfully to publish the first draft with a publisher named Cadell, who rejected it, despite the offer of an arrangement for publication "at the author's risk or otherwise" (Myer 161). Austen then turned to the writing of other books. It was only years later, when Jane's father was dead and she was in need of money, that she returned to the manuscript, revising it, renaming it, and ultimately publishing it, anonymously, with Egerton for £110 (Myer 181). Austen's fondness for the novel stemmed in large part from her partiality for Elizabeth Bennet, a "reader of characters" and a young woman who sparkled at the same time that she laughed at herself and at the foibles of others—a woman, in fact, very much like Austen.

Set in Regency England, *Pride and Prejudice* follows the fortunes of Elizabeth and her sister Jane, the eldest of the five Bennet daughters. Mr. Bennet realizes that, should he die without a male heir, his egocentric cousin, the Reverend Mr. Collins, will take possession of Longbourn, the family's only home, and disinherit Mrs. Bennet and her daughters. Yet, ever hopeful that his wife will bear a son, Bennet puts away little money as dowry for the girls. Mrs. Bennet shares her husband's hope but nevertheless grows increasingly anxious about her daughters' fate—and her own—should they have to provide for themselves. When Mr. Bingley, a young single man of large fortune, rents the nearby Netherfield estate in Hertfordshire, she believes that he is destined for one of her girls; and much of the novel's comedy arises from Mrs. Bennet's subsequent efforts to save the family from penury by her desperate matchmaking.

Bingley is soon joined at his estate by his friend Fitzwilliam Darcy, a handsome bachelor with an even more commanding fortune. At the local assembly ball, Bingley falls in love with Jane Bennet. Elizabeth, however, is snubbed by the reserved but arrogant Darcy, and she nurtures a resentful prejudice towards him, a prejudice that intensifies when George Wickham, the dashing soldier to whom she is attracted, claims that Darcy has withheld his inheritance. Meanwhile, despite his pride, Darcy finds himself more and more attracted to Elizabeth.

To make amends for his eventual disinheritance of the Bennet women, Mr. Collins becomes their houseguest, with the intention of marrying one of his fair cousins. Upon being refused by Elizabeth, however, he is accepted by her best friend Charlotte Lucas, who is practical enough to appreciate such a union; and the couple move to a parsonage in Kent on the large estate of Lady Catherine de Bourgh, Mr. Darcy's aunt.

Mistakenly thinking that Jane Bennet does not return Bingley's regard, Darcy and Caroline, Bingley's sister, press Charles to remove to London. When Jane visits her aunt and uncle, the Gardiners, in London, Darcy keeps her visit secret from Charles. Later, when Darcy travels to Kent to see his aunt, he is thrown into the company of Elizabeth, who is visiting Charlotte. Darcy proposes marriage but is rejected; deeply hurt, he feels compelled to defend his character in a letter, in which he comments on the undignified and frivolous behavior of Elizabeth's mother and younger sisters and exposes George Wickham as a seducer and gamester. Ashamed by the revelations, Elizabeth regrets her prejudice towards Darcy.

After returning home from Kent, Elizabeth is invited by the Gardiners to tour Derbyshire, where, at his Pemberley estate, she unexpectedly encounters Darcy. Impressed by the changes in his behavior, Elizabeth falls in love with him. But just when Darcy is at the point of renewing his addresses, she receives word that her reckless sister Lydia has run off with Wickham; and she is forced to hurry back home again.

To restore the Bennet family's social position, Darcy tracks down Wickham and forces him to marry Lydia. Meanwhile, Lady Catherine de Bourgh travels to Longbourn to warn Elizabeth against marrying Darcy. Despite Lady Catherine's insulting and condescending manner, Elizabeth is encouraged by the older woman's fears. Bingley returns to Netherfield to claim Jane Bennet's hand, and Darcy follows in order to risk a second proposal to Elizabeth. This time, he is successful, and everyone lives happily and prosperously—and far away from Mrs. Bennet and Wickham.

Austen's story was in many ways a natural for film adaptation, especially in the late 1930s and 1940s, when romantic comedies were very much in vogue. The first film version of *Pride and Prejudice* (Metro-Goldwyn-Mayer, 1940; dir. Robert Z. Leonard) was, however, based as much on Helen Jerome's 1935 Broadway stage script (produced from her 1934 play), which the screenwriters Aldous Huxley and Jane Murfin incorporated into their own screenplay,[1] as on Austen's novel. Several important details and episodes in the film, in fact, are borrowed directly from Jerome, such as the elimination of Elizabeth's visit to Pemberley during the trip with the Gardiners, an event significant in the novel because it changes her feelings from wounded pride and resentment toward Darcy to embarrassment, humility, admiration, and ultimately love for Darcy. Cut as well is the climactic letter from Darcy, who instead comes to Longbourn himself to explain Wickham's character. Added from Jerome's script is the dialogue of the proposal scene, since Austen wrote most of it as narration. Clearly, though, the film—shot in black and white and with a running length of 118 minutes—made a number of its own departures from the novel.

Among the most obvious of the departures was the age of the main characters. In their mid-thirties, both Greer Garson (Elizabeth Bennet) and Laurence Olivier (Darcy) were at least ten years older than the Austen characters they played. But both were such audience favorites—Olivier, for films like *Wuthering Heights* (1939) and *Rebecca* (1940), and Garson, for *Goodbye, Mr. Chips* (1939)—that viewers easily overlooked the discrepancy and accepted them in their roles. Moreover, the affectionate tension between Olivier and Garson—fueled by rumors of a former off-stage romance between the two[2]—was not only credible but also cinematically appropriate. By actually depicting Elizabeth and Darcy's furtive glances or gestures, which often contradicted the subtle dialogue, the film offered a level of sexual intimacy that the novel itself could never illustrate.

More problematic than Garson's age, however, was her beauty. Elizabeth, in the book, is described as having looks that are merely "tolerable"; in fact, suggests Austen, being less spectacularly lovely than her sister Jane forces Elizabeth to hone her wit and intellect—in other words, to develop her inner qualities. But, in the film, as George Lellis and H. Philip Bolton demonstrate, "Garson is too sweetly beautiful and has trouble putting into her performance the bite of acid skepticism that Austen locates below Lizzy's polite exterior" (47). Garson's beauty is no doubt the reason that director Robert Z. Leonard gave her more close-ups than anyone else in the film—a source of special irritation to Olivier, who objected to the steady position the camera maintained on his co-star (Spoto 144). Yet the close-ups served another important cinematic purpose by implying the existence of the character's strong inner life. Viewers not only wondered what was going on behind Garson's sparkling eyes; they also followed with fascination the range of emotions that her face conveyed. After Darcy's first proposal of marriage, for instance, when Darcy leaves the room in dismay, Garson as Elizabeth reflects emotions from complacent bemusement, to regret, to frustration. "Her expressions," conclude Lellis and Bolton, "are outer signs of the inner process which Lizzy goes through in Austen's novel as she examines, reconsiders, and ultimately modifies her judgments about Darcy and Wickham" (47).

In addition to visualizing episodes and incidents that are only "internalized" in the novel, the film draws on dialogue that clearly was not Austen's. The film's characters often resort to telling each other directly what Austen's characters simply imply. About halfway through the film, for instance, Elizabeth tells Darcy, "At this moment it's difficult to believe that you're so proud," and he replies, "At this moment it's difficult to believe that you're so prejudiced." The exchange, which reinforces the central motif of pride and prejudice, is so blatant and so obvious that it would never have appeared in the novel. Nor would other exchanges that were intended to generate cinematic humor, such as Mr. Bennet's response to his wife's bemoaning of their daughters' future poverty. "Perhaps," he quips, "we should have drowned them all at birth."

Some of the adaptive changes, however, while in themselves inauthentic or anachronistic, work effectively in the context of the filmed story. As the movie opens, for instance, Mrs. Bennet (Mary Boland) is returning with her daughters from a shopping excursion. When she learns that the wealthy—and unattached—Bingley has rented a large estate in the area, she exclaims, "That's the most heartening piece of news since the Battle of Waterloo!" Although that battle had not yet been fought, Mrs. Bennet is already plotting her own kind of Waterloo against her rival Mrs. Lucas. Rushing home to demand that her husband Mr. Bennet (Edmund Gwenn) visit Bingley to establish an acquaintance with him, she races her carriage against the carriage of Mrs. Lucas, thus foreshadowing the competition that continues between the two mothers as they try to arrange successful marriages for their daughters. But, as R. H. Chapman demonstrates, the incident is historically inaccurate in another way as well. Due to the poor state of country roads and the frequency of carriage accidents during the Regency period, people would never have raced carriages (565). Jane Austen knew of several people who had suffered carriage spills, and she even lost her best friend, Anne Lefroy, in a riding accident; hence she would never have detailed much less endorsed such risky behavior. Yet the primary audience for the 1940 *Pride and Prejudice* were Americans, who loved cars, speed, and slapstick comedy; and, in this particular scene, which was highlighted by Herbert Stothart's buzzing bee music and accented by Mr. Bennet's amused reaction to his wife's singleminded determination, that is precisely what they got.

Other such inaccuracies—and even more serious ones—occur throughout the film. At the Meryton Assembly (see Figure 12), self-

Figure 12. As the Lucases look on and as Bingley stares at Jane across the room, Caroline Bingley (Frieda Inescort) claims a waltz with Darcy (Laurence Olivier). © MGM

appointed master of ceremonies Sir William Lucas (E. E. Clive) encourages Darcy to participate. "Every savage can dance," Darcy replies. Screenwriters Huxley and Murfin, however, change his line to "Every Hottentot can dance," a reference that would have been as unappreciated by Austen's contemporaries as by the African tribe itself. Then, in the film (though not in the book), Elizabeth, having been previously snubbed by Darcy, refuses his gallant invitation to dance, an action that seems to foreshadow her rejection of his marriage proposal. And, of course, where Darcy fails, George Wickham briefly succeeds, by ingratiating himself into Elizabeth's favor. Here again, however, the screenwriters neglected to do their research. Regency etiquette, with which Austen was totally familiar, dictated that a woman who declined a man's invitation to dance was expected to say that she was fatigued and then to sit out the next several sets so as not to insult the gentleman. If, after all, eligible young men were expected to ask young ladies to dance only to suffer the humiliation of rejection, the custom of dancing would not have served its purpose. Yet it is unlikely that an American audience in the 1940s would have held Elizabeth to such a strict code of conduct or judged her so harshly for breaching it. In the film, in fact, though Darcy now has cause to resent Elizabeth, he resents only Wickham, his rival for her affection.

Austen describes a similar situation in another novel, *Northanger Abbey,* in which the young heroine, Catherine Morland, must reject an invitation to dance with a young man who really interests her, since she had already promised that set of dances to a repellent suitor, who is delayed in escorting her to the dance floor (Chapter 8). Later, she claims fatigue in order to avoid dancing with the boor again. But, in so doing, she must sit out the rest of the evening. On another occasion in that novel, when the brutish John Thorpe tries to cut in on Catherine and Henry Tilney's dance, Henry claims that a set of dances is like a marriage, implying that partners owe each other their attention and loyalty (Chapter 10).

Etiquette again comes into play at the garden party at Netherfield Park. After rescuing Elizabeth from the unwelcome attentions of Mr. Collins, a buffoon who rehearses his compliments aloud and who taps the Bennet family's porcelain and crystal to determine their worth, Darcy invites Elizabeth to engage in target practice. Assuming she has no experience with archery, he condescendingly shows her how to place her fingers and how to hold the bow. When she surprises him by shooting three bull's-eyes, he takes her instruction goodnaturedly, which she acknowledges. (It is an interesting scene, in many respects, especially since it suggests both that Elizabeth is equal to Darcy and that she knows—literally as well as metaphorically—what her target is.) Afterwards, as Elizabeth asks why he dislikes Wickham, green-eyed Caroline Bingley interrupts Darcy's defense of a gentleman's privacy. Caroline warns Elizabeth that, if Darcy says so, Wickham is dishonorable. Elizabeth responds by asking Caroline what she knows of the matter. When Caroline admits she has no specifics, Elizabeth retorts: "How clever of you, Miss Bingley, to know something of which you are ignorant. Oh, Mr. Darcy, Miss Bingley is eager for her lesson. I hope you will enjoy it, Miss Bingley, and that you will learn to direct your *darts* with greater accuracy."

Respecting the word of a gentleman and zealously guarding privacy were sacrosanct customs of the early nineteenth century. In fact, had the English during the Regency period believed in sharing their personal concerns, Jane Austen's books would never have been written. All of Austen's story lines depend on the main characters not being privy to significant information that affects their destinies. Had Elizabeth been familiar with Wickham's reputation, she would not have misjudged Darcy's behavior, and there would have been no sexual tension—and no dart-throwing—in the scene.

Historical inaccuracies are a common problem in the filming of period pieces; and a variety of such inaccuracies is apparent in this first adaptation of *Pride and Prejudice*. As Rachel King notes, "MGM's 1940 version of the novel preferred a Victorian treatment, to match public misperception of the look of Regency England" (62). In addition to the problems in locale (the film, after all, was shot not in the English countryside but in Hollywood, with indoor sets Victorian rather than Regency in period), there were costuming concerns. Adrian, the film's gown designer, fashioned clothing that was clearly inappropriate for the great walkers and horseback riders of the Regency era. "The actresses wear billowing hoopskirts rather than the columnar dresses . . . the oversized hats look out of place, the voluminous skirts menacing. The bow on Greer Garson's ringlets distracts rather than charms—she looks less like a Regency beauty than Shirley Temple with an overactive pituitary gland" (King 62). The musical score was only marginally better than the costumes. In an overture that accompanied the film's leader, musical director Herbert Stothart introduced appropriate musical themes that recurred like leitmotifs in opera for each family of characters; but some of his "old England" score was irritatingly silly. The bassoon, for example, was effective in mocking Mr. Collins (Melville Cooper) both in the opening scene and in each of his subsequent appearances, but the chicken-like parade for Mrs. Bennet set a slapstick tone for the whole film. That slapstick, which reaches its climax in the scene when Lady

Catherine calls on Elizabeth to protest her engagement to Darcy—their encounter devolves into farcical misadventures, including a tea-tray that is kicked over, a music box that is crushed by being sat upon, and a parrot that is overly talkative—creates a visual humor that vulgarizes and violates the refined spirit of the novel. It is as if the filmmakers lacked the confidence in the capacity of Austen's wit to hold the audience's interest (Lellis and Bolton 50). Despite such shortcomings, the film—enjoyable, if only adequate as an adaptation—was a resounding hit.

To accommodate the two-hour time frame of the feature film, the director Robert Z. Leonard had to sacrifice some of Austen's story line. To that end, scenes were often and usually effectively excised; others were consolidated. Elizabeth's visit to Darcy's estate, for example, was eliminated, as were some of the parties. Also excluded was the ball at Bingley's Netherfield property. Instead, Leonard substituted a large garden party at Netherfield, which allowed the characters to interact freely with each other and also revealed important aspects of their personalities. Set free outdoors, for instance, Lydia and Kitty are vulgar and loud. Darcy, proving that he can be a good friend, saves Elizabeth from the unwelcome attentions of Collins. Mary, oblivious to her lack of vocal accomplishment, suffers her father's timely but insensitive intervention. Caroline Bingley reveals herself to be wholly mercenary and heartless. And Bingley and Jane are clearly in love.

The climax of both book and film occurs at Hunsford Parsonage, on Lady Catherine's estate, where Darcy proposes marriage to Elizabeth. Purists are always curious about this scene because, in the novel, Austen never actually writes Darcy's proposal. Instead, she writes a single declaration of love and lets the omniscient narrator explain the rest. "In vain have I struggled [with the fact that Elizabeth is from an inferior family and that it would be debasing for Darcy to marry her]. It will not do. My feelings will not be repressed. You must allow me to tell you how ardently I admire and love you." A description of his scruples follows. Elizabeth's response, which is longer than Darcy's declaration, suggests controlled anger and attempted civility, despite her desire to be rid of him: "In such cases as this, it is, I believe, the established mode to express a sense of obligation for the sentiments avowed, however unequally they may be returned. It is natural that obligation should be felt, and if I could *feel* gratitude, I would now thank you. But I cannot—I have never desired your good opinion, and you have certainly bestowed it most unwillingly. I am sorry to have occasioned pain to any one. It has been most unconsciously done, however, and I hope will be of short duration. The feelings which, you tell me, have long prevented the acknowledgement of your regard, can have little difficulty in overcoming it after this explanation" (Chapter 34). Darcy's demand for clarification follows, as does Elizabeth's "endeavor at civility," a long and bitter tirade. But unlike Mr. Collins's "reasons for marrying," for example, which are detailed at great length, Austen infuses Darcy's dialogue with description. Perhaps she did this because she wrote in a highly stylized form. Chronicling Darcy's outpouring of love would have deflated the sexual tension beneath the surface and deflected the reader's attention from the comic aspects of the proposal.

To Austen's credit, she experimented with "alternate ways of rendering speech," such as "free indirect speech, . . . telescoping a long speech into a few telegraphic phrases [such as Darcy's], eschewing dialogue altogether, even at the price of disappointing the reader's expectations" (as in Emma's response to Mr. Knightley's proposal in *Emma*), and introducing "interior monologue" (Page 269). Austen could certainly have expanded on what a man says to a woman when he is deeply in love, either from her imagination or from her own personal experience. From the little that is known of Austen's own romances, apparently she flirted with a young Irishman, felt great but brief affection for a young clergyman whom she met on a seaside holiday and who died suddenly, and accepted and rejected—within the space of a day—a family friend's proposal of marriage (Nokes 157-61, 242-45, 251-58). That she chose to suggest rather than to state the particulars of the intimate conversation between her characters is clearly in keeping with the reticence of her age on such matters.

Conveyed almost entirely through narration and indirect speech, Darcy's declaration of love and Elizabeth's refusal therefore pose special challenges to playwrights and screenwriters. Helen Jerome, in her 1934 script, wrote the scene as brief lines that alternate between Darcy and Elizabeth (Act II, Scene 3). Darcy barely utters even the slightest expression of his love before Elizabeth roars back a reproof. The proposal scene in the film improves greatly on Jerome's scene by having Darcy speak at length while Elizabeth listens in stunned silence. The tension is thick, and audience sympathy is very much with Darcy. Yet the justice of Elizabeth's indignation is as palpable as the sting of her refusal. "Your arrogance, your conceit, your, your selfish disregard of other people's feelings," she tells him, "made me dislike you from the first. I, I, I hadn't known you a week before I decided you were the last man in the world I would ever be prevailed upon to marry!" As Darcy recoils from her rebuff, the film audience runs the gamut of emotions along with him, from the flattery of his proposal and the insult of its presumptuous and condescending tone to the frustration of his reluctance to tell Elizabeth what he knows about Wickham and his forced civility, in which he urges her to "accept my best wishes for your health and happiness."

In the novel, a second climax occurs when, on the day following his ill-fated marriage proposal, Darcy defends his character in a lengthy letter to Elizabeth. In his letter, he describes the inappropriate behavior of her family, which initially raised his scruples concerning the marriage; justifies his advice to his friend Bingley by explaining that he never saw evidence that Jane Bennet reciprocated Charles' affection; and exposes Wickham as a rogue. At first, Elizabeth does not want to accept Darcy's defense, but when she reads how Wickham almost succeeded in seducing Darcy's young sister in the hope of gaining her fortune, she knows that Darcy's words are true. Though not yet in love with him, she realizes the justice of his claims, regrets the tone of her rejection, admits that Jane may not have sufficiently encouraged Charles in his suit and that her own family's impropriety may have stood in the way of both her happiness and Jane's, and acknowledges that her judgment of Wickham was colored by the charming attentions he had paid her. "Till this moment," she concedes, "I never knew myself" (Chapter 36). Yet it is only when she tours Darcy's Pemberley estate, where she is surprised by his warm welcome and his desire that she get to know his sister, that she truly feels his love and begins to return it. Lydia's elopement forces her to end her visit to Pemberley prematurely and leaves her wondering if her now deep feelings for Darcy are all in vain. Given Darcy's sensitive consideration of and attention to Elizabeth's reproofs, her growing affection for him seems wholly credible.

By contrast, the film devotes insufficient time to Darcy's self-improvement and Elizabeth's change of heart. Upon learning of Lydia's disgrace, a remorseful Darcy arrives at Longbourn to reveal Wickham's true nature and to offer his services in recovering Lydia. In a single rather unbelievable instant, Elizabeth feels gratitude for Darcy's assistance, disappointment over Wickham's reckless behavior, and love. Time passes. Lady Catherine, visiting as Darcy's secret ambassador, acts the bully to test Elizabeth, who passes with flying colors. Vindicating Darcy by revealing how he found Wickham, set him up with an income, and forced him to marry Lydia, Lady Catherine reports to an anxious Darcy: "She merely refused to refuse to marry you! She's right for you Darcy. . . . What you need is a woman who will stand up to you. I think you've found her." With renewed confidence, Darcy claims Elizabeth as his just reward. The film ends with the Bennets contemplating the marriage prospects of their remaining daughters, Mary and Kitty.

Although the film falls somewhat short as an adaptation, contemporary critics were rather generous in their assessment of its merits. In contrast to *Variety*'s Flin (10 July 1940), who preferred the stage adaptation to the film ("In the stage version of the novel prepared by Helen Jerome," he wrote, "Elizabeth was properly highlighted against the restrictions of her time. In the screenplay by Aldous Huxley and Jane Murfin, she is trimmed to fit a yarn about a family, rather than about an unusual and courageous girl"), John O'Hara called *Pride and Prejudice* "a graceful costume-comedy of manners" that improved upon Helen Jerome's stage adaptation and, with its tightened plot, was "closer to the novel." While O'Hara appreciated that the film retained "a surprising amount of Jane Austen's dialogue," he nonetheless observed that "the most notable departure in the script is an inevitable bow to the box office that plays some of the subtle characterizations for broad comedy" (35). *Commonweal*'s Philip T. Hartung found some fault with Leonard's direction, which he called not "in the best cinema tradition, but . . . executed with finesse appropriate to the subtle Austen satire"; yet he concluded that Hunt Stromberg's "production of this first-rate period piece is excellent" (311). And the *New Yorker* proclaimed *Pride and Prejudice* "one of the year's best films, in large part because the writers of the adaptation "sensibly decided against trying to improve on the lady's [Austen's] prose" (37).

The casting was also the subject of much critical discussion. *Time*, which found the whole cast to be "excellent," singled out Olivier's performance: "From the moment when he, as Mr. Darcy, walks into a ballroom in provincial Meryton with a memorable sneer, the picture is in" (44). Other reviewers concurred, noting that, after his performance as Heathcliff in *Wuthering Heights*, Olivier was "back in his familiar sinister-lover vein" that he does so nicely (*New Yorker* 37). Hartung praised Darcy's invulnerability and impassive disdain, though he found "perhaps a little too much fluttering of hands even for a comedy of artificial manners" (311), a tendency also noted by Otis Ferguson. Olivier, according to Ferguson, was not properly directed by the script, but he "kept himself collected except for a startling new tendency to register emotional upsets by upward jerks of the hand" (246). For *Variety*'s Flin, however, Olivier simply appeared "very unhappy in the role."

Greer Garson's performance, on the other hand, was universally praised: she was "excellently cast" (O'Hara 35); "a perfect choice" (*New Yorker* 37); "the embodiment of Elizabeth Bennet's prejudice and wit" (Hartung 311). For Ferguson, her interpretation of Lizzy was one "I can't imagine improved upon" (246). Some of the minor characters received notice as well: Lady Catherine (Edna Mae Oliver) made "for some much needed merriment" (*Variety*) and provided "just the right mixture of the infuriating and the funny" (Ferguson 246), while Mary

Boland (Mrs. Bennet) "was out to steal the picture . . . and probably succeeded" (Ferguson 246). Philip T. Hartung, who praised not only the film's fine acting but its "beautiful sets and stunning Regency (or 1941) gowns by Adrian" (and who, like most American critics, did not realize that the costumes were often wrong for the period), nevertheless offered one of the best assessments of the film as a whole when he observed that men would find the film talky and women would find it delightful.

A more faithful if highbrow rendering was the 1979 television adaptation of *Pride and Prejudice* (dir. Cyril Coke), produced by the British Broadcasting Company in partnership with the Australian Broadcasting Company. Shown in America as a five-part series on *Masterpiece Theatre* (1980), the highly acclaimed, almost four-hour-long adaptation was scripted by acclaimed British novelist Fay Weldon, with Jonathan Powell as producer; and it was distinguished by its authentic-looking sets and costumes (Joan Ellacott), its excellent make-up (Elaine Smith), and its respect for the integrity of the original work.

Unlike the 1940 adaptation, which drew in large part on Jerome's play, the 1979 televised version drew more directly on Austen's novel but employed a commonly used stage technique, of allowing the characters to recite the lines of narration in the text that referred to them. In addition, people's thoughts were revealed by means of voice-overs, and past experiences were recalled by means of replayed actions within screen insets. Also, more time was devoted to creating a sense of the foreshadowing that was so essential to the subtle movement of Austen's plot. Charlotte Lucas, for instance, befriends Mr. Collins when the Bennet daughters want to escape his attention, although a grateful Elizabeth is unaware that Charlotte is trying to transfer his affections from Lizzy to herself. There are many times when Darcy gazes at Elizabeth; despite his denials to Caroline Bingley and Charles, it is clear to viewers that he is falling in love. And much more of Lydia's indiscreet behavior is actually depicted: the flaunting of her bosom without sufficient lace, her throwing herself in the way of officers, and her chasing men across the street. While these various devices brought viewers into the heart of Austen's story, the exquisite shots of the grounds of English country estates and the interiors of the manor houses provided viewers with a real sense of place, which beckoned them to forsake the twentieth century for an interlude in Regency times.

In her filmscript, Fay Weldon establishes her characters almost immediately. She splits Austen's famous opening line—"It is a truth universally acknowledged, that a single man in possession of a good fortune, must be in want of a wife"—between Elizabeth Bennet (Elizabeth Garvie) and her friend Charlotte Lucas (Irene Richard), who repeat it to themselves as a way of introducing their newest neighbor, Mr. Bingley. But, while Elizabeth and Charlotte share curiosity over Bingley, Weldon quickly demonstrates their differences: the former will marry for love; the latter will settle for security. There is a wonderful instance of foreshadowing when Charlotte finds Elizabeth arranging flowers. Elizabeth confesses embarrassment over her parents' behavior. Charlotte in turn wishes she could gratify her parents more in finding an acceptable husband. They discuss marriage, and Elizabeth mistakenly assumes that Charlotte shares her opinions. Although Charlotte lets her believe this without argument, the viewer can see by Charlotte's expression that she is more practical than romantic.

Whereas in the 1940 adaptation, the marriage-minded Mrs. Bennet provided much of the film's comedy (and some of its more regrettable slapstick as well), in this version Mrs. Bennet, superbly acted by Priscilla Morgan, generally plays her role straight; it is, instead, her daughter Mary Bennet (Tessa Peake-Jones) who now emerges as the family comic. Mary's bookish earnestness offers numerous occasions for humor. In a departure from the novel, Mr. Bennet (Moray Watson), recognizing an opportunity to get a laugh, baits Mary by asking whether sister Kitty's cough is ill-timed. Mary responds with deadly seriousness, "One coughs when one must, does not one?" But when the subject of conversation turns to the pride of Mr. Darcy (David Rintoul), pedantic Mary observes, "Pride is a very common failing, I believe. By all that I have ever read, I am convinced that it is very common, indeed; that human nature is particularly prone to it, and that there are very few of us who do not cherish a feeling of self-complacency on the score of some quality or other, real or imagined." And, when the elopement of Lydia (Natalie Ogle) disgraces the family and threatens the marital prospects of all the Bennet sisters, Mary reflects: "Unhappy as the event must be for Lydia, we may draw from it this useful lesson: that the loss of virtue in a female is irretrievable; that one false step involves her in endless ruin; that her reputation is no less brittle than it is beautiful." In preserving as much as possible of Mary's—and indeed most of Austen's—dialogue, Weldon also manages to preserve the novel's original and subtle comedy, a comedy all too easily lost in less graceful adaptations.

The 1979 version of *Pride and Prejudice* also conveys the sexual tension that is ever present beneath the surface in Austen's work. When Elizabeth walks to Netherfield to visit her sick sister Jane (Sabina Franklyn), she has occasion to visit with Mr. Bingley (Osmund Bullock), Miss Bingley (Marsha Fitzalan), and Mrs. Hurst as well as Mr. Darcy. All evening, Miss Bingley unsuccessfully tries to divert Darcy's attentions from Elizabeth, who sits reading. When Mrs. Hurst begins to play a reel on the piano, Darcy suddenly addresses Elizabeth. "Do you not feel a great inclination, Miss Bennet, to seize upon this opportunity of dancing a reel?" he asks; and when she fails to reply, he asks again, "Miss Bennet, I inquired—" "I heard you the first time, Mr. Darcy," Elizabeth snaps back; "but I was puzzled as how to reply. If I said yes, you would despise my taste in reels. If I said no, you would despise my taste in rejecting you. No, I do *not* wish to dance a reel. Now *despise* me if you dare!" To which Darcy quickly replies, "Indeed, I do *not* dare!" The nuanced conversation reveals the unmistakable intensity of their feelings for each other.

Weldon also offers glimpses into other aspects of Regency life; her version allows the viewer to observe the habits, conventions, and manners of the age. We see the Bennet daughters trimming hats, embroidering, and arranging flowers. They play backgammon, whist, and piquet; and they write letters, read, play the piano, sing, walk, ride, and dance. We see how proper introductions are made: fathers, brothers, or trusted male friends must introduce young ladies to other men. We learn that members of the gentry do not work. Rather, they collect rents, improve their libraries, hunt, fish, garden, dance, or play cards and billiards.

Perhaps it is because the 1979 adaptation is so attuned to the particulars of the times and the details of Austen's society that, relative to the rest of the production, the crucial proposal scene plays as disappointingly as it does. Although similar in dialogue to the 1940 version, it lacks the suspense that Austen so delicately sustains. Darcy actually looks bored by his own declaration. His appearance, moreover, fails to reflect the sting of the insults he directs at Elizabeth's family. It is clear that Elizabeth must reject him; but the absence of the usual tension between them at such a critical moment leaves the viewer unconcerned whether they will find the means to change themselves or—more importantly—whether they will ultimately find the way back to each other.

Because the proposal scene lacks intensity, the scene that follows necessarily assumes greater import. Darcy's walking away from Elizabeth at the very instant she reads his letter, to which she initially responds with resentment but with recognition of the justice of his account, becomes the real climax of this story. Enhanced very effectively by voice-overs of Elizabeth's own thoughts and by cinematic replays of the behavior of the Bennets and of Wickham (Peter Settelen), the scene ends with Lizzy's sense of her own blindness and her regret at having so vehemently rejected Darcy.

The best moment of all in the film, however, occurs during Elizabeth's tour of Pemberley, a scene that makes credible—and strikingly visual—Elizabeth's change of heart concerning Darcy. From the housekeeper, Elizabeth learns of Darcy's fine reputation among his tenants and servants and of his affectionate generosity to his sister; and with her own eyes, she beholds the tasteful furnishing of his home. When Darcy appears suddenly, she is truly embarrassed to be discovered exploring his property, especially since she had so recently rejected him and called him insensitive, ungentlemanlike, and the last person she would ever "be prevailed upon to marry." Though startled, *he* remains in control and, unbeknownst to Elizabeth, secretly thrilled at this opportunity to demonstrate how he has attended to her criticisms. He demonstrates his transformation in his gracious attentions to her and to her aunt and uncle (Barbara Shelley and Michael Lees), whom he invites to dinner and to fish, and in his desire to introduce his sister (Emma Jacobs) to them at the earliest opportunity. It is now incumbent upon Elizabeth to show that she welcomes his suit; but the news of Lydia's elopement quickly separates them—forever, fears Elizabeth. The television adaptation repeats faithfully the novel's denouement, including the warning of Lady Catherine (Judy Parfitt), the new happiness of Bingley, and the return of Darcy to Longbourn, and hints again at the sexual tension as Darcy tries to speak privately with Elizabeth. Just when all seems hopeless, Elizabeth's inquiry about Mr. Darcy's sister brings about a happy resolution for the couple.

The faithful rendering of the 1979 BBC *Pride and Prejudice* elicited just critical acclaim. John O'Connor reported in the *New York Times* that the characters were "all drawn to individual perfection," even though the production at times "gets a touch too cute with reaction shots of girlish giggles and popping eyes." There is, O'Connor continues, "a tendency for most of the characters to talk constantly in epigrammatic forms. The most ordinary observations prompt overly clever generalizations." Nevertheless, he concludes, the brittle romance "remains a model of charm, distinctively British," with splendid sets and costumes and performances of an impressively high caliber (C 32). Television commentator John Romano felt that behind the production was "a shrewd and witty observer of human nature" (11). And Gloria Emerson, who considered the story to be "slightly outdated," still found in it "a delightful reminder that women's lives have improved" in many ways (184).

It is the most recent adaptation of *Pride and Prejudice,* however, that ignited "Darcy-fever" worldwide and helped to fuel the ongoing wave of Austen-mania. Even the publicity preceding the six-hour film (1995; dir. Simon Langton) was considerable. The $9.5 million dollar cost of the production, flaunted as the most expensive costume drama to date, caught the attention of critics and fans alike (Amis 32), as did rumors of the off-screen romance between Colin Firth and Jennifer Ehle

(Koenig 494)—a relationship that recalled the rumors of romance between Laurence Olivier and Greer Garson. Reports, ultimately untrue, that the production would feature frontal nudity drew vehement protests from the Jane Austen Society. And Janeites lobbied, successfully, to have Austen's name appear in the title itself.

By the time the adaptation was shown in America on the Arts and Entertainment (A & E) network, parties of Janeites had assembled to watch the extravagant love story. In other homes, videocassette recorders taped the production for later viewing by absent residents. Austen readers placed bets among themselves as to the extent of the sexuality to be portrayed on-screen: would there indeed be a mouth-to-mouth kiss? The build-up to the broadcast was so intense, it seemed that no adaptation could satisfy audience expectations. But, in fact, the latest version of *Pride and Prejudice* not only met expectations but exceeded them.

A subtle prologue opens the film. The amiable Charles Bingley (Crispin Bonham-Carter), who is considering the purchase of the Netherfield estate, seeks the opinion of his trusted friend, Fitzwilliam Darcy (Colin Firth). The men are seen riding out to Netherfield, where Darcy gives his approval of the purchase to a self-satisfied Charles. As the two gallop back to town, Elizabeth Bennet (Jennifer Ehle), who—unobserved—has been watching the men, runs down a hill at a virtual gallop herself.

This prologue establishes a number of details essential to the story. We learn, for instance, that the handsome Bingley and Darcy are athletic young men, not dandies or fops; that Bingley relies on Darcy's opinion and solicits it before taking action; and that the enticing Elizabeth is moved both by the sight of the sportsmen who are racing through the meadow and by the natural beauty surrounding her. All three are attractive characters who exude a certain joie de vivre and sensuality.

The delightful portrait, however, contrasts sharply with a second portrait, that of the vulgar Bennet family. Mrs. Bennet (Alison Steadman) screeches; Kitty (Polly Maberly) and Lydia (Julia Sawalha) argue over a hat; and the body language of Elizabeth, Jane (Susannah Harker), and Mr. Bennet (Benjamin Whitrow) implies that there is little peace to be found within the household. Yet the intimate glances and private jokes suggest the closeness between Elizabeth and her father, a closeness Elizabeth also shares with her sister Jane, with whom she discusses her hopes of marrying for love and shares her fears that their good nature and beauty will be insufficient to attract suitable husbands. (As Garret Condon points out, this latter scene is both enlightening and confusing to American viewers, who cannot fathom the sisters' "poverty" or understand why they just don't go out and find jobs of their own [NC 17].)

Together, the two scenes—of Darcy and Bingley at Netherfield and of Elizabeth and the Bennets at home—establish the frame for Austen's comedy of manners.

Jane Austen, in a letter dated February 4, 1813, to her sister Cassandra, had herself critiqued *Pride and Prejudice*. "The work," she wrote, "is rather too light & bright & sparkling;—it wants shade;—it wants to be stretched out here & there with . . . anything that would form a contrast & bring the reader with increased delight to the playfulness and Epigrammatism of the general stile" (Le Faye 203). Scriptwriter Andrew Davies, whose previous work included the filmscripting of other classics like *Middlemarch*, obviously had Austen's observations in mind when he emphasized the drama of the story, filled out so many scenes, and invented new ones for the lavish 1995 adaptation.

Producer Sue Birtwistle and script editor Susie Conklin, in their book, *The Making of Pride and Prejudice*, described some of the other principles on which the production was based. Darcy, they suggest, fights desperately against his strong sexual desire for Elizabeth, who is blind to her own attraction to him. The story must therefore focus not only on Elizabeth's feelings but also on Darcy's emotions and his struggles to repress them (3).[3] (That is why, for example, great emphasis is placed on the dances, since they are perfect settings in which to capture the fit between Darcy and Elizabeth and the electricity ignited by their sparring.[4]) At the same time, however, the audience cannot simply observe the action from the sidelines; it has to be drawn into the drama.

As a way of involving viewers, write Birtwistle and Conklin, the ambitious production afforded glimpses of Darcy "denied to Elizabeth, thereby making us more actively involved in the story" (5). Darcy is seen not only riding but also dancing, bathing, playing billiards, writing, fencing, and swimming (thanks to the use of an underwater camera).[5] All of these actions have a common theme: they emphasize his vitality, energy, and sensuality—aspects of Darcy's character which contemporary audiences can admire and to which they can relate. In choosing to highlight these aspects as a way of bringing Darcy to life (often, ironically, through some very traditional Austen-like techniques, such as pregnant pauses, stolen glances, long stares, and gazes into mirrors), the production conveys all of the emotions—sexual energy to repressed passion to release—that Austen subtly chronicles in her novel.

Both as a way of underscoring the importance of communication and as a method of further involving the viewer in the action, most of the novel's letters are dramatized in the production. In Darcy's letter to Elizabeth regarding the inappropriate behavior of the Bennets and the development of Wickham's ungrateful, irresponsible, and hedonistic nature, a full twenty minutes is devoted to flashbacks (significantly, from Darcy's point-of-view, not Elizabeth's). And curiously, the sequence of events described within the letter itself is changed from book to film. In the novel, Darcy discusses first the improprieties of the Bennets and then the indiscretions of Wickham. But in the 1995 dramatization, Darcy stays awake all night writing about Wickham. He then waits in a grove to hand the letter to Elizabeth. Only as she begins reading does the focus shift to her family. Darcy is much more affected by Wickham's betrayal than is Elizabeth; it works, therefore, to see him suffering over his recollections as he writes. Elizabeth is more injured by the impropriety of her family, which is more appropriately featured as we see her reading Darcy's letter.

Whereas in the 1979 adaptation, it was the bookish Mary who provided the film's comedy, in this version Mary (Lucy Briers) serves a lesser role, while Mr. Collins, Mrs. Bennet, and especially Mr. Bennet are responsible for much of the humor. Delightfully perverse, Mr. Bennet's speeches expose his inability to take situations seriously; they also reveal his compulsion to ridicule his wife. When, for instance, Elizabeth rejects Mr. Collins's proposal and Jane receives confirmation from Caroline Bingley that Charles will not return to Netherfield, the discussion turns to Wickham. Mrs. Bennet, fond of him even though he has no money, berates her eldest daughters for ruining the family's prospects. Mr. Bennet tells Jane to "take comfort," and he wonders, somewhat facetiously, when Lizzy's turn will come. "You," he tells Elizabeth, "can hardly bear to be long outdone by Jane! I hear there are officers enough in Meryton to disappoint all the young ladies in the country. Let Wickham be your man. He's a personable fellow. He'll jilt you creditably!" When Elizabeth responds that a less agreeable man would satisfy her, Bennet rejoins, "True. It is a comfort to think that whatever of that kind may befall you, you have an affectionate mother who will always make the most of it." Later, after Lydia has been invited to be the guest of Colonel Forster's wife in Brighton, where the militia is to be stationed next, Mrs. Bennet is ready to buy her daughter new ball gowns. Elizabeth, however, is appalled at the idea of Lydia's disgracing the family and appeals to her father's common sense. Mr. Bennet dismisses her point with these words: "I understand your concern, my dear, but consider: Lydia will never be easy until she has exposed herself in some public place, and here is an opportunity for her to do so at very little expense or inconvenience to her family."

Director Simon Langton also subtly traces Elizabeth's trip to Derbyshire with her aunt and uncle (Joanna David and Tim Wilton). In the 1979 adaptation, when Darcy comes upon Elizabeth touring the estate, he remains in control; in the 1995 adaptation, however, both Darcy and

Elizabeth find their chance meeting equally awkward. She is embarrassed to be there, uninvited, after her stinging rejection of him; he is embarrassed by his wet and disheveled appearance. (He has been swimming in a pond, "the fever-heat of his passion . . . still in need of cooling" [Hopkins 7].) She apologizes and explains that she did not think his family was in residence; he asks, twice, after her parents' health. But once he is dressed properly, Darcy regains his composure and solicits with gracious gallantry the company of Elizabeth and her relatives. And the next morning, he brings his sister Georgiana (Emilia Fox), herself newly arrived, to the Lambton Inn to meet Elizabeth.

As the group gathers later for an evening of music at Pemberley, Elizabeth protects Georgiana from a foolish remark by Caroline Bingley (Anna Chancellor) intended to wound Elizabeth, after which Darcy and Elizabeth exchange a long loving glance across the piano. The next day, Darcy gallops to Lambton, where he hopes to speak with Elizabeth alone; but he finds her distressed over the news about Lydia and Wickham. Stunned and remorseful, he quickly takes his leave. Misunderstanding his departure, Elizabeth assumes he is casting her off to avoid an alliance with Wickham. Apparently, she has not yet learned to appreciate his sense of duty and honor.

Back at Longbourn, the Bennets attempt to cope with being outcasts: in a hilarious scene, Collins comes to condole with the unfortunate sisters; and Lady Catherine (Barbara Leigh-Hunt) launches her own dictatorial invasion. (It is interesting to note that, even in extreme situations, etiquette is observed: following the custom that the person greatest in consequence must first take notice of those beneath him or her, no one—not even Mrs. Bennet as hostess—addresses Lady Catherine until she speaks to Elizabeth.) Darcy, meanwhile, arranges Lydia's marriage to Wickham, confesses his interference in Bingley's affairs, and then encourages Bingley to propose to Jane. (Bingley's need for Darcy's approval and encouragement, after all, is suggested as early as the film's prologue.) Darcy can then return to rectify his own affairs. The film ends with the double wedding of the Darcys and the Bingleys and with a shot of the couples romantically riding off in open carriages (a somewhat incongruous detail, since there is snow on the grounds and buildings). The book, by contrast, ends in autumn, and it is unclear when the wedding takes place (Modert 54-55).

If there are any shortcomings in this otherwise outstanding adaptation, it is that little was left to the viewer's imagination. Every letter is dramatized for the fullest visual effect, and even obvious and unnecessary lines—e.g., when Lizzy worries, "I shall never see him again"—are spoken. But such quibbles are minor, to be sure, especially in a production that so fully captures the charm and delightful archness of Elizabeth and the awkwardness and pride of Darcy as he evolves into a man who is ardent and caring—and very much Lizzy's equal. (See Figure 13.)

It is not surprising, therefore, that critical response to the latest production of *Pride and Prejudice* was overwhelmingly positive. John O'Connor called the production a "splendid adaptation, with a remarkably faithful and sensitively nuanced script by Andrew Davies" (13). Although Lon Grahnke felt that the mini-series could have been "trimmed by a third with nothing lost," he nevertheless found it "pretty" and "lushly designed and photographed" (NC 49). Martin Amis praised virtually all of the performances, singling out Alison Steadman (Mrs. Bennet) for establishing "a miraculous equipoise between bitterness and boiling vulgarity," and David Bamber for conveying "a marvelously contorted and masochistic Mr. Collins" (35). Colin Firth (Darcy) was universally praised, and often in very emotional language: Kim Cunningham, for instance, referred to him as "the regally handsome British actor (*Valmont,* 1989) whose smoldering Mr. Darcy had women swooning on both sides of the Atlantic" (128). Moreover, Jane Gibson's skillful and intricate choreography provided beauty as well as privacy to several public conversations, while the excellent musical score by Carl Davis complemented rather than competed with the action.

Just as each of the three adaptations of Jane Austen's *Pride and Prejudice* offers a somewhat different perspective on the novel, each also renews the debate about the process of adaptation itself. A novel, after all, allows readers to imagine their own characters, settings, and costumes—in effect, to craft their own movies. A film, on the other hand, particularly a good film, can engage the senses, offer surprise, afford escape, and even stimulate the desire to read. Yet, while the adaptation of any novel to film requires choices and compromises, Austen's works raise special concerns. Her books, after all, were intended to be read aloud, making the dialogue paramount. Deviation from Austen's turns of phrase, the rhythm of her sentences, and the unsurpassed humor and subtle wit—the very qualities that make Austen's novels unique—can easily make for poor plays or films; yet slavish devotion to those same elements can make for lifeless imitations (Wright 423).

Robert Z. Leonard's *Pride and Prejudice* (1940), the first film version, intelligently borrows many qualities from Austen's narrative. Yet, because it falls short in depicting Elizabeth's ultimate sense of revelation and relief, as an adaptation it is merely good rather than great. Since Darcy's outward bluster and sensuality is more readily and fully conveyed than Elizabeth's inner sensitivity, "Leonard's movie"—as George

Figure 13. Jennifer Ehle (as Elizabeth) and Colin Firth (as Darcy) take a break from filming the Netherfield Ball sequence to pose for publicity shots. © BBC-TV

Lellis and H. Philip Bolton suggest—"is about pride but not really about prejudice" (51). Cyril Coke's BBC/Australian Broadcasting Company version (1979), on the other hand, apart from David Rintoul's uncompromisingly stiff interpretation of Darcy and the occasional excesses of Wilfred Josephs' musical score, is a fine example of period costume drama. A faithful if somewhat highbrow rendering of Austen's novel, Coke's *Pride and Prejudice* retains much of the dialogue and the humor of its source. But it is very much a portrait of its age: "slightly outdated," according to one critic; decidedly "brittle," according to another (Emerson 184, O'Connor C32). Simon Langton's *Pride and Prejudice* (1995) for BBC/A & E is, by contrast, the Austen adaptation for the 1990s. It succeeds in being a product both of its age and of *our* age. Drawing on the best features of the earlier adaptations, including the period realism of Coke's 1979 version and the sensuality of Darcy in the 1940 version, Langton's production depicts two fully realized characters who are the equal of each other.

The adaptations, moreover, are telling for what they reveal and conceal. A matter as simple as a kiss, for example, assumes great importance in its different cinematic contexts.[6] Although Austen was no sexually repressed or desiccated spinster, she never wrote about sexuality; she merely alluded to it. In her world, public displays of affection were considered vulgar, and intimate touching and kissing were behaviors reserved for the bedroom. As Darcy and Lizzy walk together down the lane from her home, for instance, she reassures him that her feelings for him have changed and that she now receives his assurances with "gratitude and pleasure." Austen writes simply, "The happiness which this reply produced was such as he had probably never felt before, and he expressed himself on the occasion as sensibly and as warmly as a man violently in love can be supposed to do" (Chapter 58). In the 1940 American film, produced in an era when romantic comedies with happy endings were the cinematic norm, Darcy hugs and kisses Elizabeth in the garden—though with propriety and in view of her parents, the Bennets. In the 1979 British mini-series, the affection between the two is only implied: as they walk well away from Longbourn, Elizabeth slides her arm through Darcy's, and he presses her fingers. In the more fully realized 1995 production, which best portrays the characters' range of emotions and depicts a proposal that is somewhat anti-climactic, there is no kiss, no touch, not even a smile from Darcy as he walks down the lane with Elizabeth. But it ends with a shot of Darcy and Elizabeth being driven away from their wedding in an open carriage. Slowly, they lean towards each other and engage in a very contemporary mouth-to-mouth kiss. It is, in fact, over that frozen image that the credits roll.

All three adaptations eliminate the scene in which Elizabeth informs her father that Darcy restored their respectability by paying off Wickham to marry Lydia. This information releases Mr. Bennet from having to reimburse his brother-in-law, who reluctantly appeared as the family's savior when Darcy did not want his efforts publicized. Darcy wants Elizabeth to love him for himself, not out of gratitude or obligation. And none of the adaptations, thankfully, shows a bedroom scene with the principal couples. In the 1995 production, however, it is interesting that Wickham and Lydia are depicted as bored and trapped by their lust for fornication—a novelty for contemporary audiences, who are all too accustomed to seeing instant rather than enduring relationships.

"Austen's big-time screen bonanza," suggests Garret Condon, can be explained as a quiet revolution against our rude and violent culture; "moviegoers, weary of thin characters and broad violence, are hungry for crisp characterizations, civility and romance" (17). Jack Kroll concurs: "The popularity of Austen films in an age of marriage meltdown is fascinating," he writes. "It's an antidote to the fungus infection of Joe Esterhaus (*Showgirls, Jade*)" (66). For Suzanne Fields, "The pendulum that swings toward Jane Austen . . . reflects a hunger for fine language, narratives that reflect the human heart without vulgarity or sentimentality, and a craving for moral standards and manners now driven from our daily lives" (29). It is precisely these elements—the moral standards, the fine language, the crisp characterizations, the civility and romance—that fuel the phenomenal Austen-mania in Hollywood and in literary circles alike and that continue to generate interest in the adaptation of her finest works like *Pride and Prejudice*. And for that, viewers and readers can only respond, as Lizzy ultimately does to Darcy's assurances, with "gratitude and pleasure."

Notes

1. Austen's *Pride and Prejudice* was apparently a popular work for stage adaptation. In "Jane Austen Adapted," Andrew Wright notes that there were at least ten stage versions of the novel before the 1940 movie. (For a more complete list of dramatizations and performances of *Pride and Prejudice* through 1975, see Wright, 442-46.) George Lellis and H. Philip Bolton suggest that the novel was so frequently adapted to the stage because "Austen appears to write in a dramatic, playlike manner" (45).

2. In his biography *The Real Life of Laurence Olivier,* Roger Lewis writes: "Olivier and Garson had worked together five years previously, in *Golden*

Arrow, at the Whitehall Theatre in 1935, and they had conducted an off-stage affair" (19).

3. According to Linda Blanford, when Colin Firth was asked how he decided to play Darcy, he replied: "I thought to myself: 'This is where he wants to go across the room and punch someone. This is where he wants to kiss her. This is where he wants sex with her right now.' I'd imagine a man doing it all, and then not doing any of it. That's all I did" (H 31).

4. See Lisa Hopkins, "Mr. Darcy's Body: Privileging the Female Gaze," 3, for a further discussion of the importance of the dance scenes in the Langton adaptation.

5. Cheryl Barnard writes that a stand-in for Colin Firth actually dove into the pond (15).

6. As Cathleen Schine notes, for example, most people find aberrant or inappropriate the crowded street kiss (at the reunion of Captain Wentworth and Anne Elliot) in the otherwise excellent 1995 adaptation of Austen's *Persuasion* (32).

Works Consulted

Amis, Martin. "Jane's World." *New Yorker* 8 Jan. 1996: 31-35.

Austen, Jane. *The Complete Novels of Jane Austen.* Voyager Expanded Book. System 6.0.7 and HyperCard 2.1 Computer Software. Macintosh 2 MB RAM and large display 640 x 400 pixels. Santa Monica, 1992.

Avedon, Richard. "Chameleons." *New Yorker* 13 May 1996: 64-65.

Barnard, Cheryl. "On Location: *Pride and Prejudice.*" *In Britain* Jan. 1997: 12-17.

Barton, David. "It's a Big Year for Jane Austen." *Eagle* (NH) *Tribune* 17 Jan. 1996: Arts 1, 23.

Birtwistle, Sue, and Susie Conklin. *The Making of Pride and Prejudice.* London: Penguin, 1995.

Blanford, Linda. "Beware the Insidious Grip of Darcy Fever." *New York Times* 14 Jan. 1996: H 31.

Chapman, R. W. "On Carriages and Travel." *The Oxford Illustrated Jane Austen: Mansfield Park.* Ed. R. W. Chapman. Oxford: Oxford UP, 1988. 561-65.

Condon, Garret. "Jane Austen's Tales Transport Filmgoers to More Genteel Times." *Chicago Sun-Times* 22 Dec. 1995: NC 17.

Cunningham, Kim. "They Felt the Firth Move." *People* 5 Feb. 1996: 128.

"The Current Cinema: What Is This Anyway?" (Rev. of *Pride and Prejudice.*) *New Yorker* 17 Aug. 1940: 37-38.

Emerson, Gloria. "American Morals and English Manners." *Vogue* Oct. 1980: 184.

Ferguson, Otis. "Class-A Paint Jobs." *New Republic* 19 Aug. 1940: 246.

Fields, Suzanne. "An Age in Need of Manners Turns to Jane Austen." *Washington Times* 25-31 Dec. 1995: 29.

Flin. "*Pride and Prejudice.*" *Variety Film Reviews.* 10 July 1940. New York: Garland, 1983.

Gold, Joel J. "Heady Days for Jane Austen Scholars." *Chronicle of Higher Education* 9 Feb. 1996: B3.

Grahnke, Lon. "The 'Pride' of Jane Austen." *Chicago Sun-Times* 12 Jan. 1996: NC-49.

Harris, Laurie Lanzen, ed. *Nineteenth-Century Literature Criticism.* Vol. 1. Detroit: Gale Research, 1981. 30.

Hartung, Philip T. "The Screen: Pride, Prejudice, Passion, Pango." *Commonweal* 2 Aug. 1940: 311-12.

Hopkins, Lisa. "Mr. Darcy's Body: Privileging the Female Gaze." *Jane Austen Goes to the Movies.* Special Issue of *Topic.* 48 (1997): 1-9.

Jacobs, Laura. "Playing Jane." *Vanity Fair* Jan. 1996: 74-77: 122-23.

Jerome, Helen. *Pride and Prejudice: A Sentimental Comedy in Three Acts.* New York: Samuel French, 1934.

King, Rachel. "Casting Call." *Arts and Antiques* Jan. 1997: 60-67.

Koenig, Rhoda. "People Are Talking About Firth Coming." *Vogue* Sept. 1997: 494, 498.

Kroll, Jack. "Jane Austen Does Lunch." *Newsweek* 18 Dec. 1995: 66-68.

Le Faye, Deirdre. *Jane Austen's Letters.* Oxford: Oxford UP, 1995.

Lellis, George, and H. Philip Bolton. "Pride But No Prejudice." *The English Novel and the Movies.* Ed. by Michael Klein and Gillian Parker. New York: Ungar, 1981. 44-51.

Lewis, Roger. *The Real Life of Laurence Olivier.* New York: Applause, 1996.

Modert, Jo. "Chronology Within the Novels." *The Jane Austen Companion.* Ed. by J. David Grey. New York: Macmillan, 1986. 53-59.

Morell, Ricki. "Jane Austen, A Hit in the 1990's? It Seems Proper." [Hollywood, FL] *Herald* 23 Jan. 1996: C1, C2.

Myer, Valerie Grosvenor. *Jane Austen: Obstinate Heart.* New York: Arcade, 1997.

Nokes, David. *Jane Austen: A Life.* New York: Farrar, Straus and Giroux, 1997.

O'Connor, John. "Pride and Prejudice, Sensitive Father Figure." *New York Times* 24 Oct. 1980: C32.

——. "Where the Heart and Purse Are United." *New York Times* 13 Jan. 1996: Arts 13, 18.

O'Hara, John. "Hollywood Finds Jane Austen with 'Pride and Prejudice.'" *Newsweek* 22 July 1940: 35.

"Other Versions." http://www.geocities.com/Hollywood/Set/2428/otherver htm#pap52. Jane Austen Film & Television Adaptations. Accessed 18 Nov. 1997.

Page, Norman. "Jane Austen's Language." *The Jane Austen Companion*. Ed. J. David Grey. New York: Macmillan, 1986. 261-70.

Pride and Prejudice, 1940. Dir. Robert Z. Leonard. Videocassette. MGM/UA Home Video and Turner Entertainment Network, 1990.

Pride and Prejudice, 1979. Dir. Cyril Coke. Videocassette. BBC Enterprises and CBS/Fox Video, 1985.

Pride and Prejudice, 1995. Dir. Simon Langton. Videocassette. BBC/A & E New Video Group, 1995.

"Pride and Prejudice." Rev. of Film. *Time* 29 July 1940: 44-45.

Romano, John. "Pride and Prejudice." *TV Guide* 25 Oct. 1980: 11-12.

Rothstein, Edward. "Jane Austen Meets Mr. Right." *New York Times* 10 Dec. 1995, "Week in Review": 1, 14.

Schine, Cathleen. "Jane Lives!" *Mirabella* Nov.-Dec. 1995: 32-33.

Spoto, Donald. *Laurence Olivier: A Biography.* New York: HarperCollins, 1992.

Thomas, Evan. "Hooray for Hypocrisy." *Newsweek* 29 Jan. 1996: 61.

Wright, Andrew. "Jane Austen Adapted." *Nineteenth-Century Fiction* 30 (1975): 425-53.

3

THE MULTIPLEX HEROINE:
SCREEN ADAPTATIONS OF *EMMA*

Tom Hoberg

A friend of mine, a dedicated and knowledgeable movie buff who once dragged me to the untrimmed Bayreuth film of Wagner's *Parzival,* recently confessed that, because of my enthusiastic recommendation of the story, she had started to watch the four-and-a-half-hour British Broadcasting Company (BBC) version of *Emma.* But, finding the pace maddeningly slow, she quit after forty-five minutes. "Nobody *does* anything," she complained. "Nothing *happens!*" A couple of weeks later, she read the book and was enchanted. Much more enticing, she enthused, than even her erstwhile favorite, *Pride and Prejudice;* she couldn't put it down.

My friend's dichotomy encapsulates the challenge of bringing *Emma* to the screen. In conveying a story from one medium to another, the cinematographer must choose whether to remain faithful to the original, at the risk of producing a new version that is flavorless and obscure, or—more temptingly and hence more frequently—to adapt the source with a freewheeling license that sacrifices artistic integrity to the transient whims of a particular audience (e.g., Demi Moore's desecration of *The Scarlet Letter*). Of course, occasionally an adaptation succeeds in adhering to the original without being stodgy (which I maintain to have been the case, my friend notwithstanding, with the BBC version) or in transporting the essence of the original to a completely different milieu (as is the case with *Clueless,* one of the recent interpretations of *Emma*).

Emma is doubtless the longest and arguably the most leisurely paced of Jane Austen's six novels. The only one of her works titled after a character—something that Austen's predecessors and peers did almost as a matter of course, as witness *Tom Jones, Moll Flanders, Pamela, Clarissa,* and a host of lesser works like *Belinda, Cecilia,* and *Evelina*— *Emma* is also the one most dominated by the heroine and the one in which that heroine is most controversial. (Austen, in fact, is reported to have said that Emma is "a heroine whom no one will like except myself."[1]) And, as protagonist, Emma did indeed present special challenges for Austen as both storyteller and narrator, particularly since in this novel the two are not the same.

Austen's novels can be distinguished by the absence of violence—indeed the dearth of strenuous activity of any sort—and of any long-term narrative suspense as to the outcome; essentially all six are variations on the theme announced in the celebrated opening of *Pride and Prejudice:* "It is a truth universally acknowledged, that a single man in possession of a good fortune must be in want of a wife." The intrigue comes in determining what obstacles the heroine will need to overcome and what changes she will need to make before the inevitable coupling with her hero signals a happy beginning. (Both Austen outside and her characters within are too savvy to expect "Happily ever after.") And it is as means to this end that the role of the narrator assumes special significance. On the very first page of the novel *Emma,* the narrator not only hints at the likely shape of things to come but also suggests that the misunderstandings, blunders, and equivocations that determine the heroine's fate are very much of her own making. "The real evils indeed of Emma's situation," she states:

were the power of having rather too much of her own way, and a disposition to think a little too well of herself; these were the disadvantages which threatened alloy to her many enjoyments. The danger, however, was at present so unperceived, that they did not by any means rank as misfortunes with her. (1)

Neither straightforward reporter nor invasive commentator, the narrator takes the responsibility of guiding the reader through the story, providing clues to situations and characters, as in good detective fiction. Specifically, according to Wayne Booth, she directs the "intellectual, moral, and emotional progress" of the reader by alternately offering an inside view of Emma's thoughts and feelings and an outside view of the heroine that reflects the reactions of others to her behavior (qtd. in Lauritzen 105).

Much of the activity in *Emma* centers on matchmaking and, as a corollary, on preserving the social pecking order in the bucolic, deceptively idyllic community around the village of Highbury. As the largest frog in a very small pond, Emma has no social rivals, equals, or mentors apart from the local squire and landowner George Knightley. Emma's father, a sweet, doddering valetudinarian, is not a strong parent to her (although Emma cares for him tenderly); and her former governess, too amiable to provide any firm guidance, has recently married and left for a new home. So Emma is free to meddle virtually without restraint in the lives of those around her.

For all of her meddling, however, Emma is curiously detached, like the master who revels in the game but never joins in. The theme of the novel thus involves her meaningful integration into the community. The narrator's second and even more significant role is therefore to interpret this process of integration to the reader: for if Emma is both the writer and director of her own drama, the narrator becomes the producer.

Emma's first attempt at matchmaking—between her new protégé Harriet Smith and the local clergyman Mr. Elton—is a fiasco, an outcome the reader anticipates long before Emma does; and it results in the departure of the disgruntled Elton (though he soon returns in triumph with a new bride, a brassy vulgarian who dares to vie for social leadership). Yet Emma's even more fundamental delusion, and the one that promotes her detachment, is that she herself will never marry. She has everything she wants, she tells Harriet; and besides, there is no one appropriate with whom to fall in love—at least not until the dashing, mysterious Frank Churchill appears, ostensibly to meet his new stepmother. For a while Emma is flattered by Frank's attention to her and pleased to find an intellectual and kindred spirit; but their relationship remains a mutual flirtation—and ultimately becomes, as Emma realizes to her great chagrin, a way of Frank's maintaining the secret of his engagement to Jane Fairfax, the relation of the indigent community wards Mrs. and Miss Bates. Only after Emma's cruel put-down of Miss Bates during the outing at Box Hill (the result of her carelessly clever collusion with Frank) does Emma grasp the extent to which she has been used. Harriet, on the other hand, receives the news of Frank and Jane's engagement with a disconcerting serenity; Harriet's newest interest, it seems, is not Frank—as Emma had intended—but Mr. Knightley. Even more stunning to Emma is Harriet's admission that it is all Emma's doing, that without Emma's assurances and encouragement she would have never aspired so high. At that moment, Emma realizes that she loves Knightley, that she alone should marry him, and that her own devices have caused her to lose him forever. For perhaps the first time in the novel, her insights and those of the narrator coincide; and for the first time in the novel, comedy becomes edged with tragedy, as Emma contemplates the bleak years ahead that she will spend tending her increasingly needy father and growing more and more isolated from those who might have sustained her. Nevertheless she determines to face such a fate with resolution and to conduct herself accordingly. It is this newfound sense of real responsibility, Austen implies, that makes her worthy of Knightley and that sets the scene for his proposal shortly thereafter. Meanwhile, Harriet is reunited with Robert Martin, her true and original love; Frank charms his way back into everyone's good graces; and even

Mr. Woodhouse becomes reconciled to innovation, including Knightley's decision to move his seat at Donwell Abbey to the Woodhouse home at Hartsfield. The novel's world again becomes purely comic, with each character finding some measure of the contentment and community—albeit an Emma-centric community—that is carefully nurtured by the narrator from the beginning of the story.

Since Emma is in every sense the central character in Austen's novel, her portrayal is the key to any cinematic adaptation of the novel. As with the character of Hamlet in Shakespeare's great tragedy, the other portrayals depend largely on the manner in which the actress and director combine to depict Emma, which in turn determines how the audience responds to her and how that response changes as the film proceeds. Too much, and she becomes a self-centered, officious twit, whom everyone in Highbury would be better off without—clearly a perversion of the book. Too noble or too sweet, however, and she loses her edge, and the whole becomes a kind of silly comedy of manners—particularly without the judicious interiorizing of the narrator, who balances Emma's occasional selfish, shallow, and officious conduct. Similar concerns arise with the depictions of both Mr. Woodhouse and Miss Bates. Too irritating, and they lose all sympathy; too "normal," and their unique status in Emma's community is misunderstood. So also with the portrayal of George Knightley. Too much a handsome lover, and the mentoring role is lost in straight romance. Too much the elder advisor, and the mutuality of their love is lost in embarrassing May-December-hood, his sobriety unenlivened by her ebullience.

Thus, in adapting *Emma* to the screen, the filmmaker's challenge is how to retain the inner voice that the narrator provides without resorting to gimmicks. The adaptation, moreover, must capture the feel of an age that did not look or act or think as ours does without making a distraction of anachronism or a fetish of realism (an especially difficult task in adapting a novelist such as Austen, who is sparing in her description of persons and places). Above all, it must somehow transfer, as intact as possible to a new medium, that evanescent but vital quality called "style."

Of the four adaptations of *Emma* to date[2]—*Emma* (BBC, 1972; dir. John Glenister); *Emma* (Meridian, 1996; dir. Diarmuid Lawrence); *Emma* (Miramax, 1996; dir. Douglas McGrath); and *Clueless* (Paramount, 1995; dir. Amy Heckerling)—the first is in many ways the best. The four-and-a-half-hour BBC production, originally released in 1972, was re-released by CBS in 1996 to capitalize on the author's—and the novel's—new popularity. Almost twice as long as its more recent competitors, it is ideal for home rather than cinema viewing, a fact that, in turn, substantially influences its relation with the audience by providing the opportunity for a more leisurely pace of acquaintance, a more considered intimacy with the characters. Thanks to the conveniences of even the most elementary VCR, viewers can skip ahead, ignore parts of the production that seem boring or redundant, replay scenes that seem puzzling or beguiling, and pause for minutes or even hours before returning to where they left off. In short, viewers can do all the things that readers can do when reading the book.

Not by chance, this adaptation is also the closest to Austen's book in substance and, more important, in spirit. According to Monica Lauritzen in *Jane Austen's Emma on Television,* a study of select BBC Classic Serials, everyone involved in the production "appears to have agreed that a maximum degree of faithfulness [to the book] was imperative." Director John Glenister believed that "you don't set out to improve on Jane Austen; you try to get somewhere near what she's got down on paper." And adaptor/screenwriter Denis Constanduros declared, "Now with an author like Jane Austen, my loyalty, personally, is absolutely to the book . . . not to myself, not to try to make something clever out of Jane Austen." Yet, while the faithfulness of the adaptation was no doubt due largely to the seriousness of the production team, "their work was clearly facilitated by the fact that Austen's novel lends itself very readily to dramatization" (Lauritzen 53, 153).[3]

Emma is in every scene but one, and even that scene is *about* her. Yet it is not so much that she is always center-stage as it is that the film viewer sees the things she sees, though not always as she sees them—in other words, the film provides the very perspective on events that Austen offers in her novel. Consistent with Glenister's vision for the production, in fact, all of the characters are present "in order to explore Emma's personality, and Emma's intentions, and Emma's behaviour" (Lauritzen 77).

And the viewer also sees a great deal of Emma.[4] Although in the initial scenes, this Emma (Doran Godwin) seems too perky, too elegant, too blonde, just as Mr. Knightley (John Carson) seems a bit short, a bit unstately, even a bit fussy, these misgivings prove to be as evanescent as they are superficial. Viewers quickly realize what Austen, with her extreme economy of physical description, makes readers appreciate: that manners, not appearance, are the key to character, and manners are in turn revealed, or betrayed, by intercourse with friends and acquaintances. In Emma's first encounters with Knightley, the nature of their relationship is deftly inaugurated. He is inclined to chide her and she to needle him, but more than suggesting that they are mentor and pupil, their conversation evinces the strong rapport between them. In the first big scene of the movie, the imbroglio involving Harriet and Robert

Martin, it is the dialogue and not any body language or close-up that carries character and story alike. Godwin and Carson thus become Emma and Knightley not by physical resemblance but by speaking and acting like them.

Among the other characters whom we meet early on, Harriet (Debbie Bowen) is correctly sweet and blonde and vacant at first; Miss Bates (Constance Chapman) is properly dough-faced and dumpling-shaped; and Mr. Elton (Timothy Peters) is handsome and articulate, as surely he was meant to be, and only faintly tainted by pomposity. Emma's father Mr. Woodhouse (Donald Eccles), a terribly important character to portray properly, is perfect in this production. Neither a sweet old man nor a senile ruin, he has an edge to his character. Used to having his own way, he is capable of selfishness if crossed. At the Christmas fete at Randalls, he is sincerely terrified but also crabby and importunate—and only intermittently aware of the burden he can be.

The entire cast of the BBC production, in fact, is uniformly excellent—due, at least in part, to director Glenister's tremendous attention to the particulars of character, from costumes to the "minutest details of the every day life of the period insofar as it had an immediate effect on the appearance" (Lauritzen 114).[5] Consequently, no role in the production, however minor, is a throwaway: the parts of Mrs. Ford (Lala Lloyd), unctuous proprietress of the all-purpose store, and Patty (Amber Thomas), the Bateses' harassed, overworked, and marginally competent maid, are as meticulously wrought as any of the principals. And indeed, when the credits roll, the players are fittingly listed in order of appearance rather than by the more typical commercial star system.

This BBC production's Jane Fairfax (Ania Marson) is a contrast to Emma: younger, a bit frail, and with a contained, undiffident reserve that can make Emma seem the slightest bit bumptious, especially when she is forced to contrast Jane's elegance with the tangle-footed manners of Harriet. Clearly, Emma is more in tune with Frank Churchill, the other newcomer—and the first *young* man we have seen (Mr. Elton being prematurely aged by sham dignity). Frank is charming, with nothing dandyish about him. He and Emma sparkle together, pleasurably at first, two attractive, mildly flirtatious young people; and even their mischievous by-play about Jane Fairfax and Mr. Dixon seems harmless enough. But quickly it becomes too familiar, too pseudo-intimate, too fast, too clever. As to the *real* object of Frank's affections, the innocent watcher is probably duped as much as Emma is (particularly in the absence of the reliable narrator, whose voice is lost in the translation from narrative to drama). There is none of the obvious prompting that tipped the audience off to Elton; this matter is more involved. In fact, there is an occasional visual hint that while Emma and Frank are becoming involved, Knightley has some intentions towards Jane. As to the cognoscenti who know the story, their focus *is* on Emma and her self-satisfied abetting of Frank's fun, as irony mounts upon anticipatory irony and leads to the grand revelation.

Mr. Elton's new bride (Fiona Walker) completes the female tetragon. She too is perfectly cast, with an appearance all teeth and nose and a gratingly nasal voice. The note of civilized animosity between her and Emma is struck at once, and the disparity between what is said and what is intended is exquisitely realized. The viewer can only marvel at how much hostility can go into the passing of a plate of petit-fours between the two.

Throughout these comings and—in Frank's case—goings, the relationship between Emma and Harriet is sustained superbly as well as delicately, because—as in the book—it illustrates all sides of Emma's character. There is the joy of having such an adoring acolyte; yet Harriet must show some of the sweetness and vulnerability that endears her to Emma, while Emma cannot seem just manipulative and domineering and therefore must reveal that her benevolence is unfeigned. This is achieved in a series of placid domestic tableaux in which viewers listen to Harriet twitter away and watch the spectrum of emotions flit across Emma's face.

Two-thirds of the way through the movie (as in the book), with the interpersonal dynamics firmly established, the pace of the story changes from a leisured narrative to a burst of individual and increasingly histrionic episodes. The first, the ball at the Crown, lasts longer than expected but not longer than necessary. The humiliation and rescue of Harriet is handled well. But more important is the film's eloquent presentation of a principal Jane Austen concept: the dance as social metaphor. Non-Janeites who have viewed this and other film adaptations of her works have been uniformly fascinated by the intricate grace with which the participants glide and skip through the prescribed movements, in such glorious contrast to the rugged, in-your-face individuality of today's slam dancers. The idea of dancing as at once a social grace and a communal obligation bespeaks a world in which, if a single person fails to observe the proprieties and traditions, the whole society comes unraveled. Thus, Mr. Elton's cruelty becomes a general not a particular offense, and it is important that Mr. Knightley is not only willing to dance but is able to as well.

Likewise, it is this need for mutual support and forbearance that makes Emma's heedless put-down of Miss Bates in the scene at Box Hill so reprehensible. And here, for the only time, this film disappoints. In the book, the insult is the culmination of tensions and hostilities that had been building for days and that involve Emma along with Frank, Jane, the Eltons, Harriet, even Mr. Knightley. Together with Knightley's angry reproach, it also marks Emma's social nadir as well as the eventual but defining crisis in the relationship between Frank and Jane. That moment in the novel is therefore carefully led up to—and away from. But in this movie, it occurs quickly, almost perfunctorily, as if the film's mavens were afraid that viewers would be turned off by the incivility. Moreover, by reducing the number of participants in the Box Hill episode and by eliminating entirely both Jane Fairfax and Mr. Elton, the film clearly disturbs "the neat choreography of the original scene"; lost as well is the poignancy of the tension between the characters.[6] Unfortunately, the audience is never allowed to see what Ms. Godwin and Mr. Carson could have done had they had been allowed to be angry and mortified, respectively, instead of mildly embarrassed.

Once this scene is over, however, the quality of both performances returns to its former level. In the culminating traumatic exchange, Debbie Bowen does not play Harriet with a roguishly comic air, as if to suggest that her pretensions need not be taken seriously; instead she shows some spunk and confidence—just enough to rattle anyone who has not read the book. And, in a bravura close-up performance by Doran Godwin, Emma's response shows silently but eloquently in her face. In the following episode, extrapolated from the book, Emma contemplates a rain-smeared landscape that mirrors her own future as her father, huddled shawl-wrapped by the fire, mumbles "It's a sad thing . . . when one lives from one cup of gruel to the next . . . ."

Of course, the proposal scene follows in short order, an emotional highpoint worth every minute's wait. The sense of timing, so awry in the Box Hill scene, is exquisite here. Emma and Knightley approach each other with cautious diffidence, equally fearful of inflicting hurt on, and receiving hurt from, the other. When Emma cuts Knightley off and then a long instant later begs him to speak, she makes us aware of the depth of the moment's crisis; and when his saving declaration is made and received, the palpable relief turns both tender and arch, just as in the book. The viewer, reminded of the pair's initial exchanges early in the film, is vividly shown the delicious fittingness of their union.

The 1972 BBC adaptation was followed in 1996 by *Emma* (Meridian; dir. Diarmuid Lawrence), with Kate Beckinsale (*Cold Comfort Farm*) in the title role. And, while it falls short of the BBC version, this second adaptation of *Emma*—a mere one hundred minutes long—is neither a stunted enactment that fails to repeat the letter of Austen's novel nor a distortion of a classic that undervalues its source. Rather, it is a moving and pleasing production, set to an entirely different tempo and with an entirely different rhythm.

Of all of Jane Austen's novels, *Emma,* the longest, would seem to be the most imperiled by abbreviation to a sort of adaptive synopsis that this version, by its very brevity, initially promises. In so short a time, the cinematic temptation would be overwhelming to fashion a series of high-speed, high-emotion episodes, full of emotional pyrotechnics and impatient of subtleties. Such an approach might be more supportable, perhaps, in rendering on the screen *Pride and Prejudice* or *Persuasion,* where the locations change regularly and the story is full of many different events. But the contrary is true in *Emma:* the outside comes to visit Highbury occasionally, but goes away again, and readers and viewers do not go with it. We do not travel to Weymouth, or Enscombe, or London, even though the John Knightleys live there and Frank raises Knightley's ire by "seemingly" going there for a haircut. And, as cosmopolitan as Emma can seem, she has "never seen the sea" (78)—quite an accomplishment for someone who resides in Surrey.

Moreover, though people in *Emma* are amiable or disagreeable to various degrees, there are no bounders or cads or tyrants here—no harridans or opportunists—who can be encapsulated and categorized in a few lines, or, cinematically, in a few seconds. Even the most mono-dimensional characters—Mr. Woodhouse or Miss Bates—have some substance to them; even the most stereotypical—Harriet or Mrs. Elton—can provide surprises. And, while Austen rarely details landscape, here, with Mr. Knightley's home, she waxes almost lyrical: "It was a sweet view," she writes, "—sweet to the eye and the mind. English verdure, English culture, English comfort, seen under a sun bright, without being oppressive" (282). This is the kind of place where homes are estates, and estates have titles, histories, and personalities—Enscombe, Donwell Abbey, Hartsfield, Randalls, even Abbey Mill Farm—to distinguish them from "The Coles" or "The Bateses." And it is here that Emma's fate is worked out, and here that she will abide. Of all of Austen's heroines, only Emma is not "taken away from all this" by her marriage.

The abbreviated running time of this second adaptation thus raises potential concerns and seems somewhat off-putting, as do the first glimpses of some of the characters. Beckinsale, dark and brunette and slender, looks intense rather than elegant and self-assured, the opposite of the novel's Emma who, for all her business, gets her way by being rather than by doing. Correspondingly, her father (Bernard Hepton) seems too hale and hearty, like someone who has been smuggling cakes and ale into his own diet while urging others to subsist on coddled eggs and gruel. But then the community's two gentlemen appear: Mr. Knightley (Mark

Strong) and Mr. Elton (Dominic Rolman), the former tall, stately, and dignified, the latter an increasingly unconvincing approximation thereof. And with Harriet (Samantha Morton), fluffy and breathless but no bird-brained caricature, the cast assumes a more familiar dimension.

These are the principals in Part One, which ends with Elton's sullen departure and the anticipation of Frank Churchill's triumphant arrival. Of course, some episodes are telescoped and some, like the extended absurdity of Elton's misdirected courtship, are omitted. But the essentials are preserved and even highlighted. The argument between Emma and Knightley escalates from discussion to debate into a virtual shouting match as both are angry and neither minces words. He gets in the last word, but she does not back down, and the whole not only demonstrates their past and present relationship but also points the way to the final scene. Meantime, the coach proposal moment is dealt with economically: Emma, less outraged than revolted, tries to be a lady but conveys her disgust at Elton's presumption as she watches his bewilderment turn to indignation.

As Elton exits, Frank and Jane enter—and a good pair they are, even before it is clear that they are a couple. In their first meeting at the Bateses, Jane (Olivia Williams), with her cool politeness, makes Emma seem adolescent and snippy, as intended. Frank (Raymond Coulthard), good-looking, smiling, and smooth, looks and sounds a bit callow next to Knightley. Mrs. Elton (Lucy Robinson) is characterized by a strident voice (reportedly Canadian), which apparently symbolizes her working-class, Bristol lineage; never has an articulated "R" seemed more grating.

By hints and glances, the more complex relationship between Emma and Frank is presented as rapidly as her earlier non-involvement with Elton. In a tête-à-tête just before Frank returns to Yorkshire, he drops his bantering mask and in earnest almost stammers out his engagement to Jane, while Emma waits breathless for a marriage proposal that she no doubt would have rejected. The production shows clearly that the latter relationship would never work: the two bring out the least endearing traits in each other. But the moment is recalled some time later, when Knightley opens a crucial conversation with the same hesitant constraint.

At the Crown, the characters show a different side of themselves—in their party clothes, so to speak, and at a public entertainment, with the dances so well executed as to both evoke and celebrate this society. Harriet's humiliation and salvation, portrayed minimally as an unfortunate solecism in an otherwise festive scene, are soon smoothed over and segue to her corresponding rescue from the Gypsies by Frank, her alternate hero. The action moves quickly to the critical moment at Box Hill, which this version conflates with the strawberry fete at Donwall Abbey.

The scene is given its full impact, even including a lot of the original dialogue. Frank is properly febrile, and until the moment of insult, he—not Emma—is properly given center stage. The atmosphere is sultry. The moment, in turn, is highlighted by a splendid performance by Miss Bates (Prunella Scales), who invests her response with a dignity that adds credence to Knightley's rebuke of Emma. That rebuke is short but fierce, more in anger than in sorrow, and Emma is suitably abashed.

There follow quickly a series of interscenes, depicting with compact skill the tribulations of the heroine. The snubbing by the Bateses is compounded by the revelation of the engagement and the realization of Emma's foolishness. As her anger gives way to misery during the interview with Harriet, Emma responds with poignant grief as well as self-castigation. This reflective interlude is crucial for all Jane Austen's heroines and requires that the heroine accept that all is lost and over but that she press on for the sake of those dependent on her strength. Only then is she psychologically ready for—and deserving of—happiness. When the moment of deliverance comes, it is always indirect and underplayed by the novel's narrator, contrary to the inclination of filmmakers to go for the baldest and boldest emotion. The narrator describes the golden minutes after Knightley's confession this way:

What did she say?—Just what she ought, of course. A lady always does. She said enough to show there need not be despair—and to invite him to say more himself. . . . Seldom, very seldom, does complete truth belong to any human disclosure; seldom can it happen that something is not a little disguised, or a little mistaken; but where, as in this case, though the conduct is mistaken, the feelings are not, it may not be very material.—Mr. Knightley could not impute to Emma a more relenting heart than she possessed, or a heart more disposed to accept of his. (338)

And so it is played in the film, particularly by Kate Beckinsale. Her Emma, happily dazed rather than delirious, has little to say. This big scene is not hers but Knightley's, and he does it justice, in a manner plain rather than glib. The man and woman seen and heard in so many circumstances before now find themselves in the moment for which all readers—and, by this time, most viewers—have been waiting.

But this is not quite the end. This version appends an event without parallel in the novel: a harvest festival at Donwall Abbey, at which Mr. Knightley both announces the engagement and reveals his imminent move to Hartsfield before giving the cue for general rustic merriment. It is a scene denounced apoplectically by most Janeites as totally unwarranted and irrelevant, except as a splashy Hollywood ending to a story as far from Tinseltown as is imaginable—an objection that is certainly understandable in view of the shortness of the film and the necessary elimination of so much of the novel's detail. But the scene is really the bucolic counterpart of the ball at the Crown, organized and presided over by George Knightley, not Frank Churchill. Like the finale of a more contemporary work like *Oklahoma*, it marks the end of the story rather than just the plot. And, while the scene would not have worked at all in the book—Austen is not good at big events—it has a certain appropriateness in this adaptation. The harvest festival dance serves as a metaphor for both social celebration and social bonding and as an affirmation of the abiding social values that Knightley's world embodies and that he and Emma will help perpetuate.

Unlike the two earlier versions, in which the title character was not allowed to dominate the drama, the third adaptation of *Emma* (Miramax, 1996; dir. Douglas McGrath) was designed to be a star vehicle for Gwyneth Paltrow, who plays the lead and brings to the part a resplendence, a sly refinement, an "elegance and patrician wit" (Maslin, "So Genteel" 1).[7] In some ways, this focus on Paltrow is fitting: after all, in the novel Emma clearly *is* the star, both as the main character of the narrative and as the creator within the novel of the society around her. Although Emma's aloofness from the entanglements of love does not make her an omniscient observer, it frees her to make—even invent—the kind of world that she chooses, arranging lives and choreographing relationships to bring some life and spark into the humdrum.

In adapting the novel's Emma-centrism, adaptor/director Douglas McGrath provides fairly frequent inner narratives from Emma herself, by which the audience is privy to her thoughts and feelings. The device, however, is not uniformly successful. By making Emma, in effect, the story's narrator, McGrath sacrifices the distance that the novel's narrator provides; the audience sometimes feels too chummily close to Emma to recognize her wrongheadedness.

Yet Gwyneth Paltrow almost brings it off. Elegant and glittering, impeccably dressed and coiffed, she completely dominates a pretty, bright-eyed Harriet (Toni Collette) at the same time that she strikes the right note of affection for and impatience with her protégé; and she is properly solicitous of her father (Denys Hawthorne), though he at first seems a bit too well-fed and alert to be convincing. In this version, Knightley (Jeremy Northam) is also good—though Elton (Alan Cumming) is the best of the lot—and Sophie Thompson as Miss Bates turns in a jewel of a performance.[8]

The time constraints in this version, which is only a little longer than its immediate predecessor, the Beckinsale version, are handled less well. After a clever opening sequence in which the planet quite literally spins around Emma, the first half hour or so of McGrath's film is full of irritating narrative dodges typical of soap operas, wherein the audience is provided information in a series of forced dialogues and mini-speeches, particularly about the absent but imminent Frank Churchill and Jane Fairfax.[9] Those subvocal asides from Emma, usually designed to show the difference between her public behavior and her private feelings, are intrusively irritating, as if the director mistrusted either his performers or his audience.

The strongest part of this version is the re-creation of Book One: the day-to-day intercourse between Emma and Harriet is well-realized, the relationship perfectly limned in Emma's voice when she calls the younger woman "Dear" in response to the former's "Miss Woodhouse." At least as good is the way in which Emma and Knightley interact—as old acquaintances, old friends, in a world where heterosexual friendship is a rarity. Affection, fondness, admiration: all of these are established here; all, moreover, are the keys in Jane Austen to a deep, rich, and lasting love. Emma and Knightley are friendly contestants who trade barbs and quips but who clearly enjoy the exchange. (See Figure 14.) The scene with Elton, in the coach, also finds Emma in control and formidably glacial as she bites off her words.

Of the other early arrivals, the Westons (James Cosmo and Greta Scacchi) are a minor triumph—she mature and handsome, he a comfort-

Figure 14. Emma (Gwyneth Paltrow) and Knightley (Jeremy Northam) trade barbs over Emma's patronage of Harriet Smith. © Miramax

able, amiable squire who 150 years later might be wearing tweeds and puffing a pipe. And she strikingly contrasts with Mrs. Elton, played with élan by Juliet Stevenson as a vulgar and abrasive woman who darts across the screen like a silverfish and speaks in short declarative, staccato bursts.

Production problems begin to surface and proliferate with the Second Book. Polly Walker's Jane is the best of a good lot—dark to Emma's bright, accomplished and within herself, contralto to Emma's soprano. But Frank Churchill (Ewan McGregor) is rather awful. From the moment he rescues Emma from her creek-bogged carriage (an unhappy invention of adaptor/director McGrath), he is glib and flashy, not witty, with his claims to elegance seriously compromised by a frightwig haircut. His appearance and manners seem intended to reassure the audience that he is no competition for Knightley.[10]

In fact, the rest of the movie seems designed to underscore the Emma-Knightley connection by short-shrifting everything else along the way. Unlike the telescoping of scenes that worked in the Beckinsale version because the integrity and balance of the original story were preserved, here the Frank-Jane involvement virtually disappears—except as smokescreened by some wisecracking by Emma and Knightley—as if the film could not sustain, or the viewer cope with, a parallel and analogous love subplot. In a paltry seventeen minutes, we move from the Crown Ball, the Gypsy encounter, and the strawberry fest-Box Hill parley to Emma's insult to Miss Bates. But with the connection to Frank reduced and trivialized, Emma's actions seem either incomprehensible or gratuitously mean. The impact of the scene, however, is salvaged in part by a magnificent performance by Sophie Thompson as Miss Bates, who manages in her response to show herself as vulnerable, touching, and oddly dignified. There is no doubt that Emma has done *something* here to be ashamed of. And Knightley subsequently captures exactly the right tone of angry, disappointed reproach, and Emma the silent misery of remorse to confirm her misdeed. (See Figure 15.)

The film then accelerates again. The secret engagement is exposed and substantiated without the audience's seeing or hearing either Frank or Jane, who, their work in Emma's life done, slip mutely from the scene. And the traumatic interview with Harriet is dispensed with quickly as well, apparently to allow McGrath more time for his freelancing—a series of vignettes wherein Emma plays "he loves me, he loves me not" with daisies, and "retaliates" against her erstwhile protégé by removing her portrait from its place of honor and replacing it with a picture of a dog. McGrath's diversion is more than unfortunate. An absolute key to Jane Austen's characterization is that Emma must be torn by self-

Figure 15. Knightley chastises a temporarily penitent Emma. © Miramax

blame in bringing about, ironically and inadvertently, her most considerable matchmaking triumph; but the irony must be muted. Emma must truly be made to be wretched here, for herself and for Mr. Knightley, if the denouement is to be properly triumphant. She must be capable of real wretchedness, so that her happiness a few scenes later can be correspondingly exalted. Grumbling petulance is appropriate earlier, perhaps; this is a crisis of a different order.

The resolution of the crisis thus needs to be properly anticipated; and until the mutual joyous enlightenment, in the film it is absolutely superb. The eloquence lies in the tense, fearful silences between Emma and Knightley's speeches. When he turns away from her, before she pursues him, it is one of those cinematic moments wherein—though we either know or suspect it will all work out—we want to shout at the screen at both of them to stop, talk, listen.

But once the suspense is dispelled, the talking goes on and on—for once—too long and too volubly, and it culminates in Knightley's growled proposal, "Marry me"—a jarring and mood-shattering imperative rather than an entreaty. Though there is little doubt of Knightley's intentions, the audience is nonetheless forced to witness his declaration.

But Emma is radiant afterwards, and Paltrow conveys emotions both strong and subtle with consummate skill (apart from the few occasions of real stress during which her usually impeccable accent slips, betraying the American within). And, apart from a kiss between Emma and Knightley, from which Austen purists recoiled, the film returns to the detail of the book by allowing Mrs. Elton the last word about the newly-wed Robert Martins. Her sneering observation about the plebeian accoutrements of the bride—"Very little white satin, very few lace veils; a most pitiful business!"—puts the inner joy of the couple in some sort of narrative and societal perspective.

The shortcomings of this version can be laid squarely on the shoulders of the director: Douglas McGrath succumbs to the temptation to make this a "big-screen" production and, in so doing, shows a lack of faith in an American audience to appreciate anything not tailored to its expectations. Fortunately, however, it is an intelligent audience he has in mind. *Emma* was McGrath's first attempt at directing; his previous experience included comedy writing, for *Saturday Night Live* and later for Woody Allen in *Bullets Over Broadway*. That comedic influence is often apparent in *Emma*—in the "unexpected sight gag or broadly contemporary touch"; Janet Maslin notes that "it's one of Mr. McGrath's little jokes to seldom depict servants here [in the film], even though an absurd set of props appears on the manor lawn every time a new form of dabbling—archery or stitching or writing or sketching—is under way" (Maslin, "So Genteel" 1). McGrath, however, was wise enough to recognize that "Jane Austen would be a good collaborator" (Purdum 11), and so he left a lot of the dialogue intact. That—plus the quality of the performances, particularly Gwyneth Paltrow's radiant portrayal of the title character—helped to ensure that McGrath's *Emma,* despite its shortcomings, "stands up to bigger historical sagas, and is definitely funnier than most" (Eisner 51).

The fourth and in many ways the most delightfully surprising adaptation of *Emma* is *Clueless* (Paramount, 1995; dir. Amy Heckerling), a film warmly received by all but the most intransigent of Janeites. A good comedy in its own right[11]—reminiscent of Austen, herself in the widest and best sense fundamentally a comic writer—*Clueless* replaces bucolic Georgian Surrey and its centuries-old rural culture with an aggressively urban, post-Reagan Los Angeles, where, it seems, a new sub-culture erupts every month or so, flourishes for a few weeks, and then shrivels and dies. Tidy, placid Highbury has yielded place to the raucous sprawl of mall, disco, and freeway, and its sleepy denizens to the decibel-challenging spindizzies of contemporary teenage-hood, where endless cell-phone conversations supplant social visiting. In a film review for the *Christian Science Monitor,* David Sterritt concluded that "without question, director Amy Heckerling had created an *Emma* that resonated with contemporary times" (11).

And then there is Cher (Alicia Silverstone)—poor Emma Woodhouse that was—in the center of it all. At sixteen rather than nineteen,

Cher, the happy child of a superficial culture (her mother died in "a freak accident during routine liposuction"), has neither Emma's sometimes abrasive compulsion to dominate and manipulate nor her substance. Nor does she possess the opportunity or the desire. The Valley Girl pond is a lot bigger than Emma's tranquil pool, and there are more frogs Cher's size. And her itch to manipulate is usually subordinated to her adolescent urge to conform with distinction. It is tempting to concur with her rueful assessment of herself as "a ditz with a credit card."

But Cher's similarities to Emma are more fundamental than the differences, most strikingly in that the strengths of her character are more evident and perdurable than her shortcomings. She takes kind and efficient care of her father (Dan Hedaya), here transmogrified into a dour, domineering lawyer, and of their glitzy mansion—a "classic," she tells us proudly, the pillars dating all the way back to 1972. She is tireless in support of her friends, eloquent in her own Valley-speak patois, and even superior in her studies, though shamelessly ready to scam and sweet-talk her teachers for better grades. Most of all, under her designer-fashioned surface, Cher has a solid basis of integrity and amiability. She wants to make the world—at least as much of it as she is aware of—a better place and, though she can more than hold her own in the tribal disputes and territorial feuds of her sub-society, she never knowingly hurts anyone, is never, as she would say, "way harsh." The film is remarkable to the spirit of the novel, and that is what attracts Austenites, who do not view it as a flip send-down of their favorite but as a version that validates the universality of the original.

When Cher introduces her new friend and current project—the hopelessly unfashionable, Bronx-accented Tai (Brittany Murphy)—to the high school social director and trend-maven, a supercilious lunk named Elton (Jeremy Sisto), the parallels to Austen's novel fall into place. Tai, of course, is the surrogate of Harriet, and her first love, the brain-fried skateboarder Travis (Brecken Myer), is an approximation of Robert Martin. The place of the Westons is supplied by two of Cher's frazzled middle-aged teachers (Twink Caplan and Wallace Shawn), whom—and here she *is* one up on Emma—she really *does* bring together. Mrs. Elton's role is assumed by Amber (Elisa Donovan), Cher's social rival and all-around nemesis, and Frank's by Christian (Justin Walker), a sleek, sophisticated newcomer with whom Cher briefly contemplates "going all the way." (A politically correct supplement to the original is a hip couple, Cher's best friend and co-conspirator, Dionne [Stacey Dash], and her supportively macho boyfriend.)

Most of all, there is Josh (Paul Rudd), Cher's step-brother by marriage, with whom she carries on a big-brother/little-sister badinage, behind which lies a mutual affection and trust. Josh, a handful of years older than Cher, is a college student interested in Nietzsche and environmental law. Only a little removed from the predatory oafdom of male adolescence, he is suspicious of Christian and covertly protective of Cher's person and future. Their relationship, which unfolds analogously to Emma and Knightley's, is deftly and sweetly presented; it alone would have made this film successful, irrespective of the *Emma* connection. (See Figure 16.) It is the success of that connection, however, that raises this film above the level of clever parody.

Amy Heckerling, the adaptor/director of *Clueless,* is wise enough not to insist on the parallels. And since the situational parallels are implied rather than invoked, her whole story is smoothly jointed and stands capably on its own, sort of an Oz to Jane Austen's Kansas. The Cher-Elton confrontation takes place in his car, in the wake of one of those wild, teenage rock-and-roll revels about which adults are always twitching. Afterwards, he leaves her in a drive-in parking lot, to be mugged and left for a grumpy Josh to rescue, chide, and fuss over. The big dance metaphor scene occurs at yet another party, to which Christian escorts Cher and to which the mistrustful Josh follows them; there he "rescues" Tai from social humiliation by escorting her to the mosh pit. (Unlike Knightley, Josh is a terrible dancer—at least by Cher's measure.) Christian endears himself to Tai by rescuing her—not from Gypsies, but from a pair of bozos facetiously threatening to toss her off the mezzanine at the mall. Most ingeniously, Christian is neutralized as Josh's romantic rival for Cher's affection because he is gay. He terminates her carefully orchestrated seduction with a peck on the cheek and an insouciant "We're friends, right?" ("I should have guessed," Cher admits. "He dresses good, he knows art, and he likes to shop.") There is no substitute for Miss Bates (unless it be the entire culture), no shadow of Jane Fairfax, no grim modern version of Mrs. Churchill.

But the backbone of the original story—the mutual, awakening love of Cher/Emma and Josh/Knightley—remains effectively intact. After a thoroughly wretched day—preoccupied with her various schemes, she "totally" flunks her long anticipated driver's test, then listens to Tai rhapsodize about how *she* and Josh are an item—Cher is incredulous while Tai is unrepentantly scornful ("I should listen to advice from a virgin who can't drive"). Then, contemplating the wreckage of her hopes and schemes, Cher laments, "I was just totally clueless." But suddenly she realizes, "I love Josh totally."

What to do next? Nothing less, she resolves, than "a total makeover of my soul." In the context of her world, this does not involve any somber attempt at spiritual resuscitation but a commitment to commu-

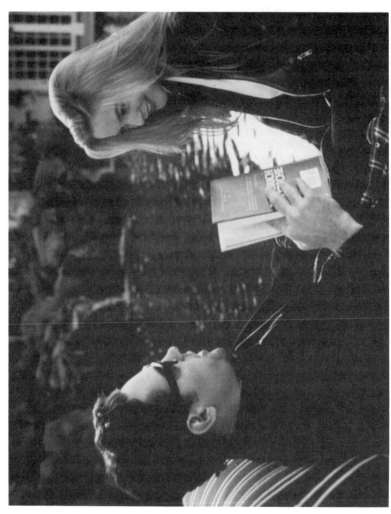

Figure 16. Cher (Alicia Silverstone) talks Josh (Paul Rudd) into interrupting his reading to drive her to the mall in *Clueless*. © Paramount

nity do-gooding (for victims of a devastating mudslide at Pismo Beach), a successful effort to re-interest Tai in a drug-free Travis, and a stint at volunteering as a paralegal gopher for her father Mel—and, coincidentally, for Josh. Mel likes and trusts Josh, alone among Cher's acquaintances and almost among humanity at large. A tiff with Mel's stuffy legal clerk brings Josh to Cher's defense and leads to a mutually enlightening exchange wherein the couple realize, and share, what each means to the other. The episode concludes with a chastely tender kiss.

The film itself ends with a wedding ("No, not that one," Cher informs us; "this is California, not Kentucky"): the long-anticipated nuptials of her teachers, Miss Geiss and Mr. Hall. "Old people," she remarks, "are so sweet." But Cher, after a lively scuffle, does catch the bridal bouquet. The ending is not quite happily ever after, of course; with Austen "forever after" is still to come.

Clueless is Alicia Silverstone's picture, as fully as the latest *Emma* belongs to Gwyneth Paltrow, and Silverstone fulfills expectations superbly.[12] Silverstone's character, more innocent and vulnerable than her counterpart, is equally appealing. Cher laughs where Emma would smile, and she expresses with many words what Emma would convey with a look. But while she can be flighty, Cher is never silly, particularly when she is speaking directly to viewers in a kind of oral diary that Amy Heckerling integrates into her script more successfully than Douglas McGrath does in his *Emma*. We care what happens to her, with an intensity not expected in an ostensibly comic film. Like Emma, Cher deserves not only to be saved but to be loved and to love as well. *Clueless* is not an imitation, not a gimmick, but a retelling of a story a lot older than Jane Austen and one that needs to be redone periodically, as successfully as it has been here.

In a scene at the outset of *Clueless,* Cher chooses her school couture by mixing and matching possible combinations on her computer screen—*this* skirt with *that* top, or *that* one, *those* shoes or the others—until she creates (after the most intense cerebration she devotes to anything connected to school) the ensemble that most satisfactorily embodies that day's Cher. After seeing the four films based on Austen's *Emma,* the viewer is tempted to play a similar game, commingling actors from the different versions and fantasizing various scenarios: how would *this* Emma go with *that* Knightley? Or what would happen if the BBC's Mr. Woodhouse had to be coddled by Kate Beckinsale's Emma? Yet ultimately the viewer must appreciate the fact that each version offers unique insights, both into contemporary culture and into Austen's society. The 1972 BBC *Emma,* the longest version, is closest to the novel both in substance and in spirit and is therefore perhaps the best. The

1996 *Emma* (produced by Meridian), on the other hand, is the shortest version; it telescopes episodes but preserves and even highlights the essentials of the story. The 1996 *Emma* with Gwyneth Paltrow, by focusing on its popular star, necessarily focuses on the character of Emma, just as Austen had intended. And the 1995 *Clueless* succeeds in transporting the essence of the original to a completely different milieu. Each adaptation thus affords interesting perspectives not just on Austen's work but on the process of adaptation itself.

In Austen's *Emma,* the people of Highbury and its environs have the leisure to converse intelligently, to give human relationships the nurture they deserve, even to be comfortably alone with themselves. Courtesy for them is not superficial; elegance is not affectation. Their admirable sense of community requires effort—"exertion" is Austen's word for it—as well as grace to endure minor foibles and frictions. Austen's fictional world certainly has a great deal to show contemporary viewers; and, judging by the many successful adaptations of *Emma,* a lot of people are watching.

Notes

1. Jane Austen, *Emma,* ed. Lionel Trilling (Boston: Houghton Mifflin, 1957) ix. All subsequent references, made by page number in the text, will be to this edition.

2. In her study of *Jane Austen's Emma on Television* (176), Monica Lauritzen notes that there was also an early BBC television adaptation of *Emma,* by Vincent Tilsley and Campbell Logan in 1960.

3. Nevertheless, as Lauritzen demonstrates, in adapting *Emma* as a BBC serial, the production group was not "aiming at a 'bookish' production"; instead, "their ambition was . . . to achieve a piece of genuine and effective television drama" (103).

4. Glenister's "explicit ambition," writes Lauritzen, was "to let Emma's point of view dominate the serial in the same way as in the novel" (79).

5. Glenister, Lauritzen writes, strove for "total fidelity," as did his production crew. Designer Tim Harvey "did research into the buildings and mode of living of the time, while [Costumes Designer] Joan Ellacott copied cuts for costumes in museums" and became familiar with properties of fabrics and dyes. Make-Up Supervisor Pam Meager "was equally attentive to the minutest details"—i.e., whether people of that era used soaps or other detergents; how often they washed their hair—and even replicated hairstyles using the paper curlers employed in Austen's day. That same attention extended to costumes and to the film sets, especially to interiors, which were scrupulously analyzed for aesthetics and colors (114, 112).

6. This scene is explored at length in Lauritzen's study. She notes, for example, that "By including Jane Fairfax in the company at Box Hill, Austen made Frank Churchill's demonstrative courting of Emma appear so cruel as to be almost unforgivable. In the serial the flirtation between Emma and Frank seems frivolous and thoughtless, but is without the more serious dimension given to it in the novel" (140-41). Lauritzen also observes that "what we get on the television screen is only the manifestation of Frank's and Emma's feelings, and as television viewers we are no more able than Mr. Knightley is in either novel or serial to look beyond the surface and perceive the true motivations for their behaviour. This is a privilege that Austen offers to her readers" (142).

7. Paltrow's performance in fact, was almost universally praised. In addition to Janet Maslin's very positive *New York Times*' review, Margy Rochlin, also in the *New York Times,* observed that Paltrow makes "it easy to be an American passing as England's most beloved heroine in a film overflowing with acclaimed British actors" (11). Ken Eisner, in *Variety,* writes that "the pic rests on the star's slim shoulders, and her work goes beyond mere charm. . . . It helps that Paltrow's accent is stunningly spot-on, but beyond that, she invokes sweetly subtle feelings" (52). And Jay Carr, in the *Boston Globe,* remarks on the "delicate balancing act" involved in playing Emma, an act that requires "project[ing] at all times an air of quality. This Paltrow does—almost genetically" (N9).

8. In his review for the *Christian Science Monitor,* David Sterritt takes a somewhat different view of Thompson's performance. Sterritt writes that "The only real disappointment [in the film] is Sophie Thompson, who badly overplays the boring Miss Bates, one of Austen's best-known comic characters. McGrath shares the blame for this, since his handling of Thompson's scenes is sadly lacking in nuance and tact" (11).

9. Interestingly, Janet Maslin likens the film to something "between finely wrought social satire and daytime soap operas" ("So Genteel" 1).

10. Maslin, on the other hand, praises McGregor's performance. "Mr. McGregor," she writes, "currently creating a sensation as the skeletal star of *Trainspotting,* is as versatile as humanly possible playing a country gentleman in a top hat. He may not know what to do with the tails of his morning coat, but he gives this performance all the requisite flirtatious spark" ("So Genteel" 1).

11. "A sleeper hit of the summer," *Clueless* was also—according to Bernard Weinraub—a "very inexpensive commercial film. At $12 million, it cost about one-third what the average studio film does" (10).

12. Silverstone, in fact, gives "a film performance that clicks. As a pampered Beverly Hills clotheshorse, she's mostly a one-joke princess," writes Janet Maslin, "but the joke happens to work" ("Teen-Ager" 9).

Works Consulted

Austen, Jane. *Emma*. Ed. Lionel Trilling. Boston: Houghton Mifflin, 1957.

Brown, Julia Prewitt. *Jane Austen's Novels: Social Change and Literary Form*. Cambridge: Harvard UP, 1979.

Carr, Jay. "Emma Gets a Clue." (Rev. of McGrath version of *Emma*.) *Boston Globe* 4 Aug. 1996: N-9.

Copeland, Edward, and Juliet McMaster, eds. *The Cambridge Companion to Jane Austen*. New York: Cambridge UP, 1997.

Eisner, Ken. "Paltrow Persuasive in Latest Austen Adaptation." *Variety* 17 June-23 June 1996: 52.

Jenkins, Elizabeth. *Jane Austen: A Biography*. London: Gollancz, 1938.

Johnson, Claudia. *Jane Austen: Women, Politics and the Novel*. Chicago: U of Chicago P, 1988.

Lascelles, Mary. *Jane Austen and Her Art*. Oxford: Clarendon P, 1939.

Lauritzen, Monica. *Jane Austen's Emma on Television: A Study of a BBC Classic Serial*. Göteborg, Sweden: Acta Universitatis Gothoburgensis, 1981.

Litz, A. Walton. *Jane Austen: A Study of Her Artistic Development*. New York: Oxford UP, 1965.

Maslin, Janet. "So Genteel, So Scheming, So Austen." (Rev. of McGrath version of *Emma*.) *New York Times* 2 Aug. 1996. Sect. C: 1.

——. "A Teen-Ager Who's Clear on Her Priorities." (Rev. of *Clueless*.) *New York Times* 19 July 1995. Sect. C: 9.

Morgan, Susan. *In the Meantime: Character and Perception in Jane Austen's Fiction*. Chicago: U of Chicago P, 1980.

Pool, Daniel. *What Jane Austen Ate, and Charles Dickens Knew*. New York: Simon and Schuster, 1993.

Purdum, Todd S. "From 'Saturday Night Live' to Jane Austen." *New York Times* 25 Aug. 1996. Section 2: 11.

Reviews of *Clueless*: *Chicago Sun-Times* 19 July 1995; *Washington Post* 21 July 1995.

Reviews of *Emma* (Lawrence version, starring Beckinsale): *London Times* 25 Nov. 1996; *Los Angeles Times* 16 Feb. 1997; *Washington Post* 16 Feb. 1997.

Reviews of *Emma* (McGrath version, starring Paltrow): *Chicago Sun-Times* 9 Aug. 1996; *Time* 29 July 1996; *Washington Post* 9 Aug. 1996.

Rochlin, Margy. "Like Emma, Setting Her World All Astir." *New York Times* 28 July 1996. Sect. 2: 11.

Sterritt, David. "Emma Rings True to Jane Austen's Novel." (Rev. of McGrath version of *Emma*.) *Christian Science Monitor* 2 Aug. 1996. 11.

Tave, Stuart. *Some Words of Jane Austen*. Chicago: U of Chicago P, 1973.

Tomalin, Claire. *Jane Austen: A Life*. New York: Knopf, 1997.

Weinraub, Bernard. "A Surprise Film Hit About Rich Teen-Age Girls." (Rev. of *Clueless*.) *New York Times* 24 July 1995. Sect. C: 10.

4

ADAPTING JANE AUSTEN'S *NORTHANGER ABBEY:* CATHERINE MORLAND AS GOTHIC HEROINE

Marilyn Roberts

The sole screen version of *Northanger Abbey* is the most controversial of all media adaptations of Jane Austen's works. That there is just one version of *Northanger*—a BBC production televised in the United Kingdom in February of 1987—may not be a surprise, for the novel is perhaps the least read and least taught of the six major works in the Austen canon. In addition, *Northanger* presents significant challenges to the screenwriter and director. With its parody and imitation of Gothic and sentimental novels and its narrative wit, *Northanger* requires a screenplay that can present its sources clearly to a modern audience and that can maintain a delicate balance between parody and romance.[1]

Northanger Abbey is one of the earliest of Jane Austen's full-length works. During the course of the narrative, Catherine Morland learns to distinguish true from false friends and suitors. To her dismay, Catherine discovers that Isabella Thorpe is a shallow flirt and that John Thorpe is a self-centered boor. To her delight, Catherine realizes that Elinor Tilney is a worthy friend and that Henry Tilney is a devoted suitor. Under Isabella's influence, Catherine has become addicted to Gothic fiction, using her free time between social engagements to read Ann Radcliffe's *The Mysteries of Udolpho,* a best seller of the period. After eagerly joining the Tilneys at their family home, Northanger Abbey, Catherine imagines that the abbey conceals dark family secrets paralleling those in *Udolpho,* and she humiliates herself by inadvertently suggesting to Henry that she suspects his father, General Tilney, murdered the late Mrs. Tilney. Yet, despite this and other obstacles, Catherine and Henry are happily united at the end of the narrative.

In their televised production of *Northanger Abbey,* writer Maggie Wadey and director Giles Foster eschew the restrained, cup-and-saucer style of other BBC adaptations of Austen and take a bold, unconventional, and campy approach to the novel.[2] According to the film's producer, Louis Marks, "we wanted to make a version 'for our times,' rather than a reverent rehash of a classic." Yet this innovative approach elicited mixed reviews from critics and dismay from many Austen scholars. The adaptation does have its problems: a severe compression of plot and cartoonlike characterizations; the lack of a world of reality to counterbalance Catherine's Gothic fantasies; and a questionable sexualizing and updating of Catherine, Isabella, and Eleanor. Yet a careful study of the production reveals a method to this apparent madness and an understanding of the problems that *Northanger Abbey* presents to its potential adaptors.

In response to the challenges of adapting *Northanger,* Wadey focuses on the Gothic roots of the novel and on a psychoanalytic approach to Catherine's character. To compress the action of the novel into one ninety-minute time slot, Wadey develops the teleplay around the fantasies and dreams Catherine experiences in response to *The Mysteries of Udolpho.* Unlike Austen's novel, the teleplay opens with Catherine (Katharine Schlesinger) taking secret pleasure in reading and fantasizing about Radcliffe's novel. Although this change eliminates Isabella Thorpe's responsibility for introducing Catherine to Gothic novels, there is a structural advantage to beginning the production this way. Several scholars assert that *Northanger* falls into two incompletely unified parts: Catherine's experiences in Bath and her misadventures at Northanger Abbey.[3] By depicting Catherine as *Udolpho*-obsessed from the outset, Wadey prepares the viewer for Catherine's response to the abbey and her fears that General Tilney is another Montoni, the chief villain of *Udolpho.*

Beginning the production with Catherine's daydream also serves to introduce the spectator to Radcliffe's novel. We see Catherine enraptured as she reads the book. Then she turns the book to view an illustration of a scene in which Emily is carried away after fainting at the sight of an apparent corpse revealed by a drawn black veil. Suddenly, the illustration comes to life, and we see Montoni (Robert Hardy) carrying Emily, who is played by a heavily made-up Katharine Schlesinger. In this and in the succeeding fantasies and dreams, Wadey conveys one of Catherine's significant traits: her desire to be a heroine. Austen develops this trait to poke fun at an ordinary young woman's ambition to experience the extraordinary romances and trials of a typical literary heroine:

She had reached the age of seventeen, without having seen one amiable youth who could call forth her sensibility; without having inspired one real passion. . . . There was not one lord in the neighborhood; no—not even a baronet. There was not one family among their acquaintance who had reared and supported a boy accidentally found at their door—not one young man whose origin was unknown. Her father had no ward, and the squire of the parish no children.

But when a young lady is to be a heroine, the perverseness of forty surrounding families cannot prevent her. Something must and will happen to throw
a hero in her way. (Austen 16-17)

The next fantasy reinforces Catherine's discontentment with her rather
dull life. In the novel, when Catherine experiences the uneventful ride to
Bath, Austen mocks the young woman's expectations of the trip: "It [the
journey] was performed with suitable quietness and uneventful safety.
Neither robbers nor tempests befriended them, nor one lucky overturn to
introduce them to the hero. Nothing more alarming occurred than a fear
on Mrs. Allen's side, of having once left her clogs behind her at an inn,
and that fortunately proved to be groundless" (Austen 19). In the BBC
production, Catherine, riding in a carriage, looks bored with her chaper-
ones, the Allens (Googie Withers and Geoffrey Chater), and begins to
fantasize about being dragged off to a castle by two men. In a significant
departure from Austen's novel, Catherine notices a real castle and learns
that the building is Northanger Abbey. This addition leads to the fashion-
ably delayed opening credits. While scholars may object to the addition
of this exciting vision to Catherine's dull journey, the sequence helps the
viewer understand the significance of the title and helps unify the two
parts of the narrative.

Catherine's fantasies about *Udolpho* appear at regular intervals
throughout the adaptation. After meeting Henry Tilney (Peter Firth),
John Thorpe (Jonathan Coy), and General Tilney (Robert Hardy),
Catherine incorporates them into her daydreams, casting them as Valan-
court, Morano, and Montoni, respectively, parallels that Austen seems to
have intended.[4] For example, in the fantasy that follows Catherine's
introduction to the General, we see Montoni's face clearly for the first
time and recognize that Catherine envisions the General as a Gothic villain. Some of these fantasy sequences include voice-over or readings
from *Udolpho* that provide the viewer with more background about Radcliffe's novel. Through such sequences, Wadey and Foster prepare viewers for Catherine's suspicions that the General murdered Mrs. Tilney,
much as Montoni causes the death of his wife.

In her efforts to unify the tone and style of the novel, Wadey integrates Gothic elements into the Bath sequences as well. While this
choice may seem unorthodox, it does have a certain scholarly basis.
According to Daniel Cottom, the heroines of both Radcliffe's and
Austen's novels "face similar problems, however differently they may be
expressed" (52). In *Ghosts of the Gothic,* Judith Wilt argues that Catherine's adventures in Bath are satiric variations on Gothic plots, "But the
middle ground of Bath . . . where unfamiliar anxieties begin, is that same

significant isolating Gothic labyrinth, subtly more frightening because it is filled with that ghostly intimidating crowd of 'no acquaintance'" (138).

One Gothic element Wadey adds to the Bath sequences is the sinister Marchioness (Elaine Ives-Cameron). An anorexic widow of a guillotined French aristocrat, the Marchioness appears in a tight black gown and heavy white, black, and gray make-up. The Marchioness is a confidante and possibly a mistress of the General and encourages his excessive gambling and marriage schemes for his children. Her character seems to be modeled on Lady Laurentini in *The Mysteries of Udolpho.* Laurentini, who is presumed dead, actually lives in a convent and haunts the environs of her deceased lover's castle with her eerie singing. She retired to the convent, suffering intense remorse after she and her lover poisoned his wife (a marchioness). Emily suspects that the ghastly figure she discovers behind the black veil is Laurentini, murdered by her kinsman Montoni for refusing to marry him. The corpselike appearance of Wadey's Marchioness and her unsavory association with the General, a Montoni figure, add to the Gothic emphasis of this production.

Other manifestations of the Gothic in the Bath episodes include more fantasies and nightmares as well as additional grotesque characters wearing overly elaborate empire gowns and tall feathered hats. It is almost as if, after leaving her home, Catherine sees the unfamiliar world of Bath through distorted Gothic lenses.

Wadey provides a psychological explanation of Catherine's obsession with the Gothic by adding Lacanian and Freudian features to Austen's characterization.[5] We can observe a kind of Lacanian *jouissance* in Catherine's responses to *Udolpho,* which fills her with an orgasmic pleasure she does not seem to comprehend. According to Lacan, "There is a *jouissance* proper to her and of which she herself may know nothing, except that she experiences it—that much she does know" (145). Austen understands the power of novels like Mrs. Radcliffe's to fill the reader with a pleasurable excitement akin to *jouissance* and allows Henry, as well as Catherine and Isabella, to admit to the grip such novels exert on the reader. As Henry confesses, "*The Mysteries of Udolpho,* when I had once begun it, I could not lay down again;—I remember finishing it in two days—my hair standing on end the whole time" (Austen 106).

Wadey's Catherine also comes across as an early nineteenth-century version of one of Freud's patients, a young woman who must conceal and repress her sexual impulses in response to a sheltered middle-class upbringing. In most of the fantasies, we see Montoni/the General carrying the unconscious Emily/Catherine away from the supposed corpse or forcing her to lie on a bed-like platform and even attacking her with a sword, a clear phallic symbol (Freud 5:356). The violence in these sequences suggests the kind of repressed attraction to the father that Freud maintains is the source of the beating-fantasies often reported by neurotic patients experiencing the Oedipal complex (17:179-204). In addition, the resemblance between Montoni and the General reflects Catherine's fears of the General's aggressive personality and his admiration of her.[6] Then, stimulated by the mysterious abbey, Catherine's fantasies develop into paranoia, leading her to suspect the real General of murder. According to Freud, such paranoia emerges when unconscious fantasies develop into conscious delusions (7:271). Near the end of the BBC production, Henry appears in a fantasy as her rescuer and carries her away on that cliché of romance, a white horse. This development is symbolic not only of a happy ending but also of the heroine's maturation, for the Oedipal phase is now complete, and Catherine's neurosis has ended or at least eased. No longer obsessed with a threatening father figure, she can abandon the Gothic and look forward to a relationship with a suitable partner.

But Catherine seems to develop a new fantasy from the old. After having been sent home by the General, she drifts distractedly away from an outdoor gathering while Mrs. Allen chatters about Bath. Catherine enters a thick mist, out of which Henry emerges on a horse. A brief dialogue leads to a proposal and a passionate kiss. While some scholars and readers feel that the novel's happy ending seems implausible, Austen's intent seems to be to reward Catherine for growing beyond the influence of the Thorpes and her obsession with the Gothic. Wadey and Foster's conclusion also suggests that Catherine has matured but implies she has traded one romantic fantasy for another.

Ingenious and spectacular as these psychoanalytic fantasy sequences are, Wadey's approach creates some serious difficulties in the production. First, the added material takes up too much time in proportion to the original narrative and characters. Among the oddest additions is a lengthy duet between Henry and a very minor character that segues to an outdoor performance of cartwheels by the Marchioness's page. Even the purpose of some of the fantasies seems excessive, for as Marilyn Butler points out, "the text of the novel does not often concern itself with Catherine's fantasy life" ("Disregarded Designs" 57). In addition, the garish sensationalism of the fantasies does not mesh with Austen's depiction of Catherine as a modest and naive young woman. In a review for the London *Times*, Martin Cropper describes the fantasy sequences as "a succession of sub-Ken Russell videos, where blood and Satanism ran riot" (17).[7]

Moreover, the luscious sensuality of Schlesinger's response to the novel goes far beyond what Austen and Mrs. Radcliffe could or would describe.[8] This updating of Catherine's sexuality seems intended to make her enticingly "relevant" to a 1980s audience. This sensationalism begins immediately, as if to allay male viewers' fears of being bored by a narrative written by an early nineteenth-century bluestocking. After an establishing shot of the church, the camera shows us a basket of plums and a wisp of white skirt. Then the camera slowly follows the skirt upward to reveal stockinged knees and calves. Next, we see Catherine's face responding with orgasmic horror to *The Mysteries of Udolpho*. This sequence leads to her first fantasy, which is interrupted by her brother's call. Catherine rebukes the child, "You do realize, Edward, you've interrupted a vital part of my education. Literature and solitude are as necessary to a young woman's development as sunshine is to ripe fruit." Then she saucily takes a bite out of a plum and chases her brother to the parsonage. Her avid enjoyment of the plum seems to promise pleasure for the male spectator, who is encouraged to make her part of his fantasies. In her classic article "Visual Pleasure and Narrative Cinema," Laura Mulvey describes how the image of woman on screen can be exploited to draw in the male viewer: "The determining male gaze projects its fantasy on to the female figure which is styled accordingly. In their traditional exhibitionist role women are simultaneously looked at and displayed, with their appearance coded for strong visual and erotic impact" (11). While Catherine is not always depicted in such a provocative way, this opening gambit sets the tone for the sexualization of the novel.[9]

Isabella (Cassie Stuart), too, is portrayed with an added dose of sexuality, looking more like a prostitute than a middle-class woman determined to marry into wealth. First appearing in a flashy red outfit and heavy make-up, Isabella so telegraphs her vulgarity that it is a wonder Catherine and Mrs. Allen would pursue their acquaintance with the Thorpes or that Catherine is surprised when Isabella jilts James Morland. This divergence from Austen's characterization is aptly critiqued by David Nokes in his review for *TLS:* "Cassie Stuart plays Isabella as a flouncing, bouncing flirt with a heaving bosom and rolling eye, who seems to have tumbled straight from the pages of *Moll Flanders* or *Fanny Hill*" (186).[10]

Thus, the problem with the BBC Bath sequences lies not in the Gothic elements but rather in the characters' grotesque campiness. Perhaps these touches satirize the excesses of upper-middle-class society then and now (for example, the conspicuous consumption of both Regency and Thatcherite England), but they do little to help the viewer understand the narrative. The strangest Bath sequence takes place in the

Roman baths themselves, where the central characters exchange snippets of dialogue as they drift through the water wearing orange bathing gowns but also their feathered hats. Possibly it was too much of a temptation to avoid paying homage to the greatest portrayal of spa life, Fellini's *8 1/2,* which features a Dantesque steam bath.[11] But the episode in the teleplay of *Northanger* is so odd and so removed from Austen's style and plot that it is difficult to listen to and piece together the telegraphic exchanges between characters. In that episode, Catherine introduces herself to Eleanor Tilney (Ingrid Lacey)—an uncharacteristic breach of etiquette—and the young women immediately arrange to go for a walk later. Even John Thorpe is there, a participant in apparently co-ed bathing.

There are also serious problems in the episodes at Northanger Abbey itself, particularly with setting, plot, and characterizations, all of which are more Gothic than in the novel. The BBC version of the abbey is more like Montoni's castle than the building Austen describes.[12] Part of Austen's point about the abbey is that, to Catherine, it is disappointingly modernized:

An abbey!—yes, it was delightful to be really in an abbey!—but she doubted, as she looked round the room, whether any thing within her observation, would have given her the consciousness. The furniture was in all the profusion and elegance of modern taste. . . . The windows, to which she looked with peculiar dependence, from having heard the General talk of his preserving them in their Gothic form with reverential care, were yet less than what fancy had portrayed. To be sure, the pointed arch was preserved—the form of them was Gothic— they might be even casements—but every pane was so large, so clear, so light! To an imagination which had hoped for the smallest divisions and the heaviest stone-work, for painted glass, dirt and cobwebs, the difference was very distressing. (161-62)

In contrast, the BBC abbey (depicted by Corsham Court and Bodiam Castle) is a gloomy, mist-enshrouded moated castle, where screeching peacocks roam. The interior contains narrow, winding staircases; old furniture; dark hangings; strange objects; and even a flock of birds that frightens Catherine as it bursts out of nowhere. While this kind of setting makes it more believable for Catherine to imagine that the abbey harbors dark secrets, it deflates the contrast between the world of reality and Catherine's fantasies.

Changes in the plot and characters intensify the Gothicization of life at the abbey. Instead of discovering laundry bills in the mysterious cabinet in her room, the BBC Catherine finds surreptitious messages that have passed between Eleanor and a lover. The BBC Eleanor is more modernly spunky than Austen's, who never challenges her father or complains of his behavior. In Wadey and Foster's production, Catherine overhears this Eleanor engaging in an angry exchange with her father and then tearfully asking Henry, "How long must I go on living in this house?" Another updating is the secret meetings between Eleanor and her lover in the late Mrs. Tilney's garden. This added mystery modernizes Eleanor by having her participate in activities that both the original character and Austen would have considered improper, thereby eroding the crucial distinction between Eleanor and Isabella.

In adapting *Northanger Abbey* as a short television program, Wadey and Foster faced a difficult task of compressing Austen's narrative while introducing *The Mysteries of Udolpho* to a modern audience. Although Wadey's choice of tightening the novel by focusing on the Gothic is consistently realized, other choices in the teleplay and direction seem sensationalistic. The updated sexuality of the young women may make them relevant and appealing to a late twentieth-century audience but at the expense of distorting their characters. Allowing the fantasy world to spill over into the "real" world of *Northanger Abbey* is the more serious mistake, resulting in excessive campiness, confusing changes in the characters, and extreme compression of plot. As Benny Green observed in his review for *Punch,* "Rendering the joke pictorial is difficult because there is a danger that the daftness of Catherine become the daftness of the production's overview" (52).

Wadey and Foster's excessive pursuit of the Gothic is also reflected in the genuinely gloomy and mysterious interior of the abbey and the genuinely secret correspondence their Catherine uncovers. In attempting to explain *Udolpho* to the viewers and satirizing its influence on Catherine, the screenwriter seems to have become drawn more to Radcliffe's novel than to Austen's. Scholars themselves have struggled to interpret the extent to which Austen parodied or paid homage to Radcliffe. As a consequence, the task of translating this complex relationship between *Udolpho* and *Northanger* will always be a significant difficulty in any screen adaptation of Austen's novel.

Despite its consistent vision, striking visual sequences, and solid performances, Wadey and Foster's adaptation of *Northanger Abbey* remains an interesting failure. More than ten years have passed since its first screening. Now is a good time for the BBC or an independent film director to grapple with the challenges of *Northanger Abbey* again. Indeed, the BBC has a new *Northanger Abbey* in production. Let us hope that this production achieves the delicate balance between the coming-of-age narrative and the Gothic parody that the novel demands.

Notes

1. Jan Fergus offers an excellent discussion of how Austen alternately parodies and pays homage to the conventions in the novels of her contemporaries (*Jane* 20-38). Benny Green points out the difficulties of rendering the Gothic parody on screen (52).

2. Both Wadey and Foster have been involved in successful adaptations of novels. Wadey wrote the script for the 1994 miniseries based on Edith Wharton's *The Buccaneers,* and Foster directed the BBC *Silas Marner* (1985) before working on *Northanger Abbey.*

3. For examples of such criticism of the novel's structure, see McKillop (60) and Butler, "Disregarded" (56-58).

4. For a discussion of these parallels, see Wilt (126-30, 132-38, 141, 144-46).

5. In his review for *The Guardian,* Hugh Hebert points out the psychoanalytic bent of the production (13).

6. In the novel, John Thorpe reports to Catherine that "the General thinks you the finest girl in Bath" (Austen 96). In the BBC production, after Catherine bursts into the Tilney's drawing room, the General stands very close to her to size her up and then comments on "the charming elasticity" of her walk.

7. Ken Russell's film *Gothic,* also set during the Romantic period, was released at about the same time as the BBC *Northanger Abbey.*

8. As Daniel Cottom demonstrates, Radcliffe's heroines and heroes feel constant pressure to behave properly no matter how extreme their circumstances. Characters who depart from standard rules of moral conduct are punished accordingly (53, 55). Judith Wilt points out that, in *The Mysteries of Udolpho,* Emily behaves with the utmost propriety (133-34). Most scholars agree that Austen was conservative in her judgment of sexual relationships and discreet in her discussion of sexuality. See, for example, Butler (*Jane* 43-45, 108-09, 180) and Brownstein (38). While Jan Fergus argues that Austen does deal with her characters' sexuality, she also states that the novelist "is interested in dramatizing sex in everyday social life—in the drawing room rather than the bedroom" ("Sex and Social Life" 66).

9. Mulvey has modified her position to account for other ways of presenting and responding to screen images of women, but she adds that "I still stand by my 'Visual Pleasure' argument" ("Afterthoughts" 12).

10. Is such sexual sensationalizing of literature a pattern in Wadey's screenplays? The resolution of Wadey's adaptation of *The Buccaneers* aroused indignation among British critics. Diverging from Wharton's notes for the conclusion of the unfinished novel, Wadey has Nan leave the Duke because of marital rape and his homosexual escapades (Bhatti).

11. David Nokes mentions the influence of Fellini on this scene in his review in *TLS* (186).

12. Bernard Richards discusses the discrepancy between the abbey as described in the novel and as depicted in the BBC production (271).

Works Cited

Austen, Jane. *Northanger Abbey*. Vol. 5 of *The Novels of Jane Austen*. Ed. R. W. Chapman. 3rd ed. 6 vols. Oxford: Oxford UP, 1969.

Bhatti, Jabeen. "How did a Wharton mini-series end up with such a happy ending?" *Current* 11 Sept 1995. Online at http://current.org/bucc516.html (1 July 1997).

Brownstein, Rachel M. "*Northanger Abbey, Sense and Sensibility, Pride and Prejudice*." *The Cambridge Companion to Jane Austen*. Ed. Edward Copeland and Juliet McMaster. Cambridge: Cambridge UP, 1997. 32-57.

Butler, Marilyn. *Jane Austen and the War of Ideas*. Oxford: Oxford UP, 1975.

——. "Disregarded Designs: Jane Austen's Sense of the Volume." In Monaghan. 49-65.

Cottom, Daniel. *The Civilized Imagination: A Study of Ann Radcliffe, Jane Austen, and Sir Walter Scott*. Cambridge: Cambridge UP, 1985.

Cropper, Martin. "A Sort of Zealotry." (Rev. of *Northanger Abbey*.) London *Times* 16 Feb. 1987: 17.

Fergus, Jan. *Jane Austen and the Didactic Novel*. Totowa, NJ: Barnes & Noble, 1983.

——. "Sex and Social Life in Jane Austen's Novels." In Monaghan. 66-85.

Freud, Sigmund. *The Complete Psychological Works of Sigmund Freud*. Trans. and ed. James Strachey. 24 vols. London: Hogarth P and the Institute of Psycho-analysis, 1953-1974.

Green, Benny. "Miss Emily and Miss Austen." (Rev. of *Northanger Abbey*.) *Punch* 25 Feb. 1987: 52.

Hebert, Hugh. "Taking Liberties with Jane." (Rev. of *Northanger Abbey*.) *The Guardian* 16 Feb. 1987: 13.

Lacan, Jacques. *Feminine Sexuality: Jacques Lacan and the École Freudienne*. Ed. Juliet Mitchell and Jacqueline Rose. Trans. Jacqueline Rose. New York: Norton, 1983.

Marks, Louis. Email to the author. 10 July 1997.

McKillop, Alan D. "Critical Realism in *Northanger Abbey*." Rpt. *Jane Austen: A Collection of Critical Essays*. Ed. Ian Watt. Twentieth-Century Views. Englewood Cliffs, NJ: Prentice-Hall, 1963.

Monaghan, David, ed. *Jane Austen in a Social Context*. London: Macmillan and Totowa, NJ: Barnes & Noble, 1981.

Mulvey, Laura. "Afterthoughts on 'Visual Pleasure and Narrative Cinema' Inspired by King Vidor's *Duel in the Sun* (1946)." *Framework* 6.15-17 (1981): 12-15.

——. "Visual Pleasure and Narrative Cinema." *Screen* 16.3 (1975): 6-18.

Nokes, David. "Shepherd's Bush Gothic." (Rev. of *Northanger Abbey*.) *TLS* 20 Feb 1987: 186.

Northanger Abbey. By Jane Austen. Adapt. Maggie Wadey. Dir. Giles Foster. With Katherine Schlesinger and Peter Firth. BBC/A & E, 1987.

Richards, Bernard. Letter. *TLS* 13 March 1987: 271.

Wilt, Judith. *Ghosts of the Gothic.* Princeton: Princeton UP, 1980.

5

HER FIRST AND HER LAST:
AUSTEN'S *SENSE AND SENSIBILITY,*
PERSUASION, AND THEIR SCREEN ADAPTATIONS

Tom Hoberg

When Jane Austen published *Sense and Sensibility* in 1811, she was in the prime of her creative vigor; seven years later, when she completed *Persuasion,* she was dying, and by the time it reached the public, she was dead, her active career spanning less than seven years. Much is made by some critics of her remarkable development over that span. The youthful vigor and exuberance—and emotional imbalances—of her first book and its young heroines contrast with the smoother and sadder resonance of her final work and its autumnal heroine. Yet the separation between the two books is not as great as is sometimes made out, and certainly not as basic as their fundamental similarities. Both works deal with the same world, its denizens and their tribulations and triumphs; and both reflect the concerns and values of the same narrative genius. More particularly, they are two of Austen's dark novels (the other being *Mansfield Park*) where satire is biting rather than genial, where the good are overpowered by the bad, and where, in the end, the heroine and her husband do not triumphantly preside over a rejuvenated society, but are forced to flee a society grown hopelessly corrupt and cruel.

Certain assumptions, therefore, are common to *Sense and Sensibility* and to *Persuasion.* One is that a suitable marriage is the only life option for a woman—and that a secure and substantial income is essential to the success of that marriage. In the words of Austen scholar Louis Kronenberger:

As always . . . money (or the lack of it) was to be of decisive, if sometimes unspoken, importance, and marriage, as always, whether for the young people or their match-minded elders, was to be the mainspring of the plot. (7)

That a young woman's desirability or a young man's eligibility is reckoned by the size of his or her annual income—an income, moreover, which must be settled or inherited, not earned—is revolting to modern romantic sensibilities. After all, in fiction if not in life, it is love that is supposed to conquer all.

But love does not conquer all. Economic realities and practicalities, important today, were even more important two hundred years ago, especially among the gentry about whom Austen chose to write. To enter marriage without sufficient financial security was an exercise in folly, for marriage was regarded as an investment, and attention to fiscal considerations was not avarice, but simple prudence. Moreover, and of equal importance, marriage gave women not only social status but also social establishment: the care of a husband and household and the rearing of children. This is not to minimize the necessity of affection, including physical attraction: any woman marrying solely for status or security was begging for trouble. But these former were not principal desiderata and, at any event, were often cultivated after the more mundane negotiations had been completed. And only with all these elements in place could a rich and happy union begin. Playing out such a process was the function of courtship. And such is the story of the Dashwood sisters, which Austen unfolds in *Sense and Sensibility*.

Indeed, in her first novel, Austen presents two courtships from inception to culmination, involving very different women and their chosen men, and the very different ways the choosing is effected. The enigmatic title of *Sense and Sensibility* (an earlier draft, now lost, was called *Elinor and Marianne*) suggests categorical contradictories, one emblematic of the positive, the other of the negative. In the novel, Elinor, the embodiment of *sense,* is the putative "good sister," while Marianne, the incarnation of *sensibility,* is ostensibly the flighty, impetuous, and troublesome one. But to read the novel in terms of this dichotomy—as numerous literary critics have—is to reduce a social comedy to a moral allegory. In fact, sense and sensibility are complementary, not opposed, and any reasonably complex human being, whether in flesh or fiction, has some of each, with the realistic elements of his or her nature balancing with the romantic, rather like the humors of medieval physio-psychology. Otherwise, in *Sense and Sensibility,* one sister would be reduced to a bloodless drudge, the other dismissed as an overheated airhead, and neither would be fit subject for anything but satire.

The characteristics of these two states of soul are better illustrated in the actual than debated in the abstract. Austen portrays Elinor as possessing "a strength of understanding and coolness of judgment which qualified her, though only nineteen, to be the counselor of her mother. . . . She had an excellent heart; her disposition was affectionate, and her feelings were strong; but she knew how to govern them; it was a knowledge which her mother had yet to learn, and which one of her sisters had resolved never to be taught." Marianne's abilities "were in many respects quite equal to Elinor's. She was sensible and clever, but eager in everything; her sorrows, her joys could have no moderation. She was generous, amiable, interesting: she was everything but prudent. The resemblance between her and her mother was strikingly great" (18).

If the sisters sound like characters from a fairy tale or melodrama, they are—as long as we acknowledge that there is nothing wrong with melodrama *per se*. Their story, on the one hand, is replete with secret engagements, blighted troths, unrequited attachments, passionate rivalries, financial double-dealings, life-threatening illnesses, even a duel (though that happens, so to speak, off-stage). On the other, their story reveals how both sisters, through their own exertions, are united with the men they have chosen to love, in lives that promise happiness, if not always absolute bliss.

Elinor's beloved is Edward Ferrars, a quietly genteel man of no independent fortune, dependent on his selfish termagant of a mother, whose ambitions for him reach far beyond the likes of the portionless Elinor. As diffident as he is reserved, Edward is also bullied by his sister Fanny Dashwood, whose husband John, half brother to Elinor and Marianne, is largely responsible for the sisters' penury. Circumstances, believes Elinor, make her engagement to Edward unlikely—a belief confirmed by the revelation of his secret engagement to another woman, Lucy Steele.

Prospects initially seems brighter for Marianne, who has fallen violently in love with John Willoughby and he, apparently, for her—or so it seems, until he departs abruptly for London, where he becomes engaged to an heiress with nothing to distinguish her but her fortune. Waiting to console Marianne is another admirer, Colonel Brandon. A landowner of considerable fortune and impeccable character, he is in his mid-thirties—an age Marianne considers on the brink of senescence—and his prosaic, sober reticence makes him difficult for Marianne to accept. Only after Brandon (along with Elinor) helps to restore Marianne to health after her illness and depression over Willoughby does she agree to marry him. Her passion for Willoughby replaced by admiration and gratitude for Brandon, her sensibility mitigated—if not supplemented—by sense, Marianne prepares, at the novel's end, to become mistress of the estate at Delaford.

Elinor, too, is ultimately rewarded for her constancy, when she learns that Lucy Steele has wed not Edward but his brother Robert Ferrars, whose financial prospects prove more promising. Freed from his obligation, Edward proposes to Elinor, marries her, and carries her away with him to the new rectory home provided by Brandon and situated next to her sister's.

A happy, sappy ending? Hardly. Unlike in *Emma,* in *Sense and Sensibility* there are villains aplenty; and, at the end, they are still out there, and for the most part they seem to have triumphed. The John Dashwoods do not receive their comeuppances; Lucy and Robert manage to weasel into the good graces—and secure the fortune—of Mrs. Ferrars; and even Willoughby's loveless marriage has its tolerable moments. The little community around Delaford seems less an Elysium than a fortress, wherein its denizens take refuge from a world where greed and nastiness are the requisites for success.

Of the two film productions of *Sense and Sensibility*[1]—a 1981 BBC production directed by Rodney Bennett (re-released by CBS FOX on video in 1995) and the more recent and publicized 1995 version produced by Columbia Tri-Star Pictures from an Oscar-winning screenplay by Emma Thompson and directed by Ang Lee—the Columbia blockbuster attempts to ameliorate the bleakness of a world in which only moderate expectations are honored and only moderate feelings are tolerated by burnishing the portrayals of the three "sense" characters, casting Hugh Grant as Edward, Alan Rickman as Brandon, and Emma Thompson as Elinor. Grant brings to Edward a boyish vulnerability, a suppressed sense of fun, that contrasts with Elinor's seriousness. His diffidence seems genuinely good-natured rather than listless. He tells jokes; he smiles; he actually grins. He has the potential to enjoy life and, marvelously, might even help Elinor do the same. This muted joie de vivre is demonstrated in his by-play with Margaret, the youngest Dashwood sister, almost a cipher in the novel, but here given a more important role as a foil for Edward's cheerful whimsy.[2]

Alan Rickman's Brandon is even more impressive, in that—by his own nature and by the nature of the story—he has few lines, yet he conveys his feelings through his powerful presence. Rickman's character is a strong man who is, with some effort, holding his feelings in check. His voice is a baritone growl, an implied contrast to the pleasant tenor of Grant's Edward; and he is most expressive when his features silently reflect his emotions.

Both Grant and Rickman give bravura performances, but whether these performances enhance the impact of the story is questionable. In the film, Elinor cannot help but love such a charming Edward; and Brandon is such a patient yet powerful force that there is no doubt he will prevail with Marianne. But in the novel, the imprecise nature of the relationships generates more suspense about the outcomes: Elinor and Brandon share an even more obvious and suggestive rapport; and, for a while at least, Brandon seems unlikely to win the hand of his true love Marianne in marriage. By lessening much of the circumstantial suspense, the film dilutes the grim uncertainties of the novel in the interests of a conventional love story.

As the Dashwood sisters, however, Emma Thompson and Kate Winslet succeed brilliantly in bringing their characters toward the emotional center. (See Figure 17.) In lesser hands, Marianne could have dwindled to a hyper-emotional adolescent who passes from drooling infatuation to scenery-chewing hysterics, offering little for the audience to sympathize with, let alone respect, and becoming simply another burden for Elinor to shoulder and, at the end, a much depreciated kewpie doll for Brandon to be content with. But Winslet's portrayal of "the high-flying romantic who gets her wings burned" (McCarthy 51) is sympathetic rather than irritating. Like Rickman, she has a wonderfully expressive countenance when she is in repose and when she is trying to show the world an emotion at utter odds with the one inside. Her performance here rivals her Ophelia to Kenneth Branagh's Hamlet.[3]

Yet it is Emma Thompson who is best of all. Despite the handful of ultra-orthodox Janeites who grumbled that she was too old to portray the nineteen-year old Elinor, her performance is nothing short of "ideal" (McCarthy 51). Although Thompson's Elinor is the articulate and responsible one—for example, she deals with the servants at the ancestral estate at Norland, while her mother and sisters alternately glower and weep from the sidelines—she is no automaton, and still less a martyr. Elinor has seen little of life on which to build illusions, but the considerable happiness of which she shows herself capable is clearly more natural, if not more authentic, than her sister's febrile romanticizing.

The relationship between the two sisters—director Ang Lee called it "the balance" (Elias 15)—is the heart and soul of the film, as it is in the novel, and the nuances of that relationship are depicted superbly. When the dashing Willoughby thunders into Marianne's life, she gives herself to him with an unrestrained ardor, condensed cinematically into a series of vignettes that make their love seem even more impetuous. He and Marianne are a heedless but attractive pair; viewers who did not know the original story would wish them romantic godspeed. In this sequence, Thompson's Elinor is relegated to a role that is not just supporting but also supportive: she likes the engaging Willoughby, laughs at his jokes, smiles at his high jinks, and clearly wishes the young couple well, even as she cautions her sister against headlong behavior. And Winslet's Marianne admires and leans on her sibling, even as she is fondly—and, once

Figure 17. The Dashwood women in a rare moment of tranquil accord: Elinor (Emma Thompson), Marianne (Kate Winslet), and Mrs. Dashwood (Gemma Jones). © Columbia

or twice, sharply—impatient with Elinor's restrained "affection" for Edward.

The dynamics of the sisters' relationship, and of the whole Dashwood family, is underscored after Willoughby's first defection. Screenwriter Emma Thompson and director Ang Lee make optimum use of the visual medium to convey in seconds what in the book required minutes of dialogue. (Todd McCarthy, in his *Variety* review, applauded their efforts to preserve "the necessary niceties and decorum of civilized behavior of the time while still cutting to the dramatic quick" (51) and while still keeping "an eye out for the comedic possibilities in any situation" [51].) In one scene, for example, Marianne spurns Elinor's offer of a healing cup of tea and rushes off inconsolably to her room. Her mother, distraught that Marianne will not confide in her, locks herself weeping in her room. And Margaret, hurt that no one is listening to her, shuts herself up—sobbing—in hers. As the scene fades, Elinor plops down on the stairs, sighs, and drinks the tea herself.[4]

The visual medium improves upon the book in certain other ways, especially in contrasting the spacious, sunny idyllic countryside with the claustrophobic gloom of reconstructed Regency London. Austen, famous—or notorious—for the sparseness of descriptive passages, leaves much to the imagination of her readers; in the film, however, the visual presentation of the city provides a metaphor for its emotional and communal poverty. At the traumatic meeting between the former lovers, which occurs after Marianne has been feverishly awaiting a letter or visit from Willoughby, he greets her with a cold punctiliousness that pulverizes her romantic dreams. The crowded London rooms with their wavering lights give Willoughby a perfect hiding place, and even after being momentarily flushed out to confront and devastate Marianne, he can scurry again back to his "party," from which his frigidly elegant London lady can mock Marianne and her friends and their "country fashions." Indeed, the only individual comfortable in these rooms is Edward's dandyish brother Robert, who engages Elinor to dance and rhapsodizes to her about the "simplicity" of the palatial "country cottage" he has always coveted.

As other Austen adaptors have, director Ang Lee, executive producer Sydney Pollack, and the other creators of the film in fact use the dance as metaphor. But the dance in *Sense and Sensibility* is employed for an entirely different effect. In *Pride and Prejudice, Northanger Abbey,* and the various versions of *Emma,* for instance, the dance represents a social engagement, an act of community and harmony. Here, in the mahogany vastness of the London ballroom, the effect is rather of anonymity and isolation. Each couple performs the correct numbers, but there is little sense that the dancers are aware of anyone beyond themselves—a genteel eighteenth-century version of slam-dancing. When Mrs. Jennings' party must leave to deal with Marianne's collapse after the unpleasant encounter with Willoughby, the festive ranks close behind, and no trace of them remains.

Furthermore, in the anonymity of London, with Willoughby gone from Marianne's life (their relationship terminated by his viciously formal missive and his return of her letters) and with Edward not yet arrived, the filmmakers are able to develop further the relationship between the sisters. By this point in the film, the rapport between the two performers is such that their intimacy seems natural. (Uncannily, they have even contrived to *look* related.) It is, however, Marianne's turn on center stage, as her increasingly manic behavior over Willoughby's rejection plagues everyone in Mrs. Jennings' household, where the Dashwood sisters are guests.[5] Although the ever-burdened Elinor finds it harder to cover for Marianne's lack of the barest civility, her love for her sister becomes manifest, as does the melancholy fact that, in such an environment, they have only each other on whom to depend.

The sisters' mutual love, intensified during Marianne's decline in London, reaches a peak when she collapses and almost dies in Somerset. The emotional responsibility that rested on Marianne in the first half of the film now shifts to Elinor, and Emma Thompson carries it magnificently. In a series of remarkably moving scenes, she waits at the bedside of her dangerously ill sister and, later, attends to her during her convalescence. (Indeed, in her screenplay, Thompson excised one of Austen's most dramatic scenes—the confrontation between Elinor and Willoughby, in which he confesses, with a questionable degree of penitent sincerity, that he has always loved Marianne and that he now realizes his mistake—perhaps as a way of keeping the emotional focus on the women.) And it is in these scenes of sisterly care, not in the final marriages, that the film makes the most hopeful statement about the goodness of its characters.[6]

The powerful scenes with Marianne overshadow, though they do not eclipse, Elinor's other fine moments, especially in the meetings with the two men in her life, Edward and Colonel Brandon. When Brandon, in the latter instance, comes to impart the news of Willoughby's inveterate infamy in seducing, impregnating, and abandoning the Colonel's teenaged ward (and, in so doing, reveals his own tragic past), Rickman's Brandon and Thompson's Elinor play so strongly off each other that the viewer wishes, at least briefly, that they could be more than compassionate friends. The former, in which Elinor plucks up all her sense of righteousness to make Brandon's offer of a rectory home to Edward, thus removing the only impediment to his marriage to Lucy Steele, is an even more quietly moving scene. It is the first time in the entire film that Elinor and Edward remain together, uninterrupted, since their first acquaintance. As in the book, the episode is portrayed with few words. There is no way that Edward can escape without appearing awkward and humiliated; yet Elinor cannot seem to be a plaster saint, nobly subordinating her own happiness to some higher good. The pain and reluctance with which she carries out her mission is obvious, and she takes scant comfort in Edward's effusions. "Edward will marry Lucy," she later tells Marianne, "and you and I will go home"—or, more accurately, to Cleveland, and to Marianne's nearly fatal relapse.

That collapse is brought on in a burst of cinematic pyrotechnics, by a piece of extravagance that has no textual justification from the novel but that works gloriously in the film. Originally, Marianne just desiccates, until a wasting fever can gain a hold. In the film, however, after a long interlude of wan, tight-lipped, dry-eyed wretchedness in London, Marianne celebrates their arrival in the country by dashing off in a driving deluge to stand on a hillock looking down on the lights of Combe Magna. Tears and rain obscuring her features, she whispers a favorite Shakespearean sonnet into the blast as the camera pans up and out to leave her a forlorn miniature, a kind of Turneresque effect. Although purists objected to the high-decibel histrionics, the scene itself is remarkable. In her despair as in her rapture, it is just the thing Marianne would do—what she would have felt obliged to do—and it is an effective metaphor of the magnificent folly of unbridled passion. Much later, a subdued and pensive Marianne learns of Willoughby's visit from Elinor, and the bond between the sisters grows even stronger.

The rest of the film, much of it interpolated by Thompson's script, is anticlimatically low key. Marianne learns to tolerate, then anticipate, then cherish the attentions of Brandon, who sends to London for a magnificent spinet piano, to which he appends his love and his Christian name. Marianne's acceptance of both makes them declared lovers. Through all of this, Brandon visits the Dashwoods as a welcome guest, honored by mother and sisters, but still a transient in their determinedly domestic women's world.

When he appears at Barton Cottage, apparently as Lucy's husband, Edward is decidedly an interloper. What remains penultimately is to rejoin the emancipated Edward with Elinor, which is done in a scene reminiscent in its choreography of the earlier scene in London among Edward, Elinor, and Lucy. The hidden apprehension and initial exchange of stupefying banalities are the same; but this time they are followed by the news that frees Elinor to vent her past misery and to express her present happiness in a fit of unrestrained bawling. (See Figure 18.) Appropriately, the first strong emotion to which she gives release is joy.

Figure 18. At long last, Edward (Hugh Grant) and Elinor (Emma Thompson) exchange expressions of mutual esteem. © Columbia

In the novel, the wedding that follows is almost an afterthought, a necessary prelude to the formation of the new community around Delaford, with such romantic love as has survived taking second place to a chummy fraternity. But the film portrays the wedding both lavishly and properly. Elinor and Edward are there, in the middle ground, but the day belongs to Marianne and to the Colonel. Resplendent in scarlet regimentals, Brandon joyously tosses handful after handful of coins into the crowd of his tenants. Not a coherent word is spoken in the scene, nor in the one that effectively ends the movie: high on a hill, a solitary horseman overlooks the communal celebration—counterpart to Marianne's earlier isolation—then wheels and gallops away. That horseman, of course, is Willoughby.

Austen's novels are assumed to be not only about but almost exclusively for women, and a great measure of the surprising popularity of Thompson's version of *Sense and Sensibility* is doubtless due to its outstanding portrayal of those women, who—in an intelligent contrast—are emotional superiors in a world in which men still maintain social hegemony. Their story, which in bare outline seems hopelessly old-fashioned, is in fact not so much conventional as traditional; and it is a story driven by characters, as are all of Austen's stories—and as are all good stories in general. As scripted by Thompson, those personations are allowed to dominate cinematically as well.

The earlier version of *Sense and Sensibility,* however, is manifestly directed to a different audience and elicits a much different emotional and artistic response. Produced in 1981 by the BBC and re-released by CBS FOX in 1995, the BBC *Sense and Sensibility* is longer and more leisurely than the Thompson version; yet, paradoxically, although it unfolds itself without shortcuts, it requires a knowledge of the novel in order to be fully savored. Thus it assumes a relatively small and sophisticated audience and makes comparisons with the Thompson blockbuster largely invidious.

The BBC production of *Sense and Sensibility* (the first film adaptation of the novel) is inescapably a woman's vehicle, though in a much different way than Thompson's film. Perhaps in an attempt to be more faithful to the essence of Jane Austen, it depicts the female characters as making much more of an impact than their male counterparts. For one thing, there are more of them. Although Margaret, the youngest Dashwood sister (rather a cipher in the novel), has been sacrificed, Lady Middleton has been reborn; Lucy Steele's birdbrained sister Anne is back; and there is a even a brief but memorable appearance by the imperious Mrs. Ferrars senior, who is present in the book only by reputation.

Moreover, the women are presented as a much more psychologically centrist group. Fanny (Amanda Boxer) and Lady Middleton (Marjorie Bland) are cut from the same cultural cloth, and Mrs. Ferrars (Margot Van Der Bergh) reveals how Fanny will look—and sound—in a score of years. All three are impeccably well-bred, the sort who would carefully choose the right fork with which to stab a person in the back. Lucy Steele (Julie Chambers) has her harpy side, to be sure, but also demonstrates a vulnerability that stirs at least a faint answering sympathy from viewers. Edward is all she has to save her from turning into a social clone of her sister, and she is anxious and defensive—not just uniformly sadistic—in the presence of the more polished Elinor. Even Mrs. Jennings (Annie Leon) is trimmed from Wagnerian dimensions to a dumpy, well-meaning creature who on the occasion of Marianne's illness rises almost to heroism. Into this group, the three Dashwood women (Irene Richard, Tracy Childs, and Diane Fairfax) are set as members of the sorority, not detached and opposed; and the effect is to present them in the aggregate, rather than as discreet individuals, and to put this collective into psychological as well as social charge of the narrative agenda. The men are outnumbered, and outdone, in virtually every scene.

Likewise, Edward (Bosco Hogan) is genuinely awkward and self-denigrating, not boyishly and winsomely reticent—more in spirit with the initially colorless picture of him in the novel. Even while rooting for Edward to be successful, the viewer cannot help but be irritated at his almost masochistic conviction that he is going to destroy any relationship or social moment he is called upon to enter, a conviction that makes him retreat at the slightest hint of disapprobation. Even his brother, the coxcombly Robert Ferrars ("Choosing the right clothes is the labor of my life"), played by Philip Bowers, suggests that Edward has "no polish; he is gauche; awkward, clumsy."

Brandon (Robert Swann), while tall and stately, lacks the commanding presence of Alan Rickman's character; Swann's Brandon appears mostly as a person of benevolent power, the only potential lover not financially challenged or dependent upon the whims of a rich old female relative. Similarly, the depiction of Willoughby (Pater Woodward) is less impressive than in the Thompson version: he is less impeccable, less assured, seemingly more teenaged. Until the revelation of his villainy by Brandon and his meeting with Elinor, in which he belatedly pleads his love for Marianne, Willoughby seems more heedless than calculating. Even at the painful farewell scene at Barton Cottage, he acts like a schoolboy caught in the perpetration of a prank.

Thus, while this is emphatically not a man-bashing film, the males are usually relegated to the background. As in the Thompson version, the most important ongoing relationship in the film is between the two

Dashwood sisters, who learn to understand and respect each other. And it is precisely in its portrayal of both women as individuals with strengths and vulnerabilities, neither being merely an embodiment of the ethical abstractions of the title, that the film shines. The sisters' empathy grows stronger as each becomes the other's sole emotional support in time of crisis, through Edward's apparent betrayal as well as Willoughby's evident perfidy.

This mutuality is illustrated in the interview scene with Willoughby, which (unlike the Thompson film) this version not only includes but also highlights. In that scene, Elinor is her own concerned self as well as a surrogate for her sister; she not only has to listen and judge for both of them but also has to serve as emotional conduit, to intuit as best she can Marianne's likely response to Willoughby's confession of love, to guess whether in time she should even tell Marianne about the event at all. Marianne's long-term well-being is now another of Elinor's responsibilities, just as one of Marianne's burdens is her failure to be available for Elinor during her romantic afflictions.

And Marianne's atonement takes the form of penitence by exertion, by her attempt to free herself from the memory of Willoughby and from her own depression and lassitude. In a series of scenes extending through Marianne's convalescence—too leisurely done, perhaps, for an impatient American audience—the greatest tribute Marianne can pay her sister is to emulate Elinor's hard-sustained resilience, and the most efficacious way Elinor can reciprocate is to open to Marianne her own complex emotions. Here, there is no rush to romantic closure, no flamboyantly dramatic ending, as in the Thompson version. Here—and this is emphatically true to Austen—the sisters seem resigned to continue on, Elinor deprived forever of Edward and Marianne still unable to warm to the Colonel as a potential lover.

Such a conclusion, however realistic, is intolerable; and so the story proceeds. In the BBC version, since the main barriers to Edward's union with Elinor are external ones, his revelation is handled with understated and convincing economy, as is the proposal. The espousing of Marianne and Brandon, on the other hand, is of more interest. Not a done deed even with the neutralization of Willoughby, it requires a fundamental change in Marianne and a lesser one in Brandon. At first, a recovering Marianne receives the Colonel's attentions with an uneasy civility; though her savior, he nonetheless seems a dull hero. The change occurs when he begins reading, even quoting, to her poetry—Shakespeare and Milton, the giants of time and tradition—before whom the likes of Scott and Cowper, whom she and Willoughby had shared, appear pale and transitory.

Nor is their marriage realized within the film. Curiously, and appropriately, it is the elder "sensible" sister who makes a daring and comparatively impetuous marriage, and the younger "romantic" one whose union is allowed to ripen and who utters that great comment, "I shall have hundreds of questions to ask you." The ending is not the more showy Hollywood-style ending of the Thompson adaptation; but it is certainly true to Jane Austen, who respects her characters enough to give them not just a dramatic ending but a hopeful beginning. And it is the women who will make it so, even more emphatically than in the Thompson adaptation. Both Edward and Brandon are promising husbands with undeniable virtues; but it is Elinor and Marianne who will actualize that potential and make their marriages a mutual adventure rather than merely a comfortable slide into domesticity.

Though the BBC version was not—and was not intended to be—the kind of commercial blockbuster that Emma Thompson's adaptation was, it has found its own audience, including many who were led to it on video by the later film, and who found it equally—though differently—attractive. Whereas Thompson and Lee gave their film a more immediately general appeal by retailoring their characters to make them relevant to contemporary audiences, the earlier BBC version gives viewers something closer to Austen's original people, who make the story itself appealingly universal. Moreover, the absence of big-name actors—and the consequent lack of distraction by star turns and personalities—makes the BBC *Sense and Sensibility* even more accessible. Likewise, the more leisurely pace and the fuller representation of the historic milieu make the earlier adaptation a more texturally satisfying, if less intense, cinematic experience.

Whereas the main obstacle to reader—and viewer—rapport in *Sense and Sensibility* is the inadequacy of the "heroes" as proper objects for the heroines' love, the initial difficulty in Austen's last novel *Persuasion* is the reverse. Royal Navy Captain Frederick Wentworth is a quintessential romantic hero, almost to the point of caricature. Eight years earlier, the dashing but impecunious Frederick had proposed marriage to Anne Elliot. Then about the same age as Elinor Dashwood, Anne—believing her friend Lady Russell's fears that he could not provide properly for her—refused his offer; and since her refusal, she has declined into premature spinsterhood, tending to her vain and stupid father Sir Walter and her elder sister Mary, and being alternately imposed upon, patronized, bullied, and ignored by other relatives and acquaintances. "Her word had no weight," the narrator observes; "her convenience was always to give way:—she was only Anne" (5).

Particularly when compared to the romantic Frederick, Anne, at least initially, seems a rather unpromising heroine—a heroine, to paraphrase Jane Austen on *Emma,* that no one else would call a heroine. Yet, writes Austen, she possessed "an elegance of mind and sweetness of character, which must have placed her high with people of any understanding" (5). When Walter's improvidence forces him to relocate and to let the ancestral manse Kellynch Hall to Admiral Croft, Anne again encounters Frederick, who is Mrs. Croft's brother. Now dashing, handsome, and rich, Frederick callously belittles his former flame as "so altered that he should not have known her again" (60).

On a junket to the resort of Lyme Regis, Anne meets a pair of Frederick's old cruise mates, the invalid Captain Hargrove (with family) and his guest Captain Benwick, and comes to the aid of her sister-in-law Louisa Musgrove, who, in an attempt to impress Frederick, leaps off the sea wall, knocking herself concussive and senseless. In the ensuing chaos Anne takes efficient charge and—it would appear—reignites Frederick's interest in her as well as her interest in herself.

While Louisa recuperates, with the excruciating slowness nineteenth-century novelists found so convenient, Anne rejoins her father's household in Bath, where her attentions are soon monopolized by William Elliot, the heir presumptive to the Elliot name and fortune. But, learning of William's iniquitous past, she distances herself from him at the same time that she begins communicating to Frederick—without violating the rules of feminine decorum—the true nature of her strong feelings for him.

To remain true both to her characters and to narrative plausibility, Austen scripted the novel's reconciliation scene with scrupulous care. Interestingly, in fact, she wrote two such scenes, the first appearing as the penultimate chapter in the original edition, the second published as a "cancelled" chapter in the *Memoir* her nephew wrote fifty years after her death. A clumsy bit of manipulation occurs in the first version: Frederick is commissioned by Admiral Croft to confirm the imminence of Anne's marriage to Mr. Elliot, since the newlyweds will surely take possession of the ancestral manse at Kellynch and require the Crofts to vacate. Anne seizes the chance to repudiate Croft's notion; and, emboldened by hope, Frederick bursts forth in an ardent protestation of his love.

Whatever Austen's final intentions, the "second" version—incorporated into the second and all subsequent editions—is by any reckoning the better. Anne, Frederick, and Captain Harville are together in the apartment of the Musgroves Senior, who have brought their whole family to Bath to outfit their daughters for their upcoming weddings. While Frederick writes a letter at a nearby *escritoire,* Anne and Harville are drawn into a discussion of the relative fidelity of men and women to the memory of lost loves. Each is the advocate of his or her own sex, and the result is a forensic standoff, with Anne claiming the last word: "All the privilege I claim for my sex," she declares, "is that of loving longest, when existence or when hope is gone" (240).

Whether Anne connives that Frederick should eavesdrop on her declaration or whether fate simply intervenes, Frederick does overhear, and, in a hastily penned note, renews his vows of love and devotion. Soon the couple is exchanging "again those feelings and those promises which had once before seemed to secure everything, but which had been followed by so many, many years of division and estrangement" (240). Hearing of the engagement, Elliot decamps for London, apparently hoping to preserve his claim to the family name and ancestral home; significantly, in terms of the endings of Austen's novels, the scoundrel will probably succeed.

But Anne does not care and, finally, neither does the reader. For this, the last and most mature of Austen's heroines, is also the most intrepid as she throws in her lot with the new order, symbolized by the Crofts, the nation's new meritorious elite, and one diametrically opposed to the hereditary landed gentry best represented by the sorry Sir Walter. Emulating Sophie Croft, Anne is ready to follow her husband wherever fate and duty may lead them. Far from affirming the cultural conservatism that seems to secure the happiness of her other heroines even as it guarantees the sedentary perpetuation of its domestic values, Austen shows Anne embracing a refreshing new set of values as she does a new set of friends, even with the uncertainty that inevitably goes with them. "She gloried in being a sailor's wife" (252).

The nature and character of the heroine is paramount to *Persuasion*. And, in adapting *Persuasion,* the cinematic challenge is how to play her: too competent, Anne becomes self-sufficiently unromantic; too meek, she becomes a milksop, a dutiful drudge, the nightmare of romances, the unmarried relative. In the story's early stages, Anne is less doing than done to; she defines herself (or allows herself to be defined) by those around her, as a kind of universal social solvent. Yet, in a fiendishly difficult role to execute in a visual medium, the lead actresses in both adaptations of *Persuasion*[7]—the early BBC version (1971) and its 1995 successor, a British telefilm released under the auspices of SONY Pictures Classics—succeed admirably.

Amanda Root, in the second film version, however, meets the challenge with special skill and panache. Root positively scintillates as the resilient Anne; and it is in great measure due to her performance that *Persuasion* is arguably the best of all the Austen adaptations, better even than Emma Thompson's *Sense and Sensibility* and the six-hour BBC version of *Pride and Prejudice*. Janet Maslin spoke for many film critics when she called it brilliantly incisive, "spartan," and "the most thoughtful new Austen adaptation" (Maslin 15).

As in Thompson's *Sense and Sensibility*, the other characters in the SONY Pictures version of *Persuasion* are etched rather than penciled around the heroine, but this time with even more visual vividness: Sir Walter (Corin Redgrave), the clueless, arrogant clotheshorse who seems to swagger even when standing still; his antithesis, the genial weather-beaten Admiral Croft (John Woodvine), who always looks more the real gentleman whenever the two are juxtaposed; Charles Musgrove (Simon Russell Beale), a bright-eyed little badger of a man, who usually appears displaced when forced to remain indoors; and, of course, the majestically sexy Captain Frederick Wentworth (Ciaran Hinds), resplendent in Navy dress blues, in glorious contrast to the foppery or untidiness of the other male characters, including his own officer comrades. Only William Elliot (Samuel West) seems a bit miscast, too patently smarmy to be a convincing threat.

Even more sublimely delineated are the women characters, who—and here the movie draws on an abiding strength of Jane Austen—array the complementary embodiments of the Feminine while simultaneously preserving their uniqueness as individuals: Anne's elder sister Elizabeth (Phoebe Nicholls), whose elegance is already becoming stiff and angular; Mary (Sophie Thompson), her younger sister distinguished forever by her red nose and her continual ill-mannered sniff; the freckled, heavy-footed, buck-toothed Mrs. Clay (Felicity Dean), always half a beat behind the conversation; Lady Russell (Susan Fleetwood), like Sir Walter always outrageously overdressed, even at Bath; the wonderful Mrs. Croft (Fiona Shaw), with her attractive, hopelessly unfashionable sun-and-wind-burn, her graceful, rolling carriage, and her ravishing contralto laugh; the chirpy, eager twitchy Mrs. Smith (Helen Schlesinger), confined to her chair; and Nurse Rooke (Jane Wood), every inch the competent, sly attendant. Memorable, even, is the lacquered, mummified Lady Dalrymple, a hollowed-out title, who fittingly stands mute for the entire production.

And, of course, there is Anne, perfectly conceived and portrayed by Amanda Root, who fulfills Austen's intentions and the viewers' expectations as her character's resignation gradually yields to hope and fear. As Caryn James notes, "Ms. Root makes Anne sad but never self-pitying or forlorn" (18). There are three brief moments when Anne stops to peruse herself in a mirror (a clear analogue to her father's incessant, vainglorious posturing), the first after she has been informed of Captain Wentworth's callous jibe about how "changed" she is, the last before the moment at the inn, in Bath, after she has all but convinced herself that

Frederick still loves her. The audience can see how in the interim she has revived and bloomed. While invariably gracious and accommodating, she never gives the impression of being a victim (although it is clear that she has never quite forgiven herself for following Lady Russell's advice and almost losing Frederick forever). Anne can be firm, even impatient, with the sufficiency of the good and ill-natured fools with whom she is surrounded, and, once self-interest has again supplanted mere self-preservation, is as determined in the pursuit of her happiness as social decorum will allow. When Frederick stalks angrily out of a concert after finding her in William's company, she rushes after him and all but entreats him to remain, heedless of the looks of some of the other music lovers. And when she reads Frederick's letter, her instinct is not to lapse into rhapsodic reverie but to insist, and insist again, that his invitation to the Elliot soirée be reconfirmed and reissued.

Despite its brevity, *Persuasion* is the most "mobile" of the Austen novels; it takes its heroine through four locales that are widely disparate socially and culturally, if not geographically, and that suggest a brisk pacing that the SONY Pictures production was quick to exploit: the rush from Lyme Regis to Thrushcross and back, with news of the injured Louisa, or the gallop of Lady Russell's coach into Bath. The filmmakers even add a prefatory scene aboard a British man-o-war during which Admiral Croft announces the capitulation of Napoleon, an initial framing that anticipates the movie's final scene. The faintly overripe ornateness of Kellynch, the cluttered domesticity of the Musgrove home at Uppercross, the bracing elementalism of the sea wall at Lyme Regis, and finally, in contrast to them all, the febrile, tinselly glitz of Bath—all provide eloquent backgrounds for Anne's rejuvenation.

Nor do the filmmakers attempt to create any artificially romantic suspense. It becomes clear early on that William is no serious rival for Frederick and that neither of the Musgrove sisters offers Anne serious competition. Thus the dramatic tension, as it always does for Austen, involves problems in resolving the misunderstandings and the personal anomalies of her primary lovers, as in the subtle but powerful recognition/reconciliation scene. The screenplay adheres faithfully to the original dialogue, while the camera angle shifts between Anne, discoursing to Captain Harville, and Frederick, trying to listen intently while pretending not to listen at all. And once Anne and Frederick finally understand each other, all external difficulties dissolve; and the happy couple walks away, metaphorically, into the sunset.

A lot of purists have denounced the ensuing scene, which involves the pair moving obliviously against the raucous flow of traffic following a circus parade—a gratuitously gaudy embellishment, the purists complained, on the novel's ending. But the scene does much more than that. Not without its own charms, the carnival is emblematic of the spirit of Bath, of Kellynch, of William's machinations, and even of Lady Russell's snobberies. Yet the carnival holds few charms for Anne and Frederick, who have earned some privacy from a world whose incessant meddling almost separated them forever—a world to which, uniquely among Austen's triumphant lovers, they need not and will not return.

In fact, the film abounds in such visually delicious moments, as "the camera"—according to Caryn James—"becomes the visual equivalent of Austen's rich, commenting voice" (18): Sir Walter's wardrobe, which becomes more progressively outrageous until in one scene his morning suit looks as if it would have been more at home on a couch; the contrast between the elegantly turned Mrs. Croft and the mannequined Lady Russell, between the graceful elegance of Frederick's uniform and the exquisite dandyism of William; Mary's whining about her delicate health, given the lie by her stevedore appetite; Captain Wentworth's brief encounter with his nemesis, in which he puts into the phrase "Lady Russell!" eight years of animosity and frustration. Most memorable perhaps is the scene in the drawing room at Camden Place, lit with smoky inadequacy by candlelight, and the claustrophobic cardroom, into which Frederick strides to rescues Anne, once and for all, from all that it represents—a fitting conclusion for a cinematic retelling of Austen's *Persuasion*.

Designed though it was for a general audience, the SONY Pictures version—"brilliantly captured" and "profoundly truthful" (James 18)—was undeniably superior to the earlier and more "faithful" BBC rendition (at 224 minutes, more than double SONY Pictures' 104). In adapting Austen to film, longer is not necessarily better (as both the BBC version of *Emma* and the recent six-hour *Pride and Prejudice* attest). In the BBC interpretation, strange though it may sound when discussing an Austen novel and its adaptation, there is too much talking. The dramatic tempo moves from the leisurely to the sluggish and is slowed by long prosy conversations—mostly between Anne and Lady Russell—about the danger Mrs. Clay poses and the rightness or wrongness of the marriage that never happens. At its most tedious, the conversational device is reminiscent of those episodes in television serials, where one character presents a laborious synopsis of past events which, while it might gratify the truant viewer, tramples on any notion of dramatic plausibility.

Far worse, it creates the wrong impression of Anne's character, a lapse that the movie takes a long time to put right—longer, perhaps, than some viewers are willing to give it. As the film progresses, the audience does eventually warm to the interpretation of Anne (Ann Firbank). But what distinguishes Anne from Austen's other heroines is her fundamental alienation from the society in which she is immersed, an alienation that calls into question that society's most basic values and that finally results not in reconciliation but escape. (Caryn James calls Anne not only "the most mature and possibly the most poignant and autobiographical" of Austen's heroines but also "the sane center around which Austen constructs the most bitter and redeeming of her social satires" [18].) In contrast, for instance, to Emma, whose triumph comes when she reintegrates herself into her world, Anne must free herself from a world in which she never really belongs and in which there is nothing left for her. And it is crucial to the integrity of the story that this quest for freedom be made clear from the outset.

While Amanda Root's portrayal conveys this, Ann Firbank's does not. In the first half of the production, Firbank's Anne is generically indistinguishable from her sisters, except that, on the whole, she seems happier than they are—wholesome, almost perky, smiling benignly as she copes with the selfishness of others, bravely as she plays the piano so that everyone else can dance. The audience is told several times, mostly by Lady Russell, that Anne is "out of spirits," though she does not seem to be so. "Dear Anne" to some, "Only Anne" to others, she sounds and acts as if she belongs here among her peers, despite her tribulations.

In fact, this homogeneity—with due allowances for age and sex—characterizes the production's other *personae* as well. Mrs. Croft looks and sounds like Lady Russell, who is in turn hard to distinguish from Mrs. Musgrove. More disquieting is the fact that the younger male characters appear almost interchangeable in this story in which a sharp distinction must be made between the men of the Navy and those of the civilian sector. Captain Wentworth (played by Bryan Marshall) seems the perfect society gentleman, as do Captains Harville and Benwick (Michael Culver and Paul Chapman), and Mr. Musgrove and Admiral Croft (Richard Vernon) are both variations of the Elderly British Gent from central casting or from a first-class repertory company. Indeed, as the first half of this adaptation unfolds, it is difficult not to feel (as in so many outstanding BBC productions) that the cast of players was the given and that the characters had somehow to be adapted to fit the players' personalities.

Moreover, this sense of a stage production modified for the screen pervades the entire film. The interior scenes—from Kellynch through Camden House—are uniformly bright, and the accoutrements have a suspiciously modern look to them, as if some contemporary decorator had done up the rooms for period atmosphere. And many of the urban exteriors have clearly been filmed elsewhere and spliced in as needed. The "atmosphere" shots of Lyme in particular have a Potemkin Village air about them, its nautical ambiance conveyed by a pair of Jolly Jack Tars conspicuously posed at a corner or a spotless fishing boat drawn up on the strand in picturesque isolation.

All of this is not to suggest that the production is without merit. Particularly in the first two hours, it falls short only in comparison with its nearly flawless successor. And while Ann Firbank's interpretation does not measure up to Amanda Root's, interpretation can—and here must—be distinguished from performance; and by any standards Firbanks is a splendid actress, who, once well into the part, performs admirably. In an early scene, when Mrs. Croft (Georgina Anderson) announces that her brother has recently married—her brother, the curate, that is—the changing and contrasting expressions that flit across Anne's face represent a moment of acting sublimity. The audience wishes for more such moments; and in the second half of the production, they abound.

The film is divided by the traumatic accident on the Cob at Lyme, when Anne takes command after Louisa's fall and Frederick begins to see her as she really is. Anne's action is that of someone fit to be a sailor's wife, a peer of Mrs. Croft and Mrs. Harville, and contrasts with the hysterics of Mary and the collapse of Louisa. From that moment, this Anne comes increasingly alive; when she arrives in Bath and learns that Frederick is still available, she goes after him with new vigor and confidence, as their mutual awkward caution turns to confidence and candor. Her rendering of the conversation with Captain Harville is flawlessly poignant, as is her flurried reaction to Frederick's letter. And if the denouement is a little prosy, it also depicts her as finally, unqualifiedly happy, and that is worth waiting for.

The BBC company of actors, composed of first-rate performers, from principal to walk-on, is of the high and consistent quality found almost exclusively in Britain, where acting is still a craft to be acquired rather than an extended photo opportunity to be seized. Down to the battalions of extras who appear as maids and footmen, coachmen and waiters and linkboys, a phenomenon apparently inspired by the idea that no role is unworthy, there is not a bad or mediocre performance: even Bryan Marshall as Frederick, the production's most disappointing performance, is praiseworthy. In two middling roles, Charlotte Mitchell and Polly Murch are superb as, respectively, Mrs. Clay and Mrs. Smith. While Morag Hood is a bit too petite and a trifle too elegant for Mary Musgrove, she admirably conveys the character's bone-headed selfishness. And no one could better Basil Dignam's bravura performance as

Sir Walter. Yet, whereas the acting is strong, the sense of sexual tension between the lovers is fairly weak—a complaint countered by Austen fans, who assert that Austen left such matters implied and understated so that the reader could furnish the technicolor.

And, indeed, in such contraries lies the final evaluation of the two film adaptations of *Persuasion*. Both films, by transforming Austen's early nineteenth-century novel into a late twentieth-century film, are a double translation—from age to age and from medium to medium. And, unlike the recent reprehensible distortion of *The Scarlet Letter* or the butchering of *Great Expectations,* neither adaptation cheapens its source by aiming for a low contemporary denominator. The 1971 BBC version, however, attempts to be faithful to the letter of the original; the 1995 SONY Pictures film strives to capture its spirit. And ultimately, as with *Sense and Sensibility,* while the earlier version of *Persuasion* is a more technically accurate adaptation of the book, the later version is a better movie.

In reviewing the recent film adaptations of Austen's first and last novels, Roger Ebert gave both positive notices; but he preferred the actual story of *Persuasion* to that of *Sense and Sensibility,* noting correctly that Austen was not yet a great novelist when she wrote *Sense and Sensibility;* he concludes that, while *Sense and Sensibility* is entertaining and amusing, *Persuasion* is the one true Austen lovers will prefer. There are, to be sure, numerous similarities between the two works, from the appealing maturity of the heroines to the richly depicted rhythms of English country life. And neither novel, at the end, offers complete resolution; in both, difficulties remain to be coped with and problems to be solved, since the bad are merely banished or chastised to the point of being neutralized. In *Sense and Sensibility,* for instance, Lucy Steele Ferrars, John and Fanny Dashwood, even Willoughby are discomfited only to the extent that they must live with their own unpleasant personalities; and in *Persuasion,* Anne and Frederick leave behind them a world in which venality, cruelty, and stupidity rule triumphant.

In *Sense and Sensibility,* however, there is a stronger sense of roots, a love of the perdurable. John Dashwood's barbarism, for example, can be measured by the depredations he visits on the estate at Norlands, the ancestral home he has usurped. Yet the Dashwood women are able to replant their roots at Barton Cottage, whose humble charms attract even the worldly Willoughby. And the Delaford estate, hereditary seat of the Brandons and settling place for all the deserving in the novel, is a positive contrast to London, where few come to any good. Conversely, in *Persuasion,* all the homes, both traditional and transitory, are either garish or shabby. Bath comes across as a papier-mâché mockery of

London, a Regency Las Vegas, full of hologram people, where Sir Walter expends a day cataloguing people into good- and bad-looking. The Uppercross cluster is a monument to discordant rural tedium, and Kellynch Hall, which in other stories would have been the goal and the reward of the heroine, passes from the Crofts upon their return to their natural element, eventually to be graced by the graceless heir and his wife, the solicitor's daughter. What is liberation in *Persuasion* would be folly in *Sense and Sensibility;* what is security in *Sense and Sensibility* is virtual incarceration in *Persuasion*.

Anne, moreover, begins where the heroines of *Sense and Sensibility* end, and her story details the means by which she unravels the society that has surrounded her. Elinor dutifully subscribes to and practices the social virtues advocated by her society, and Marianne learns—or is coerced—to do the same. And their conventional reward is a life of settled, if limited, contentment in the securely rooted community around Delaford, with their settled, if limited, spouses. By contrast, Anne has initially been reduced to a stereotype, almost a caricature, of the dutiful, other-directed female that the world purports to cherish; her adherence to the societal limitations prescribed by her mentor Lady Russell lands her in this untenable situation in the first place. As Ebert observed, forced into prudence in her youth, she had learned romance as she grew older. And the romance she finds, or rather rediscovers, is embodied in a curious hero, a hero curiously unlike Austen's other heroes. It is not just that Frederick is the antithesis of both the men in *Sense and Sensibility;* he is fundamentally different from other, more dynamic Austen heroes, like Knightley or even Darcy. Aggressively swashbuckling, almost to the point of parody, he seems the male hero most able to contend with a bold and adventurous female counterpart; instead, he is won by Austen's most mature and reflective heroine, who comes alive in the course of the novel. And the world into which the couple goes together is both an untraditional and a precarious—albeit a very fulfilling—one, as demonstrated by the Crofts, who are happily unencumbered by estate, offspring, or other conventions of the social establishment. In the novel, as in the films, there is little doubt that Anne will be more comfortable and happier aboard her husband's ship than in the chilly reaches of Kellynch Hall or the cheapjack elegance of Bath.

In his *Variety* review of the Thompson adaptation of *Sense and Sensibility,* Todd McCarthy suggests that "Austen's sudden ascendancy after decades of neglect by Hollywood . . . has something to do with strong stories, rich characters and astute class observations" (McCarthy 51); Janet Maslin, noting in her review of the same version the wealth of Austen's "tartly etched secondary characters," calls Austen "the movies' most welcome new moralist" (15). And in an interesting essay entitled "Ideas and Trends: Jane Austen Meets Mr. Right," Edward Rothstein writes that it is no accident that Austen's novels' "finely detailed accounts of moral and social education should inspire such interest at a time when conservative criticism of American culture is increasingly concerned with failures in those areas" and suggests that, in her efforts to define the elusive and ever-changing notion of manners, Austen is as contemporary as William Bennett or Gertrude Himmelfarb in their search for "values," the term that "has come to stand in for manners, narrowing the discussion and distorting it." Sometimes, he writes, "manners deceive, creating illusion; sometimes they are worthy of mordant irony. But as Austen keeps showing, again and again, the language of gesture and counter-gesture ultimately reveals a person's deepest nature" (1). Yet, as the adaptations of Austen's novels "remind us, Austen was not just a novelist of manners and education but one who also dramatized the beginning of their dissolution." Rothstein suggests that Elinor and Marianne represent not just the opposing poles of the title but "two distinct eras, Elinor speaking with the voice of the Enlightenment, Marianne welcoming the burgeoning world of Romantic sentimentality in which manners begin to seem dated and out of place. Austen's allegiance is with Elinor, but in her late novel, *Persuasion,* a change is evident. Elinor wouldn't have had a hope in this more familiar, pre-modern world in which manners are turned into caricature. They are far less reliable than they once seemed; irony verges on satire. The gentry pants after the stuffy aristocracy and the most authentic gentleman turns out to be a sea captain. The critic Tony Tanner has written that in the world of this novel 'the usual sources, strongholds and tokens of social values' have 'dried up, collapsed or been eroded or travestied into meaninglessness.'" This may indicate another way in which Austen's tales subtly work their way into the modern consciousness, by showing how fragile the circumscribed world of manners can be. Austen's characters "learn through ambiguity and pained disclosure, through error and misjudgment. It may be that we are now looking toward them [especially in the recent film adaptations of *Sense and Sensibility* and *Persuasion*], in the hope of doing the same" (1).

Jane Austen's world—sometimes good and transcendent, sometimes grubby and venal—is all the more interesting for such complexities. And that is why, whether it be two hundred years ago on the page or only a few years ago on the screen—Austen's works remain objects, not of veneration, but of joy.

Notes

1. According to Monica Lauritzen, in her study of *Jane Austen's Emma on Television,* there was also an earlier BBC-TV version of *Sense and Sensibility,* which aired on BBC2 in 1971.

2. As Janet Maslin points out, Margaret serves another subtle but significant role in the film. As Elinor explains to her the inheritance laws that are the reason for the Dashwood women's dispossession, Margaret is hidden in her treehouse. "Houses go from father to son, dearest, not from father to daughter," Elinor (Thompson) says. Margaret stays hidden, but—as Maslin writes—"she yanks up the treehouse ladder to show what she thinks of inheritance laws like that" (15).

3. Interestingly, Winslet was originally scheduled to read for the role of Lucy Steele. As producer Lindsay Doran recalls, "When Kate walked in, not even having read the book or the script, I just assumed she had been sent in to read for Marianne. So I sat there selling her on it [the part of Marianne], telling her all about the script, the character, and she was saying: 'This sounds just like me. This is exactly who I want to play.'" Emma Thompson has a similar memory. "We thought Marianne was going to be the most difficult person to cast," Thompson remembers, "and then Kate walked in. At the end of the interview she turned her great, headlamp eyes on me and said: 'I wish you would let me do this. I know how to play her.' When she left, I said: 'That's Marianne. No question'" (Elias 15).

4. Another such moment in which the visual medium conveys in seconds what was developed at length through dialogue in the book occurs a scene or two later, when Elinor's new acquaintance, Lucy Steele, binds her to the secret of her engagement to Edward. Objectively, nothing is said by either woman that sounds exceptionable. Yet Lucy, played with bright-eyed, reptilian malice by Imogen Stubbs, shows very clearly with every smirk that she knows what torment she is inflicting on her rival, while a determined Elinor almost succeeds in not letting her own hurt and anger show.

5. Critics have uniformly praised this aspect of Winslet's performance. Todd McCarthy, writing in *Variety,* found Winslet's portrayal of "a reckless romantic who can't abide her sister's restrained propriety" to be "outstanding" (51). And Janet Maslin called Winslet "spirited and striking" (15).

6. Thompson herself observed that the success of the film rested in its "quieter scenes." "You can show being ill; you can show being angry. That familial relationship," she said, "that bread-and-butter familiarity, that's what's hard" (Elias 15).

7. Monica Lauritzen, in her study of *Jane Austen's Emma on Television,* notes that there was also an earlier BBC-TV version of *Persuasion* in 1960; but,

apart from the notation, Lauritzen provides no further information about that television version.

Works Consulted

Brown, Julia Prewitt. *Jane Austen's Novels: Social Change and Literary Form.* Cambridge: Harvard UP, 1979.

Butler, Marilyn. *Jane Austen and the War of Ideas.* Oxford: Clarendon P, 1975.

Carr, Jay. "*Persuasion* Convinces." *Boston Globe* 6 Oct. 1995. Arts Sect.: 91.

Copeland, E., and J. McMaster, eds. *The Cambridge Companion to Jane Austen.* New York: Cambridge UP, 1997.

Duckworth, Alistair. *The Improvement of the Estate: A Study of Jane Austen's Novels.* Baltimore: Johns Hopkins UP, 1971.

Ebert, Roger. Rev. of *Persuasion. Chicago Sun-Times* 27 Oct. 1995.

Elias, Justine. "Kate Winslet: No 'Period Babe.'" *New York Times* 10 Dec. 1995. Sect. 2: 15.

Gilbert, Sandra M., and Susan Gilbert. *The Madwoman in the Attic: The Woman Writer and the Nineteenth Century Imagination.* New Haven: Yale UP, 1979.

James, Caryn. "Austen Tale of Lost Love Refound." *New York Times* 27 Oct. 1995. Sect. C: 18.

Jenkins, Elizabeth. *Jane Austen: A Biography.* London: Gollancz, 1938.

Johnson, Claudia L. *Jane Austen: Women, Politics, and the Novel.* Chicago: U of Chicago P, 1988.

Kronenberger, Louis. "Introduction." *Jane Austen. Sense and Sensibility.* New York: Collier, 1962.

Lascelles, Mary. *Jane Austen and Her Art.* Oxford: Clarendon P, 1939.

Lauritzen, Monica. *Jane Austen's Emma on Television: A Study of a BBC Classic Serial.* Göteborg, Sweden: Acta Universitatis Gothoburgensis, 1981.

Maslin, Janet. "In Mannerly Search of Marriageable Men." (Rev. of Thompson version of *Sense and Sensibility.*) *New York Times* 13 Dec. 1995. Sect. C: 15.

McCarthy, Todd. "Austen Makes Big Screen 'Sense.'" *Variety* 4 Dec.-10 Dec. 1995. 51.

Moers, Ellen. *Literary Women.* New York: Doubleday, 1976.

Morgan, Susan. *In the Meantime: Character and Perception in Jane Austen's Fiction.* Chicago: U of Chicago P, 1980.

Mudrick, Marvin. *Jane Austen: Irony as Defense and Discovery.* Princeton: Princeton UP, 1952.

Nardin, Jane. *Those Elegant Decorums: The Concept of Propriety in Jane Austen's Fiction.* Albany: State U of New York P, 1973.

Rothstein, Edward. "Ideas and Trends: Jane Austen Meets Mr. Right." *New York Times* 10 Dec. 1995. Sect. 4: 1.

Spacks, Patricia Meyer. *The Female Imagination: A Literary and Psychological Investigation of Women's Writing.* New York: Knopf, 1979.

Tave, Stuart. *Some Words of Jane Austen.* Chicago: U of Chicago P, 1973.

Tomalin, Claire. *Jane Austen, A Life.* New York: Knopf, 1997.

Weldon, Fay. "Jane Austen and the Pride of the Purists." *New York Times* 8 Oct. 1995. Sect. 2: 15.

Wiesenfarth, Joseph. *The Errand of Form: An Assay of Jane Austen's Art.* New York: Fordham UP, 1967.

6

SYMPATHY FOR THE DEVIL:
THE PROBLEM OF HEATHCLIFF
IN FILM VERSIONS OF *WUTHERING HEIGHTS*

Lin Haire-Sargeant

When, in her 1847 novel *Wuthering Heights,* Emily Brontë created the pivotal character Heathcliff, she set herself a daunting challenge: how to tell the story of a brutal, calculating sadist, the bane of two families over two generations, in such a way that by the end of the book the reader's horror is overwhelmed by sympathy. At first, critical reaction seemed to indicate that she had failed: most reviewers attacked the brutality of the book, saving their worst condemnation for Heathcliff. The *North American Review*'s pronouncement was typical: Heathcliff was a brute "whom the Mephistopheles of Goethe would have nothing to say to, whom the Satan of Milton would consider an object of simple disgust" (Oct. 1848). But over the next decades attitudes changed. Readers became fascinated with Heathcliff's villainy, as imitation in lesser works made him the prototypical hero of Gothic Romance. Eventually the allure of his evil was recognized as part of the power of Brontë's book.

In the next century, when a novel as famous as *Wuthering Heights* was bound to be made into a movie, the stakes for a favorable response to Heathcliff grew higher. It was not only sympathy for the devil that was required of us; it was love—a necessary generic condition of the feature film, where characters project as gods, the movie screen irresistibly our Olympus, our Sinai. There, even our darkest demons must show as angels dancing bright. Historically, the films of *Wuthering Heights* have met this challenge in two ways: either by changing the story so that Heathcliff's evil deeds are lessened or mitigated, or straight on, as Emily Brontë does, directing the reader/viewer to absorb the totality of Heathcliff's evil and good within his human situation.

Of course, there is much more to *Wuthering Heights* than Heathcliff. This is, of novels, among the elect, judged to be great by critics and the reading public alike. For the latter, its greatness lies in the love story between Heathcliff and Cathy; critics are more likely to cite the structure: the elegant symmetry and precision of the plot (as in C. P. Sanger's 1926 "The Structure of *Wuthering Heights*") or the even more elegant patterns of repetition of phrases and tropes (as in J. Hillis Miller's chapter "*Wuthering Heights:* Repetition and the 'Uncanny'" in his 1982 *Fiction and Repetition*).

Brontë's means to greatness were linguistic; the filmmaker's must be visual. Inevitable differences follow. Where the novelist's words spark individual, intimate mind pictures in each reader, the filmmaker must define the image on the screen, the same for all viewers, and in doing so ground the story in time and space—the time and space in which the movie is filmed, not that in which the story is set. In these ways and others, the filmmaker creates a work of art separate from its "original" yet connected in an intimate way. So the question is not "does the movie replicate the book?" since that is an impossibility. More interesting questions: does the movie communicate something of the book's art? And how, by what means, is that art communicated, since it must be communicated by analog? Finally, the most important question of all: does the film succeed as a work of art in its own right? If it does, it creates its own sufficient reason for being. If it does not, it can be criticized not only as a failed film but as a failed adaptation: every departure from the novel becomes a fault. And even a great movie based on a novel has one irredeemable flaw: it is not the novel.

The events of this novel are complex, even in summary: in 1801 a London man, Lockwood, rents Thrushcross Grange, an estate in Yorkshire. Arriving at his landlord's house Wuthering Heights in a snowstorm, he receives a churlish welcome from its occupants: the reclusive Heathcliff; beautiful but unfriendly Catherine Heathcliff, widow of Heathcliff's dead son; the brutish Hareton Earnshaw, Heathcliff's ward and cousin to Catherine; and a crabbed old servant, Joseph. During the night Lockwood is awakened by the ghost of Catherine Earnshaw Linton, mother of the present Catherine, trying to get in his bedroom window. "Twenty years I've been wandering!" she wails. In the early morning Lockwood flees the Heights and struggles through the snow to the Grange, where he is taken ill.

During Lockwood's long convalescence, Grange housekeeper Nelly Dean, longtime servant to the Earnshaws and the Lintons, regales him with the history of the Heights and its strange inhabitants. Nelly's story goes back thirty years, to 1771: old Mr. Earnshaw brings a mysterious foundling, Heathcliff, to Wuthering Heights to raise as a brother to his son Hindley and daughter Catherine. Cathy and Heathcliff form a strong attachment that survives Heathcliff's brutal demotion to servant status by Hindley after Mr. Earnshaw's death. But Cathy is attracted to the wealth and grace of Edgar Linton, scion of a neighboring aristocratic family. Though she loves Heathcliff, she agrees to marry Edgar. Overhearing Cathy tell Nelly her plans, Heathcliff runs away.

Three years later, in 1783, he returns. He has mysteriously transformed himself into a rich gentleman—but too late; after nearly dying from grief over Heathcliff's loss, Cathy has married Edgar and lives with him and his sister Isabella at Thrushcross Grange. Heathcliff begins to lay the groundwork for revenge. He gambles and wins from Hindley Earnshaw, who has become a drunkard and a wastrel since his wife's death. Heathcliff moves into the Heights with Hindley and his young son Hareton. At the same time, he begins to court Isabella Linton, though he still professes total love for Cathy and reproaches her bitterly for preferring Edgar to him. Cathy, torn between Heathcliff and Edgar, goes on a hunger strike and sinks into delirium. In the meantime, Heathcliff and Isabella elope.

By the spring of 1784, the unhappy couple has returned to reside at the Heights while a pregnant Cathy lingers near death at the Grange. Heathcliff forces Nelly to let him into the Grange, where he has an emotionally violent reunion with Cathy. They manage to communicate to each other the strange nature of their mutual love before Edgar returns and Cathy loses consciousness. She gives birth to a daughter, Catherine, and dies. A few days later, Heathcliff, mad with grief, attacks and nearly kills Hindley, who has tried to kill him. Isabella runs off and moves to London, where in the autumn she bears Heathcliff's son Linton. At about the same time Hindley Earnshaw dies, having mortgaged all his property to Heathcliff. Heathcliff takes over both Wuthering Heights and Hareton, Hindley's son: "We'll see if one tree won't grow as crooked as another, with the same wind to twist it!" (Chapter 17). Edgar, grieving for Cathy, devotes himself to bringing up young Catherine.

By 1800, Isabella has died and Linton is living with his father Heathcliff and cousin Hareton at the Heights. Heathcliff begins the final phase of his revenge by snaring Catherine into friendship then romance with her frail cousin Linton. Edgar's health is failing, and Catherine keeps her involvement with Linton from her father and Nelly, who are alive to Heathcliff's malevolent intentions. Finally, with both Edgar Linton and Linton Heathcliff perilously close to death, Heathcliff kidnaps Catherine and forces her to marry Linton. When Linton and Edgar die, because of the male bias of property laws Heathcliff is undisputed master of the Grange and Catherine is a penniless dependent.

This is the point at which Lockwood makes his visit to the Heights. Upon recovering from his illness, Lockwood goes back to London. He returns to the Grange only in the fall, when he finds that many changes have taken place. Some time in the spring Heathcliff began to act strangely. He stopped eating, and told Nelly that the ghost of Cathy was constantly in his presence. He even lost interest in thwarting the growing friendship of Catherine and Hareton. Eventually he was found dead in the haunted bedroom, in the bed he and Cathy shared as children. Catherine and Hareton, restored to their inheritances, have fallen in love and plan to marry. Lockwood ends his narration by musing over the graves of Heathcliff, Cathy, and Edgar, wondering "how anyone could ever imagine unquiet slumbers for the sleepers in that quiet earth" (Chapter 34).

The five film versions of *Wuthering Heights* discussed here (several filmed versions of *Wuthering Heights* were not available for this review: a six-reel 1920 British silent film that has apparently not survived; four BBC treatments [1948, 1953, 1962, and 1967]; and a French production, *Hurlevent*) vary in mood and meaning, following shifts in time, national origin, and the artists' interpretation. My analysis proceeds chronologically, beginning with William Wyler's *Wuthering Heights,* filmed in the United States in 1939.

In his adaptation, Wyler goes a long way towards solving the problem of Heathcliff with his casting: Laurence Olivier plays Heathcliff like Heathcliff playing Laurence Olivier. The young Olivier delivers a bravura turn as an anesthetized brute whose intelligence takes him on forays into psychologizing sympathy ("You're lonely, he comforts Isabella [Geraldine Fitzgerald]. "It's lonely sitting like an outsider in so happy a household as your brother's. . . . You won't be lonely any more"). On the page this is almost laughably far from Brontë's Heathcliff, but paradoxically, of all the Heathcliffs, the Wyler/Olivier version gives the strongest analog of Heathcliff's felt emotion, the injustices endured and absorbed, the repressed passion and rage.

This is accomplished partly through Olivier's performance (of which more later), and partly through Wyler's brilliantly conceptualized and realized artistic direction. The film is holographic; every frame, in narrative content and composition, contains the whole story. Wyler controls a black-and-white palette of exquisitely shaded tonality; even on a TV screen the numinously glowing whites, the engulfing blacks, and the shimmering grays eloquently express emotional and spiritual nuance.

The story is considerably truncated in this 103-minute version. It begins with Lockwood's arrival: "A stranger lost in a storm." Lockwood (Leo G. Carroll) runs the gamut of snarling dogs and unanswered knocks to finally gain shelter in Wuthering Heights. The family he encounters is not second generation Earnshaws and Lintons—that story has been cut. Rather it is Isabella, Nelly Dean (Flora Robson), Joseph, and a softened Heathcliff—who, when, reminded of his manners, responds with urbane irony: "I hardly know how to treat a guest—I and my *dog*" and himself offers Lockwood lodging. After Heathcliff, galvanized by Lockwood's dream of Cathy (Merle Oberon), bursts out into the blizzard to seek her, Nelly tells Lockwood the tale of the first generation of Earnshaws and Lintons. The conventional voice-over ("It began forty years ago when I was young") along with the track into a tight close-up of Nelly's face anticipate the dissolve to the long-ago scene of the boy Heathcliff's arrival at Wuthering Heights. The story of the entanglements of Heathcliff, Cathy, Edgar (David Niven), and Isabella, with occasional voice-over commentary by Nelly, is followed through to Cathy's death. Then there is a return to the frame story. As Nelly concludes her tale, Dr. Kenneth comes in out of the blizzard. He has found Heathcliff's body by Pennistone Crag after first having seen a vision of him with Cathy. The film ends with a long shot of Heathcliff and Cathy ascending Pennistone Crag together.

Paradoxically, Wyler and cinematographer Gregg Toland tell this tale of tightly caged violence through visuals that emphasize open space. In contrast to the description of a disorderly, cramped household in the novel, Wyler's Heights interiors, filmed deep focus, open an airy palatial zone behind the viewing screen. When Lockwood arrives, the camera follows him across uneasy expanses of floor while the family, huddled at the fireside, stare. Eventually Joseph leads Lockwood to his lodging for the night, Cathy's old bedroom. To get from Joseph's presentation—"the bridal chamber"—to Lockwood's reaction, the camera pans across what seems an immense expanse of dingy, candle-lit wall. The meaning of this emphasis on space is not the claustrophobia of the interlocking narratives and the closed worlds of the Heights and the Grange that really exist in Brontë's pages, but rather an edgy agoraphobia that at once contains its opposite and suggests its transcendence.

Another paradox: in the novel, Heathcliff and Cathy are characterized by violent movement—motion equals emotion. In the film, Cathy and Heathcliff, most tempestuous of lovers, are portrayed through the poetics of immobility. Olivier moves through much of the film with his trunk and arms stiff, his eyes fixed and unfocused, like a somnambulist who does not dream. This of course makes his occasional outbreaks of movement—two slaps across faithless Cathy's face, a plunge of bare knuckles through window glass—the more violently emotive, though ultimately we are taught to experience Heathcliff's giant rage most intensely in its tethering. Similarly, Merle Oberon's snow-queen Cathy, herself motionless, with each unmoving second builds charged emotion like a dynamo. She sits frozen at table while Hindley abuses Heathcliff, then flies from the house, over a wall, and up Pennistone Crag to a tryst with Heathcliff impelled by a blast of primal desire usually confined by this Cathy's strong proprietary and propertarian good sense.

There is one scene in the film that brilliantly deploys the narrative's two lines of emotional symbolism, the agoraphobic use of space and the burning paralysis of the lovers. In a scene that does not appear in Brontë's book, Edgar and Cathy give a ball at Thrushcross Grange. The scene begins with dance music, then a fade to a moving shot as the camera pans up over a stone wall for an exterior view of Thrushcross Grange, recalling an earlier scene where prelapsarian Heathcliff and Cathy spied on just such a ball. With Cathy's marriage to Edgar she has become part of this world, while Heathcliff, though mysteriously trans- formed into a gentleman, remains shut out. Through brilliantly lit win- dows we can glimpse dancing couples. Then there is a fade to the inte- rior scene shown through an ornate mirror. The restless camera pans rather jerkily away from the mirror, across expanses of mechanistically dancing couples, other mirrors, crystal chandeliers. The effect is of a giant music box; artifice, not humanity, is the key. The camera roves ner- vously above the dancers, a questing, disembodied point of view. Light- ing is high key, focus is deep. The camera fixes its gaze on the entrance door; the footmen admit Heathcliff, in impeccable evening dress, a tall black column against the hard white surfaces of the ballroom. A bit later he stands immobile behind a seated Isabella; a harpsichordist begins to play a Mozart sonata. A crane shot circles above the frenetically pound- ing harpsichordist, surveys the immobilized audience. There is an extended close-up of a somber Heathcliff; we know where his unswerv- ing gaze is directed. Cut to a close-up of Cathy. She is a snow woman with her white bared shoulders, and her apparel might as well be ice. The dress is highly polished white satin; diamonds sparkle from neck- lace, earrings, and tiara. She is like an ice sculpture, especially when Heathcliff's gaze freezes her. Then, though she struggles against it, her eyes are drawn to him. Such is the force of his gaze that it draws not only Cathy's notice but the notice of the crowd. The resulting voyeuristic heat is extraordinary. Will Cathy melt? Cut to an extreme close-up of the harpsichordist's hands banging away at the coda like jackhammers, invoking the brutal mocking mechanism of the social trap caging the lovers.

In Wyler's rationale for fabricating this scene we see his genius as a filmmaker. In the book *Wuthering Heights,* writing and reading, inscrip- tion and its decoding—the carving of Cathy's name on the wooden shelf in her bedroom, her palimpsistic writings in the book of sermons—these are the channels into the text, for the inside reader Lockwood, then for us outside readers. Part of the peculiar power of this device is that the medium doubles the message. For the book, the act of reading is an act of power and connection. First Lockwood's reading, then ours, becomes a process of spying on these distant lives; we catch ourselves brushing Lockwood's shoulder as we lean over to make sense of the words, and the distant lives become not so distant. For the film, Wyler translates this participatory mechanism to the visual. Passion, for Wyler's Cathy and Heathcliff, is always ocular, their gaze a conduit for voyeuristically charged eroticism—as is our gaze when we watch theirs. (See Figure 19.) Our complicity must give us sympathy for the devil—except that under Wyler's gentlemanly direction Heathcliff is no devil, but a great heart more sinned against than sinning.

After the dancing resumes, Heathcliff's continued gaze compels Cathy to turn to him. They walk out to the veranda, a zone halfway between the Grange's caging civilization and the freedom of the natural world. Cathy chides Heathcliff for his somber air. "Don't pretend life hasn't improved for you." "Life has ended for me," he replies. As he leans toward Cathy with words of love, she turns away, and the howl of a cold wind from the moors overtakes the waltz music. The camera retreats through the leaves of the trees into darkness. By freezing his actors within open, uneasily shifting space, Wyler has shown both the spiritual connection of Cathy and Heathcliff and the terrifying emptiness of the universe for the one without the other.

In 1954, a quarter century after *Un Chien Andalou* and a decade before he was to father his second generation of great surrealist films, Luis Buñuel made a low-budget black-and-white adaptation of *Wuthering Heights* called *Abismos de Pasion*. Buñuel has no problem buying sympathy for Heathcliff, in this version called Alejandro (Jorge Mistral). He makes him a much better person than Emily Brontë did, and he makes the Edgar Linton character (Eduardo, played by Ernesto Alonso) much worse. But these are among the least of the departures from Brontë's text: *Wuthering Heights'* Yorkshire moor is here transformed to a Mexican desert, with corresponding changes in climate, architecture, costume, local color, even codes of behavior.

Abismos de Pasion covers a narrower time span than any other version of *Wuthering Heights*. Dispensing with frame narratives, the second generation's tale, and even with the childhood of the principals (except as backstory developed through dialogue), the film begins at the point of Alejandro's return and ends in Catalina's (Catherine's) tomb, a few days

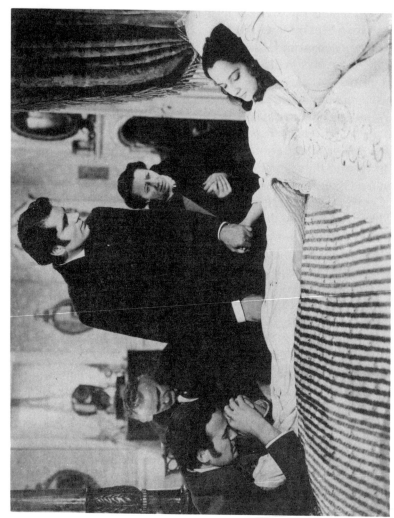

Figure 19. Ocular passion at Cathy's deathbed: Laurence Olivier's erotically charged gaze cannot awaken Merle Oberon now. © Samuel Goldwyn Productions

after her death. This gives Buñuel space to explore what clearly interests him most: the mesh of emotions among the five love-and-hate entangled siblings and lovers Alejandro, Catalina (Iraseme Dilian), Isabella (Lilia Prado), Eduardo, and the Hindley character Ricardo (Luis Aceves Casteneda). Buñuel's version is unique in that the latter three characters are as fully developed as the first two. The five-character ensemble is at times presented operatically: static camera and total depth of field that replicates an audience's view of a stage; groupings and regroupings of characters in confrontational "duets," "trios," and "quartets"; impassioned extended speeches like arias; even declamatory physical stances of divas presenting themselves to best advantage. As if to underline the operatic connection, Buñuel borrows leitmotifs from Wagner's *Tristan and Isolde*. Most strikingly, Buñuel's conception of the characters is operatic. He both simplifies and moralizes their stories (in such a way as to remind us that opera's conventions are more in tune with Buñuel's Spanish culture than Brontë's Anglo-Celtic roots), valorizing the heroic instinctual masculinity of Alejandro on one hand, the faithfulness of the wronged wife Isabella on the other.

The opening of the film sets Buñuel's simplifying moral tone. As the titles scroll, there is a long shot of a gnarled tree silhouetted against the sky. We are offered this introduction: "These characters are at the mercy of their own instincts and passions. They are unique beings for whom the so-called social conventions do not exist. Alejandro's love for Catalina is a fierce and inhuman feeling that can only be fulfilled through death." A gunshot rings out, and a flock of buzzards flaps from the tree.

"Inhuman," "instinct," and "fierce" are key words here, for the pervading trope in this movie is animal. All the principal characters are identified both as animal predators and as prey—visual correlatives of their cruelty to each other. Catalina is the hunter whose shot scatters the buzzards. "I kill them with one shot," she says in the discussion of cruelty that introduces the characters. "They pass to death's liberty without feeling anything." This in contrast to Eduardo's manner of killing a butterfly, shown to us in close-up—he crushes its body with his fingers. Catalina keeps a bird in a cage. Eduardo asks why she doesn't release it—or kill it. She coos to the bird, "Isn't my love enough so you won't mind being locked up?" In the meantime, dogs are barking. "It must be those buzzards again." In fact, the dogs bark at Alejandro, whose association with the dog ("Canaille!" Eduardo calls him) and the buzzard (scavenger, death) is established here to be used later.

Animal imagery follows human interaction throughout the story, glossing the characters' increasing cruelty: the buzzards' quick death followed by the crushing of the butterfly, and a bit later, the leisurely piercing of the insect with a pin (we are reminded that in Aztec lore, butterflies were souls of the dead). Still later, Ricardo's primitive old manservant tries to exorcise an evil spirit (Alejandro) from the house by immolating live frogs in a smoking charcoal brazier (another Aztec custom). The climax of cruelty occurs at the moment when Catalina swears to Eduardo that she will never again seek out Alejandro. Close-up of her proud smile; cut to the grimace of a terrified pig being roughly dragged to the slaughter. We escape its screams only as its throat is slit.

Less pointed, but equally effective, is the creepy display of Eduardo's insect collections in the background of various interior shots as silent commentary on Eduardo's and Catalina's marriage. First we see only panels of butterflies and moths, neatly ordered, hundreds and hundreds of them. Later we are shown a wall of flying beetles and wasps, and finally, with the household in crisis, the camera pans over ranks of scorpions and spiders. Periodically we see Eduardo handling his collection and his jars of anesthetizing gas with dreamy orgasmic absorption. All this takes place in Eduardo's house. At "The Farm" (Wuthering Heights), the collections come to life; Ricardo feeds flies to a spider that lives in a crack in the wall. Sooner or later, all characters in this story emerge red in tooth and claw.

If Buñuel's staging is operatic, if his use of animal symbolism is essentially literary, still his most masterful effects are achieved through purely cinematic means. Through subtle manipulation of light and the repetition of similarly composed shots, he builds up our sense of the transcendent relation of Catalina and Alejandro, and in doing so gains sympathy for Alejandro.

Catalina, in close-up, is often cocooned by gauzy light shading to dark toward the edge of the frame. Depending on context, this suggests either her anesthetized entrapment in the marriage with Eduardo or a spirituality that transcends worldly situations. That such spiritual transcendence is, for Catalina, linked to Alejandro is also shown by the symbolism of light. After Alejandro's return, Catalina stands at her open bedroom window to gaze out over the night-enshrouded valley. The next shot reveals Alejandro's answering gaze from the opposite side of the frame, at dawn. He raises his ecstatic face towards the luminous clouds of sunrise, and towards Catalina. For each of these lovers, the source of light and life is the other.

From the start Alejandro is associated with thresholds; there are repeated shots of him entering or looking through passageways, doorways, staircases, windows, arches. After barking dogs disturb Eduardo's household early in the film, there is a tracking shot away from the building—in this and all other film versions of *Wuthering Heights,* a signal of demonic presence. And now Alejandro comes—in night rain and shadow, passing silhouetted through a lit stone archway. The next day, Catalina and Alejandro set out to revisit their childhood haunts, running hand-in-hand through a sun-streamed archway toward "places only the two of them know about." At "The Farm," on several occasions Alejandro walks up a dark staircase with a light at the top, as though drawn like a moth. The last such incident follows his fight with Ricardo after Catalina's death, when he disappears up the arched stairway with the demented concentration of one entering his own mind. In none of these threshold shots do we see Alejandro arriving. He is in shadow, seeking the light. What is his luminous destination?

After grieving for Catalina for three days, Alejandro goes to the cemetery where she has been interred. It is night. He wanders among crosses and tombs, searching for her grave. He is weak and faltering. We are shown a gun training upon him. Clearly now he is the prey of a yet unidentified predator. Alejandro finds the tomb, a raised catafalque with a large metal lock. With difficulty, he breaks the lock, raises the stone lid, and sees a staircase leading down to an underground tomb. There is a shotgun blast and Alejandro falls. We see that it is Ricardo, Catalina's brother, who is the hunter.

But Alejandro is only wounded. The staircase before him is lit by a dim radiance. He staggers down steps like those he has climbed before and reaches the inner tomb where the coffin of Catalina lies. There is Catalina in an earth-covered veil. He lifts her stiffened hand; when he lets go it snaps back. Then, as he raises the veil and kisses her dead face, Catalina in a glowing white wedding dress appears behind him at the bottom of the stairs. It is she, of course, who is the source of light; it is her radiance pouring through archways, from stair tops, that Alejandro has always been seeking, hers the sacred presence on the other side of the threshold. She holds out her arms. Alejandro raises his face joyously. But in a flash Catalina transforms into Ricardo, with an aimed gun. There is an explosion, and Alejandro's body falls over Catalina's in the coffin.

There is a cluster of images and associations here: Catalina equals light, and light stands for absolute union with the beloved, the kind of union that is impossible except in memories of a shared childhood paradise, and in death. This equation holds true in Brontë's book too. In the spirit, if emphatically not in the letter, Buñuel has been true to Brontë.

Robert Fuest's version of *Wuthering Heights* came out in 1970, less than two decades after Buñuel's, but there is more than a generation's worth of difference in the look of the two. Where Wyler had filmed mostly in Hollywood studios, and Buñuel shot his version in Mexico, Fuest was part of a growing trend to film on location, in this case, the Yorkshire moors. Add candy-colored, careening tracks and zooms and television-influenced longshot-close-up pulses, and Fuest would seem at first to blast slow, subtle Buñuel along with the restrained Wyler into sepia-tinged storage. But a more measured response would teach us the danger of undue haste, both in film pacing and in critical judgment.

Perhaps the most strikingly contemporary note is struck by Fuest's treatment of Heathcliff. He cast a very young Timothy Dalton, creating the handsomest Heathcliff in the Pantheon and in some ways the most appealing, though not as nuanced psychologically as any of the other Heathcliffs. Dalton strikes two character notes. Early in the movie, before he leaves, teenaged Heathcliff is vulnerable, affectionate, direct. He lays his head trustingly on old Earnshaw's knee, nuzzles Cathy with innocent ecstasy in their Pennistone Crag's hideaway. Though this is only one aspect of the complicated creature Emily Brontë presents to us in her novel, it is an authentic aspect, and Dalton portrays it strongly. But in the balance of the film, the Fuest/Dalton Heathcliff is made to exude the menace and cynicism of a rock star. There is no doubt about it: this Heathcliff, with his high-decibel sexuality, seduces not only Anna Calder-Marshall's Cathy (in a stunning departure from Brontë's text!) but his audience as well. If this handily solves Heathcliff's negative appeal problem, it creates others, perhaps more serious.

Like Wyler and Buñuel, Fuest limits the story to the first generation of Earnshaws and Lintons, and like Buñuel cuts out Lockwood, his visit to the Heights, his visitation by the ghost of Cathy, etc. Nelly Dean's narration survives only in an introductory voice-over, soon abandoned. There are plot, character, and motivational changes as well, mainly resulting from the sexualization of the story. For instance, Nelly Dean (Judy Cornwall) is a simpering big-haired flirt who is in love with Hindley (Julian Glover); she is ridiculously (for a farm worker) squeezed into a breast-billowing corset. Then there is Heathcliff and Cathy's sex scene, which takes place in Thrushcross Grange Park right after Heathcliff's return from his mysterious three-year absence. A little later, Edgar (Ian Ogilvy) is comically surprised when the doctor informs him that Cathy is with child; it has been implied before that Edgar is impotent, so Cathy's baby is probably Heathcliff's ("Edgar's waitin' to see the color of its eyes," Joseph [Aubrey Woods] tells Heathcliff with a leer, as Heathcliff leers back). In keeping with this plot twist, Edgar cuts a pathetic figure all around. He seems more interested in his books than he does in his young wife. When Cathy goes on her hunger strike, Edgar cruelly refuses Nelly's pleadings for her. He is portrayed as cold, selfish, pompous, and not too bright—a fool made dangerous with power.

If in nothing else, Fuest follows his predecessors in his ending for the film. After Cathy's funeral, a drunken and furious Hindley lies in wait for Heathcliff inside Wuthering Heights, gun ready. In the cemetery, Heathcliff flings himself on Cathy's grave, plunges his hands into the soil, and curses her: "Catherine Earnshaw, may you not rest while I am living!" He hears her call teasingly, "Heath-cliff!" When he looks up, he sees her ghost beckoning him to run after her. She draws him toward the Heights, where Isabella (Hilary Dwyer) connives with Hindley for Heathcliff's destruction. Cathy's ghost, with a come-on smile, lures Heathcliff to a shuttered window, where Hindley waits with his gun. As in Buñuel, the image of Cathy is replaced by that of the gun's barrel just as it blasts. And as in Wyler, the film leaves us with the image of apparitional Cathy and Heathcliff together on the moors.

Perhaps because of its privileging of the physical over the spiritual, visually this film is more grounded in the time of its making than are the Wyler or Buñuel versions. Male and female characters alike are bodied forth smooth surfaced and hard edged. Make-up style favors a rubbery Halloween-mask look, with high '60s magic-marker eyes and bubble gum lips. The women's hair is ratted up and varnished smooth. Men's coiffures are early Beatles. Costumes—solid-colored, generally clean, always unwrinkled—are probably polyester.

The set design extends the cartoon-like hard edges. Fuest's physical rendering of the house Wuthering Heights is the cleanest on record. Departing from the other sets' homespun look, this one abounds with straight lines, 90-degree angles, and gleaming, unmarred surfaces. Even Hindley's drunken roisterings seem to leave no mark; food and liquor spills disappear overnight, as though the Heights had been sprayed with Scotchguard. The general tidiness is literally highlighted by predominantly high-key illumination, even of Heights interiors, traditionally so murky. One example: the scene in the kitchen when Cathy tells Nelly of Edgar's proposal as Heathcliff eavesdrops. Other directors invoke the pathetic fallacy with prophetic shadows, a passionately flaring kitchen hearth, eureka lightning flashes ("Nelly, I *am* Heathcliff!"). But here the kitchen is suffused with a steady yellow glow, not quite the sunlight of reason banishing the storm clouds of Romanticism, more an assertion of reality and relevance and, above all, physical presence—yes, these are real people, looking three-dimensional and solid in the familiar light of every day.

Fuest's insistence on physicality may have governed his casting. Anna Calder-Marshall's Cathy is against type: she is cute, pert, short, and chunky—not in the least like almost anybody else's idea of Catherine Earnshaw. But the very wrongness of her looks makes her the more emphatically present to the audience. And somehow her eager, clumsy, boyish movements communicate Cathy's mercurial intensity perfectly; she is human, flawed, accessible. Oddly, the sketchiness of her beauty gives her an appeal that airbrush-perfect Merle Oberon and Juliette Binoche lack.

Physicality is also emphasized by dynamic camera movement, with many panning, zooming, and tracking shots. The film's signature shot pattern starts with an extreme close-up of an object, then pulls back to reveal a whole scene. For example, we are shown Heathcliff's dung-crusted boots, then (pull back, pan) Joseph towering up on a hill, enforcing labor from resentful, muddy, abject Heathcliff, low man on the class totem. A similarly managed shot a half-hour later fills the screen with impeccably groomed leather boots, pans suspensefully up the column of spanking new black suit and brilliant linen, then pulls back to reveal Heathcliff asking Hindley and his fellow wastrels what has happened to Cathy. Now Heathcliff has risen far above Joseph to Hindley's class level, and perhaps beyond—as he looms contemptuously above the carousers and tosses his fat bag of money onto the sordid gaming table. Significantly, Fuest's is the only version in which the audience experiences the shock of Heathcliff's return and class apotheosis from Hindley's point of view. In this film, the magic triangle of sex is all male—Heathcliff, Hindley, Edgar—with females Cathy, Isabella, and Nelly often sidelined as trophies in the males' strutting competitions for alpha position.

Of course Heathcliff wins, here and elsewhere, but Fuest/Dalton diverge from their forerunners in physical signals for his victory. Where Olivier's passion vibrates out of stillness, Dalton's emotion is all motion; where Mistral's Alejandro weakens and falters for love, Dalton is ever puissant. In fact, decades before *The Living Daylights* and *The Rocketeer,* in Heathcliff Dalton was playing an action hero. We can see this in the spirited orchestration of Heathcliff's escape from the Grange after a confrontation with Edgar. In the space of a few seconds Heathcliff smashes a lock with a poker, knocks down two attacking manservants, chases a flurry of maidservants out of the house, vaults over a balustrade, smashes a greenhouse, evades Edgar's pistol fire, and (in one breathless take) runs into the orchard, leaps over a fence, kisses a fortuitously-placed Isabella, and bounds onto his horse. This is the sort of thing that Fuest does well, and so does Dalton. But the scene's James Bondish self-congratulation—the masculine mastery of time and motion to the end of dominance—cheapens not only Romance, but even romance.

For, in the balance, Dalton's Heathcliff is not only cruel; he is a smooth-talking rough-sex schemer. Worse, he turns both sex and violence against Cathy, first in the stable when, reproaching her for visiting the Lintons, he smacks her down into the muck and kisses her roughly; then, when after his return he again knocks her to the ground before having sex with her. This goes beyond the formal duel-like slaps Olivier delivered to Oberon into something more like rape; it is unequivocally wrong. Part of the essence and the genius of *Wuthering Heights* is that Heathcliff's overt violence is always deflected away from Cathy to her surrogates—to Isabella, to Hindley, to Cathy II, to Linton Heathcliff, to Hareton—as overt sex is displaced to Isabella. Fuest and Dalton degrade Heathcliff with their reading of his character.

Though Robert Fuest's *Wuthering Heights* tells its story with economy and clarity, through effective visual means, it is not the story Emily Brontë wrote. That is true of all the versions, but Fuest's distortions are the most disturbing of all. They trivialize Brontë's chief metaphysic: the uncanny, incorporeal love between Cathy and Heathcliff. Furthermore, Fuest shrinks or altogether dismisses subplots that in Brontë add their own metaphysical overtones: the story-within-story repetitions that teach and suggest so much about the nature of narrative, the second generation's reworking of their parents' drama that mimes the regenerating tragicomedy of the human condition. Finally, what Fuest's version does best is show us how Brontë's great story has become the type for a debased though appealing genre: the Gothic romance, with Dalton's Heathcliff a triumphant example of its menacing swashbuckling hero.

1978 brought the most ambitiously authentic version of *Wuthering Heights* to date: a five-part television adaptation for the BBC directed by Peter Hammond. In its loyalty to Brontë's story line and text, the Hammond film is also the most ambitious in its portrayal of Heathcliff. Besides pleading (as other movies do) his good qualities and the cruelties heaped upon him by fate and enemies, this version more than any other shows his vile acts plain. Actor Ken Hutchison gives the bloodiest and basest rendition of Heathcliff on record. Neither noble victim, vampire lover, brooding rock star, nor smirking action hero, Hutchison's is the hardest Heathcliff to love but, in the quotidian specificity of his flaws, the easiest to believe. The script, by Hugh Leonard and David Snodin, allows Hutchison to portray the full range of Heathcliff's personality: besides the usual leitmotifs of obsessive love for Cathy and hatred for almost everyone else, less common melodies echo: Heathcliff's rather naive pride in possession, his odd vulnerabilities (especially to Nelly's judgments), his superstitious fears (even of Cathy's ghost!), his contempt for small kindnesses, his self-destructive susceptibility to blind rushes of greed and rage. Following Brontë, Hutchison's Heathcliff challenges the viewer's human understanding: can it expand to contemplate petty sins as well as great, give the hobgoblin as well as the devil his due? If the challenge fails, it is not Hutchison's fault.

To build such a round character takes time, and this version has it: between four and five hours. Happily, Hammond replicates story lines with little distortion, including the full second-generation tale of Cathy II, Hareton, and Linton Heathcliff. Also included are the frame story of Lockwood's initiating stopover, with his vision of ghostly Cathy trying to reenter the Heights, and his ending visit, where he witnesses the happy romance between Cathy II and Hareton and sees the three graves in the churchyard. Dramatists Leonard and Snodin, faithful stewards of Brontë's language, usually draw dialogue directly from the original. There are departures from Brontë; neither Lockwood nor Nelly acts directly as narrator, though their narrative stances are sometimes sketched by Nelly's gossip with neighbors or Lockwood's occasional ruminating voice-overs. But these are quibbles: clearly the production's aim was that tantalizing impossibility: the truly faithful adaptation.

Faithful to Brontë, too, are the physical components of the production. Sets and setting have been designed to replicate not only the Yorkshire Emily Brontë created but also the Yorkshire in which she lived. In all its artifacts, the film gives a vivid sense of time, place, and history. Director Hammond takes his quest for verisimilitude far beyond Fuest's exterior location shots of moors and crags. For interior shots of the Heights, Hammond appears, at least, to have crammed his actors and cameras into a real Yorkshire house, with narrow stairs and awkwardly placed windows. In doing so, he equally serves historical accuracy and Brontë's symbolic subtext. The contrast between the agrarian, almost savage world of Wuthering Heights and the Enlightenment world of Thrushcross Grange is starkly drawn: walls, windows, furniture at the Heights are worn, crooked, and dirty; preserved food hangs in the smoky rafters of the kitchen; clothes and linens are homespun and colored with indigenous dyes; all seems crabbed and warped, like a tree rooted in rock. In contrast, the Grange interiors and furniture—painted panels, papered walls, gracefully limbed furniture—clearly did not grow out of anything; they were measured, sawn, sanded, and polished into architechtonic Reason. Some visual elements jar but are right nonetheless. The profile portrait of Cathy, for instance, looks ugly and awkward to the modern eye, but in fact faithfully renders actress Kay Adshead's likeness as, say, Branwell Brontë might have painted it.

The look of the actors too—whether achieved through cast selection, acting, make-up, or costume—satisfies both Brontë's descriptions and historical likelihood. With the exception of Caroline Langrishe (Isabella Linton), there are no perfect beauties in this cast, but real people with double chins, gaping teeth, bad skin—all contributing to a sense of rich authenticity. Hutchison's lantern-jawed rather fleshy face, framed by long matted black hair, is far removed from the pretty-boy casting of other Heathcliffs, and in its individuality the better able to show a more spiritual beauty—or a more gripping viciousness. Hutchison plays with his whole physical instrument, expressing Heathcliff's crabbed malice through stiff angles between head, neck and back, the vigor of his rage by occasional berserker dashes, his love for Cathy in the musicality in his high, tight voice when talking to her or of her. Hutchison is obliterated: Heathcliff lives. In high contrast but just as effectively, David Robb plays Edgar with narrow-shouldered eighteenth-century grace, face classical and cold as a coin Caesar. He makes us see Edgar in a new and better light. We understand how his tender reason must always crumble before Cathy's unprincipled histrionics, and that with him capitulation is not a sign of moral weakness. As for Cathy, Kay Adshead communicates her nerviness, selfishness, and outright insanity better than it has ever been done. Like Heathcliff, she sacrifices audience sympathy with some aspects of her portrayal (her manipulative temper tantrums, for instance), but she regains it with others. With brimming eyes and trembling lips she plays the heroine of sensibility to perfection; when on the brink of death she says that she is yearning to escape to that glorious world, we believe her, and believe too in the petulant ghost who returns to torment her demon lover. Pat Heywood's brilliant Nelly Dean is warm, impulsive, earthy, her humanity and sympathy fully engaged in the lives of those she serves. She is a magic mirror that reflects the other characters to the viewer in a truer, fuller light.

Yet, with all these virtues, the film fails, and fails dismally.

Why? After watching fifteen minutes, any viewer will be able to answer that question. The filming itself—camera angles, camera movement, lighting, editing, and especially framing—has been woefully mismanaged.

For example, there is the scene where the transformed Heathcliff returns. As in the novel, we do not directly witness his first reunion with Cathy. Instead, we watch Edgar watching them through the window. Stiff-faced, he walks to a wall mirror and gazes uncertainly at himself. The camera shows the mirror reflecting his face and thoughts: how will he measure up to Heathcliff in Cathy's eyes? So far, so good. But when Heathcliff finally enters, the camera lingers awkwardly on Edgar's back for a few seconds, then, nervous, zooms in to an extreme close-up of Cathy's and Heathcliff's hands clasping, then Edgar's hands (forced by Cathy's) joining theirs. There is a zoom out to frame all three in the mirror—a move that unfortunately dilutes the message of the previous mirror framing. Close-up of Catherine: her lips tremble; she is so excited she is unable to speak. The audience longs to see how Heathcliff is reacting, but when he is shown, his face is swallowed by the glare of a candle flame.

Obscurity rules throughout this film. Actors' heads and feet are routinely cut off and we are left to follow their talking torsos—though it is often difficult to hear what they are saying. When there is an indoor shot, the fire roars. When there is an outdoor shot, the wind howls. Frames of shots often act more like masks, veiling what they are supposed to emphasize. Dirty windows, bunches of drying herbs, keyholes, hanging rabbits bleeding at the mouth, branches leafy in summer and barren in winter, sheets whipping on a clothesline, jaws of stone griffins—all these and more come between our eyes and the action. Finally, there is the climax of Cathy's death scene, when the faces of the tortured lovers are blurred by the red blossoms of a potted geranium in the foreground.

It is possible to make a case that Hammond and his crew were carrying their experiment in authenticity into the realm of viewer reception: could they make the audience experience what it would have been like, *really,* to have been there, in windy inclement Yorkshire during the last decades of the eighteenth century, observing the agonies and the ecstasies of two squirearchical families? To find out what is happening, the film viewer must (like any eighteenth-century eavesdropper) squint against the glare of a flaming hearth, or peer into the gloom past a candle, or struggle to make out the indistinct outlines of hero and villain alike through the ever-present hearth haze.

A more likely explanation? A loss of nerve. Having made the daring decision to follow Brontë's book closely, using most of her story points and much of her actual language, Hammond, finally, could not trust the text. Perhaps he worried about drowning the audience in literary dialogue; the visual medium disdains "talking books" but eagerly devours image and movement. So Hammond decided to provide visual diversion artificially, counterpointing the progress of Brontë's great drama with seventy-times-seven camera tricks.

Some might say that Hammond was right to distrust the text, that it is his faithfulness to Brontë that defeats him, that too many words, even when they are words of genius, spoil a medium where artistry is visual. Such critics might assert that the film fails first and foremost because it is talky and rambling. In fact, Leonard's and Snodin's script does succeed, and it succeeds because it follows the strong contours of *Wuthering Heights'* intrinsic dramatic structure. The actors uniformly achieve complex, book-true characterizations. Responsibility for the film's failure must be assigned to artistic and technical direction, ultimately Peter Hammond's domain. Had a director with the artistry of a Wyler or a Buñuel realized this script with these actors, a masterpiece might have resulted. As it is, though Ken Hutchison may be the only actor to have solved the problem of Heathcliff in a way Emily Brontë would have approved, his performance is history, and only history. Unavailable in commercial video and seldom shown on TV, the Hammond version of *Wuthering Heights* is sinking into a fate as murky as its soundtrack.

In the early '90s, Peter Kosminsky directed *Emily Brontë's Wuthering Heights,* a 104-minute British production. A 1992 release in the U.S. was hyped, then canceled; the film had been trashed in England, perhaps in part because of the unpopular casting of French film star Juliette Binoche as the quintessentially English Cathy. A few years later the film was shown on American cable TV and has recently been released to U.S. video markets.

The problem of Heathcliff is turned on its head by another controversial casting: Ralph Fiennes. With his fair coloring, refined features, and lithe, well-proportioned body, Fiennes looks more an Edgar than a Heathcliff. He has to work hard at being bad—luckily a specialty of his. The virtuosic cosmic evil of Fiennes's Nazi in *Schindler's List,* the all-for-love moral myopia of his title character in *The English Patient*—both are anticipated here. Yet bad as Fiennes gets, he never loses his appeal. Rather than asking how we are made to like him at all, we might better inquire why we do not hate him more thoroughly. The answer perhaps reflects more luster on the movie's psychology than on the moral soundness of its audience.

The keynote of the Kosminsky/Fiennes's Heathcliff is sadism. He is neither the raging, cruel maniac of Hammond/Hutchison nor the sad, half-mad sufferer of Olivier/Wyler, but a quiet, smiling torturer at play. This is a character strand clearly present in Brontë: Kosminsky pulls a quote from the book when he has Heathcliff tell Cathy that while she was gone at the Lintons he put a wire mesh over a brood of fledgling lapwings and starved them. This neatly sets up Heathcliff's signature *modus operandi:* when Cathy hurts him, he will hurt, and hurt worse, something or someone that Cathy cares about. Watching a smiling, controlled Fiennes jerk a puffy-lipped Isabella (Sophie Ward) by the wrist as he tells her how much he detests her is much more painful than watching parallel scenes in Wyler and Hammond.

This is daring. The cruelty of the Fiennes's Heathcliff cannot be excused as an act of temper or seen as one part of a complex pattern of personality, as in the Hutchison or Olivier Heathcliffs. Fiennes's harshness does not move with the tidal pulls of sex or heroism, as do Dalton's and Mistral's. This Heathcliff's sadism freezes hotter emotions, and the production bets on Fiennes's ability to project, from his essence, an ironic, depressed, bitter, modern intelligence, one with which the audience must feel complicity, however uneasily.

But the audience is likely to be looking elsewhere. More than in any other version, it is Cathy, not Heathcliff, who carries the film. First, the script gives her more development and power, in a balance with Heathcliff more closely reflective of Brontë's intentions. But the more important factor is the strong charisma of Binoche, who plays both Cathys, mother and daughter. When she is on a screen she owns it, though her characterizations are almost annoyingly eccentric. Binoche as Cathy I laughs, charmingly and shockingly, at everything. Somehow this distracting tic is a fit psychological aberration to put beside Heathcliff's controlling sadism. Binoche's Cathy just laughs it off.

Binoche's smile, so defiantly merry, eerily mirrors Heathcliff's sadistic grin; in fact, by nature or artifice these two actors look very much alike in this film. This resemblance of course brings out the submerged incest theme in their love affair, for Heathcliff and Cathy were brought up as brother and sister, and may in fact have been so. It is a fault of this version that it slides too quickly over their shared childhood. Their early paradisiacal relationship should be established using child actors, as in Wyler, Fuest, and Hammond, but Kosminsky dispatches the youngsters in seconds. Instead, suddenly we are confronted with Binoche and Fiennes, fully and embarrassingly adult, giggling through a scripture lesson, then off to their shared bed to play (of all things!) a guessing game about flowers and trees. These scenes are so obviously wrong that their inclusion seems like wanton sabotage, but Kosminsky will not give screen time to peripheral actors. He wants to drench us immediately with the glorious light of his big stars, and he wants to keep us in that light without distraction.

Sometimes that light is very beautiful. The most engaging scene in the movie is one of the few that allows Cathy and Heathcliff to be happy. Early in the film, we are shown the two standing in a strange blasted landscape: a lava field serrated like the folds of the brain, with here and there a gnarled tree growing up out of it. Heathcliff enfolds Cathy in his arms. He is boasting, making himself out to be some kind of wizard. "I'll send your spirit into the tree. Listen!" Birds fly out, squawking.

She laughs. "How did you do that?"

"I can do a lot of things," he says. Squinting up at the rays of sun pouring out of a bright cloud, Heathcliff tells Cathy to close her eyes. "If when you open your eyes the day is sunny and bright, so shall your future be. But if the day is for storms, so shall be your life."

When Cathy looks, she laughs to see sun. But thunder growls behind them. They turn to find a horizon of roiling thunderheads. "What have you done?" Cathy breathes. Then she shouts defiantly to the sky, "I don't care! Do you hear? I don't care."

Here we have the visual analog for the animistic magic so vital to the metaphysic of Brontë's book, as voiced by Cathy, "If all else perished, and he remained, I should still continue to be; and, if all else remained, and he were annihilated, the Universe would turn to a mighty stranger. . . . my love for Heathcliff resembles the eternal rocks" (Chapter 9), and Heathcliff, "In every cloud, in every tree—filling the air at night, and caught by glimpses in every object by day, I am surrounded with her image!" (Chapter 33). Their lives, too large to require nuance or explanation, are inscribed in rocks, in trees, in clouds. They are nature gods. (See Figure 20.)

Kosminsky's essentialism, his emphasis on painting the right strokes very broad, is his greatest strength—when he can pull it off. His stubborn concentration on the spine of his story makes for marvelous efficiency. Unlike Wyler (103 minutes), Buñuel (90 minutes), and Fuest (105 minutes), Kosminsky includes both Lockwood and the second generation, all in 104 minutes. Only Hammond does as much, in more than twice the time. In fact, as indicated by his title, Kosminsky adds another frame story—a bold stroke that unfortunately goes wrong. Emily Brontë herself wanders catatonically through opening credits into the ruins of Wuthering Heights, wondering who lived there. "My pen creates stories of a world that might have been, and here is one that I will tell," she mutters. Her puzzlingly monotone narration intrudes several times during the action, and the film closes with a shot of her wandering out of the house again, still robotic. While this framing does remind a viewer/ reader of the Chinese box narratives-within-narratives of the book, it proves at best a distraction and at worst an undercutting of the "reality" of the film world. Perhaps Kosminsky's motive was to save time with Brontë's strategically placed voice-over explanations. On the contrary: her presence scatters time along with viewer concentration.

But often Kosminsky's chic streamlining works brilliantly. Early in the film Kosminsky sets up an association between the first Catherine and a burning candle when Cathy II gives a candle to Lockwood at the door of the haunted bedchamber and tells him not to set it in the window. Of course he does, unwittingly summoning the ghost of the first Cather-

Figure 20. Animus and Anima: Ralph Fiennes and Juliette Binoche play a cosmically connected Heathcliff and Cathy. © Paramount

ine. Thereafter, living and dead, she is recalled by a candle flame; in one scene late in the movie the effect is particularly stunning. It begins with a close-up of Heathcliff at Cathy's window, staring at a candle. He speaks slowly and intensely: "Catherine—Why have you not come back to me? Every day I wait for you. My one waking thought has been of you." Then cut to Cathy II at the Grange reading a letter as Heathcliff's words continue in voice-over, and we realize that Heathcliff is dictating a love letter to his son Linton, sadistically forcing Linton's courtship of his cousin as Heathcliff works toward final revenge. But of course more strongly Heathcliff is calling out to Cathy I to come back to him as a ghost—which at the climax of the film she will, at that very window. Viewing this scene, we feel pleasure, the pleasure that comes from the concentration, then release, of emotion and understanding. Kosminsky has built meaning through the careful repetition of tropes (candle, window) and now deployed them in a scene that does double duty for two generations. This is accomplished visual story telling.

Another reward of sound filmic economy is that expression of a character's emotion can be intensified by condensing a scene. For negative proof one has only to go back to Fuest, that prodigy of motion. Recall Fuest's version of the confrontation between Heathcliff and Edgar in the kitchen of the Grange. There the Dalton Heathcliff's escape was choreographed as swashbuckling action, all flash and dash, its emotion squandered in gaudy, expansive display. In Kosminsky this is condensed to a few quiet seconds: when Edgar hits Heathcliff, Heathcliff lifts a poker. He is frozen by one shake of Cathy's head. Icy eyes narrowing, Heathcliff brings the poker down on the lock of the door instead of the skull of his enemy. He walks out quietly, his anger compact as a fist.

But Kosminsky's less-is-more philosophy works against as much as for him. The story reads like shorthand; events pass so swiftly that we can scarcely comprehend some of them. Several five-second shots may be sufficient to remind a Brontë scholar of the ins and outs of an incident that takes twenty pages to develop in the book (i.e., Heathcliff's courtship of Isabella and their subsequent elopement), but they can hardly do more than sketch a plot point for even the most alert non-literary filmgoer. Furthermore, the movie's rapid pace does not allow character development for anyone but the two principals. It is difficult to tell, for instance, why Nelly Dean keeps turning up. Frances, Hindley's wife, dies before we are sure just who she is, and Hindley fades away off-screen without our caring. Even Heathcliff and Cathy are moved along too fast. As has been noted, the childhood of the first generation Earn-shaws is passed over so quickly that it is barely present, an important loss. Kosminsky gives us little chance to plant our emotions.

But this is the way we want our stories told these days. Leisurely examination, lingering mood pieces, careful development of complexity—these are too often read as boring, pompous, and—worst of all—plain slow. Now condensation, implication, collage are preferred in all storytelling, visual or textual. In film, snappy, economic editing is favored—group-bursts of split-second takes swinging into sequences of longer takes, cuts for point-of-view switches in the middle of gestures or words. These Kosminsky gives us, in a treatment that also manages a flowing lyricism. It is altogether a chic, stylish production. In fact, Kosminsky's cinematography is so much of the moment and *in* the moment that it is hard to isolate its most significant elements. Their kinship to the prevailing ideology—the hot quick fix of the '90s, the cool rush onward—renders them almost transparent.

Ralph Fiennes's Heathcliff, then, is a Heathcliff for our age, not Brontë's. His taut physical grace, the edge of irony to his sadism, his emotional aloofness, even his depressive personality—all these mark him as our own. In him some of the supposedly negative aspects of masculinity are delineated, and redefined as positive. In fact this has always been true of the film Heathcliff. He occupies mental space more often filled by woman: he projects as a voyeuristic object, a spectacle. He is a trap for the fleeting animus, a shadow man showing viewers, female and male, what it is we need of darkness. Looking back, we can catch the shade of the male Zeitgeist behind each screen Heathcliff. In 1939, from a world playing out a relentless historical tragedy, the Olivier Heathcliff, driven by fate, asserted the noble necessity of causing pain and enduring it. Buñuel's reactionary 1954 post-war Alejandro sought to escape the rigors of civilization by turning back nostalgically to a more personal, primitive code of masculine honor, where wildness and elementalism conquered refinement. Riding the boom-time 60s, Dalton's 1970 expansionist Heathcliff reveled in his command of screen spatials and erotics, defying the limitations of evil. Eight years later, at the crest of the self-realization movement, a psychologizing Hutchison turned inward, plumbing evil in search of authenticity. Now, in the '90s, Fiennes's Heathcliff displaces authenticity from Knowledge into Being; evil justifies itself; in its existential energy it becomes an object of desire.

Sympathizing with the devil, we are likely to locate him very close to home. Will we then exorcise him? Perhaps. But it is more likely that we will find we like his company.

Acknowledgment

The author would like to acknowledge help from Larry Berman, Jeri Freedman, Bob Gerst, Sage Green, Barbara Lupack, Annie MaCaulay, MaryKay Mahoney, Mark Meadows, Candice Rowe, Rebecca Saunders, Margaret Turner, and Peggy Walsh.

List of Film Versions of Wuthering Heights

*Wuthering Heights. Dir. A. V. Bramble. With Milton Rosmer, Colette Brettel, Warwick Ward, and Anne Trevor. Six reels. British production, 1920.

Wuthering Heights. Dir. William Wyler. With Laurence Olivier and Merle Oberon. Samuel Goldwyn, 1939.

Abismos de Pasion. Dir. Luis Buñuel. With Jorge Mistral and Iraseme Dilian. Producciones Tepeyac, 1954.

Wuthering Heights. Dir. Robert Fuest. With Timothy Dalton and Anna Calder-Marshall. American International Pictures, 1970.

Wuthering Heights. Dir. Peter Hammond. With Ken Hutchison and Kay Adshead. BBC, 1978.

*Hurlevent. Dir. Jacques Rivette. With Lucas Belvaux and Fabienne Babe. French production, 1985.

Emily Brontë's Wuthering Heights. Dir. Peter Kosminsky. With Ralph Fiennes and Juliette Binoche. Paramount, 1992.

*Not available for this review.

Works Cited

Brontë, Emily. *Wuthering Heights*. 1847. Boston: Bedford, 1992.

Miller, J. Hillis. *Fiction and Repetition*. Cambridge: Harvard UP, 1982.

Sanger, C. P. "The Structure of 'Wuthering Heights.'" *The Brontës: A Collection of Critical Essays*. Ed. Ian Gregor. Englewood Cliffs, NJ: Prentice-Hall, 1970.

7

FEMINISM IN BRONTË'S *JANE EYRE* AND ITS FILM VERSIONS

Kate Ellis and E. Ann Kaplan
(with a new *Postscript* by E. Ann Kaplan)

Charlotte Brontë's *Jane Eyre* is the story of a woman who understands instinctively the inequities of patriarchal structures but who cannot, finally, move entirely beyond them. Published in 1847 at the height of the Victorian era, the book won immediate popular acclaim, along with some harsh criticism.[1] But it is the intense ambivalence toward male domination on the part of Brontë and her heroine that speaks so strongly to present day feminists, who have claimed Brontë as one of the "foremothers" of the contemporary women's movement.[2] Jane's strength comes to the reader through the clear, strong voice of the first person narrative as she describes her situations: analyzing them, commenting on them, and giving us her thoughts and reactions at every point. Neither the 1944 nor the 1972 film version is ultimately able to retain the centrality of Jane's point of view, though there is, in Stevenson's 1944 version, a voice-over narration that is a very much watered-down version of Brontë's strong diction. This dilution of Jane's rebellious vision has partly to do with the limitations of film form, but mainly it is a result of a reversion on the part of the two directors, Robert Stevenson and Delbert Mann, to accepted patriarchal structures so that Jane is seen, for the most part, from a male point of view.

In allowing Jane to narrate her own story, Brontë allows her heroine the complexity of a double vision. On the one hand, we see Jane chafe against the constrictions and inequities of the patriarchal spaces within which she is placed: Gateshead, Lowood School, Thornfield Hall, and finally Marsh End. She is "thrilled with ungovernable excitement" as she declares to her aunt, in words very close to those she will later say to Rochester, "You think I have no feelings, and that I can do without one bit of love or kindness; but I cannot live so" (Chapter 4). This declaration will be, in fact, the motif of Jane's life, drawing her away from the Reeds, away from Lowood, toward and then away from Rochester and the ascetic St. John Rivers, until she finally finds, at Ferndean, a love and kindness that do not patronize her. On the other hand, when she discovers that she might have "some poor, low relations called Eyre," she will not leave Gateshead to go to them.

"Not even if they were kind to you?"

I shook my head. I could not see how poor people had the means of being kind; and then to learn to speak like them, to adopt their manners, to be uneducated, to grow up like one of the poor women I saw sometimes nursing their children or washing their clothes at the cottage doors of the village of Gateshead: no, I was not heroic enough to purchase liberty at the price of caste. (Chapter 3)

Again at Lowood, we see Jane raging against the submissiveness of Helen Burns, but also learning from it. When Miss Scratchard pins the word "Slattern" on Helen, Jane tells us:

I ran to Helen, tore it off, and thrust it into the fire: the fury of which she was incapable had been burning in my soul all day, and tears, hot and large, had continually been scalding my cheek; for the spectacle of her sad resignation gave me an intolerable pain at the heart. (Chapter 8)

At the same time she has her first real experience of love and kindness there from Miss Temple and Helen, and this causes her to declare: "I would not now have exchanged Lowood with all its privations, for Gateshead and its daily luxuries." Therefore she stays on there for two years as a teacher (a post she rejects in both film versions) and leaves only when her "motive" for staying is taken away by the marriage and removal of Miss Temple.

Brontë gives us the same juxtaposition of need and contempt in Jane's view of Thornfield. Explaining why she does not want to leave in the wake of her master's purported marriage to Blanche Ingram she says:

I love Thornfield—I love it because I have lived in it a full and delightful life— momentarily at least. I have not been trampled on. I have not been petrified. I have not been buried with inferior minds, and excluded from every glimpse of communion with what is bright and energetic, and high. I have talked, face to face, with what I reverence; with what I delight in—with an original, a vigorous, an expanded mind. (Chapter 23)

But she sees the necessity of leaving, acknowledges that this place that has given her her first real experience of a home is an appropriate setting for the kind of life Rochester will have with Blanche Ingram. But "I

would scorn such a union," she says, "therefore I am better than you—
let me go!" When Rochester offers her a form of "union" that in her
view is just as debased as this one without love, she does scorn it.
Finally, she scorns Rivers's offer of marriage based not on mutual affection but on dedication to a higher cause. Jane extricates herself from this
temptation, yet it is only because Rivers insists on marriage that she
refuses. While she lives under his roof she notices that "I daily wished
more to please him: but to do so, I felt daily more and more that I must
disown half my nature" (Chapter 34). She sees that she cannot give her
body as well as her soul to him, yet she freely consents to go with him as
his fellow missionary. Clear-headedly she reasons: "I should suffer
often, no doubt, attached to him only in this capacity: my body would be
under a rather stringent yoke, but my heart and mind would be free." Yet
she is not immune to the attraction of heroic action. It was she, after all,
who in her first months at Thornfield looked out at the skyline and
"longed for a power of vision that might overpass that limit; which
might reach the busy world, towns, regions full of life I had heard of but
never seen" (Chapter 12).

The question is: does she relinquish this restless side of her nature
when she gives up her independent life and career to care for a blind,
dependent man? In some ways, Brontë is simply following the narrative
demands of her genre, which imitate the dominant bourgeois code. She
brings the lovers safely back together, the woman firmly back in her
place caring for the man. Yet Rochester's blindness suggests a fundamental weakness in men that belies the original harsh, invulnerable, controlling exterior that Rochester presents. Ultimately, he is terribly
dependent on Jane, needing her more than she, with her newly inherited
income, needs him. She, on the other hand, turns out to be the stronger,
thus fulfilling the symbolism of their first meeting where she helps him
up after a fall from his horse. Yet this strength of hers is little more than
the strength that mothers have in caring for their children: one wonders
if this was the only alternative model that Brontë had to the traditional
"he for God only, she for God in him" paradigm of male-female relationships. That is to say, Brontë offers only the alternative of women
feeling subordinate and vulnerable to men, living with them "as sisters"
or without them altogether, or undertaking a nurturing, mothering role
that gives them all the control. Here we see Brontë's ambivalence
toward the institution (as opposed to the experience, to borrow a distinction from Adrienne Rich) of marriage that becomes increasingly unmistakable in her later work. Then again, perhaps she is simply saying that
it takes rather drastic events (blindness on the male side, a large inheritance on the female) to equalize, even in a place as far from "society" as

Ferndean, the drastic sexual inequalities with which her age presented her.

What is interesting, from our point of view, about the film versions, is the ways in which Stevenson in 1944 and Mann in 1972 liquidate Brontë's ambivalence toward patriarchy. The Stevenson film was made in the post-World War II period when *film noir* was dominant. Having played active roles in the public sphere during the war, women were now being told to go back into their homes and care for their husbands and children. It is thus not surprising to find Joan Fontaine playing a very meek, docile, and submissive Jane in the second half of the film. Interestingly enough, the first half of the film, prior to Orson Welles's appearance as Rochester, sticks close to the novel in showing Jane's rebelliousness and defiance, first toward the Reed family and then at Lowood. Stevenson uses expressionist, nonrealist cinematic techniques to show the monstrosity of the Reed family and the vulnerability of Jane by using high and low angles. Mrs. Reed and John lower over her menacingly, or we see her small, pathetically cooped up, in the Red Room. But Jane fights back against these looming figures, putting up a brave, if pointless, fight. The camera angles thus express some of the Gothic terror that emerges from Brontë's description.

The use of high contrast in this black and white film also brings out the Gothicism of a book in which the room where a man died is filled with secrets and a mad woman is confined to an attic. In this film, as in the novel, a sadistic Mr. Brocklehurst enjoys piling hardships on his pupils in the name of religion, and has no remorse even when Helen Burns (Elizabeth Taylor) dies as a result of harsh rules carried out by an equally unrelenting Miss Scratchard. The one mitigating female presence in the novel, it is important to note, is replaced by an added character, the kindly Dr. Rivers whose name is taken from the novel's stern St. John Rivers who does not appear in the film. Dr. Rivers tries to circumvent Brocklehurst's insane regulations and to explain their danger for the girls. But even though he is a man confronting another man, he is powerless to effect a change. While he comforts Jane, his role is essentially to teach her her place, to beg her to conform, to submit to the will of God. Like the Rivers of the novel, this essentially virtuous male figure sees no possibility for changing the omnipresence of male domination, and he tries to undermine Jane's independent spirit. In the novel it is Miss Temple who objects strongly to the rules and sometimes breaks them. Her warm, nurturing presence offsets the horror of Lowood for Jane. But even more importantly, she provides a powerful model for both Jane and Helen of a principled and intelligent, if ultimately powerless, woman.

One can only speculate on the reasons for a change like this: balancing the hateful Brocklehurst with the kindly Rivers mitigates an absolute condemnation of male authority that might be implied. Rivers is the good father to Jane canceling out the bad one. Yet Brontë had been more interested in Miss Temple as the good mother balancing out Mrs. Reed, the bad one. The film, in removing one side of this balance, represses the mother who in the novel brought about Jane's growth. Male authority is thereby left supreme.

While Jane's point of view is given prominence in the Lowood section of the film, the tension comes from the way it shows male authority trying to silence it. But once Joan Fontaine replaces Peggy Ann Garner, as Jane arrives at Thornfield Hall, the directing consciousness becomes Rochester's, in a complete reversal of the situation in the novel. This is partly because Orson Welles, who plays Rochester, always dominates whatever scene he is in. But it also has to do with the camera work, about which Welles may possibly have had some say. Cinematically, Jane is placed as Rochester's observer: she yearns for him, waits upon him, watches him from the window, the stairwell, a corner of the room, hiding her tears from him behind closed doors. We retain Jane's point of view, but her gaze is fixed on Rochester as object of desire, an odd reversal of the usual situation in film where the male observes the woman as object of desire in such a way that the audience sees her that way too. (See Figure 21.) Interestingly, the reversal of the look does not give Jane any more power: Rochester comes and goes, commands and manages, orders Jane's presence as he wishes. Jane's look is of a yearning, passive kind as against the more usual controlling male look at the woman.

Jane's subordination and passivity are particularly marked in the scenes where Blanche Ingram and Rochester's other guests come to Thornfield. Jane then skulks around with Adele, shot often behind the guests, in the rear of the room, glimpsed behind a door, or through the richly dressed, loud party. Rochester places her in the impossible position of forcing her to be present, and then ignoring her and relegating her to the status of an observer of his love affair with Blanche. Since her voice-over commentary is silent at this point, we do not get her thoughts and analysis or the contempt for the situation that Jane's point of view in the novel so strongly registers. When the pain is intolerable she does of course ask to leave and, as in the novel, thus precipitates the marriage proposal. But overall we see Jane as passive and long-suffering, putting up with this treatment without complaint.

Jane's passivity is heightened by the naturally subservient and self-effacing style of Fontaine the actress. While this manner may have suited her role in Hitchcock's 1940 film *Rebecca,* it is quite unsuitable

Figure 21. Cinematically, Jane (Joan Fontaine) is placed as observer of Rochester (Orson Welles). Her gaze is fixed on him as object of desire. © Twentieth-Century Fox

for Jane. But reinforcing this is the equally natural bombast of Welles, who dominates his co-star in a way that Olivier did not in *Rebecca*. Yet Welles's baroque sensibility is in many ways suited to the Gothic elements in the original novel, and on this score Stevenson's version does much better than the later Mann one, largely due to Welles's influence. While he sometimes overplays his hand in an embarrassing manner—for instance, by the macho riding-off into the snow-swept landscape, storm blowing, and huge mastiff at his side (Jane meanwhile looking on passively from a window with a diminutive Margaret O'Brien as Adele, one sewing, the other painting)—he *has* caught the tenor of Brontë's image, the swashbuckling Byronic overtones of her male character. Anachronistic as is the medieval castle that constitutes the set for the Thornfield section, it again fits Brontë's Gothic imagination. And while the film cannot reproduce the symbolism of Bertha in the novel, where she embodies the repressed parts of Jane, in not letting us see her properly, Stevenson surrounds her with mysterious and sinister elements.

The omission of the St. John Rivers sequence in this film seems to fit in with the subordination of Jane's point of view. In the novel, it is through her experiences away from Rochester that Jane learns to be strong and to function effectively on her own. The delay between the romantic passion and its fulfillment enables her to mature and return to Rochester as an equal. Stevenson deals with the necessity of sending Jane somewhere, after she has left the still-married Rochester, by moving forward the brief return to the Reed household that Jane in the novel makes prior to Rochester's proposal. In the novel Jane comes as a result of this visit to pity her former tormentors, and the freedom from them that she thereby acquires is a necessary prelude to her ability to understand and express her feelings about Thornfield and its owner. But in the film Jane falls into the same passive, observing, subordinate role that she had at Thornfield. Dr. Rivers appears again as the emissary between herself and Rochester, and as a storm swirls around her she hears the voice of Rochester that calls her to his side. It is significant, we think, that they meet in the burned shell of the castle, the charred remnants surrounding them menacingly. Welles limps through the ruins but is hardly the mellowed, chastened Rochester (could Welles ever appear chastened?) of Brontë's closing chapters. Their coming together simply represents the typical lovers' reunion, with male and female traditionally placed. Jane is overjoyed to be back with Rochester and he is relieved at her return to take care of him. One has no sense of real change having taken place in either of them.

Delbert Mann's 1972 made-for-television version of *Jane Eyre* makes an interesting contrast to the 1944 film. The dominance of *film noir* as a film form in the postwar period enabled Stevenson to re-create quite effectively some of the Gothic aspects of the novel: *film noir* looked back to expressionism, which in turn drew on the Gothic revival and romanticism for its themes and styles, so that the line from Brontë's novel to 1940s film aesthetics was reasonably direct. On the other hand, the ideology of the same postwar period in relation to women was partly responsible for the omission of Brontë's feminist leanings. But Mann's version, made in the period when the new wave of feminism was in its most exuberant, optimistic phase, humanizes Rochester and Bertha Mason, and removes much of the conflict from the relationship between Rochester (George C. Scott) and Jane (Susannah York). (See Figure 22.) In doing this the characters become much more human and familiar, or at least familiar as film characters. But by the same token, the theme of personal growth through struggle and hard-won self-knowledge, which makes Brontë's novel an important document for feminists still, is swept away in a tide of rich, sensuous images.

To begin with, the lush, colorful photography is completely at odds with the Gothicism of the original. All is bright, colorful, and unmysterious. Mann has a strong feeling for textures as well as colors, and on this level the film appeals strongly. The inmates in Lowood wear uniforms and nightgowns that could have been designed for the pages of *Vogue*. Thornfield is now an elegant mansion fitted out with magnificent eighteenth-century objects, furniture, and a stunning staircase. George C. Scott's Rochester is a humane, sympathetic character: instead of the charismatic, blustering Welles we have a tired, jaded, and aging man worn out by a life of too much easy pleasure, seeking in Jane the freshness of a young, innocent woman. His grief about Bertha is stressed, and to make this convincing, Mann lets us into Bertha's prison after the aborted wedding, as Stevenson did not. A desperate Rochester insists that the priest, Jane, and Bertha's brother Mason follow him to see the wife now preventing his happiness with Jane. Bertha is beautiful but catatonic, in contrast to the violent, "unchaste" creature described in Brontë's novel and implied in Stevenson's film. Rochester sits wearily down beside her and asks what they should do that night, making it clear that it is her incapacity for companionship that has driven him away in despair. His words thus highlight not only his utter loneliness but also her total isolation. Bertha has a strange kind of magnetism, and Rochester's words to Jane that he loved Bertha once as he now loves her give the relationship a compelling dignity. Similarly the separation between Jane and Rochester after the marriage is realistically and touchingly done. We have a sense of two equal people, each determined to press for what he or she wants and thinks is right.

Figure 22. By removing much of the conflict in the lovers' relationship, director Delbert Mann makes Rochester (George C. Scott) and Jane (Susannah York) more familiar and more human. © Viacom

Having omitted the Reed family at the beginning, Mann includes the Marsh End section of the novel, and this enables him to show a different, more charismatic type of man. Black-haired and starkly handsome, Rivers represents a force that Jane must learn to withstand, and it is when she does so that she hears Rochester's mysterious call. The final reunion is extremely real and touching in this version. Rochester is humbled, not expecting anything, and fully supposing her to be married already. When he realizes she wants to stay with a blind, crippled man, his pleasure is quietly expressed in their embrace. Fittingly, the reunion happens not in the Gothic ruin Thornfield but in the peace and quiet of Ferndean, and here Mann is closer to Brontë than Stevenson was, conveying that sense of peace and transcendence with which Brontë ends.

In humanizing Rochester, Mann comes closer to portraying an equal relationship, but the camera still favors Rochester and shows Jane looking up to or being looked down upon by a male observer. Structurally Rochester is still in command, and it is significant that the equality comes not from Jane's rebellion or his questioning intelligence, but simply from the fact that Rochester's weaknesses are on the surface right from the beginning. While Welles made Rochester's anger at Jane's departure come from a defensive wounded pride, Scott makes us see the utter loneliness and loss that Rochester experiences—a loss that seems equal to Jane's in a way that it does not in either Brontë or the Stevenson film. Mann allows us to see more of Rochester's pain than Jane sees (she is not there when he tries to converse with Bertha, for instance) so that we become sensitive to his view of things, which thereby becomes the dominant point of view in the film.

It is worth dwelling a moment on the significance of the humanizing of Rochester in the Mann version in terms of what it does to the original Gothic pattern. The Gothic is premised on the father's being distant, unknown, unapproachable, commanding. Once he is known, his threat diminishes and the premise for Gothic emotions is removed. Patriarchal structures are premised on the mysterious father's defining woman's place for her. Once he is no longer mysterious, once he enters into the structure as a human entity, his power is lost and the woman has room to interact, to enter the sphere from which she has been excluded. Scott's Rochester is thus (to answer Freud's question) what women want: a vulnerable, open, accessible father who is not afraid to reveal his weakness or the depth of his needs. A daughter may not have the same power in the world that a father has, but if they are equal in their need for one another, and can express this equally, then the differences in age and experience (which are the only ones Rochester insisted on in the novel) are not oppressive. The fantasy of "marrying daddy" comes out from behind its Gothic trappings in Mann's film, but it is there in Brontë too, as well as in the innumerable contemporary "drugstore Gothics" on the market today. Behind this gruff, male exterior, it says, lies true love, unable, for the most part, to express itself, but there nevertheless. He may seem distant, dazzled by charms that are beyond your reach, and bound to another, but in fact it is really you that he has loved all along.

A much more blatant departure from the Brontëan Gothic is the fact that Susannah York's Jane is in no way the plain heroine conceived by an author who, Mrs. Gaskell tells us,

once told her sisters that they were wrong—even morally wrong—in making their heroines beautiful as a matter of course. They replied that it was impossible to make a heroine interesting on any other terms. Her answer was, "I will prove to you that you are wrong; I will show you a heroine as plain and small as myself, who shall be as interesting as any of yours."[3]

Brontë lived in a society that rewarded pretty women but not plain ones; so do we. Fathers have become more casually accessible to their children since the Stevenson movie was made, and certainly since Brontë wrote. And for a brief time in the late 1960s and early 1970s, feminists were caught up in a belief that the world they wanted was right on the horizon: that the fate of pretty women in this culture could be distributed equally, that men could throw down their burdensome defenses, and that age-old struggles could be done away with through a change of consciousness. Fortunately for us now, Charlotte Brontë knew better.

Postscript by E. Ann Kaplan: When Kate Ellis and I wrote our essay on Brontë's *Jane Eyre* and its film versions in the early 1980s, we came to our task very much within the specific intellectual and political context of America in that historical moment. And our corner of that moment was the feminist movement, and Feminist Studies in particular. Most of the prior essays on film adaptations of Brontë's novel (except that by Sumiko Hagashi) had dealt more narrowly with contrasts and comparisons between novel and adaptations in terms of historical film/fiction studies.

Ellis and I were at pains to tease out Jane's voice—so loud and clear in Brontë's novel—in the two film adaptations we looked at. We were interested in how far patriarchal codes—and a naturalized male dominance—influenced film presentations of Jane and Rochester. Whose cinematic point of view was privileged? How far did Jane's point of view prevail? How far was she silenced? How did each adaptation deal with Brontë's ambiguous ending to the narrative—with Jane returning to a maimed Rochester, who was now able to forgive her as she was free now to love him? Did this return compromise 1970s feminist concepts of independence?

We noted the age-long appeal to women of the search for stories of romantic love within a patriarchal society: in these stories, the heroine finally wins the affections of a highly placed, exciting, rich but accessible man, who begins by wanting to use her and is led gradually to appreciate her values and integrity. We noted the longing for the absent, distant father that underlies some of the unconscious pleasure in these stories, as part of a psychic constellation produced by patriarchy. We argued that the later Delbert Mann film version images a new kind of father, less distant, more approachable, perhaps partly the result of 1970s feminist challenges to patriarchy.

If these were our 1980s questions, what are those for the late 1990s? Too complex a question to answer adequately in this brief note, let me just suggest three directions to look for answers. One would be the achievements of recent feminist movements; another, postcolonial studies' influence on canonical scholarship; a third, the 1990s cultural fascination with the great realist novel as witnessed by the many new film and television adaptations. Let me address each of these very briefly in relation to a 1997 BBC/A & E collaboration on a television version of *Jane Eyre* (dir. Robert Young):

1. Feminist Achievements:

There has been a significant change vis-à-vis American culture's awareness of feminine ways of being—female sexualities and desires, emotions, social conflicts, reproductive and caring roles. Women scholars have produced a wealth of new knowledge about women, *and in the process about men too,* in the last thirty years—knowledge which has increased feminists' own abilities to understand women and men in ways more multiple than the prior patriarchal analysis allowed, as well as increasing general awareness about women in American culture.

In line with the interest in adapting Victorian novels to the screen, in 1997 the BBC and A & E collaborated on yet another *Jane Eyre* version. Less melodramatic than the 1944 Stevenson film, and less naturalized than the 1972 Delbert Mann version, the 1997 BBC/A & E *Jane Eyre* seemed both to get the proper historical distance on the story and at the same time to avoid sentimentalizing and overdramatizing the events. Samantha Morton's quiet, controlled Jane comes closest to my own understanding of Brontë's original character. Ciaran Hinds' Rochester is more passionate and emotional than Brontë's hero, but he makes Jane's interest in him more believable. Instead of being the remote Gothic fantasy of a young romantic girl that Brontë still was when she wrote this novel, Hinds' Rochester is a complicated but ultimately moral man, who becomes genuinely intrigued by, and then in love with, the quiet, genuinely unpretentious and Christian governess. This Rochester is far from the cold, distanced, even cruel Rochester of earlier versions and even of

Brontë's novel. His desire for Jane is evident quite early in the story in the scene where Jane saves Rochester from "Grace Poole's" attempt to set him on fire.

Very interesting in this scene—and a departure from prior versions, I think—is the focus on Jane's obviously overwhelming sexual arousal. Her virginal situation vis-à-vis a first powerful sexual desire is dramatized in the camera's catching her face as Rochester touches her hand, in her abrupt departure from the room, and in the following scene where she is found crying and rocking herself on her bed, unable to sleep. The blanched visual appearance of Jane and her room here mime her desperate inner conflicts about her desire for Rochester. Meanwhile, Rochester too is seen emotionally torn and conflicted about his also socially inappropriate desire for his governess.

Thus, by 1997 in the wake of the feminist cultural intervention, it was possible for BBC and A & E to construct a *Jane Eyre* version less about patriarchal domination, Gothic fantasies and oedipal traumas than about a man and a woman caught in impossible social constraints and social codes that prevented their love from expression. In this context, their coming together finally at the end, after their diverse tragic experiences, seems quite plausible and no longer much of a capitulation by Jane to patriarchy.

2. Impact of Postcolonial Studies on Readings of Victorian Fiction:

In any reading of *Jane Eyre* in the late 1990s, in the wake of pioneering work by Edward Said and many others, I would want to question (as Victorian scholars are doing) what assumptions about class and race remain unquestioned in *Jane Eyre,* even as Brontë struggles to draw attention to Victorian gender constraints as they hampered female possibilities. What obvious assumptions about the exploitation of peoples within the British Empire—at its height as Brontë writes—enter into the novel and into Jane's consciousness? What class biases does Jane herself carry as cultural baggage? Note the quotation we inserted in our essay, where Jane talks about the working classes as a different caste! Brontë could not see outside the prevailing race and class biases in her mid-nineteenth-century British culture, although, out of her personal experience, she was beginning to understand female oppressions. Her heroines, too, are limited by what Brontë could, and could not, see.

Unfortunately, the 1997 television version still did not develop the implicit issues about class, race and the British Empire that I would love to see a version of this novel address at some point. Perhaps one is in the making as I write. . . . Certainly, as noted, the critical and theoretical apparatus is now available for such a *Jane Eyre.*

Interesting in the context of both sets of 1990s questions examined so far is a recent classroom experience I had with *Jane Eyre*. This was during a visit to a session of the novel being taught by a Comparative Literature graduate student from Taiwan. The young instructor was deeply engaged in a close reading of Brontë's novel with multicultural Stony Brook students. The cross-cultural implications of all this lie beyond my task here, but I should note the interesting questions the context raised about what this very British, very Victorian novel can mean for students coming from different ethnic and cultural backgrounds.

Perhaps precisely because of the cultural gap she sensed between students in the class (white students included, of course) and Brontë's particular historical, cultural, class and racial context, the instructor used class time to focus on helping students understand Jane's changing emotional states, the motivations for her actions, and the motivations for those acting upon her. It seemed that specifically feminist approaches no longer needed foregrounding, or perhaps they are now simply assumed.

I hope our piece will at least reinsert those perspectives self-consciously into discussions, if only to debate their ongoing relevance. Can we say that American culture is no longer largely patriarchal in its basic assumptions about gender, even if more attention is being paid to the oppressions of specific men and women? But I would also hope that the whole political and social context of nineteenth-century British culture, deeply influenced by Britain's still huge Empire, would be addressed.

3. Why the Victorian Novel Now?

Why *now* are scholars and the media returning to *Jane Eyre?* Of course, this last question also goes for many other 18th-century, Victorian, and early 20th-century British novels avidly being turned into films, including novels by Jane Austen, Henry James, and recently Virginia Woolf's *Mrs. Dalloway*. I cannot answer this question properly in this short note, but perhaps scholarly interest is less surprising than the media focus on these texts. Scholars continue research on canonical works, and as long as the canon continues to be taught in high schools and colleges, there will be a need for pedagogical tools like this volume. As cultures change, so new perspectives are continually needed to illuminate canonical works.

But what about the media, whose pulse is always on public consciousness? I suspect the haste to make the great realist novel into film and television versions has to do with a cultural anxiety about the continuity of both genres—realist fiction and illusionist film—in an era of rapidly developing digital technologies, such as websites, internet, virtual reality and CD-ROM technologies. All these raise questions about the future of film and canonical fiction.

A second linked reason may be worries about the loss of humanistic values in our postmodern, highly technological era—values embedded in much of the fiction being made into film. Presumably a volume such as this one will permit Brontë's *Jane Eyre* to gain new life in the classroom, and this is certainly a good idea. Hopefully, critical approaches will be situated in their specific historical, national and racial contexts; and hopefully, our own post-feminist historical moment, along with awarenesses newly brought to consciousness by Postcolonial and Media Studies, will find their way into discussions of *Jane Eyre*.

Notes

1. For a favorable contemporary review see G. H. Lewes, "The Reality of Jane Eyre," *Fraser's Magazine,* Dec. 1847: 690-93; the most famous hostile review is Elizabeth Rigby, *Quarterly Review* 84 (Dec. 1848): 162-76.

2. See Adrienne Rich, "*Jane Eyre:* The Temptations of a Motherless Woman," *Ms.* 2.4 (Oct. 1973): 69-73; Helene Moglen, *Charlotte Brontë: The Self Conceived* (New York: Norton, 1976); Sandra Gilbert, "Plain Jane's Progress," *Signs* 2.4 (Summer 1977): 770-804.

3. Elizabeth Gaskell, *The Life of Charlotte Brontë* (London: Dent, 1960) 215-16.

8

UNCLE TOM AND AMERICAN POPULAR CULTURE:
ADAPTING STOWE'S NOVEL TO FILM

Barbara Tepa Lupack

"So this is the little lady who made this big war," Abraham Lincoln reportedly remarked upon meeting Harriet Beecher Stowe. While *Uncle Tom's Cabin* did not cause the Civil War, Stowe's classic novel certainly flamed the embers and ignited passions on both sides of the conflict. Even today, almost one hundred and fifty years after its publication, it remains among the most painful yet powerful portraits of a vital period in Southern—and, indeed, in American—history.

Uncle Tom's Cabin appeared first as a series of installments (from June 5, 1851, through April 1, 1852) in the *National Era,* a small abolitionist journal published in Washington, D.C., and edited by Stowe's acquaintance, Dr. Gamaliel Bailey. There it found a limited but very receptive audience. At the instigation of his wife and against his own better judgment, publisher John P. Jewett, of Jewett and Company of Boston, soon acquired the rights to the book and issued it as a two-volume set, bound in cloth at one dollar fifty per set, in paper at one dollar, and in "cloth full gilt" at two dollars (Rugoff 322). Released on March 20, 1852, the first edition of five thousand copies sold out in two days, an especially remarkable achievement since no advance review copies had been sent out. Sales of 50,000 sets followed in the next eight weeks; within the first year, sales in America soared to more than three hundred thousand, and in England and its colonies, where there were no copyright prohibitions, a million and a half copies were in print.

By every measure, the book—whose critical acclaim equaled its popular appeal—was a success. Stowe's admirers included such distinguished contemporaries as William Dean Howells, who recorded in his personal reminiscences that *Uncle Tom's Cabin,* drawing on "all the inspirations and traditions of New England," is "almost the greatest work of imagination that we have produced in prose" (Andrews 8); James Russell Lowell, who remarked on the novel's "genius"; and Henry Wadsworth Longfellow, who congratulated Mrs. Stowe on a great moral as well as literary triumph. (In his diary, Longfellow noted almost ruefully: "At one step she has reached the top of the staircase up which the rest of us climb on our knees year after year" [Rugoff 326].) Henry James referred to Stowe's novel as "that triumphant work"—triumphant specifically in that it had reached readers of all classes (*UTC* Afterword 482). George Sand, who observed that "In matters of art there is but one rule, to paint and to move," wondered "where shall we find conditions more complete, types more vivid, situations more touching, more original, than in *Uncle Tom?*" Ill in Paris, Heine said it led him back to the Bible and to faith; and Tolstoy ranked *Uncle Tom's Cabin* with *Les Misérables* and *A Tale of Two Cities* as high moral art (Rugoff 326-27).

No simple tale of by-gone Southern life, the novel consisted of parallel plots, one a plot of compliance, the other of defiance. In the first, Uncle Tom, the black retainer faithful not only to God but also to his master and his fellow slaves, is forced from his pleasant home on the Shelby plantation in "Kentuck" as payment for his irresponsible master's debt. Shipped down river to New Orleans with other slaves, he saves a young girl, Little Eva, from drowning, and is purchased by her grateful father, the kindly Augustine St. Clare. After several years of devoted service, Tom is offered manumission; but before realizing his promise to Tom, St. Clare is killed and his property, including his slaves, sold off. Taken to a slave auction, Tom is purchased by the wicked and vicious Simon Legree, on whose Red River plantation he suffers many abuses before finally being beaten to death.

The second plot also involves a journey. Unlike Tom's devastating and ultimately doomed journey south, however, a journey that takes him away from his beloved wife and children, this one is a journey north, to freedom and to reunion of the young family threatened by evil masters and greedy slave brokers. Mulatto George Harris, an accomplished mechanic, has been forced out of his factory job and into the most menial labor by his cruel and jealous owner, who punishes him severely for imagined transgressions. Realizing that his owner's wrath can lead only to his own death, George escapes. Meanwhile, George's wife Eliza flees the Shelby plantation after overhearing her master's plan to sell her young son as well as old Uncle Tom to Haley, a slave trader. Aided by numerous people—including a former slave owner; Senator Bird, a supporter of the Fugitive Slave Act, whose heart is softened by the recent loss of his own son Henry; and numerous Quakers, whose principles of religious tolerance and openmindedness allow them to provide assistance not only to the escaping slaves but also to less savoury types like the wounded slave catcher Tom Loker—Eliza, George, and Harry eventually make their way to Canada. And, at the novel's end, after George is reunited with his long-lost sister, he and his family travel to France, where George receives the education that he has long sought, and ultimately to Liberia, where they undertake a new struggle for freedom.

Tom and George, in many ways, are diametrical opposites. Tom is loyal, even to Legree, and harbors no resentment toward his white masters for separating him from his family or for abusing him; intensely and enthusiastically religious, he accepts his lot, drawing others to him because of his innocence. A pacifist, Tom refuses to harm anyone; when Legree, for instance, insists that he flog Emmeline, Tom refuses and consequently incurs a terrible beating himself (Andrews 73). George, on the other hand, is hot-headed and independent. Atheistic, he believes in nothing but himself. No pacifist, he plots his escape from his master; and when that escape is threatened, he grabs a gun and wounds one of his pursuers and frightens the others away. Even after achieving his dream of an education, he chooses to fight for freedom again, this time in Africa.

The saintly martyr Uncle Tom and the openly rebellious, obviously intelligent slave George are part of the new spectrum of fully human and sympathetic black characters that Stowe introduced into her portrait of mid-nineteenth century life. Stowe, to be sure, drew on existing types— the earth mother (Aunt Chloe), the pet or entertainer (little Harry), the clown and prankster (Sam, who misled Haley at the Shelbys in order to give Eliza time to escape), and the dandy (Adolph, the St. Clare valet, who was elegant, arrogant, and presumptuous to his master but correct in his duty) (Andrews 74). But Stowe imbued even her familiar character types with vitality and dignity, and she created minor characters every bit as memorable as her major ones. The lively Topsy, for example, is just as engaging as the pious and sanctimonious Little Eva. And the doomed slave Prue, who drinks to forget her sorrows and who is beaten and left to die in a fly-infested cellar, is as tragic a figure as Tom—perhaps even more so, since her death lacks the redemptive, reaffirming aspect of his.

Stowe's innovative portrayals are not limited to the novel's black characters; her depictions of the novel's slave owners, in fact, are often as complex, as contradictory, and ultimately as balanced as those of the slaves themselves. Arthur Shelby, Tom's first master, for instance, is a genial Southerner who values his slave's constancy but whose improvidence nonetheless forces Tom's sale and Eliza's flight. Although at first Shelby tries to avoid confronting Tom, he manages to overcome his moral cowardice and even to recognize his responsibility to honor his family's commitment to buy back Tom and return him to Kentucky. Just as Arthur Shelby initially rationalizes the sale of Tom as essential to the survival of the other slaves in his possession, his wife Emily rationalizes their slave-holding by her suggestions that she is actually providing for the blacks' education and welfare. Nevertheless, her affection for Tom, Chloe, and Eliza is sincere, and it is at her instigation that the slave trader Haley is hampered in his pursuit of Eliza and her son. Even the brutality of Simon Legree (who, significantly, is not a native Southerner but rather a transplanted Northerner) is mitigated somewhat by the guilt and loneliness that shaped his early life and by his awareness of the cruelties that he has inflicted on others.

The redemptive power of faith and love, from Tom's overtly messianic sacrifice to more subtle conversions like St. Clare's, is in fact the underlying theme of Stowe's novel. Yet, as Hannah Page Wheeler Andrews has demonstrated, not all readers found such changes and metamorphoses in Stowe's characters to be credible. Nineteenth-century Southern critics argued that Stowe's portraits, while instinctively correct about human nature, were extremely inaccurate about factual details of life, language, and behavior (e.g., the ineffectuality of the Shelbys or the self-involvement of Marie St. Clare). Stowe's Tom and George Harris, they added, were really monstrous exaggerations or idealized simplifications of reality. Twentieth-century critics, on the other hand, seemed less preoccupied with external details but more concerned about the artistic internal consistency of the characters. For them, the abrupt abandonment of long-held principles and sudden shifts of philosophy or in behavior due to love or religious repentance—Topsy's instant moral correctness upon hearing Eva's declaration of affection for her, Miss Ophelia's sudden embrace of her ward, Cassy's relinquishing of her hatred for Legree, Augustine St. Clare's turning from agnosticism and despair to an awareness of God's love—were utterly unrealistic. For them, Stowe's compromising of the subtle complexity of her vision by making it conform to familiar and comforting myth, especially in her arbitrary announcements of resolutions and happy ending, violated the integrity and complexity of her characters (Andrews 100-02). Yet even the novel's critics conceded its strengths.

Stowe's original purpose in writing *Uncle Tom's Cabin* had been to protest the September 1850 passage of the Fugitive Slave Act, which enforced the return of escaped slaves to their owners. Harriet—as the daughter of the distinguished Calvinist preacher Reverend Lyman Beecher, as an assistant at her sister Catharine's school for young women, and as the wife of Professor Calvin Stowe—could appreciate the implications of that act in a more deeply personal way than many others could. She had witnessed race riots, endured the cries of runaway slaves being returned to their masters, and heard the stories of sympathetic Northerners who worked as part of the Underground Railroad. After sister-in-law Isabella had poured out to Harriet her anger at the Southern slave-hunters—"Hattie," wrote Isabella, "if I could use a pen as you *can,* I would write something that will make this whole nation feel what an accursed thing slavery is" (Rugoff 319)—Harriet apparently did precisely that. During a Communion Sunday in February of 1851, Stowe had a vision during which she conceived the image of a brutish white master and two equally brutal black slaves flogging an old white-haired slave who betrays neither his fellows nor his faith in Christ and who even prays for his murderers as he dies (Rugoff 320)—the essence of the tale of *Uncle Tom's Cabin.* Over the next weeks and months, Stowe added to that central image details from her imagination as well as from her own experiences, including her assistance to the young black servant Eliza Buck (fictionalized as Eliza Harris), who worked for the Beechers in 1837 and who—with the help of Harriet's brother Henry Ward, husband Calvin Stowe, and Quaker neighbor John Van Zandt—escaped the master who had come north to reclaim her.

A tale so humbly conceived and sentimentally told could scarcely have been expected to grip the popular imagination. Even the publisher John P. Jewett expressed reservations about printing a novel that might alienate the Southern audience; in fact, he asked Stowe to bear half of the initial publishing costs, in turn offering her half the profits. (The Stowes, unable to assume such financial risk, settled for the standard author's royalty of 10 percent and thereby lost a fortune.) But grip the popular imagination *Uncle Tom's Cabin* did. Even before the final serial installment of the novel appeared in the *National Era*—and well before the novel was published in book form—dramatizations of *Uncle Tom's Cabin* were already being mounted and performed.

The first known theatrical adaptation, notes Harry Birdoff in his comprehensive study *The World's Greatest Hit: Uncle Tom's Cabin,* was written by a Southern playwright, identified only as Professor Hewett. Based on the early serial installments of *Uncle Tom's Cabin* from *National Era* and called *Uncle Tom's Cabin as It Is, or the Southern Uncle Tom!,* the play premiered in Baltimore on January 5, 1852, and was staged again briefly in Richmond, Virginia. Another theatrical version quickly followed. Written by actor and playwright Charles Western Taylor, it opened in August, 1852, in New York. But that version proved just as incomplete as Hewett's: it included only two of Stowe's original characters, eliminated entirely Tom's martyrdom, and had a happy ending. Neither version was a hit, critically or financially.

The next month, a short play, *Uncle Tom's Cabin, or Life Among the Lowly,* written by another actor, George L. Aiken, opened to much greater success. It too, however, was far from complete in adapting Stowe's tale: intended as a vehicle for the four-year-old daughter of Aiken's cousin George C. Howard, the owner of a theater in Troy, New York, the play ended with the death of Little Eva, a scene powerfully portrayed by Cordelia Howard. Aiken's play was certainly a family affair: Howard himself played St. Clair [*sic*], and Mrs. Howard was Topsy. Interest in the story proved so high and audience reaction so favorable that Aiken was prompted to write *The Death of Uncle Tom, or the Religion of the Lowly*, a sequel that covered the events between the death of Little Eva and the death of Uncle Tom. That second short play was performed independently for only one month (from October 26 until November 15, 1852). It was then paired with the original play and staged as a full six-act piece,[1] with remarkable results: the combined version, now called simply *Uncle Tom's Cabin*, ran for 100 nights and was viewed by 25,000 people, a performance record both for Troy (then a city of 30,000) and for any American production up to that time (Birdoff 54). From Troy, George Howard moved the production to New York, where it proved just as popular. The cast was forced to perform as many as twelve to eighteen shows per week in order to keep up with demand, and they even took their meals in the theater.

In light of the success of the Aiken adaptation of *Uncle Tom's Cabin* during its New York run, other New York theaters began producing dramatic versions. Not surprisingly, one of the most lucrative and spectacular was a production mounted by the great American showman Phineas T. Barnum and scripted by Henry J. Conway. As all of the earlier versions had, Conway downplayed much of Stowe's story and softened what he considered "the [novel's] many crude points"; Birdoff notes that "Topsy was a pointless caricature, . . . and the dramatist omitted the final tragedy, and added a happy ending, with Uncle Tom rescued by George Shelby from Legree" (86).[2] In fact, when Stowe later saw the Conway adaptation in Hartford, she sat "profoundly surprised," was "taken aback" by the strong language of a new character named Penetrate Partyside, and eventually "left the theatre in disgust," complaining to her neighbor and theater companion Charles Dudley Warner that "she couldn't follow the plot at all" (Birdoff 87).

Among Howard's and Barnum's rivals was an adaptation staged at the Bowery Theatre beginning in January, 1854. That production, which departed from its competitors only in its introduction of a Yankee and a horse, did offer one innovation: the casting of renowned black actor "Daddy" T. D. Rice, "the father of Ethiopian minstrelsy . . . [and] *the* pioneer" of black actors in the role of Uncle Tom (Birdoff 102). Rice's Uncle Tom proved to be a real draw. Not to be outdone, Captain Purdy, the owner of Captain Purdy's National Theater, countered with festive black musicians, singers, and dancers (and, occasionally, even fireworks), an audience attraction that other theaters quickly imitated and a gimmick that anticipated the musical Tom Jubilees of the 1870s and 1880s.

The popularity of *Uncle Tom's Cabin* in New York led to productions in other large cities. Several competing versions of the drama were soon being performed in Philadelphia; other productions followed—in Boston, in Baltimore, in Saint Louis, in Chicago—until, as Birdoff observes, *Uncle Tom's Cabin* had become a virtual institution. Throughout "the continent, a foundation was being laid which all the masons in the world could not dislodge" (121). One measure of the degree to which Stowe's story had permeated the American popular culture was the frequency with which *Uncle Tom's Cabin* was lampooned or parodied. "The Bowery Theatre boasted an *Uncle Crochet's Parlour,* and minstrelsy was responsible for such burlettas as *Uncle Dad's Cabin, Happy Uncle Tom, Uncle Tom and His Cabin,* and *Aunt Dinah's Cabin.*" H. Plunkett's *Black and White, or Abroad and at Home,* performed at Burton's Theatre in New York toward the close of 1853, set its scene in England and contrasted "English miseries with the so-popular Southern variety." *Uncle Tom in England: A Proof that Black's White; a* [sic] *echo to the American "Uncle Tom"* was another "flubdub," purportedly the dying confession of Emmeline whose ultimate fate, according to the playwright, should have been left to the readers' imagination. There were even ethnic take-offs, such as the Irish *Uncle Pat's Cabin* and *Uncle Mike's Cabin* (Birdoff 121-22).

The tremendous audience interest in *Uncle Tom's Cabin* had other repercussions. One of the most significant was the legitimizing, in America, of "the Negro" as serious stage material and not just as the subject of travesty. (Black roles, however, for the most part, continued to be played by white actors in burnt-cork make-up, a tradition observed even in the early cinematic adaptations of *Uncle Tom's Cabin.*)

Another interesting development was the internationalizing of Uncle Tom. In England, the "Tomitudes"—the name Brits gave to the *Uncle Tom's Cabin* craze in their country—led to the marketing of numerous Tom products, including such improbable items as "Uncle Tom's pure unadulterated coffee," "Uncle Tom's china," "Uncle Tom's new and secondhand clothing," and "Uncle Tom's shrinkable woolen stockings." British productions of Uncle Tom's story proliferated: the Standard Theatre featured *The Slave's Life in America;* the Olympic, *Negro Life in America;* the Vic, *The Fugitive Slave;* still another playhouse, *Life among the Lowly.* Other productions followed: *Uncle Tom,* at Astley's Royal Amphitheatre, integrated equestrian feats into the play[3] (a novelty soon imitated by the Royal Pavilion Circus and by the City of London Theatre, which provided Topsy with a trick donkey named Tom Tit), while *Eliza and the Fugitive Slaves; or, Uncle Tom's Cabin,* at Francon's Cirque, introduced even more spectacle. The familiar and usually plotless British Christmas pantomimes took on the Uncle Tom theme: Drury Lane's opening feature during Christmas of 1852 was E. Fitzball's *Uncle Tom's Cabin; or, the Horrors of Slavery;* the Pavilion Theatre brought out Frederick Neale's grand pantomime, *Uncle Tom and Lucy Neal; or Harlequin Liberty and Slavery;* and both the Standard Theatre and Sadler's Wells offered their own Tom versions. In fact, as Birdoff notes, "Hardly a playhouse in the United Kingdom did not, at some time or another, succumb to a dramatization of the popular story" (Birdoff 144, 147-49, 157). Not surprisingly, in 1853, when Harriet Beecher Stowe made her visit to England, she was mobbed by crowds, who hailed her as the "deliverer of the American Negro."

Uncle Tom's Cabin's popularity was not limited to England; it actually swept the continent. Paris went mad for the story: Parisian playwrights adapted it, albeit often liberally (one version even featured Niagara Falls as a backdrop),[4] while French shops and restaurants reinterpreted their usual fare *à l'Oncle Tom.* Uncle Tom was soon a familiar figure in more than twenty languages, from Danish and Finnish to Bohemian and Polish, from Spanish and Swedish to Greek and Wallachian. "The exotic tale of negro life," writes Glenn Hughes, "was of course a factor in the play's foreign popularity, but probably an even greater factor was the human sympathy which it aroused—a universal feeling for the downtrodden and abused" (303). Harry Birdoff summed it up even more succinctly: "The simple tale stung the world's conscience" (182).

Ironically, although *Uncle Tom's Cabin* became the longest running play in theatrical history, Stowe herself realized no profits from any of the adaptations. Only when a road show brought the play to Hartford did she even receive a free box in the theater. Perhaps because of the positions that her preacher father and husband had taken against the theater, Stowe initially had reservations about adapting her work to that medium. In 1852, when Asa Hutchinson, a "temperance singer" with whom Stowe had a slight acquaintance, approached her to request permission to adapt her novel for the stage, she demurred. His adaptation, she admitted, would in all likelihood be harmless, but it would set a bad precedent: "If the barrier which now keeps young people of Christian families from theatrical entertainments is once broken down by the introduction of respectable and moral plays, they will then be open to all the temptations of those who are not such" (Gossett 261). According to Hannah Page

Wheeler Andrews, Stowe considered the stage too immoral a place for her public and felt that her story of slavery should not be used to legitimize it (106).

Curious about the way various dramatists brought her characters to life, Stowe eventually overcame her reluctance. (In fact, she even attempted her own dramatization of a portion of *Uncle Tom's Cabin,* called *The Christian Slave.*[5]) While Stowe did not record any impressions of her first attendance at a theater, a performance of the Howards' version of *Uncle Tom's Cabin* at the National Theatre in Boston in 1854, her companion Francis R. Underwood, founder and managing editor of the *Atlantic Monthly,* recalls: "It must have been for her a thrilling experience to see her thoughts bodied upon the stage, at a time when any dramatic representation must have been to her so vivid. Drawn along by the threads of her own romance, and inexperienced in the deceptions of the theatre, she could not have been keenly sensible of the faults of the piece or the shortcomings of the actors" (Birdoff 191). Stowe's expression—according to Underwood—was "eloquent," with "smiles and tears succeeding each other through the whole"; and she seemed especially moved by the powerful performance of Mrs. Howard as Topsy.

Meanwhile, a phenomenon even more exciting and uniquely American than the legitimate theatrical adaptations of *Uncle Tom's Cabin* was occurring. In the years after the publication of Stowe's novel, as American theater developed, its growth influenced by various factors (e.g., the extension of the railroad throughout the West, the tremendous growth in population, and the application of American big-business methods to all forms of public entertainment [Hughes 228]), stock companies formed to take the various versions of the *Uncle Tom's Cabin* plays on the road. At first, these companies toured in the summers and returned to their permanent homes for the off-season. By the 1860s, however, the companies became largely itinerant. Known as "Tommers," "Tomming troupes," "Tom shows," or simply "UTCs," the traveling shows varied widely in the size of their casts (from several hundred to family groups of five), in the quality of their costumes and scenery, and in the level of their authenticity and credibility (Andrews 113-14). "Mammoth" shows traveled in specially-built railway cars and carried scores of people involved in the production; little shows transported all of their equipment on a few wagons and staged their plays in tents that they brought along with them. Some companies were so poor that their members would walk from one town to another, perform their plays in town halls or barns, and offer "comps" (complimentary tickets) to the local people who gave them hog fat for footlight torches or who lent them furniture or other articles to be used as stage props (Birdoff 214, Gossett 368).

The shows soon became the major forms of entertainment in many of the towns that they visited; their arrival was often announced by hand-bills, colorful posters, and even advance musical performances by the show's major actors. Soda fountains hung up signs, advising the locals to "Try our Topsy Tipple or our Uncle Tom specials" and to "Taste the Little Eva Sundae." Songs like "The Ghost of Uncle Tom" became popular hits; even Stowe's own publisher issued "Little Eva; Uncle Tom's Guardian Angel," with words by John Greenleaf Whittier and music by Manuel Emilio (Birdoff 4, 79).

As the number of Tom shows increased, the rivalry between companies grew more intense and led to increasingly extravagant spectacles and self-promotions. Tom Jubilees, which featured black dancers and musicians playing "genuine plantation music" on homemade fiddles, sheepskin banjos, and tin horns, became a requisite part of the performances in the mid-1870s. Audiences, enthralled by this authentic touch of Southern history, created a kind of jubilee furor, to which the more established Tommers responded by engaging groups like the Centennialities, "thirty colored ladies and gentlemen from Fisk University," and "Sawyer's Original Jubilee Singers, one hundred colored folks." To meet the growing demand for "'Jubilee Singers' of Negro extraction," one New York newspaper advertised the immediate need for "100 octoroons, 100 quadroons, 100 mulattoes, and 100 decidedly black men, women, and children capable of singing slave choruses" (Birdoff 227, 228-29). The success of the jubilees—along with the popular but more low-cultural minstrel and burlesque shows[6]—not only established a place for Uncle Tom in American musical culture but also helped to take the Tom plays in yet another new direction: the Tom operas of the 1880s.[7]

Though black singers and dancers remained a popular part of the show's tradition, the jubilee craze soon gave way to other extravaganzas. During the 1880s, for example, when Tomming was already rooted deeply in American culture, the Jay Rial Ideal Company enhanced the shows' circus parade tradition by adding animals to the productions: hunting dogs barked ferociously as Eliza fled with her child, and Lawyer Marks and other slave catchers rode in on the backs of horses and donkeys. A few years later, the Ed Davis company expanded on the circus aspect by featuring a four-block-long parade prior to the show itself consisting of wagons, bands, horses, dogs, and cakewalkers. But even this spectacle was surpassed by the Al W. Martin shows, whose motto was "Too Big for Imitators—Too Strong for Rivalry!" and whose parade included a "Lady Zouave Drum and Bugle Corps, 18 Real Georgia Plantations Shouters, Mlle. Minerva's New Orleans Creole Girls' Fife and Drum Corps, the 'Original Whang-doodle Pickaninny Band,' Eva's

$1500 gold chariot, a log cabin, floats, phaetons, carts, ornate banners, dazzling harnesses and uniforms, 3 full concert bands, the drum major an 8-foot colored boy, 10 Cuban and Russian ferocious, man-eating hounds, 25 ponies, donkeys, oxen, mules, horses, and burros, all trained as entertaining tricksters" and all carried in three "70-foot magnificently equipped palace" railway cars, including a special diner (Hughes 301). Unsurprisingly, such elaborate Tom productions not only resembled but also outrivaled the circus.

Even the size and number of the dogs used in the Tom shows became a matter of competition among the companies. Instead of harmless bloodhounds chasing Eliza across the ice floes, there began to appear more unusual and exotic breeds: Great Danes, English mastiffs, and Russian wolfhounds.[8] The Wellesley & Sterling troupe proudly listed their dogs' special attributes directly on the playbill below the cast list: "The wonderful dogs, Sultan, Caesar and Monarch, for which Buffalo Bill makes a standing offer of $5000., or $3000. for Sultan alone, take part in the play. To see these wonderful dogs is worth the price of admission" (Birdoff 298). For additional authenticity, managers resorted to rubbing their Elizas and other characters with the essence of fox, a trick that occasionally backfired when the canine performers knocked their human counterparts to the ground or took their chase into the orchestra pit, where they frightened away portions of the audience. The dog mania also led to even more unsavoury behaviors, such as the stealing or poisoning of prize dogs.

Although the Tommers were often disdained by legitimate actors and considered a tradition apart from the mainstream of American theater, they not only survived as an institution and made money but also provided the early training ground for many actors who later became major figures in American theater and even early American cinema, including David Belasco, Otis Skinner, Pearl White, Harry Carey, Belle Bennett, Mary Pickford, Lillian Gish, and Spencer Tracy (Birdoff 402-03). After all, successful Tommers (some of whom spent their entire careers on the Tomming circuit, moving from one part to another in the shows—little Evas, for instance, growing into plantation mistresses) had to be flexible: they needed to possess various skills, from improvisation to adaptability in adjusting to changing performance conditions, scripts, and casts; and they had to be prepared to perform in places ranging from elegant opera houses to tents, wagons, even open fields. Other Tommers had to accommodate themselves to different types of gimmickery, such as "doubling," which became popular in the 1880s. Tom show performers were already used to doubling up on responsibilities within their own troupes: actors, for example, would often assume the role not just of other actors but also of other members in the company (e.g., singers, dancers, ticket takers, even animal handlers) (Birdoff 309, Andrews 115-16). But a very special kind of doubling arose from the merging of the circuses of P. T. Barnum and J. A. Bailey in 1881. The resultant advertising of "two circuses for the price of one" or "everything double but the price" encouraged Tom show managers to attempt a similar stunt. One enterprising Tommer immediately began advertising two Topsys and two Markses; other companies added twin Elizas, Simon Legrees, and Uncle Toms; and soon "doubles" were being performed throughout the country. As Hughes writes, "One Topsy accompanied with banjo the other's song and dance, amicably dividing the lines . . . ," there was "a duplex whipping by bloodthirsty Simon Legrees," and "the firm of Marks & Marks, Lawyers, found one of them devoted to pantomime as his partner did the talking." Probably nothing more fantastic than this simultaneous double-casting is to be found in theatrical history. But it drew crowds, and it provided at least some justification for the use of such grandiloquent names as "Smith's Double Mammoth Uncle Tom's Cabin's Company" (302). Since the average Tom show manager owned more than one road company, he could "double" his troupe with ease, a move that often resulted in the immediate crushing of smaller rival performers. "The typical Yankee fetish for bigness" (311), as Birdoff notes, led to other short-lived stunts, such as the "tripling" and "quadrupling" of Topsys, Markses, and Toms, but such experiments, no doubt because of the logistical complications, never enjoyed the success of the double shows, or "Double Mammoths."

All of the Tom shows, however, as Hannah Page Wheeler Andrews observed, had certain key elements in common. They

were a staple, and in many instances, the only staple of American theater for their patrons outside the metropolitan centers during the second half of the 19th century. Their theatrically unsophisticated audience thrilled to the parade, the animals, and the poignant speeches. The patrons, young and old alike, literate and illiterate, never seemed to tire of the pathos or be bored by the sometimes crude and tawdry theatrical trappings. (116)

Moreover, as a play created out of a national dilemma, *Uncle Tom's Cabin* was also "colored by the sentiments of time, moulded and remoulded through years of use, handed down from one troupe to another as actors intermingled until it became truly an American folk classic—perhaps the only one we have" (Slout 140). And indeed, as a folk play very much in the oral tradition, in its various versions *Uncle Tom's Cabin*—according to Birdoff—never much resembled "Mrs.

Stowe's novel, but [was as] native as a patchwork quilt. . . . Some characters were built up into flesh and blood and sinew, others cut down to the grim essentials, or jettisoned" (5). Like Topsy, the Tom shows "just growed"—into something uniquely a part of American popular culture.

By 1879, estimates Glenn Hughes, there were approximately fifty Tom shows on the road, and the demand for them seemed unlimited. "During the eighties the number increased with every season, and in the nineties there were between four hundred and five hundred companies in operation" (300). In the final years of the nineteenth century, as the houses that sponsored the traveling shows began to shrink, the number of shows was reduced correspondingly—although, as late as 1902, a reviewer estimated that in that year alone, one out of every thirty-five Americans would see a production of the play (Gossett 371). And even into the 1920s, more than a dozen Tomming companies remained on tour.[9] In 1931, an American magazine asserted that at last, after seventy-eight years "of continuous performance, here, there, and everywhere," the play had breathed its last in a final performance (Gossett 371, 385). Immediately readers from various parts of the country wrote in to point out that there were Tom shows playing in their towns at that very moment. And, as late as 1935, a manager of a small traveling theatrical group was quoted as saying that his company still presented the play quite often because "it invariably brought more money to the box office than any Broadway show" (Gossett 385).

While the Tom shows continued with the turn of the twentieth century, the adaptation of Stowe's novel took several other significant directions, the first of which was the stage revival of the play. Major revivals included William A. Brady's 1901 production at the Academy of Music in New York, which was so extravagant that its arrival scene at the St. Clare plantation included at least fifty to seventy-five singing and dancing black cast members as well as a barouche and team of live horses (Andrews 120). Another major revival, by the Player's Club at New York's Alvin Theater in the spring of 1933, starred former Tommer Otis Skinner, by then a well-known legitimate actor, as Uncle Tom. While Skinner's dignified and sympathetic performance garnered much favorable attention, the play, like the Brady version before it, focused little on the issues central to Stowe—the moral and social implications of slavery for blacks as well as whites.

During the latter half of the 1930s and throughout the 1940s, however, cultural attitudes toward *Uncle Tom's Cabin* as a play changed markedly among both blacks and whites. During this time, as Andrews notes, "especially the role of Uncle Tom became regarded as a limiting cultural image to upwardly mobile blacks, who felt that he represented servile submission to and compliance with white culture at the expense of his own" (121). Over the years, in fact, demonstrates Thomas F. Gossett, the various productions of the play had probably done more to hamper than to help the cause of blacks in the United States. Even in its earlier productions before the Civil War, *Uncle Tom's Cabin* had been vulgarized and carried a message substantially different from the novel's strong condemnation of slavery. The process of vulgarization became more widespread and more thorough after the war, as audiences seemed inclined to take the play's black characters less seriously. Those audiences "could abandon themselves both to the pathos of Uncle Tom's plight and to the humor of such characters as Topsy without asking themselves whether either of these things had any serious meaning" (387).

Those producers and playwrights who continued to be fascinated by the story of Uncle Tom, especially into the twentieth century, were clearly more sensitive to the play's social issues and concerns. Playscripts, such as the one by Vernon L. Slout, used by an Ohio-based company during the summers of 1933-34, and another prepared by William Bale for an academic theatrical revival in 1952, portrayed blacks more seriously and came closer to Stowe's honorable portrait of them (Andrews 123). In 1936, George Abbott staged a musical version in New York, in which he introduced a major change in the ending: rather than concluding the play, as earlier producers had, with the arrival of the Union army in the South and the freeing of the slaves, Abbott tried to emphasize what freedom had specifically meant for blacks. "There was," as Gossett notes, "a parade of modern blacks across the stage at the end of the play. Some of them had menial occupations, but others were representative of such professions as law, medicine, and teaching" (386). A ballet version of *Uncle Tom's Cabin,* with choreographic direction by e. e. cummings, followed in 1936, and was important for recognizing—and addressing—a defect in earlier versions, in which blacks were shown as if they were wholly unresentful of the wrongs committed against them. In the cummings' ballet, after Uncle Tom enters the gates of heaven, a "monstergoddess" appears and dances the "dance of avenging Africa." The attempts to combine racial politics with showmanship, however, occasionally had odd results, as in the proposed reverse-casting of Martha Raye as a white Topsy in a new version of the story (Cripps 156).

More recent theatrical attempts have included an unproduced "steamboat version" written in 1975 by Harry Birdoff, the noted authority on Tom plays; a 1975 musical version by black playwright Lionel H. Mitchell, which portrayed Tom as Stowe had—a proud heroic martyr figure who chose to die rather than betray or hurt his own people (Andrews 125-26); and *Uncle Tom's Cabin: A History,* a play adapted by Adrian Hall and Richard Cumming from the novel and from the Aiken version of the play, which attempted to portray what the play version had become in its long history of performance—drama that patronized its stereotyped black characters. (In a fantasy sequence in *Uncle Tom's Cabin: A History,* Tom departs radically from his meek role and shoots Augustine St. Clare simply because he is Little Eva's father, and Eva had wanted "to change mah skin an pull de racial kink from out mah hair. She gone to Heben talkin' mighty big 'bout wooly pates an' pigments an' designs" [Gossett 406].) And a new production, *Uncle Tom's Cabin or Life Among the Lowly,* which premiered late in 1997 in New York City, tried not to re-create the past but "to bring the past to life in present theatrical terms that embrace history, manners, morals, stereotypes, ideals, fears and aspirations." As "derived by" Floraine Kay and Randolph Curtis Rand, the show was a collage, alternately funny and genuinely moving, that included dramatized scenes from the book, bits and pieces of six different stage adaptations, critical commentaries, minstrel show versions, and excerpts from slave narratives (Canby 6). Like the new ballet, *Last Supper at Uncle Tom's Cabin/The Promised Land,* also premiering in late 1997, in which Bill T. Jones sought to "acknowledge a move beyond the apparent schisms between his African-American history, his mother's Christian faith and his 60's countercultural utopianism" (Daly 44), Kay and Rand's theatrical production demonstrates the intelligence and timelessness of Uncle Tom.

Even more significant than the dramatic adaptations of Stowe's novel—the Tom and minstrel shows as well as the legitimate plays, revivals, and new adaptations—are the cinematic ones. With the development and evolution of cinema around the turn of the twentieth century, *Uncle Tom's Cabin*—already the "world's greatest hit" theatrically—soon became a success in a new medium. It was common practice for early filmmakers to turn to well-known literary stories and novels for their story material, and in this respect Stowe's novel was a natural. Familiar to thousands who had read the book or seen it performed as a play, it was quite literally a black and white tale, in which the evil was easily delineated and the plot required little exposition to establish. But just as the many theatrical versions had, early films often distorted significant aspects of Stowe's novel and characters.

Perhaps the most important of the early Tom films, and one of the most important of all early silent films, was Edwin S. Porter's *Uncle Tom's Cabin* (Edison, 1903). Comprising a prologue and fourteen scenes or tableaux modeled after the *tableaux vivant* or living pictures popularized by French film artist Georges Méliès, it ran 1,100 feet and was both the longest and the most expensive film made up to that time. The producer vouched that "The story has been carefully studied and every scene posed in accordance with the famous author's version," and he explained his approach as "a departure from the old methods of dissolving one scene into another . . . by inserting announcements with brief descriptions" (Birdoff 396).[10] The tableaux, an episodic series of highlights that provided little plot summary, however, assumed the reader's familiarity with the story of the Christian slave Uncle Tom.

In the first tableau, "Eliza Pleads with Tom to Run Away," Eliza goes to Uncle Tom's cabin at night, during a heavy snow; Chloe calls her husband Tom to the door; and after Eliza explains that she is planning to escape, Tom shakes her hand and wishes her well in her journey. As "Phenias Outwits the Slave Traders" in the second tableau, Eliza and her child exit through the window in the very room in which the traders are gathered. "The Escape of Eliza" (tableau 3) depicts the rapidly moving ice floes on the Ohio River, on to which Eliza leaps to escape the four hounds that are pursuing her. One of the slave traders chases her on to the ice but falls into the water and is rescued by his colleagues. Eliza survives the river's hazards, and "The Reunion of Eliza and George Harris" (tableau 4) occurs at the home of friendly Quakers. The scene then shifts to the "Race Between the Rob't E. Lee and Natchez" (tableau 5), an episode never depicted in Stowe's novel, and to the "Rescue of Eva" (tableau 6), which occurs as passengers debark the winning boat. Eva slips off the Lee's platform and is saved by Uncle Tom, who is purchased on the spot by Eva's grateful father. In "The Welcome Home to St. Clair Eva Aunt Ophelia and Uncle Tom [*sic*]" (tableau 7), happy slaves await the return of their master; the centerpiece of the tableau is a very lively Topsy, who dances almost maniacally and waves a long ribbon, causing obvious consternation to Ophelia. Happy slaves appear again in "Tom and Eva in the Garden" (tableau 8), where Eva falls ill and is carried away by Tom, who joins her grieving family at the little girl's bedside as she ascends into heaven in the "Death of Eva" (tableau 9). (See Figure 23.) A distraught St. Clair, with Tom standing solemnly at his side, then drowns his sorrow at a saloon, where a slave trader strikes Tom in the face. As "St. Clair Defends Uncle Tom" (tableau 10), he is mortally wounded; the distressed slave can only raise his eyes— and arms—to heaven. At the "Auction Sale of St. Clair's Slaves" (tableau 11), young slave boys and girls dance merrily in front of the auction block as a couple of black men shoot dice and a group of black women dances and sings. After the auction begins, the evil Legree buys two new slaves: a young woman, Emaline [*sic*], whom he drags away

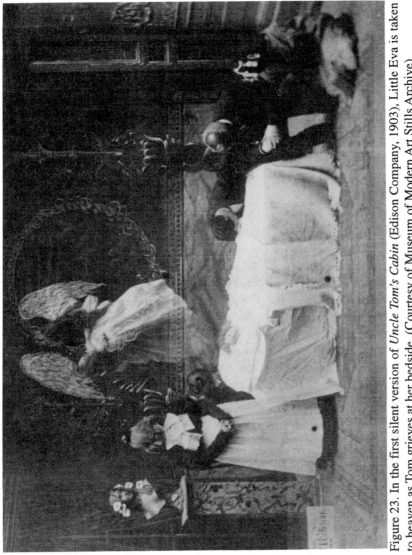

Figure 23. In the first silent version of *Uncle Tom's Cabin* (Edison Company, 1903), Little Eva is taken to heaven as Tom grieves at her bedside. (Courtesy of Museum of Modern Art Stills Archive)

roughly, and Tom. As Legree grasps his chattel firmly, both slaves fall to their knees, in servitude or prayer—or both. Once at the Legree plantation, "Tom Refuses to Flog Emaline" (tableau 12) and, after being tied to a whipping post, is severely flogged until Emaline grabs the whip and threatens to retaliate against the overseers. In the next scene, Tom is beaten again, this time by Legree himself, but "Marks Avenges Death's [*sic*] of St. Clair and Uncle Tom" by shooting the evil slaveholder on his own veranda. The film closes with "Tableau Death of Tom," in which the dying Uncle Tom has a vision that includes images of a heavenly angel, of gallows-bound abolitionist John Brown embracing a child, of the Civil War dead, of Lee and Grant shaking hands, of Lincoln the Emancipator, and of a society at peace.

Among the most significant new dimensions that this first filmed version of *Uncle Tom's Cabin* brought to motion pictures was Uncle Tom himself, the American movies' first black character. Yet, as Donald Bogle observes, ironically Porter's Tom was not black; he was "a nameless, slightly overweight white actor made up in blackface" (3). The use of whites in black roles was then a common practice, a tradition carried over from the stage and maintained throughout the early days of silent films. Nevertheless, with Porter "the first Negro character had arrived in films, and he had done so at a time when the motion-picture industry itself was virtually non-existent" (Bogle 3)—when the movies were without stars or studios or sound, when there were no great directors or writers, and when the community of Hollywood had not yet come into being.

That "first Negro character," however, was quickly metamorphosed into one of the earliest and most enduring black caricatures or stereotypes: Porter's saintly Uncle Tom became "tom," the first in a long line of "socially acceptable Good Negro[es]." As Bogle notes, although the toms are chased, harassed, hounded, flogged, enslaved, and insulted, "they keep the faith, n'er turn against their white massas, and remain hearty, submissive, stoic, generous, selfless, and oh-so-very kind. Thus they endear themselves to white audiences and emerge as heroes of sorts" (4, 6).[11] Though these types of toms appear in other early films, such as *Confederate Spy* (ca. 1910), in which dear "Uncle Daniel" is shot by a Northern firing squad but dies happy, knowing that his service as a spy was for the sake of "massa and little massa," and *For Massa's Sake* (1911), in which a devoted retainer sells himself back into slavery to aid his master, their sharpest depiction occurs in Porter's film and in the subsequent adaptations of the work from which the stereotype takes its name.

While white actors in blackface played the central characters, Porter's *Uncle Tom's Cabin* featured a number of black actors in minor roles, including a group of black performers doing a "cakewalk," a dance made popular during this period in the United States and Europe by the famous team of Bert Williams and George Walker (Sampson 122). The dancers, as Daniel J. Leab points out, were yet another early but rapidly developing stereotype of the movie black. The 1894 Edison peep-show catalogue, for example, "lists *The Pickaninnies Doing a Dance;* two other items—one in which blacks do a buck-and-wing, the other a cakewalk—are described as 'the best negro dancing subjects yet taken' and 'amusing and entertaining.' This 'dancing fool' caricature of the black," Leab concludes, found particularly strong expression in the 1903 *Uncle Tom's Cabin,* in which "one scene begins with a long cake-walk sequence that has absolutely nothing to do with the action preceding or following" (13-14).

Porter's film, moreover, reinforces this particular stereotype by the frequency of its use. Dancing slaves appear at St. Clair's estate to greet their returning master; in the next scene, they keep on dancing into the garden,[12] where the doggedly-devoted Tom attends Little Eva. Slaves also sway and dance on the shore as they await the docking of the Rob't E. Lee. And—most incongruously—there is great revelry among the blacks in the auction scene. Their gleeful gaming and dancing is interrupted only by the appearance of the auctioneer, who puts the first slave on the block and begins the auction.

These notions of the contented and adoring slave and his master, the genteel squire, were an integral part of the cinematic romance—and the cinematic artifice—of the Old South, whose mystique had crept into the national psyche. Before, people had only imagined or seen in prints or paintings the magnificent mansions and the romantic steamboats; but Porter brought a certain reality and vitality to their vision. His appealing plantation tale, full of splendor, diversion, and local color, was—to be sure—a far cry from Stowe's harrowing abolitionist account and indictment of slavery. In Porter's South, masters leap heroically to the defense of their loyal slaves; slave women (Topsy excepted) are well-coiffed and wear long white dresses as they pick cotton in the fields; children lead idyllic existences, attended by loyal family retainers; and even the lawyers act ethically. Early moviegoers, drawn to escapist entertainment rather than serious fare, enjoyed and accepted the sentiment behind such mythology—a mythology that, in fact, persisted in virtually all of the *Uncle Tom's Cabin* film versions until the mid-1960s (Campbell 12-14).

Only a few months after Porter's *Uncle Tom's Cabin,* Sigmund Lubin released his version of *Uncle Tom's Cabin* (1903). As Porter and the Edison Company had, the Lubin Company presented an elaborate panorama comprised "of a grand estate graced by comfortable Negroes, singing and dancing," that attempted more to glorify than to examine critically the Old South. In a publicity booklet, Uncle Tom's attractive abode was labeled "a typical Southern log cabin," and the tale of his trials was called "one of the prettiest stories ever written" (Campbell 39-40). The booklet itself was adorned with a picture of Abraham Lincoln as a way of generating a sense of national pride in a film with decidedly regional leanings.

While neither the Edison nor the Lubin release was intended to hold up the South as a model society, in effect that was the result. As long as traditional antebellum legend and contemporary black stereotyping complemented one another and remained acceptable and profitable, the South continued to be portrayed as a graceful agrarian society, which knew best how to control blacks and to make them contented with their situation. In fact, as Edward D. C. Campbell, Jr. observed, "the movies eventually placed the burden of secession and war not on the Southern system, but on the few who abused it, such as Legree and other radicals" (40).

In 1910, the ever popular *Uncle Tom's Cabin* was remade again, by two different companies: Thanhouser and Vitagraph (1910; dir. J. Stuart Blackton). Donald Bogle writes that these remakes "had little in style or treatment to distinguish them" (6). Harry Birdoff, however, noted some interesting differences between them. The Vitagraph version, advertised by the Vitagraph Company as "The Most Magnificent, Sumptuous and Realistic Production Ever Attempted of *Uncle Tom's Cabin,*" promised "the real thing in every respect—real ice, real bloodhounds, real Negroes, real actors, real scenes from the real life as it was in the antebellum days." It was produced in three parts, of one reel each (approximately 1,000 feet to a reel), that corresponded to the Aiken play. Part One depicted Uncle Tom at the Shelby plantation, complete with the memorable crossing of the icy Ohio River by Eliza and her child; Part Two concerned Tom's rescue of Eva, his life at the St. Clare home, and Eva's death; and the final part was structured around the events at Legree's plantation, including attempts to capture the escaping Cassie and Emmeline, and the death of Uncle Tom (Slout 144-45). The movie industry at the time, however, could only release the film piecemeal, so several days elapsed before the public saw it in its entirety (Birdoff 396).

Yet, in realism as well as length, Vitagraph's film surpassed Porter's. Shot on location, it depicted characters in motion—on foot and on horseback—in the out-of-doors (Andrews 133).[13] But the film offered "little promise of avoiding the clichés of antebellum plots," according to Edward D. C. Campbell, Jr. Although the film is not extant, the promotional lobby cards "hinted at the view to come." One, for instance, shows a nude female slave leaning to kiss a child as she is about to experience that "most cruel of all the tortures of slavery—the separation of mother and child"; another portrays Uncle Tom and Aunt Chloe in their "comfortable cabin" on the Shelby estate (the caption is: "His pickaninnies live in happy ignorance of their fate"). When Tom is led away by Haley, he persuades his compatriots to "Obey the good mas'r—for obedience to Him alone is the first step to the kingdom of Heaven." And, confirming the belief that kindly whites know what is best for their slaves, Topsy is given to her new mistress Ophelia; the lobby card depicting that scene is bordered by drawings of watermelons (Campbell 41).

The Thanhouser version (extant, unlike the Vitagraph version), released at virtually the same time as Vitagraph's, was billed as "The Prize Thanhouser Classic"; and it claimed a tremendous triumph over its rival in so far as it was "Not a Tedious Drawn-Out, Continued-in-Our Next Affair, but COMPLETE IN ONE REEL" (Birdoff 397). Frank Crane starred as Uncle Tom, and child star Marie Eline, the extremely popular "Thanhouser Kid," was Little Eva. The scenes between the two were among the most poignant in the production. As a contemporary reviewer noted in *The Moving Picture World* (30 July 1910), the last act of Eva's life is to present Tom with a little locket containing her picture. "Just before he dies, he presses to his lips the locket with the picture of his beloved mistress, and in a vision sees her in the clouds, holding out her arms to him that he, too, may enter with her the pearly gates, inside of which all souls are equal, and all free."

Two other productions of *Uncle Tom's Cabin* followed in 1913.[14] Little is known about Kalem's 1913 two-part "Special," with Anna Q. Nilsson as Eliza and Hal Clemmons as Legree (whose performance one critic called "the greatest portrayal of the part that this reviewer has seen anywhere" [Slout 145-46]) and which seemed to follow closely the outline of Stowe's novel, from Eliza's flight and Tom's purchase by St. Clare to Eva's death and Uncle Tom's brutal flogging by Legree, "who drowns the humiliation of the blow in drink and dies in a delirium shortly afterward" (*The Moving Picture World* 13 Dec. 1913).[15] But the Universal-Imp (Imperial Company) release, "a four-reel, super-super-special" directed by Otis Turner, "was the most pretentious *Uncle Tom's Cabin* adaptation up to that time. Many of the scenes were taken on the Sacramento River, with the ice 'shots' at Mt. Wilson" (Birdoff 397); other interesting "shots" included George Harris and slaves hauling logs out of a swamp and the death of St. Clair in a saloon brawl. According to a review in *Variety* (5 Sept. 1913), "the playlet is a veritable scenic and costume panorama of the old ante bellum [*sic*] South . . . [with] vistas of cotton country, stretches of far Southern rivers, kinetic glimpses of old side-wheel steamboats, freighted with passengers of the period, the women in crinolines, the men in quaint frocks and sombrero shaped hats, the children in ruffled pantalettes." The humorous scenes—of Marks trying to "open his umbrella to stem the tide of bullets aimed by Harris' defenders" and "the wench [Topsy] skedaddling with the ribbon trailing behind like a flying rein"—are counterbalanced by more "realistic bits of staging," such as Tom's rescue of Eva from the turbid waters of the Red River and (in a scene original to the film) the slave branding of George Harris with the sizzling initial of his owner. Prominent players included Robert Z. Leonard (Legree),[16] Eddie Lyons (Marks), Gertrude Short (Eva), Harry Pollard (Tom), and Margarita Fischer (Topsy). (Worth mentioning here as well is a third film, also released in 1913. *An Uncle Tom's Cabin Troupe* [Biograph] was not strictly a version of Stowe's story but rather "a semi-documentary which established a film record of a stage production of the classic" [Campbell 41]—and part of the corollary tradition of Tomming films, discussed later.)

A more distinctive film version of *Uncle Tom's Cabin* was the five-reel 1914 production by the World Film Corporation. Directed by William Robert Daly and written by Edward McWade, the film again starred the rising child star Marie Eline (the "Thanhouser Kid") as Little Eva, as well as Sam Lucas, Irving Cummings, Theresa Michelena, Roy Applegate, Paul Scardon, Boots Wall, and Fern Andra. Using "good judgement in his presentation," noted the reviewer from *The Moving Picture World* (15 Aug. 1914), Mr. Daly "has chosen to follow the book rather than the stage version";[17] and he has incorporated a variety of realistic details into his film. "It is no stage ice," for instance, "on which Eliza crosses the river. The real article is present in abundance."

But the main reason that the production company could claim greater authenticity than any of the earlier movie versions was its casting of seventy-two-year old actor Sam Lucas, "described by the New York *Age* as the 'dean of the colored theatrical profession'" (Leab 13), in the title role. Lucas became the first black man to play a leading role in a movie; "thus," as Peter Noble writes, "for the first time, a film about Negroes actually used coloured actors [although, significantly, in the film Topsy and Eliza were played by whites in blackface], and thenceforth with notable exceptions like 'The Birth Of A Nation' and 'One Exciting Night' the practice of using burnt-corked whites to play Negro rôles gradually fell into disuse" (31). Lucas, considered the "Grand Old Man of the Negro Stage," lent his authority and skill to the *Uncle Tom's Cabin* production. Contemporary reviewers commented on the fact that he "is the center of interest throughout the picture" and that "his work is dignified and displays a grasp of dramatic values" (*The Moving Picture*

World). The casting of Lucas, however, was not without its perils. It seems that during the filming of the scene where Eva is rescued by Uncle Tom, a strong undertow drew both players under the stern-wheel steamer, and Little Eva, contrary to the story, had to hold up the septuagenarian until aid arrived (Birdoff 397). And, while the casting of Lucas as Uncle Tom was almost universally applauded, a subtle racism was directed against the other black actors, as is evident in the tone of at least one of the reviews, in which Daly was praised for "his fine discrimination in depicting pathos so that it never verges on bathos—and this all the more notable by reason of the fact that of necessity he was using many colored players" (*The Moving Picture World*).

Uncle Tom's Cabin was soon remade again, in 1918, this time by Famous Players-Lasky Corporation (which later became Paramount). The five-reeler, directed by J. Searle Dawley, starred Marguerite Clark, a white actress in the dual roles of Little Eva and Topsy (a trick accomplished by the use of double exposures), and Frank Losee, long identified in Tom shows with Simon Legree, as the pious Uncle Tom. The film also featured J. W. Johnston, Florence Carpenter, Phil Riley, Harry Lee, Walter Lewis, Augusta Anderson, Henry Stanford, Ruby Hoffman, Susanne Willis, Mrs. Priestly Morrison, Thomas Carnahan, Jr., Jere Austin, and John Sutherland. The production was particularly interesting for its geographic scope: it not only reproduced the "underground railroad" but also included "thrilling sequences covering many States, from Louisiana to Canada." Dawley apparently "traveled thousands of miles for the actual localities," and the company even went to Louisiana to shoot "on the original site" (Birdoff 397). Yet, while the photography was "particularly attractive, and several of the scenes were according to the generally accepted idea of what they should be" (e.g., picturesque plantation exteriors, old-fashioned paddlewheelers plying up and down the river), "there was so much left out it appeared more like a series of episodes than a running story" (*Variety* 9 August 1918).

Surprisingly, almost a decade passed before the next remake; but *Uncle Tom's Cabin* (Universal Pictures, 1927), directed by Harry A. Pollard, had some interesting connections to earlier Tom films.[18] Pollard, now a noted director, had starred as Uncle Tom in the 1913 Universal "super-super-special four-reeler"; his wife Margarita Fischer had appeared as Topsy in that production. As Birdoff writes, "Many of the scenes in the 1913 picture were taken outdoors, and Pollard could recall how they were hampered by unfavorable weather. The Eliza sequence, for instance, petered out when the ice thawed on location, and they had to resort to canvas-covered soap boxes on rockers. The sets, too, had been crude, the painted drops substituting for the St. Clair [*sic*] mansion, a cotton field, etc. The whole arrangement had been boxed-in, dominated by the influence of the stage. And for fourteen long years Pollard cherished the hope of doing the movie realistically" (398).

His opportunity came when Carl Laemmle decided to film the classic story. (See Figure 24.) The $2,000,000 budget allocated for the project broke all records. (By contrast, the 1913 film had cost only $15,000.) Technicians were dispatched to the many towns and places described in Stowe's novel; they spent eight months traveling throughout the South and researching archives and other data to ensure that even the most minute props employed in the film (e.g., the slaves' drinking cups hollowed out of gourds, the twisted papers used as tapers to light the fireplaces in the mornings) would be accurate. Later, exact replicas of buildings were erected. According to Birdoff, the St. Clair home was constructed at a cost of $70,000, the Shelby home at $62,000, and the Legree plantation, in its run-down condition, at $40,000. All were furnished with period furniture. The Shelby estate even had a "slave street," complete with parallel rows of squalid cabins, authentic down to the cobwebs and the quaint utensils inside the huts. Over one quarter of a million feet of lumber was used; more than one hundred tons of plaster went into the walls. Instead of the grass matting usually used for exteriors, 1,000 full grown trees were hauled in from the mountains of southern California, and fifty bales of Spanish moss were transported from Mississippi. "The 10,000 artificial magnolias, oleanders, and other varieties were intermingled with tens of thousands of jasmines, Spanish dagger, all the flowers native to the old South" (Birdoff 399).

Pollard and his company reportedly journeyed over 26,000 miles to find the appropriate locales. The ice sequences were filmed in Plattsburgh, New York, before the spring thaw melted the ice floes in the Saranac River; but it took four months—and over 4,000 miles—to chase the ice jams up and down the river. Even the dogs received special attention. Unhappy with the usual mastiffs or Great Danes, Pollard insisted on "real bloodhounds" and paid a record price of $20,000 for a team of registered bloodhounds from England, whose bloodlines could be traced back to slave days in Virginia (Birdoff 399). The detail was so great, in fact, that it even involved the refurbishing of a noted side-wheeler, the "Kate Adams" (rechristened "La Belle Riviere," as in the novel), which exploded and burned immediately after the filming.

For further authenticity, Pollard cast an actor true to Stowe's original as Uncle Tom—the handsome, forty-year-old black James B. Lowe. Congratulating itself on its liberalism, writes Bogle, Universal sent out press releases about "its good colored star." Lowe, asserted Universal, "has made history. A history that reflects only credit to the Negro race,

Figure 24. The movie poster from the lavish Carl Laemmle 1927 production announces all of the key players, including celebrated black actor James Lowe as Tom and Margarita Fischer, wife of director Harry Pollard, as Eliza. © Universal

not only because he has given the 'Uncle Tom' character a new slant, but because of his exemplary conduct with the Universal company. They look upon Lowe at the Universal Studio as a living black god. . . . Of the directors, critics, artists, and actors who have seen James Lowe work at the studio there are none who will not say he is the most suited of all men for the part of 'Tom.' Those who are religious say that a heavenly power brought him to Universal and all predict a most marvelous future and worldwide reputation for James B. Lowe" (6).[19]

Lowe, however, was not the first choice for the part; the talented black actor Charles Gilpin, who had created the part of Emperor Jones, was initially cast as Uncle Tom. But, according to Noble, Gilpin, an intelligent, proud and sensitive person, had many heated discussions with director Pollard about the manner in which the novel should be filmed and the beloved Negro character portrayed. Finally, "as a protest, Gilpin left the cast and returned to New York, where it is said he went back to his old job as lift-man rather than play a well-paid screen role, the treatment of which, in his opinion, helped to malign his people." Gilpin's protests apparently had some effect, even after his departure; as Edith Isaacs remarked in *Theatre Arts,* "Uncle Tom in this 1927 version seems to wear his ball and chain with a difference" (Noble 32-33).

Nineteen months after production began, Pollard's film, which ran a record-breaking 977,000 feet (twelve reels), was completed.[20] The production had employed 5,000 players and utilized sixty-five sets (as opposed to the eight or nine required for other big productions) (Birdoff 400). Yet, as much as Pollard had sought realism in the other aspects of the production, he—"spinning out three plots and a comic line" in a script that "plodded on for over two hours" (Cripps, *Slow Fade* 160)— apparently took some great liberties with the story itself. Eliza, played by his wife Margarita Fischer, got all of the close-ups in the film; thus, Uncle Tom (filmed in long shot during the first half—and infrequently at that) became a secondary character. Moreover, whereas Stowe wrote her novel in 1851-52, Pollard carried the plot to the end of the Civil War. Birdoff notes that "some of the new situations—purely cinematic— revealed a brief flash of Lincoln, and Sherman's march to the sea, with Atlanta under shell fire and in flames; then a martial finale, when the General stopped long enough in the internecine strife to rescue Eliza and Cassy from Legree's clutches; startled by the sudden appearance of the Union Army, Legree fell out the window." Given these changes, Birdoff concludes, "Pollard's epic should have been called *The Exploits of Eliza, or How Eliza Was Saved from a Fate Worse than Death by the Union Army*" (400-01). In his review in the *New York Times* (5 Nov. 1927), however, Mordaunt Hall—like other reviewers—found much to praise in the production, particularly the scenes between Topsy and Eva ("presented with unusual skill") and the realism of "the harrowing details," such as Eliza's flight across the ice or Legree's beating of his slaves. (Legree, for example, is so zealous with his whip that he bloodies himself; the viewer sees "a stream of blood running from his temple.") Even Thomas Cripps concedes that, despite a picaresque plot that winds "through years and miles too improbably with coincidence, too laden with Yankees to effectively indict the Southern 'peculiar institution'" and other cinematic faults that cutting could not redeem, "the picture spreads wide a vision of blackness that had not been seen in years. Lowe's Tom, while not abandoning the accretion of sentimentality that had crusted like barnacles over Mrs. Stowe's character, restored some of his strength"—enough, at least, to make white Southerners grumble, Yankees exult, and blacks feel that "their cause was represented as well as possible" (*Slow Fade* 160-61).[21]

According to Cripps, when Pollard and his crew took their Southern sojourn during the film's production, the *Amsterdam News* cheered: "Never before has the Southern Negro had the good fortune to be selected to take part in a clean cut motion picture." And when *Uncle Tom's Cabin* was released in 1927, "many Negroes saw it as the highest achievement of blacks in the cinema" (*Slow Fade* 159, 150). But over the years, perspectives changed; and when Pollard's *Uncle Tom's Cabin,* with a prologue by Raymond Massey and a new soundtrack, was reissued by Jules B. Weill and Carroll L. Puciato of Colorama Features, Inc., in 1958—a time when sit-ins were erupting in the South and other civil rights protests were occurring nationwide—"many wondered if by reissuing this film Universal Studios hoped to remind the restless black masses of an earlier, less turbulent period, when obeying one's master was the answer to every black man's problem" (Bogle 7).[22]

At the time of the original release of Pollard's *Uncle Tom's Cabin,* a rival picture was already in production, United Artists' *Topsy and Eva* (1927; dir. Del Lord). Considered by many film historians to be the worst of the Tom adaptations or spinoffs, it perpetuated a stereotype as demeaning and, regrettably, as enduring as that of the tom: that stereotype was of Topsy, an amusing pickaninny whose far-fetched meanderings won mass audience approval (Bogle 8). "Ignorant, thieving, superstitious, undisciplined, and given over to swearing and biting" (Zito 72),[23] Topsy—despite being "one of the most damning examples of racist portraiture in the American film"—quickly became a favorite among white viewers. Her portrayal in *Topsy and Eva* seemed to confirm what Thomas Cripps called "the insuperable obstacles Afro-Americans needed to overcome in Hollywood," where the studios remained not so much vicious as "sentimental and ignorant of black criticism" (*Slow Fade* 162-63).[24]

How then did a film as overtly racist as *Topsy and Eva* find its way to the screen? Rosetta and Vivian Duncan, the popular blonde Duncan Sisters, were "clever San Franciscans who knew nothing of the Negro world but much of the minstrel tradition from which they had fashioned their blackface sister act" (Cripps, *Slow Fade* 163). That act had grossed well over nine hundred thousand dollars a year, an extraordinary amount for the time, and had played in twenty-three major American cities over a three and a half year period (Birdoff 401). After deciding to bring their routine to the screen, they engineered a deal with First National; Blanche Merrill was engaged to write the screen story from the Catherine Chisholm Cushman play. When the original deal fell through, United Artists took over the project, but problems persisted. Lois Weber, brought in to direct, soon quit when she learned that she would not be allowed to shape a serious drama from the sisters' vaudeville act. The studio then hired Del Lord, a director for Mack Sennett's comedies and serials (and eventually for the Three Stooges). When Lord reportedly started making "a mess of it," the producers turned to a director with more experience and reputation, D. W. Griffith, who claimed he had always wanted to do a Tom show. In ten days, Griffith reshot, recut, and patched *Topsy and Eva* into "a pathetic, regressive, burlesque of his racial beliefs" that proved to be a tribute more to Tom shows than to Tom himself; in this way, according to Thomas Cripps, "Griffith's racial cant found its way into yet one more American film" (*Slow Fade* 163, 165). Even as the picture was opening, the studio still hoped to save it by bringing in Mary Pickford's cutter; nevertheless, the results were largely disastrous.

Drawing rather loosely on incidents and details from Stowe's novel, the film opens with several original miniature shots. A white stork races—and beats—the doctor to the St. Clare home to deliver the beautiful Little Eva on St. Valentine's Day. Two months later, a black stork raises havoc by flying through rain and lightning; after being turned away from the crude homes of several "colored folks," the stork simply drops Topsy into a barrel of trash. Above, in the "Colored Department" of Heaven, two black angels roll dice while another registers Topsy's birthdate, April Fool's Day.[25]

The remainder of the film follows the two girls' comic—and often intertwined—adventures. After moneylender Simon Legree forecloses on the Shelby estate, no one at the slave auction is willing to bid on Topsy, so Eva purchases her for a single nickel. Miss Ophelia undertakes Topsy's education, which, given Topsy's penchant for chewing tobacco and for mischievous acts, is no easy task. After the St. Clare cotton crop burns, Legree redeems the unpaid note by claiming all the estate's slaves, including Topsy. Hoping to stop Legree, Eva runs after his wagon but collapses in the snow.

After Topsy escapes, she is pursued by Legree and his hounds (a pack that includes an improbably affable St. Bernard) and chased up a tree. But the real comedy begins with her own madcap chase, as she flies downhill on a pair of borrowed skis, lands atop a snowshoe-wearing horse, and leaps onto a cake of ice that floats away down the river. In Keystone-Kop-fashion, Legree follows her, jumping from one cake to another until he slips and is carried over a waterfall. Topsy arrives at the St. Clare home in time to restore the rightful fortune of Marietta De Brie, Shelby's sweetheart and Legree's former ward, and to bring Eva back to life. ("Oh, Lord, don't take little missy!" reads Topsy's subtitled prayer. "Take me instead. You got plenty of white angels. Have a black one!" [Birdoff 402].) Eva, of course, recovers instantly and falls asleep alongside Topsy in an affectionate embrace.

The story clearly belongs to Topsy,[26] who is "all over the screen most of the time." Yet, while the film offers "great opportunities for comedy," Rosetta's vaudevillian efforts are too often crude and grotesque. In one scene, for example, just before she mounts the auction block, Topsy bites some of Simon Legree's chewing tobacco and becomes sick, turning away from the crowd to get rid of the cud—a "nauseus [*sic*]" gag, said *Variety,* and "nothing pleasant to witness on the screen." As Eva, Vivian Duncan "looked nice, but her role called for little acting." And, although Gibson Gowland (Simon Legree) is as villainous as his familiar role demands, Uncle Tom (played by the fine actor Noble Johnson, who tries unsuccessfully to preserve Tom's dignity) is almost incidental: relegated to minor scenes in the film (e.g., he is sold at the same auction as Topsy is, and he is later removed along with her from the St. Clare plantation by Legree), he has "little chance to shine. He played in the meek fashion of the play and had no big moments to get over" (*Variety* 22 June 1927).

Reviews of the picture as a whole were less than enthusiastic. *Variety* noted that as long as the film was shown on the same bill as the performing Duncan Sisters themselves, it would make money. But "in houses where the Duncan girls do not appear [it] is going to be a different story. The picture is not going to draw heavy grosses and is not going to please all around"; its most promising audience, concluded *Variety* (22 June 1927), would probably be "the kiddie matinee." *New York Times* reviewer Mordaunt Hall observed that the picture is confused, sometimes striving "for tears and on other occasions [for] broad farce." No time is wasted "on anything like characterizations. Eva, in a white frock and socks, looks like flour and molasses, while Topsy, with white lips, blackened face and her hair in curl papers strives to keep the fun pot boiling" (8 Aug. 1917) as she crawls endlessly under Aunt Ophelia's voluminous skirts or attempts (rather anachronistically for a film about the South) to put snowshoes on a horse. Yet, despite its vulgarity and garishness, the film—according to another reviewer—"had the same and inexplicable success as *Abie's Irish Rose*" (Leab 52).

Though *Topsy and Eva* was released after Pollard's *Uncle Tom's Cabin,* it is the latter that was the last of the significant Tom films and one of the last great silent film extravaganzas. Over the next few decades, new versions of *Uncle Tom's Cabin* were discussed but never made. In the late 1930s, for instance, producer David O. Selznick (who in 1939 released another plantation saga, *Gone with the Wind*) proposed a new Uncle Tom film—and even, to that end, filed with the MPPDA (Motion Picture Producers and Directors of America)—but nothing ultimately came of his plans (Cripps, *Making Movies Black* 11). In 1944, Metro-Goldwyn-Mayer also considered making a new movie version. According to Thomas F. Gossett, Lena Horne was suggested for the role of Eliza, Margaret O'Brien for Eva, and Lewis Stone for Augustine St. Clare. But "there was so much objection among black organizations and liberal groups generally that the plans were cancelled" (404).[27] Almost the only way the story could be produced during these years in this country, it seemed, was by parodying it or by using it, as the Rodgers and Hammerstein 1951 musical *The King and I* (and the subsequent film version, *The King and I* [1956; dir. Walter Lang]) did, in a comic ballet sequence. That sequence, "The Little House of Uncle Thomas," with its memorable choric refrain of "Run, run, run, Eliza, run!," demonstrated the reception of the novel at the royal court of Siam in the 1860s, the time during which the musical and movie are set; but it also deftly decried the suppression of individual liberties and the various types of slaveries in any age.

Unsurprisingly, perhaps, the next film version of *Uncle Tom's Cabin* (1965/American distribution, 1968) was produced not by an American company but by a West German one, Melodie-Avala. *Onkle Toms Hütte* (dir. Géza van Radványi)—released in two versions, the original at two hours, the second edited to one hour—was filmed in Yugoslavia and included Eartha Kitt as one of the players and Ella Fitzgerald as a "dubbing voice." Full of self-righteous indignation that no American company had wanted to film the Stowe classic, Kroger Babb, the film's distributor, "exclaimed that his version 'told the story of slavery in the Deep South with amazing accuracy and tremendous spectacle,' and that it also 'explained what no teacher can'" [Campbell 183].[28]

In fact, *Onkle Toms Hütte* offered some spectacle but little accuracy. As the reviewer for *Variety* noted, the production is "full of anachronisms and liberties with the Harriet Beecher Stowe hardy perennial melodrama." The Yugoslavian cavalry are unconvincing as "southern plantation types"; the red-faced Serbian farm workers look so unintentionally ridiculous in blackface that they "may just possibly push American audiences out of their cottonpicking minds with unintended amusement." Chases and barroom brawls "come off, at best, as stereotypes from some American Western." Green pastures depict Kentucky's harsh winter (although directly in the next scene Eliza jumps onto an ice floe). But there are other, even grosser misrepresentations, the most serious being the "innermost lack of veracity that purports to picture the American scene, e.g. the re-enactment of the Lincoln assassination, here included in the story," and the thinly disguised slaying of Saint Claire [*sic*] as an analogue for the John F. Kennedy tragedy, also replete with "false detail" (*Variety* 19 May 1965).

The alterations to Stowe's novel are both radical and immediately apparent. Radványi's film opens with a close-up image of Lagree [*sic*] (played by Herbert Lom), whose badly scarred face reflects his moral decay. Purportedly a guest in the Shelby household, in fact Lagree is there to collect on Shelby's bad investment in a gold mine—ten slaves (including Uncle Tom [John Kitzmiller], who asks to be sold as part of the biblical invocation "to lay down his life for a friend") in trade for the ten notes Lagree holds. Unable to take Eliza (Catana Cayetano), whom he covets, Lagree claims her young son Harry as one of the ten—but a newly-freed Eliza escapes before Lagree can take Harry away. Eliza's husband Harris (Harold Bradley), sold by slave owner Morrison to Lagree, also escapes, leaving Lagree to claim Harris's sister, the slave Cassy (Olive Morefield), instead.

En route to his plantation, situated in Natchez (not on the Red River in Louisiana, as in the book), Lagree meets his neighbors, the Saint Claires. After Lagree refuses to give Eva (Gertraud Mittermayr) Uncle Tom as a gift, she convinces her father to buy the old slave. Tom spends some pleasant moments at the Saint Claire home before Eva dies, in a surprisingly subdued death scene without the usual angels and other hoopla (apart from her dying wish to "Free Uncle Tom . . . Free all of them"). Saint Claire (O. W. Fischer)—who, in this version, precipitates Eva's death by an affair with his mistress, Harriet (Mylene Demongeot)—is true to his word and makes arrangements to free his slaves. But on the very day—Independence Day—that the freeing is to occur, he is shot by Lagree, who blames the murder on a young black barman, who is promptly lynched by a mob of slave owners.

Meanwhile Cassy, now Lagree's reluctant mistress, has inexplicably managed to locate Eliza and her son and to hide them—in Lagree's house! Believing that Cassy is sheltering a man, Lagree casts her out to work in the fields. As she defiantly walks away, he whips his team of horses and tries to run her down. Tom throws himself in front of the animals and stops them, but his selfless act causes him grave injury. Aware that he is dying, Tom urges the other slaves to run away and to open the levee as they go so that Lagree's dogs will be unable to track them. After Cassy sets fire to Lagree's home, she leaves for a monastery with Eliza, where they are soon joined by Harris, who has returned to free them.

Uncle Tom dies, although not before the sudden arrival of George Shelby (Thomas Fritsch). At the monastery, Cassy is shot, but the revolt is ultimately successful. As the slaves depart on a boat that Harris has chartered for them, the voice-over announces, cryptically and incongruously: "Only God fully understands these United States. Soon after Lincoln gave the Negro freedom from slavery, the President was shot. God alone guides our destiny."

Apart from its absurd departures from its source and its own plot inconsistencies, *Onkle Toms Hütte* is memorable only for the gruesomeness of some of its scenes, like the death by alligator of the young slave Napoleon after he jumps ship, and for its recasting of the Old South as the Wild West. Not simply a bad reinterpretation of Stowe's novel, *Onkle Toms Hütte* is a bad film—and certainly not "The Eye-Witness Story of Slavery" that the opening credits promise.

In 1987, Showtime/Edgar J. Scherick Associates Production, in association with Taft Entertainment Television, released its version of *Uncle Tom's Cabin,* directed by Stan Lathan and starring Avery Brooks (Uncle Tom), Phylicia Rashad (Eliza), Samuel L. Jackson (George Harris), Edward Woodward (Legree), and Bruce Dern (St. Clare). According to executive producer Scherick, Stowe's novel was "a good yarn," and he felt that it was time to revive it. Scherick was also interested in correcting the misimpressions about the story, which had "changed from an antislavery novel into an anti-Negro play." By restoring the strength and virility of the original character of Tom, Scherick hoped to make people "understand why this novel had the tremendous social and political impact that it did" (Farber 50).

The first American sound version of *Uncle Tom's Cabin*—and the first new American version since Pollard's film sixty years before—Scherick's Showtime adaptation was not only contemporary but also occasionally revisionist. Eliza, for instance, escapes the slave traders by riding a frail raft across a stream, not by leaping across ice floes on the river;[29] Little Eva (whose signature blonde locks here become reddish-brown) dies a relatively pedestrian death rather than the more character-istic teary, melodramatic one; and "Stowe's wise, often witty observa-tions fall by the wayside in a production that seems overawed by its plantation surroundings" (*Variety* 17 June 1987).

Yet in other significant ways, Showtime's *Uncle Tom's Cabin* fol-lowed closely the plot of Stowe's novel—more closely, in fact, than pre-vious versions did. As John O'Connor noted in his *New York Times* review, the film attempted to go "back to the original source and to set the record straight." By toning down the stereotyping and paring away the broad theatrical elements, the script by veteran television writer John Gay got "back to the core" of the actual people about whom Stowe wrote and effectively distilled her compassion and moral outrage (O'Connor C-30). "As a portrait of slave life," concluded another reviewer, "'Uncle Tom's Cabin' does show slaves singing to ease their burdens; [but] it also has the strength to show much of that burden" (*Variety* 17 June 1987).

Shot in and around Natchez, Mississippi, the film strove for realism in the depiction of its characters: Uncle Tom is portrayed not as old and long-suffering but as young, dignified, and courageous—a man whose behavior is governed by his religious convictions, a man whose body may be bought but whose soul cannot be touched (O'Connor C-30). Edward Woodward's Simon Legree is "poor-white mean and downright stinging" (*Variety* 17 June 1987), a legendary villain who is actually believable. And Cassy (Paula Kelly) and Emmeline (Troy Beyer), both victims of Legree's brutality, convey the urgency of their plight and the precariousness of their plan to escape. (The Cassy and Emmeline episode, so crucial to the book, is downplayed or even eliminated in ear-lier adaptations. In the World Film version directed by William Robert Daly, for instance, the women appear as Legree's "housekeepers," not his unwilling mistresses.)

Director Stan Lathan admits that he initially had reservations about taking on the project. Lathan, who is black, had already directed other literary projects, including an award-winning television adaptation of James Baldwin's *Go Tell It on the Mountain.* Yet friends warned him "to leave [*Uncle Tom's Cabin*] alone"; even the Hollywood chapter of the NAACP was apprehensive about a new adaptation. But Lathan "liked the challenge this production presented: a black man's interpretation of a white woman's interpretation of black reality—a reverse of 'The Color Purple'" (O'Connor C-30). And, like Scherick, he felt motivated both by the importance of the book itself, which "pointed out the horrors of slav-ery [and the fact] that black Americans have strong human qualities," and by the desire to retrieve Stowe's original conception of Uncle Tom, "an admirable figure . . . a man of God with a sense of community and a strong sense of family . . . an inspiration to everyone around him" (Farber 50).

In Avery Brooks, the film found precisely the kind of hero that Scherick and Lathan envisioned. Starring at the time as the formidable Hawk in the television series "Spenser: For Hire," Brooks based his remarkably forceful performance in large part on the life of Josiah Henderson, a slave who escaped to Canada and then published an autobiography in 1846. Brooks' Tom is steadfast in his principles and resilient in his spirit; his nuanced—yet always powerful—portrayal contributes to what *Variety* called the innocence of the first part of the film and the momentum "that capture[s] the imagination" in the second.

Just as Stowe's novel did, the film effectively utilizes contrasting images: the congenial atmosphere at the St. Clare home vs. the wretched desolation of Legree's house, for instance, or the humane treatment that Eliza and George receive at the hands of the Quakers (see Figure 25) vs. the brutality that Tom experiences from Legree. And while the film devotes considerably less attention to some of the novel's particulars—the details of Tom's pleasant life with Aunt Chloe at the Shelby plantation, the developing relationship between Tom and Eva before her illness (which occurs much earlier in the film than in the novel), the way in which Tom finds his religion again at Legree's, the background and beliefs of Ophelia, the philosophic ruminations between characters about slavery—it nonetheless evokes the essence of the classic story, especially by visually emphasizing Stowe's themes (e.g., the theme of redemption, reinforced by the image of Tom being strapped to a cross and flogged). Lathan's film thus becomes a vision not just of its own age but of Stowe's as well.

Almost as fascinating to American audiences as the adaptations of the actual tale of *Uncle Tom's Cabin* were the tales of the Tomming troupes, who spanned the continent performing the familiar story. Tomming films, in fact, soon became virtually as much of a staple of early cinema as did versions of the novel itself. Moreover, most of the Tomming films featured performances—or portions of performances—of *Uncle Tom's Cabin* as part of their plots and in this way introduced Stowe to new audiences.

As early as 1903, the year that both the Porter and Lubin versions of *Uncle Tom's Cabin* were released, the Selig Polyscope Company produced *Uncle Tom's Cabin's Parade,* a short polyscopic film 125 feet in length that depicted a traveling Uncle Tom's Cabin company. Though, like so many of the early silent films, no copy of it is available today, according to the *American Film Institute Catalogue: Film Beginnings,*

Figure 25. In the first non-silent American version of *Uncle Tom's Cabin* (Showtime, 1987), Eliza (Phylicia Rashad), George Harris (Samuel L. Jackson), and their son (here named Jimmy) are happily reunited. © Showtime

1893-1910, Uncle Tom's Cabin's Parade was a "picture [that] pleases the children and is very clear . . . [It] shows Uncle Tom, Little Eva, Marks [the lawyer] and the tallest colored man in the world, together with the blood hounds, donkeys and everything connected with a production of

Uncle Tom's Cabin" (1122). The short was important in documenting the ongoing American preoccupation not only with Uncle Tom but also with the actual Tomming troupes.

Other similar films soon followed. In 1905, for example, the American Mutoscope and Biograph Company released *The Barnstormers,* a four-reel "comedy-drama" that depicted the adventures and misadventures of an impoverished theatrical troupe, commonly called "barnstormers." The film, however, focused more on the romantic attachments that developed among the characters than on their performances. On vacation in New York City, wealthy hotel owner Adam Green (William W. West) becomes infatuated with soubrette Nell Lavelle (Myrtle Tannehill). Later, when her troupe stops at Adam's hotel, Mason (True Boardman), the leading man, and Eppstein (Frank Jonasson), the manager, persuade Adam to finance them, an arrangement to which Adam agrees, on the condition that Nell becomes the female lead. Meanwhile, Adam's son Jack (William Brunton), whose earlier romance with Nell ended because she would not give up the stage, quarrels with her and leaves. On the road, Nell discovers Mason and Eppstein's scheme and quits. After the men kidnap Adam to get money from Jack, Nell rescues Adam, who then gives money to all the members of the troupe to return home, except Mason and Eppstein, who have to walk. Preparing to propose to Nell when he learns of her romance with Jack, Adam conceals his love and offers his blessing, as Nell, now sick of the stage, becomes Jack's wife (*American Film Institute Catalogue: Feature Films, 1911-1920* 47). Directed by James W. Horne, the film is memorable only for its portrayal of the hardships endured by some of the traveling Tommers and other turn-of-the-century acting troupes.

Tommers, writes Harry Birdoff, were certainly not above criticism in these early cinematic efforts. In *The Troubles of a Stranded Actor* (Lubin, 1909),[30] "a Mr. Shakespeare attempted Little Eva, but the unappreciative citizens of Windsor greeted him with over-ripe tomatoes, and ran him out of town. The last seen of him was in Mr. Bug's Sanitarium, where he enacted Little Eva with impunity. In *An Uncle Tom's Cabin Troupe* (Biograph, 1913), a local proprietor was so impressed by a Tom show that he gladly swapped his hotel for it, but the hardships entailed in the enterprise made him admit later, in a subtitle, 'Evil the day that I became an actor!' A more favorable view was presented in *The Open Road* (Reliance, 1913), wherein a millionaire's disinherited son took to the highway and got a job pasting posters for a Tom troupe. Under the influence of the bracing life, he regretted his dissipated youth, and married one of the pretty Tom show actresses" (Birdoff 395-96). And in *The Death of Simon La Gree* (Universal L-Ko, 1915), a group of barnstorming Tommers hits a small town, where the actor performing La Gree [*sic*] captivates a little country maid by throwing her a rose from the stage. The maid's jealous suitor, Fatty, obtains a copy of the play and begins rehearsing himself at the opera house. The whole town turns out for Fatty's debut, which goes well until Little Eva's ascent to heaven is ruined by the property man (Billie Ritchie), who slips on the rope hauling her up and lands on the stage himself, "all ending in side-splitting fashion" (Birdoff 396) as Fatty winds up rolling down a hill in a hogshead and taking several of the principal players with him. Similar mischief occurs again later in the two-reel Paramount-Mack Sennett comedy, *Uncle Tom without a Cabin* (1919), directed by Ray Hunt and starring Ben Turpin, Ford Sterling, Marie Prevost, Charles "Heinie" Conklin, Charles Lynn, Eva Thatcher, Charlie Murray, and Teddy the dog.

When Do We Eat? (Artcraft, 1918), a five-reeler directed by Fred Niblo, also took a comic approach to Tommers and their adventures. After performing *Uncle Tom's Cabin* on the small town route, a hungry Little Eva (Enid Bennett), known off stage as Nora, leaves town by way of a freight car. Alarmed by the attentions of the tramp who is her traveling companion, she jumps off the train, lands in a farmer's field, and is immediately arrested as a "suspicious character." Kindly Ma Forbes takes Nora under her wing, but trouble nonetheless ensues. Two of Ma's boarders are crooks who are waiting for a chance to rob the village bank, where Ma's son, James Watterson Forbes (Al Ray), works. Impersonating a "lady cracksman," Nora gets the vault combination from James, gives the alarm that leads to an amusing chase in which the entire village participates and the crooks are caught red-handed, and is acclaimed a heroine; after marrying James, she becomes Mrs. Forbes and goes hungry no more. According to a contemporary *Variety* review (25 Oct. 1918), "*When Do We Eat?* is a pleasing and original picture," with Miss Bennett doing "very good work as the little barnstormer." Well played to the last extra, concluded the reviewer, "such pictures are not seen often enough"—a reference, no doubt, to the quality of the film itself and not to the quantity of films on the topic.

Little Eva Ascends (Sawyer-Lubin Pictures for Metro, 1922) adapted to film Thomas Beer's story of the same title, originally published in the *Saturday Evening Post*. The action centers around a barnstorming troupe that is performing *Uncle Tom's Cabin;* the troupe's manager (Univa Vin Moore) is a woman whose two sons are in the company, the younger (Gareth Hughes) reluctantly playing the role of Little Eva. When the troupe reaches a small California town, the proprietor of their hotel (Ben Haggerty) turns out to be the boys' father, whom his wife had deserted when the children were very young. After a disastrous performance, he arranges a large cash settlement for his wife and reclaims his sons, taking them under his wing to live with him at his ranch. The film won praise for its juvenile lead, whom reviewers singled out for "developing strong comedy"; and though "the story is draggy in spots, too much time being devoted to the performance of 'Uncle Tom's Cabin,'" *Variety* concluded that "in other respects it is interesting and well mounted" (*Variety* 27 Jan. 1922).

As late as 1925, Universal released *Uncle Tom's Gal* (Universal, 1925), a two-reeler that offered a slight variation on the familiar theme: it was not simply about a Tom show but about a second-rate movie company filming a Tom show. As actors in the real Tom shows often did, Edna Marion assumed multiple roles, playing Topsy, Eva, Eliza, and a farmer's daughter. A year later, "Our Gang" appeared in *Uncle Tom's Uncle* (Pathé/Our Gang, 1926). "The important common ingredient" in all of these films in which "Tom became a touching part of sentimental business in a larger picture," writes Thomas Cripps in his seminal study *Slow Fade to Black,* "was a warm, nostalgic, glowing spirit" (157).[31]

Less warm, more stereotypical, and more overtly racist treatments of Uncle Tom occurred in various film shorts and cartoons. In the early Edison short *Uncle Tom Wins* (1909),[32] for instance, Tom—described in *The Moving Picture World* (8 May 1909) as "an old colored man"—is rewarded for his persistent pursuit of the Goddess Fortune by a $20,000 lottery win. Although Tom rejoices over his new wealth, two men soon follow him and try to discover its hiding place. Tom has to keep moving the money, from a trunk to a carpet-bag to an old chair in the garret. Ultimately, as Tom removes the money and leaves, the men are chagrined to learn that they had been sitting on his stash.

The easily recognizable character of Tom was also featured in *Uncle Tom's Caboose* (Century/for Universal Films, 1920), a two-reeler directed by Jim Davis; *Alice Gets Stage Struck* (Walt Disney/M. J. Winkler Productions, 1925), a live action frame story, in which the popular Alice plays Little Eva in an *Uncle Tom's Cabin* show that she has staged;[33] two animated shorts by Walter Lantz, *Colonel Heeza Liar in Uncle Tom's Cabin* (J. R. Bray, 1923; dir. Vernon Stallings) and *Dinky Doodle in Uncle Tom's Cabin* (Bray Studios, 1926; dir. Walter Lantz), featuring the familiar characters Colonel Heeza Liar and Dinky Doodle; *Uncle Tom's Crabbin'* (Educational Films, 1927), in which Felix the Cat outwits Simon Legree; *Topsy Turvey* (Paramount, 1927), whose hero is another feline, Krazy Kat; *Uncle Tom and Little Eva* (alternatively titled *Pickaninny Blues* (1932); *Uncle Tom's Bungalow* (Warner Brothers, 1937), a Merrie Melodies Cartoon; and *Uncle Tom's Cabaña* (Metro-

Goldwyn-Mayer, 1947), which climaxes with Uncle Tom opening a "chicken shack" at the corner of Hollywood and Vine.[34] As Thomas Cripps writes, the patently backward-looking cartoons proved "a particular nettle" to black audiences, especially black activists, who saw in the exaggeration of black style and idiom (e.g., the "mix of jive-talk, hepcat body english, and flashy zoot suits") a return to the Jim Crow tradition and a jarring offense to black sensibilities (196-97).

Although no new adaptations of *Uncle Tom's Cabin* were made during the thirties and forties, Uncle Tom—a cinematic standard, by virtue of both its legitimate and parodic presentations—continued to be a familiar motif in American films. In *Dimples* (1936; dir. William Seiter), for example, Twentieth Century-Fox Pictures recast the early history of *Uncle Tom's Cabin* into an entertaining film starring a young Shirley Temple. *Dimples* related the story of a broken-down old rapscallion actor (Frank Morgan), whose little granddaughter attracted the attention of a young producer who was launching the memorable play at the National Theatre. As Eva, Temple has numerous opportunities to shine: in the sequences with Topsy in the attic room; in a later scene, in which she and Tom engage in the famous discussion of the New Jerusalem; and, in the deathbed scene, where she is conveniently propped up to deliver Eva's final words: "I can see those great gates made of pearl, and they're opening wide—and there are the angels—they're calling me! I'm coming! I'm coming!" There is also some backstage humor, reminiscent of the Double Mammoth days, when the grandfather, after palming off a fake watch on his hostess (Helen Westley), tries to evade the police "by blacking up as Uncle Tom, and the audience at the National Theatre was regaled by two Uncle Toms entering the stage from opposite wings!" (Birdoff 407). In *Everybody Sing* (1938; dir. Edwin L. Marin), Judy Garland stars as Judy Bellaire, a precocious youngster of thirteen who is kicked out of the Colvin School for Girls. She returns home to her nutty theatrical family, which is trying, unsuccessfully, to mount a new show. Without her parents' knowledge, she auditions for the producer; dressed as a black-faced Topsy, she sings a swing version of "Swing Low, Sweet Chariot" ("Uncle Tom's got a new routine; Eliza crossed the ice in a limousine, while Simon Legree shakes a mean tambourine. . ."). Of course, her talent ultimately saves the show (though not this otherwise awful movie). In *Can This Be Dixie?* (Twentieth Century-Fox, 1936; dir. George Marshall), another child star Jane Withers, as Eva, belts out "Uncle Tom's Cabin Is a Cabaret Now," while the same treatment is given to the double Topsys—Betty Grable and June Haver—in *The Dolly Sisters* (Twentieth Century-Fox, 1945; dir. Irving Cummings) (Birdoff 407). And in *The Naughty Nineties* (1945; dir. Jean Yarbrough), a film memorable mostly for its classic "Who's On First?" baseball routine, Abbott and Costello outwit the villains who want to steal a showboat from its kindly and honest owner. The film ends with a showboat-style production of *Uncle Tom's Cabin,* in which Abbott and Costello, as Simon Legree and Eva, suffer the typical theatrical mishap of the broken rope during Eva's ascension to heaven.[35]

J. C. Furnas wrote of *Uncle Tom's Cabin* that it was like a three-stage rocket: it was first powerful as a novel, then as a play, and eventually in the twentieth century as a film (56). Uncle Tom's ubiquitousness is indeed a testament to his iconic status—sometimes beloved, sometimes despised—in American popular culture. From saintly Tom to the stereotypic "tom" to the "splendid black Christian Prometheus, epic in his grandeur and simplicity whose attitude toward injustice anticipates . . . the Christianity of Dr. Martin Luther King, Jr." (Gossett 402),[36] Harriet Beecher Stowe's kindly slave has "rocketed" his way into the national consciousness. And, in his numerous cinematic incarnations—from Edison's 1903 portrait of the devoted family retainer to the quiet dignity of Sam Lucas's portrayal in World Film's 1914 version; from Pollard's 1927 "liberal" vision of the "exemplary" James B. Lowe, who wears "his ball and chain with a difference," to the racist image of an almost incidental Tom in *Topsy and Eva* (1927); from the jive-talking, zoot-suit-wearing, chicken-eating hepcat in the jarring Jim Crow tradition of MGM's 1947 *Uncle Tom's Cabaña* to the proud, unbowed patriarch of Showtime's 1987 adaptation—he has continued to serve as a mirror of the American soul.

Notes

1. Aiken's play of *Uncle Tom's Cabin,* which combined the original play that covered events of the first two-thirds of the novel, concluding with the death of Little Eva, and the sequel, a second play that carried the action of the novel from the death of Little Eva to the death of Uncle Tom, was "a very long play," according to Thomas F. Gossett. "Later it was made still longer, with seven acts and thirty-four scenes. All between-the-act-performances and the short comedy after the play were omitted, a change which represents a turning point in the tradition of the American theater. More and more plays were presented as the only feature of an evening's entertainment" (263).

2. "Shorn of its salient points," observes Harry Birdoff (86-87), Conway's play "derived new interest through excellent scenery—'scenes in living pictures.' A grand panorama by C. Lehr, in the second act, representing a moonlight view of the Mississippi (a reverse movement of the canvas giving apparent

motion to a steamer on her way to New Orleans), surpassed anything the Bostonians had seen in years." As an additional inducement to audiences, when the Conway adaptation began performances at Barnum's American Museum on November 7, 1853, Barnum invited the public to see the giraffes, the Bearded Lady, and all of the curiosities, "without extra charge."

3. A runaway horse in the early action of the two-act drama typified the animal "that loves liberty" and provided a clear parallel to the human characters. Perhaps the most spectacular of the equestrian feats performed in this production was Eliza's escaping across the ice on the Mazeppa steed (Birdoff 148).

4. Among the more popular dramatizations were *La Case de l'Oncle Tom,* by MM. Dumanoir and D'Ennery; *L'Oncle Tom,* by Edmond Texier and L. De Wailly; and *Élisa, ou un Chapitre de L'Oncle Tom,* by Arthur de Beauplan. Parodies included *Casine de l'Oncle Thomas,* by Dormeuil, and *Cave de l'Oncle Pomme,* attributed to Paul Michel. The novel itself was imitated as *Noir et Blanc, ou le Nègre fugitive* and Jules Rostaing's *Voyage dans les deux Ameriques ou Les neveux de l'Oncle Tom;* the *Revue Britannique* serialized *Une Nièce de l'Oncle Tom ou l'Afrique Blanche.* (For a more detailed discussion of continental interpretations of Uncle Tom's Cabin, see Birdoff, "On the Continental Stage" 166-85.)

In terms of the liberties taken by French playwrights, Thomas F. Gossett writes that "The French took more liberties than the English in adapting events of the novel for the stage. In one version, Uncle Tom, Eliza Harris, Topsy, and Cassy escape from Simon Legree's plantation. The plantation is in Kentucky, not Louisiana. The fugitives float down the Ohio River on a raft accompanied by George Harris in a canoe and pursued by Tom Loker, the slave catcher, in a boat. In one of the last scenes, they are all shown approaching the 'rapids' of the Ohio River. On the backdrop of the stage, there is a large picture of Niagara Falls, a suggestion that this is the direction in which the fugitives are heading. In a later scene farther down the river, raft, canoe, and boat are seen again, the implication being that they had all gone over Niagara Falls. The boat of Tom Loker, however, is empty and he apparently has drowned, but the others have all made the descent over the falls without mishap. There is another surprise in the play for anyone familiar with North American geography. The fleeing slaves, still on the raft and in the canoe, float farther down the Ohio River and finally arrive in Canada! A placard is placed on the stage announcing 'Canada—Terre Libre'" (282-83).

5. The full title of the dramatization was *The Christian Slave, A Drama Founded on a Portion of "Uncle Tom's Cabin"* (1855); it was an adaptation for dramatic reading performed by Mrs. Mary E. Webb, a black woman. While *The Christian Slave* received favorable reviews, according to Thomas F. Gossett, "it did not become popular; in fact, it was apparently never performed by anyone else" other than Mrs. Webb in 1855 (262).

6. It is worth noting that, whereas Stowe's novel was a harsh indictment of slavery, some of the earliest "Uncle Tom" minstrel and burlesque shows actually glorified slavery with song and dance. The playbill for an August 18, 1861, performance of *Sanford's Southern Version of Uncle Tom's Cabin,* for example, emphasized the distinction with this rhyme:

> *Oh! White folks, we'll have you to know,*
> *Dis am not de version of Mrs. Stowe:*
> *Wid her de Darks am all unlucky,*
> *But we am de boys from Old Kentucky.*

> *Den hand de Banjo down to play,*
> *We'll make it ring both night and day;*
> *And we care not what de white folks say,*
> *Dey can't get us to run away.* (Birdoff 142)

7. For more on the Tom operas, see Birdoff 323-24. Gossett also briefly discusses musical treatments of *Uncle Tom's Cabin.*

8. In addition to the more exotic dogs being introduced into some of the productions, stage settings themselves became more elaborate. They included "scenes of mountains, an old-time slave market, a great plantation festival, a steamboat race on the Mississippi, and the apotheosis of little Eva—all of which were, of course, 'masterpieces of stage painting.' One production had a real cascade of water on stage and another had an orange grove with 'real fruit.' One traveling show of the 1880s had fifty actors, twelve dogs, a mule, and an elephant. A production in 1891 had alligators to snap at Eliza and Harry when they crossed over the Ohio River" (Gossett 369).

9. Interestingly, beginning in the 1890s, some of the productions of *Uncle Tom's Cabin* in the North "ended not with Uncle Tom approaching the gates of heaven but with the Union armies triumphing over the Confederates. There would be a tableau showing Lincoln signing the Emancipation Proclamation. Sometimes in the grand finale, the men in blue would carry the American flag while they sang a patriotic song. During the Spanish-American War, a version of the play was presented with military uniforms modernized to correspond with the times. Now northerners and southerners were triumphing together over Spain, not engaging in fratricidal war" (Gossett 382-83; also mentioned in Birdoff and other sources).

10. In fact, the film was based as much on George Aiken's popular stage version, then the most frequently performed play in the history of the American theater (Hansen 45), as on Stowe's classic novel.

11. Donald Bogle notes, moreover, that, "when the first film versions of *Uncle Tom's Cabin* were released in the South, advertisements announced that

the black actors were portrayed by white actors. Even at this stage, the evolving film industry feared offending the dominant white audience" (17).

12. In one instance, the dancing becomes rather sensual, as a young woman lifts her leg atop her partner's bended knee.

13. According to Edward D. C. Campbell, "the film even utilized Negroes, though the important roles were still taken by white actors in blackface" (41). In the starring roles were Florence Turner (Topsy), Marion Oramount (Eva), and Julia Swayne Gordon (Cassy).

14. Campbell writes that, in 1913, "the American studio" produced a new version of *Uncle Tom's Cabin*. Campbell's, however, appears to be the only reference to this production (41).

At one time, Powers, an independent film company whose features were distributed by Universal, had planned a version of *Uncle Tom's Cabin* as well. That version, billed as a "Three Reel Powers" and listed as "Almost Ready for Release" in several issues of *The Moving Picture World* (2 Aug. 1916 and 16 Aug. 1913), was produced by Otis Turner. The brief summary of the film, published in *The Moving Picture World* (3 May 1913) while the film was still in production, suggested that it would be "a special three-part feature offering" and that "producer Otis Turner deserves credit for what is, on the whole, an artistic picture." The summary also praised the film's good "character drawing" and its "marked Southern atmosphere in the home of the St. Clairs and in the steamboat scene." There is no record, however, of the actual release of the Powers' film version. In fact, the reviews of the 1913 three-reel Imp version "directed" by Otis Turner suggest that the "Three Reel Powers" was released not by Powers but by Imp-Universal. (At the time, Universal served as the distributor for a number of smaller independent film companies, including Powers and Imp.)

15. After the death of Uncle Tom and of Legree, "[young master] Shelby reverently takes Uncle Tom's body back to the old plantation, where it is laid away near the old slave's cabin" (*The Moving Picture World* 13 Dec. 1913: 1316).

16. Leonard would go on to direct feature films, including the first adaptation of Jane Austen's *Pride and Prejudice* (1940), with Laurence Olivier and Greer Garson.

17. Andrews disputes this point. She writes that "the World Film version varied considerably in its plot from the earlier films because it was based on a novel written by Edward Wade which drew upon, but did not copy Stowe's story, rather than upon the Aiken playscript" (133). The review from *Variety* (4 Sept. 1914), however, includes a summary of the film; and it seems clear that the film is indeed based very much on Stowe's novel. "The story," writes *Variety* reviewer "Sime.," is fully described "in the programed [*sic*] synopsis, which follows: Geo. Shelby is forced to sell his faithful old slave Tom and the infant son of Eliza Harris in order to save his property from Haley, the slave trader and

holder of the mortgage. Eliza, hearing she is to be separated from her baby, makes her escape to join her husband, George Harris, who, with Vance [Jim Vance, his would-be servant], were well on their way to freedom. Learning of the departure, Haley immediately puts the hounds on her trail. The searching party arrives on the river bank in time to see Eliza leaping over the broken ice, upon which the dogs and men feared to tread. A second party is organized by Lawyer Marks, but fails to capture the fugitive, who has been befriended by a kindly Quaker and has in the meantime joined her husband. During the sail to Haley's plantation Tom's attention from his Bible, is attracted by the cry of 'Overboard.' Making a bold rush, this wonderful old man leaps into the water and brings little Eva St. Clair [*sic*], who had wandered from her Aunt and fallen overboard, to safety. This noble deed caused his purchase by St. Clair, who treated him with every kindness, making him a companion for his small daughter Eva, who joyed in Uncle Tom's explanation of the Bible. Sadness finally came, when little Eva dies, and a second calamity when her father is killed while separating two roughs in a quarrel. This necessitates the sale of his slaves and property. Uncle Tom falls into the hands of Simon Legree, the most brutal slave owner of the South. His life here is simply a matter of how long it can last under the terrible strain and treatment he receives. The final blow came when Legree's housekeeper, Casey [*sic*], and his favorite slave, Emmeline, escaped during one of his debauches. Going to Tom, he demands to know their whereabouts. Being unable to give this information, Tom is flogged and cast into a corner to die. Young Shelby, now a man, searched the South to fulfill his youthful promise to buy Tom. He reaches the little hut just in time to cheer the dying hour of his old slave, who has just enough life left to show his gratitude."

There are, however, variations from the text. Some are small: Emmeline, for the sake of propriety, is introduced as Legree's new "housekeeper" rather than his mistress. Other variations are more significant: at Legree's plantation, Tom is forced to whip not Casey but instead an unnamed young male slave. Later, that young man, moved by Tom's earlier protectiveness of him and upset by the older slave's subsequent punishment, takes a gun and shoots Legree to death. Before dying, Tom has a vision of Little Eva. And, in the film's final scene, Abraham Lincoln is depicted freeing the slaves.

18. In addition to Margarita Fischer (Eliza), the film also starred James B. Lowe (Uncle Tom), Virginia Grey (Eva), George Seigmann (Legree), Eulalie Jensen (Cassie), Arthur Edmund Carew (Harris), Jack Mower (Shelby), Vivian Oakland (Mrs. Shelby), J. Gordon Russell (Loker), Mona Ray (Topsy), Lassie Lou Ahern (Little Harry), Aileen Manning (Ophelia), John Roche (St. Clare), Lucien Littlefield (Marks), Gertrude Astor (Mrs. St. Clare), and others.

19. Noble continues: "Although a 'heavenly power' may have been with actor Lowe, it had little effect on his interpretation of the role. Tom still came off as a genial darky, furnished with new color but no new sentiments. Yet to

Lowe's credit, he did his tomming with such an arresting effectiveness that he was sent to England on a promotional tour to ballyhoo the picture, thus becoming the first black actor to be publicized by his studio" (6).

20. Cripps disagrees on this point: in *Slow Fade to Black,* he writes that the final film came in at fourteen reels—"less than half its intended length" (159).

21. Compared to previous interpretations, the story, according to Campbell, "did expose certain plantation evils. In one shot a brutally beaten Uncle Tom appears in a crucifixion pose, after which a likeness of Christ is visible. Legree is grotesque, stumbling about with food drooling from his mouth and blood trickling from his forehead. In a revised conclusion Legree gets his just retribution at the hands of William Sherman's troops. However, when contrasted to the rest of the picture these scenes did little to counteract what had become a standard view of the plantation" (67).

22. The "narration by Raymond Massey, in front of an old barn at Mrs. Stowe's birthplace in Litchfield, Connecticut," wrote William L. Slout, "prepared modern viewers for the antique picture" (149).

23. Stephen Zito notes that Topsy also "eats bugs . . . and butts heads with a goat" (Leab 22).

24. An additional criticism of the film was the casting of a white performer in a popular black role. That ignoble tradition had a long Hollywood history, which included the casting of Marguerite Clark, a popular actress, as both Little Eva and Topsy in the 1918 Paramount production, which proved to be "an artistic and public relations tour de force" (Leab 52).

25. The publicity for the film, notes Edward D. C. Campbell, Jr., "was as disrespectful as the plot. One publicity release revealed that 'the money paid for the huge amounts of burned cork bought for the use of Rosetta Duncan . . . would buy four dozen pairs of ladies' silk stockings of a very fair grade'" (71).

26. Film audiences of the time, it seems, were as fond of angelic Evas as they were of obstreperous Topsys. As Harry Birdoff writes, around the time of *Topsy and Eva*'s release, MGM was screening the film *Girl in the Show,* based on *Eva the Fifth,* with Bessie Love in the lead role of Eva. The "precocity of Evas," according to Birdoff, was well known to movie fans. "There was Pearl White, of a thousand breath-taking, death-defying exploits in serials, who had made her debut at six, in a Tom company in Greenridge, Mo., when the Eva was down with the measles. Lillian Gish, like many Evas before her, had an awful time trying not to giggle when the straps under her robe tickled her, and her little ribs could hardly stand the strain. Belle Bennett, earlier in her career, played the sainted child, and at one performance could not be found, but was eventually discovered curled up with a delinquent bloodhound, both sound asleep. Helen Holmes, at the tender age of eight, first showed the spark in a Tom show, and later fanned it into full glow in Kalem railroad pictures. Dolores

Costello enacted the part in the Edna May and Cecil Spooner Stock Company, at the Bijou Theatre, Brooklyn. Another famous Eva, Mary Pickford, first learned her lines in 1896, at the King George Opera House, Toronto, where Joe Barnum coached her on his knee" (402-03).

27. Peter Noble, in discussing the "just depiction of the Negro in American films," also noted that MGM "was contemplating screening *Uncle Tom's Cabin*." Though Noble dates the protests to 1946, not 1944 (as Gossett did), he writes that the NAACP and IFRG (International Film and Radio Guild) "led a campaign that resulted in that studio's decision to abandon" the project (218).

28. Babb also alleged that his important effort was "equally as entertaining and informative" for children as for adults, black and white. Yet the poster for *Uncle Tom's Cabin* seemed neither entertaining nor informative: it was "dominated by a very scantily clad slave girl in the eager clutches of Simon Legree" (Campbell 185).

29. John J. O'Connor notes that the "significance is that Ms. Rashad was pregnant at the time of filming, and Mr. Lathan decided to make the crossing considerably less perilous" (*NYT* 12 June 1987: C-30).

30. Another Lubin film, *The Crushed Tragedian* (1908), featured a chief protagonist very similar to Lawyer Marks, who—according to Harry Birdoff— "trashed the tradition-bound, moribund profession." In this film, he is called Mr. Dandaly, but his make-up is "similar to the Markses of thousands of Tom shows" (393-94).

31. As Harry Birdoff writes, "There is a modern defense of Tom shows in Edmund Wilson's play, *Winter in Beach Street*. The same interest is manifested in the following: Ben Hecht's comedy, *Actor's Blood*, where two decrepit-looking hounds from a Tom show track down poor old Widow Cagle's murderer; Jack Bechdolt's novel, *The Vanishing Hounds*, which has the old folk play setting; August Derleth's *Sweet Genevieve*, which narrates the vicissitudes of a Mississippi Tom Show boat; William G. Burleigh's novel, *Uncle Tom's Mansion*, in which the former Uncle Tom and Eliza of a Tom troupe reveal the perils in re-enthroning King Alcohol. Vincent Minelli's [*sic*] *The Show Is On*, in 1936, ended climactically its first act with a Tom Show arrival, and this idea was carried on in *Bloomer Girl*, but with additional scenes from the historical play. In *The Darktown Jamboree*, by James Reach, the finale highlighted 'Uncle Tom's Harlem Cabin'" (439).

32. Little is known today about *Uncle Tom Wins*, which was registered on April 30, 1909, as a short (600 feet). Henry T. Sampson, one of the few critics even to mention the film, notes that no specific data is available about the cast, other than that it consisted of whites in blackface.

33. *Alice [Gets] Stage Struck* was one of Disney's many popular "Alice" productions. According to Russell Merritt and J. B. Kaufman in *Disney in Wonderland: The Silent Films of Walt Disney*, in this silent short, which premiered

on June 23, 1925, at the Rivoli Theater in New York City with *The Light of Western Stars* (Paramount), "Alice and the gang stage an Our-Gang style *Uncle Tom's Cabin* show. Playing the part of Little Eva, Alice is accidentally knocked out, and dreams herself in snowland with Julius [her cat], who is building a snowman. They run afoul of Pete the Bear who chases them into a winter cabin and across ice floes" (138). The silent film was later reissued with sound, and the main title of the sound version read *Alice Gets Stage Struck;* but studio records for 1925 give the title simply as *Alice Stage Struck.*

34. Thomas Cripps, in *Making Movies Black,* notes that the climax of *Uncle Tom's Cabaña,* the opening of Tom's chicken shack, "had already been a bit in the liberal revue *Jump for Joy,*" and blacks wondered "how it would play Azuza [a pejorative term for squares]" (197). In *Slow Fade to Black,* Cripps discusses at greater length *Jump for Joy,* "a liberal romp that ran for three months" and was attended by "Hollywood celebrities, 'middle-class ofays,' 'dicty Negroes,' and just plain folk." In the satire, "Uncle Tom's deathbed is surrounded by his children singing 'He lived to a ripe old age. Let him go, God Bless him!' as a brace of producers struggle to keep him alive by pumping adrenalin into his arms. The first act finale was a comic song in which Uncle Tom's Cabin becomes a drive-in 'chicken shack' at Hollywood and Vine. In case anyone might miss the point, the program helped the 'square' to become temporarily 'groovy' by providing a handy glossary of black urbane idiom" (374-75).

35. *Uncle Tom's Cabin* reached other media as well. With the inception of radio, serious treatments (e.g., *The Gray Spirit,* by the Ohio State University, over the Blue network, NBC, in February, 1937) as well as travesties (e.g., *Uncle Tom's Cabaña,* by Al Barrie's "Mellerdrammers," over WNYC in September, 1937) found their way to the air waves. Even Al Jolson performed the venerable old Tom (the "Star Spangled Theatre," on NBC-Blue [WJZ], August 10, 1941) (Birdoff 439).

36. Similarly, Kenneth Rexroth argued that Uncle Tom is "by far the strongest person in the book. Although he is whipped to death by the psychotic Simon Legree, his end is not only a tragedy in Aristotle's sense, the doom of a great man brought low by a kind of *holy hubris,* but like Samson, he destroys his destroyer." For Rexroth, the death of Martin Luther King, Jr., in 1968 was comparable to the martyrdom of Tom. "As for Uncle Tom," wrote Rexroth, "he was assassinated in Memphis, and has been before, and will be again, until something like Mrs. Stowe's secular, evangelical humanism, or Whittier's or Whitman's wins out at last, or the Republic perishes" (Rexroth 103-07; quoted in Gossett 402-03).

Bibliography

Andrews, Hannah Page Wheeler. *Theme and Variations: "Uncle Tom's Cabin" as Book, Play, and Film.* Unpublished Doctoral Dissertation. University of North Carolina at Chapel Hill. 1979.

Birdoff, Harry. *The World's Greatest Hit: Uncle Tom's Cabin.* New York: Vanni, 1947.

Bogle, Donald. *Toms, Coons, Mulattoes, Mammies, & Bucks: An Interpretive History of Blacks in American Films.* 3rd ed. New York: Continuum, 1994.

Campbell, Edward D. C., Jr. *The Celluloid South: Hollywood and the Southern Myth.* Knoxville: U of Tennessee P, 1981.

Canby, Vincent. "A New 'Anne Frank' Still Stuck in the 50s." (Rev. of *The Diary of Anne Frank, Uncle Tom's Cabin,* and *The Sunshine Boys.*) *New York Times* 21 Dec. 1997. Arts Sect.: 5, 6.

Cripps, Thomas. *Black Film as Genre.* Bloomington: Indiana UP, 1978

——. *Making Movies Black: The Hollywood Message Movie from World War II to the Civil Rights Era.* New York: Oxford UP, 1993.

——. *Slow Fade to Black: The Negro in American Film, 1900-1942.* New York: Oxford UP, 1977.

cummings, e[dward] e[stlin]. *Tom.* New York: Arrow Editions, 1935.

Daly, Ann. "Conversations About Race In the Language of Dance." (Rev. of *Last Supper at Uncle Tom's Cabin/The Promised Land* et al.) *New York Times* 7 Dec. 1997. Arts Sect.: 1, 44.

Farber, Stephen. "Cable Service Dusts Off 'Uncle Tom's Cabin' for TV." *New York Times* 13 June 1987: I-50.

Furnas, Joseph Chamberlain. *Goodbye to Uncle Tom.* New York: Sloan, 1956.

Gossett, Thomas F. *Uncle Tom's Cabin and American Culture.* Dallas: Southern Methodist UP, 1985.

Hall, Mordaunt. Rev. of *Topsy and Eva. New York Times* 8 Aug. 1927: 10.

——. Rev. of *Uncle Tom's Cabin* (Pollard version). *New York Times* 5 Nov. 1927: 16.

Hansen, Miriam. *Babel and Babylon: Spectatorship in American Silent Film.* Cambridge: Harvard UP, 1991.

Hildreth, Margaret Holbrook. *Harriet Beecher Stowe: A Bibliography.* Hamden, CT: Archon, 1976.

Hughes, Glenn. *A History of the American Theatre: 1700-1950.* New York: Samuel French, 1951.

Lauritzen, Einar, and Gunnar Lundquist. *American Film Index, 1916-1920.* Stockholm, Sweden: Film-Index, 1984.

Leab, Daniel J. *From Sambo to Superspade: The Black Experience in Motion Pictures.* Boston: Houghton Mifflin, 1975.

Merritt, Russell, and J. B. Kaufman. *Disney in Wonderland: The Silent Films of Walt Disney*. La Giornate Del Cinema Muto. Distributed by Johns Hopkins UP, 1993.

Niver, Kemp R. *The First Twenty Years: A Segment of Film History*. Los Angeles: Locare Research Group, 1968.

Noble, Peter. *The Negro in Films*. New York: Arno P and New York Times, 1970.

O'Connor, John J. Rev. of *Uncle Tom's Cabin* (Showtime version). *New York Times* 12 June 1987: C-30.

Rev. [Advance Summary] of *The Death of Simon La Gree*. *Moving Picture World* 16 Jan. 1915: 426.

Rev. [Advance Summary] of *Uncle Tom's Cabin* (Thanhouser version). *Moving Picture World* 30 July 1910: 267.

Rev. [Advance Summary] of *Uncle Tom's Cabin* (Vitagraph version). *Moving Picture World* 6 Aug. 1910: 313.

Rev. [Advance Summary] of *Uncle Tom's Cabin* (Universal-Imp version). *Moving Picture World* 23 Aug. 1913: 880.

Rev. [Advance Summary] of *Uncle Tom's Cabin* (Powers version). *Moving Picture World* 3 May 1913: 490.

Rev. [Advance Summary] of *Uncle Tom's Cabin* (Kalem version). *Moving Picture World* 13 Dec. 1913: 1316.

Rev. [Advance Summary] of *Uncle Tom's Cabin* (Daly version). *Moving Picture World* 15 Aug. 1914.

Rev. of *Little Eva Ascends*. *Variety* 27 Jan. 1925. In *Variety Film Reviews, 1921-1925*. Vol. 2. New York: Garland, 1983. N.p. [Rev. signed "Hart."]

Rev. of *Onkle Toms Hütte*. *Variety* 19 May 1965. In *Variety Film Reviews, 1964-1967*. Vol. 11. New York: Garland, 1983. N.p. [Rev. signed "Afka"]

Rev. of *Topsy and Eva*. *Variety* 22 Jan 1927. In *Variety Film Reviews, 1926-29*. Vol. 3. New York: Garland, 1983. [Rev. signed "Ung."]

Rev. of *Uncle Tom's Cabin* (World Film version). *Variety* 4 Sept. 1914. In *Variety Film Reviews, 1907-1920*. Vol. 1. New York: Garland, 1983. N.p. [Rev. signed "Sime."]

Rev. of *Uncle Tom's Cabin* (Universal-Imp version). *Variety* 5 Sept. 1913. In *Variety Film Reviews, 1907-1920*. Vol. 1. New York: Garland, 1983. N.p. [Rev. signed "Corb."]

Rev. of *Uncle Tom's Cabin* (Re-issue of 1927 Pollard version). *Variety* 27 Jan. 1958. In *Variety Film Reviews 1954-1958*. Vol. 9. New York: Garland, 1983. N.p. [Rev. signed "Land."]

Rev. of *Uncle Tom's Cabin*. *Variety* 17 June 1987. In *Variety Television Reviews*. Vol. 14 (1987-1988). New York: Garland, 1990. N.p. [Rev. signed "Tone."]

Rev. of *Uncle Tom's Cabin* (Pollard version). *Variety* 9 Nov. 1927. In *Variety Film Reviews 1926-1929*. Vol. 3. New York: Garland, 1983. N.p.

Rev. of *Uncle Tom's Cabin* (Famous Players version). *Variety* 9 Aug. 1918. In *Variety Film Reviews, 1907-1920.* Vol. 1. New York: Garland, 1983. N.p.

Rev. of *Uncle Tom's Cabin* (Dawley version). *Variety* 9 Aug. 1918. In *Variety Film Reviews, 1907-1920.* Vol. 1. New York: Garland, 1983. N.p.

Rev. of *When Do We Eat? Variety* 25 Oct. 1918. In *Variety Film Reviews, 1907-1920.* Vol. 1. New York: Garland, 1983. N.p.

Rexroth, Kenneth. "Uncle Tom's Cabin." *The Elastic Retort: Essays in Literature and Ideas.* New York: Seabury P., 1973.

Rugoff, Milton. *The Beechers: An American Family in the Nineteenth Century.* New York: Harper and Row, 1981.

Sampson, Henry T. *Blacks in Black and White: A Source Book in Black Films.* 2d ed. Metuchen, NJ: Scarecrow P, 1995.

Sherwood, Robert E. "Uncle Tom's Cabin." (Rev. of Pollard version.) *Life* 90 (15 Dec. 1927): 26.

Slout, William L. "*Uncle Tom's Cabin* in American Film History." *Journal of Popular Film* 2.2 (Spring 1973): 137-51.

Stowe, Harriet Beecher. *Uncle Tom's Cabin.* With an Afterword by John William Ward. New York: Penguin/Signet Classic, 1981.

9

FILMING THE NINETEENTH CENTURY:
LITTLE WOMEN

Shirley Marchalonis

When we as scholars and critics discuss literature from an earlier time, we bring to it our own late twentieth-century knowledge and insights, hoping that what we say or write will further illuminate the work. But if that is all we do, it is not enough, for a work of fiction grows out of its author's culture. If we ignore that culture—its attitudes, beliefs, values, and assumptions—our analysis cannot be complete.

Nothing shows differences in cultural climate so clearly as the transformations of earlier fiction into films designed to appeal to a modern popular audience. An examination and comparison of Louisa May Alcott's *Little Women* (1868) with its film adaptations not only reveals what has been left out, emphasized or de-emphasized, changed, reinterpreted; it also highlights differences and offers insight into past values and beliefs that we as scholars and critics all too often ignore or reject because they differ from present-day attitudes. For those who believe that a text has an important life of its own, there is an obligation to present that text in a way that preserves its integrity.[1]

A novel cannot do the same things or evoke the same responses from a reader as a film can from an audience. Consequently, devoted readers will always be somewhat disappointed in filmed versions of their favorites. The recent Jane Austen films are a case in point: most of them are impeccably done and faithful to the text, so they are acceptable, even enjoyable, but they lack what Austen's admirers most value, the wit and dry elegance of her language.[2] At the other extreme is the horror felt by those who grew up on the works of L. M. Montgomery at the atrocities perpetrated on her texts by the recent CBC films.[3]

The four extant film adaptations of *Little Women*[4] do try to follow Alcott's text, but they interpret that text on their own terms, or perhaps according to their own vision of what life should be or should have been. Like filmed versions of older novels in general, they reject or ignore the view of life that is at the center of the novel. Thus, the differences between perceptions and standards then and now stand out.

Published in 1868, *Little Women* was followed by *Good Wives;* since then, both parts have usually been presented as a single work. The tale of four young women growing up during the Civil War, *Little Women* is comprised of small and undramatic "events," since the important point is the interior journey of each sister. In the absence of their father who is serving in the war as a preacher, the financially-impoverished March girls—Meg, Jo, Beth, and Amy—find great solace and warm affection in the company of each other, of their mother "Marmee," and of Laurie, the boy next door who is infatuated with Jo. As entertainment, the girls produce plays and publish their own newspaper; but they also learn valuable lessons—about exclusion, revenge, anger, discipline—from the experiences of their daily lives. For instance, after the sisters plan an excursion without inviting her along, an upset Amy burns a notebook of Jo's stories. Jo retaliates by failing to warn Amy not to skate on thin ice and thus endangers her sister's life. The occasion, however, does not end sadly; rather it becomes another opportunity for Alcott's characters to learn about self-control and moral growth.

Although Beth dies prematurely, Meg eventually marries and begins her own family; Amy travels to Europe to study art and soon becomes engaged to Laurie; and Jo pursues her writing career in New York, where she achieves some measure of the financial security she has sought and where she meets the awkward but gentle Professor Bhaer, who becomes her husband. Upon Aunt March's death, Jo inherits her home, Plumfield, which the Bhaers intend to turn into a school for young men.

The films, too, combine both parts of Alcott's best-known work, although—given the necessity of compression and rearrangement when a novel is adapted—they tend to pick and choose from the second. The early Hollywood versions, for instance, are as true to the details of the narrative as the films' length permits, but generally they omit a great deal from the second part, *Good Wives,* focusing there on moments that make drama, such as Beth's death and Jo's experiences in New York.

Little Women was first adapted to the screen in 1918 as a silent film, produced by William A. Brady and directed by Harley Knowles.[5] Starring Lillian Hall, Dorothy Barnard, Florence Flinn, and Isabel Lamon as the four March sisters, Kate Lester as Marmee, and Conrad Nagel as Laurie, the so-called "photoplay" apparently was a successful attempt at "picturizing" a widely beloved novel. "Of course," noted a contemporary reviewer, "Louisa M. Alcott's famous story cannot be told on the screen completely, and no doubt many of those who love it will consider any attempt to turn it into a 'movie' as a sort of sacrilege; but leaving these considerations aside, . . . one must say that it is good." Produced in cooperation with the Alcott family and the Alcott Memorial Committee, the film was shot "in and about the author's home in Concord, Mass."; it therefore teemed with "the atmosphere of a New England home in the sixties" and provided "charming glimpses of the period." Although the acting consisted of "too much conscious posing and a lack of character delineation," faults that became less "conspicuous as the story proceeds and heightened interest supplies deficiencies" (*NYT* 4 Nov. 1918), the 1918 *Little Women* was nonetheless hailed as "a picture out of the ordinary" (*Variety* 15 Nov. 1918). Unfortunately, the film is no longer extant and has, in fact, been lost for many years.

The earliest extant film version of *Little Women* was released by RKO Studios in 1933. Directed by George Cukor (who found Alcott's novel "very strong-minded, full of character, and a wonderful picture of New England family life"[6]), it starred Katherine Hepburn as Jo, Frances Dee as Meg, Jean Parker as Beth, Joan Bennett as Amy, and Spring Byington as Marmee. Featured were Edna May Oliver as Aunt March, Douglass Montgomery as Laurie, and Paul Lukas as the Professor. "A profoundly moving history of youth . . . [whose] deeply spiritual values are revealed with a simple earnestness," Cukor's production—suggested one contemporary review—seemed designed more for mature audiences who recalled Alcott's classic with fondness than for "the younger generation," who might find its sweetly sentimental appeal "a little dated" (*Variety* 21 Nov. 1933).

The film, carried largely by Hepburn (described in *Variety* as "one of the most debated and provocative figures on the current screen" and in the *New York Times* as "the personification of sincerity, a thorough human being"), took on the personality of its star. The almost androgynously appealing Hepburn fit the image Alcott's readers had of Jo as an intelligent and ambitious woman who seeks not just marriage but personal fulfillment. In the novel, as Carol Gay writes, Jo is steadily persistent "in her progress as a moral pilgrim," and that progress "enables her to become strong, independent, and so sure of her own individuality that she is able to offer it to Bhaer and to others without fear of submerging it" (36). Hepburn's performance suggests some of these same qualities, even though—as Gay notes—she "turn[s] to jelly at the sight of Bhaer" and "loll[s] shamelessly against the piano" as he sings.

Throughout the film, the acting is mannered, the pace is slow, and a few casting flaws are apparent, especially in the ages of some of the actresses: Amy (played by a pregnant Bennett, then in her twenties) is too mature, her face too worldly; even Marmee, with her gray hair styled severely, looks more matronly than the mother of the little women should. Yet, this chronicle "without a hero, or even a villain . . . causes one to be quite content to dwell for the moment with human hearts of the old-fashioned days" (*NYT* 18 Nov. 1933). After all, as Kate Ellis noted, "In times of economic and social upheaval, the sphere of home and mother is always there to fall back on" (62). And the March family's unity and homemade pleasures do indeed contrast favorably with the harsh modern horrors of grim bread lines and Hoovervilles and give "a heartening strength to the film's vision of courage in the face of want" (Hollander 11).

The 1949 Metro version, directed by Mervyn LeRoy, was essentially a remake of Cukor's film, even down to the same musical score and Christmas-card settings. The similarity is perhaps unsurprising, since the same writers—Sarah Y. Mason and Victor Heerman—wrote the screenplay for both versions.[7] (A third writer, Andrew Solt, was added to the writing team for the LeRoy production, "presumably," as Carol Gay suggests, "to bring things up to date." Viewing both films, she notes, "gives one the impression that the directors are using basically the same screenplay with few but distinct changes in dialogue, thematic focus and emphasis" [32-33]—changes like the omission of Beth's death and of the poverty of the neighboring immigrants, changes that do not improve upon the earlier version.[8]) Technicolor tinting added charm and nostalgic allure to LeRoy's *Little Women,* which starred June Allyson (Jo), Janet Leigh (Meg), Margaret O'Brien (Beth), and Elizabeth Taylor (Amy), and featured Mary Astor as Marmee, Rossano Brazzi as Professor Bhaer, and Peter Lawford as Laurie.[9] An "old-lace classic" whose crinoline bustles "hobble the pace and lessen its dramatic impact," the film tried to be faithful to such an extent to Alcott's text that critics complained "The sentiment is too meticulously preserved in the picture, a bit out of joint for our times" (*Variety* 23 Feb. 1949). Some viewers and reviewers, however, found a topical economic message underlying the more overtly romantic one; Anne Hollander, for instance, wrote that, unlike the 1933 version, which celebrated the joys of the home and the hearth, the 1949 version used the impoverished Marches to celebrate "the fresh postwar pleasure of acquiring sleek new possessions." The girls rush to the general store to spend their Christmas money, first on themselves and ultimately on presents for Marmee ("no homemade presents from these dedicated young consumers") (11, 21). But others felt that the film was more retrogressive than progressive, that—in keeping with postwar American gender politics—it downplayed the ambitions of Alcott's women.

Just as Cukor's film is defined by the personality of Katherine Hepburn, LeRoy's film is defined by June Allyson's. As Jo, Allyson has a crisp, bright sparkle that is attractive; *Variety* observed that "her thesping dominates the film" and imbues it with much joie-de-vivre. The chief casting flaw, however, as in the earlier version, is that the actresses look too old for their parts. (See Figure 26.) This is particularly true of Amy, played here by a very buxom-bodied Elizabeth Taylor (who, in fact, was only seventeen at the time).[10]

If the criterion for judging adaptations of *Little Women* is faithfulness to the text, the 1970 BBC version, directed by Paddy Russell and shown in the United States as a production of *Masterpiece Theatre,* is the winner. Starring Angela Down (Jo), Jo Rowbottom (Meg), Sarah Craze (Beth), and Janina Faye (Amy) and featuring Stephanie Bidmead (Mrs. March), Stephen Turner (Laurie), and Frederick Jaegar (Professor Bhaer), the BBC telefilm is, of course, much longer than the earlier Hollywood versions; it includes all the events of the plot, somewhat rearranged; and it gives equal time to the second half of the story. It is excellent, for example, on the developing relationship of Amy and Laurie in Europe and newlywed Meg's attempts to adjust to marriage; and it is the only adaptation that gives nearly equal time and emphasis to all four daughters.

The most interesting and immediate of all the adapations, however, is Columbia Pictures' *Little Women,* released in 1994 and directed by Gillian Armstrong. Not simply a tepid remake of earlier versions, it establishes its own identity. Visually beautiful, with authentic clothing and sets, it uses many long camera shots and features less "action." The predominant soft browns throughout create an effect of coziness and warmth. Starring Winona Ryder (Jo), Trini Alvarado (Meg), Claire Danes (Beth), and Kirsten Dunst and Samantha Mathis (younger and older Amy) and featuring Susan Sarandon (Marmee), Gabriel Byrne (Professor Bhaer), and Christian Bale (Laurie), Armstrong's film was the first version to be directed by a woman. The screenplay, written by Robin Swicord, may also have contributed to the at-times jarringly modern feminist slant. As several reviewers have noted, the film "glides" over some of the story's more mawkish moments by applying "a dusting of contemporary feminism" (*Variety* 21 Dec. 1994) and supplants what it considers to be Alcott's "dated fictional efforts" with "a 1990's sensibility" (Hollander 21).

Like the earlier films, this one tells the story of Jo March against the background of her sisters rather than the story of the four March daughters; unlike the earlier versions (and the text), the most recent one presents young women who are all but perfect—they already know everything that the novel shows them learning. The great strength of the film is its successful portrayal of family love and closeness among the five women—love that reaches out to include others.[11] Yet its great weakness is its failure to portray the sometimes difficult process of

Figure 26. In the 1949 MGM production, the bounciness of Jo (played by then-32-year-old June Allyson) contrasts with the lush beauty of Amy (17-year-old Elizabeth Taylor). © MGM

growth, a process that involves frequent and significant interactions among the characters, particularly between the girls and their mother.

Nineteenth-century fiction tends to present mothers as vital members of society. Few of Alcott's narratives are without mothers, good or bad. Her good mothers, like Marmee, radiate love, but they also have the self-denying virtues and the will to pass these qualities on to their children. Bad mothers, like Mrs. Shaw in *An Old-Fashioned Girl,* are caught up in society and have no time for family; having themselves no self-discipline or judgment, they cannot pass on these attributes and therefore guide their children to happy, useful lives. In that novel, when trouble hits the Shaw family, it is to Polly, reared by a high-principled mother, that they turn for comfort and direction. Mrs. March is indeed important, a role model for her daughters and the center of the atmosphere of love, tenderness, and caring that the film emphasizes. But Armstrong's film fails to establish what Alcott, through her character, insists on: the sometimes painful lessons of self-sacrifice, self-discipline, and moral strength that the daughters must be taught.[12]

A few examples make the point: in Alcott's text, the sisters are ready to sit down to their unusually lavish Christmas breakfast when Marmee enters, tells them about the poor German family, and asks them to give up their festive meal to the Hummels, presenting them with the extremely unwelcome opportunity for the sacrifice they know is right. By contrast, in the 1994 film Hannah, the maid, tells the girls where their mother is, and, after exchanging a few rueful glances, they fairly cheerfully decide to take their breakfast to the poor family. The difference is not minor; given the thesis of the novel, this early key scene spells out Alcott's message: it is necessary to sacrifice and feel pain in order to achieve goodness.

Again in Alcott's text, the adult Amy, who has always vowed she will marry a rich man, finds in herself her reasons for rejecting her wealthy British suitor. She also, applying the principles by which she was reared, can honestly despise Laurie's undisciplined, self-centered, and self-pitying conduct. And, just as she can face the fact that her talent is not strong enough to make her the kind of artist she dreamed of being, she can objectively analyze Laurie's behavior, even at the risk of giving real offense. Only after that, as Laurie sees the truth of her words and pulls himself together, can the affection between them develop into love. Handled offstage in early versions and beautifully by the BBC, this segment in the 1994 film displaces both plot and values, resulting in a superficial portrayal that provides no sense of growth; characters are robbed of credit for the moral strength that enables them to make right choices.

In both of these examples, and throughout, Gillian Armstrong and the other Columbia filmmakers either do not wish to show the painful learning process, have not themselves understood it, or have assumed that audiences will reject it. Mother is important as a source of love and security, but another parental role is ignored: the obligation to bring up a child to be a responsible adult, capable of taking a place in her world, by teaching manners, self-control, and the standards of the society she will enter. By comparison, the two earlier versions of *Little Women* emphasize much more the element of sacrifice, perhaps because audiences in the 1930s and the 1950s were better able than audiences in the 1990s to face such concepts without embarrassment.

Similarly, Jo's "tomboy" behavior, which differentiates her from her sisters and shows her discomfort with some of the conventions that affected young ladies of her day, is almost overplayed in the two early films. The shouted "Christopher Columbus!" does not ring true. But such behavior hardly appears at all in the 1994 Armstrong version, where Jo is played simply as the strongest of the sisters and a budding writer. Although the film script inserts feminist observations on the restrictions by which young women must live, Meg, Jo, Beth, and Amy—except for their sexual innocence—are essentially very nice late twentieth-century young women dressed in the clothing of the 1860s. With no attempt to set them in their period through speech, behavior, or the standards by which they are trying to live, Armstrong suggests that they could exist any place and any time.

For the most part, that film's subversions of the text are subtle; the major glaring anachronism occurs in the scene in which Jo and the Professor, unchaperoned, attend the opera, and, seated in a semi-public place, have a tender love scene, including kisses. In 1868 and for many years afterward, such behavior would have forever ruined Jo's reputation, and surely the Professor was too much of a gentleman to have taken such advantage of a young lady's unprotected status. What may seem of little consequence to a modern audience was in fact a real issue of propriety and morality for Alcott and her society.

For the film's content, it is not important that James T. Fields rather than Roberts Brothers is named as the publisher of Jo's novel, or that the illustrious publisher is moved from Boston to New York. In her "biography" of *Little Women*, Sheryl A. Englund suggests several possible reasons for the change: "an implicit attempt to link Louisa May Alcott to Fields' list of canonical authors" (199) or to "deregionalize" Alcott and connect her novel "to the current source of most literary publishing in the United States" (200). Englund notes that the title page as shown in the film lacks the date, which "furthers the project of universalizing, and at the same time, modernizing a novel that is essentially specific to its time and place" (200). Since it is unlikely that any but scholars of nineteenth-century American literature would recognize the error or, indeed, the significance of being published by Ticknor and Fields or Fields, Osgood, the analysis Englund offers seems logical and supports the view that the 1994 film, like its Hollywood predecessors, refuses or is unable to transmit the climate in which the novel originated.

What is much more important is that in Armstrong's adaptation, as in the other filmed versions, the core of Alcott's story is missing. The structure of her novel is the ancient and universal metaphor of life as journey, but Alcott roots her metaphor in that book so popular in the nineteenth century, John Bunyan's allegorical *Pilgrim's Progress,* the book that Mrs. March gives her daughters and whose message is spelled out in the first chapter. In Bunyan's tale the main character, Christian, forced to leave home, sets out on his journey to the Celestial City. On the way there are encounters that help or hinder him; Bunyan as storyteller personifies these versions of the Seven Deadly Sins—Vanity Fair, The Slough of Despond, the monstrous Apollyon. Each is a temptation or terror in the path of the hero's quest. For much of the way, Christian carries a burden, which impedes his progress. His burden, of course, represents his sins (a term that frightens the late twentieth century, although "crime" does not).

Alcott's four characters start out with their own burdens, and in fact getting rid of the burdens, or mastering the sins inherent in their natures, is what the story is about. The opening chapter is titled "Playing Pilgrims"; subsequent chapters are structured so that each young girl meets her own particular temptation, fails at first to master it, but continues to try until she can, if not overcome, at least control her nature: the chapters "Beth Finds the Palace Beautiful," "Amy's Valley of Humiliation," "Jo Meets Apollyon," and "Meg Goes to Vanity Fair" deal with Beth's shyness, Amy's pride, Jo's temper, and Meg's worldliness.

Later, in a chapter called "Experiments," the sisters are allowed to do exactly as they please for a week. By the last day they have learned that an idle existence is not pleasant: "It was astonishing what a peculiar and uncomfortable state of things was produced by the 'resting and reveling' process" (161). At the end of the chapter, Marmee drives home the message of duty and responsibility:

Work is wholesome, and there is plenty for everyone; it keeps us from ennui and mischief, is good for health and spirits, and gives us a sense of power and independence better than money or fashion. . . . Have regular hours for work and play, make each day both useful and pleasant, and prove that you understand the worth of time by employing it well. Then youth will be delightful, old age will bring few regrets, and life become a beautiful success, in spite of poverty. (172)

This passage is typical of the novel; but in the film, Marmee teaches, if at all, by example rather than by precept.

The BBC version does indeed mention the concept of burden/sin: when Beth is ill, Mrs. March reads to her from *Pilgrim's Progress*. Similarly, in Cukor's 1933 version, Marmee reminds her daughters of the game of pilgrim's progress that they used to play as children, and she notes that they still have their burdens. Both of these sequences, however, are brief; otherwise the idea is completely ignored, as is the value of work and duty, so that the struggles of each character with her own temptations become simply amusing events in their story. The concepts of burden, work, and duty are even further diminished in the 1994 version, in which Marmee is the center of love, but not strength; the film even has her say "I can't give you moral courage." (See Figure 27.) But in the text it is exactly moral courage, as defined by her times, that she teaches to and exemplifies for her daughters. After her temper has endangered Amy's life, Jo and her mother talk over what happened: "in that sad but happy hour, she [Jo] had learned not only the bitterness of remorse and despair, but the sweetness of self-control and self-denial" (122). Alcott's vision certainly shows the importance of love, but puts equal emphasis on self-discipline. As in so much nineteenth-century fiction, growing up involves more than loving and being loved; it involves training sinful or savage human nature into acceptable and rewarding behavior, and "human nature" and "reward" must be defined in their terms, not ours.

The tendency to shy away from the more difficult moral questions that nineteenth-century novelists like Alcott regularly raised and to substitute instead simple, even sentimental solutions is evident in another recent adaptation of Alcott's work. *Louisa May Alcott's "Little Men"* (1997/Allegro Films, released by Legacy; dir. Rodney Gibbons), a film far more disappointing to viewers than Alcott's novel was to readers, attempts to transfer to the screen the novel's episodic structure: a boy gets into trouble, then the problem is solved.[13] Nat and Dan are two street boys who end up at at the Bhaers' school, Plumfield. Never before having learned right from wrong, Nat soon adapts, the security of Plumfield and the love from Jo making him eager to conform. But streetwise Dan is a more difficult case: Jo fears that they may have to send him away and thus destroy him, while the Professor fears that by not sending Dan away they will destroy the school. In a pat plot resolution, both

Figure 27. Surrounded by her daughters, Marmee (Susan Sarandon) is the center of love in the March home. © Columbia

boys experience conversions, if not real learning; and, at the film's very contrived end, they lead the group in a singing of "Amazing Grace." Yet the virtues integral to the novel *Little Men*—self-knowledge, self-control, a clear definition of right and wrong—are never really articulated in the film; rather they are assumed. Moreover, they tend to be external, unlike the more interior journeys that the March girls in Alcott's novel (and, to a lesser degree, in some of the film adaptations) must make. The nostalgia for a simpler past in the film of *Little Men* thus betrays the deeper appreciation and understanding of virtues such as learning and self-sacrifice that underpinned nineteenth-century social behavior.

To be sure, this tendency by contemporary filmmakers, as well as literary critics, to reject or refuse to see the moral and religious belief that informs Alcott's world and to impose current values and concepts on her texts goes to the heart of any real discussion of adaptation.[14] Alcott's novels, like so much good nineteenth-century fiction, seldom separated themselves from didacticism, though the actual degree of didacticism might vary. Nineteenth-century readers expected a "moral" from both prose and poetry and often judged a work by its ability to interweave lesson and plot: the Horatian precept that the way to get a message across was to enclose it in a good story. Alcott put her message in Marmee's words; the action carried out the ideas. The individual behaviors depicted took place within a frame that Alcott (and her contemporaries) could take for granted, since they were writing for audiences who shared their language and found their message satisfying. Nearly all nineteenth-century fiction, and especially that written by women, was, at some level, "about" religious belief, or perhaps it is better to say it took place in a world where religious belief was understood, shared, and perfectly acceptable. Novels seldom preached a specific dogma, nor did they attempt to impose a system on others; they simply took for granted common understandings, especially about religion.[15] In *Little Women,* the religious frame is Christianity, at a time when the precepts of the New Testament gospels were replacing the rigidity of the Old Testament.

Alcott's nineteenth century saw a loosening of dogma, a movement away from the rigid restrictions of Puritanism, but that easing did not mean a lessening of a religious cultural frame. The resulting religious ambiance was too varied to be rigid; rather, it involved personal, individual beliefs based on standards that made right and wrong, or good and evil, clear. Children grew up going to Sunday School and hearing Bible stories and precepts in a church-going society; whatever each personal modification of belief might be, everyone shared a body of knowledge, a frame of reference. The easing of Puritan rigidity allowed more freedom to explore and examine the meaning of religion, and often the emphasis shifted to familiarity with and individual reinterpretation of the main text, the New Testament.

Nor did the loosening of dogma mean an easy slide into sentimentality, for following New Testament precepts was not easy, as Jane Tompkins has shown in her satisfying examination of Susan Warner's *The Wide, Wide World.* Tompkins defines what Ellen Montgomery goes through as a "psychological death . . . a sloughing off of the unregenerate self" (*Sensational Designs* 182). It is a painful process: "The education of the sentimental heroine is no more a fairy story than the story of Job or *Pilgrim's Progress.* Rather it is an American Protestant bildungsroman, in which the character of the heroine is shaped by obedience, self-sacrifice, and faith" (184).[16] Alcott was certainly not as harsh with her characters as Susan Warner is with Ellen, but her goals were similar, and readers understood them.

Perhaps, more than a century later, such discussion of religion—especially in the medium of film—seems unsophisticated; perhaps the public face of contemporary religion makes the topic anything but appealing; perhaps the religious climate of most nineteenth-century fiction makes filmmakers and critics uncomfortable. Nevertheless, for nineteenth-century novelists, especially women novelists, the shared religious knowledge and experience created a climate and a language that established community.[17] It was a language not only of belief, but of knowledge: allusion and reference based on common understandings. Equally important, it was a language that could communicate across the divisions of gender, race, and class, creating a unity. Unfortunately, it is a language that twentieth-century adaptors do not always share; and it is a language that they generally fail to interpolate in their films.

In the novel *Little Women,* the sisters, by conscious effort, must work through their burdens—sins—to achieve maturity and happiness. In the most recent film adaptation, the underlying message is that love solves everything, a message that the late twentieth century finds acceptable. Marmee creates an atmosphere of love around her daughters. Perhaps that is why Armstrong's film as well as the other three versions of *Little Women* reproduce one particular visual effect: the early scene in which Mr. March's letter is read aloud. As Mrs. March sits in her big chair, the daughters gather, forming a circle with their mother at the center and creating a picture of love and unity. But the lack of moral strength makes the teaching incomplete by the standards of the novel's time and place; perhaps the filmmakers' belief that love solves everything is its own kind of naive sentimentality.

The rest of the novel's message seems even less appealing to contemporary audiences: the austere virtues, the non-glorification of self, the idea that the self needs training in restraint and control. But the nineteenth century had no doubt of the need for such training; it did not really believe in the essential goodness of human nature, Rousseau and Wordsworth notwithstanding. Rather it saw human nature as something that had to be controlled and trained according to culturally-shared standards of right and wrong. Jo March's "feelings" involve bad temper and anger that bring her sister into danger, and her insistence on speaking her feelings without regard to the effect she makes costs her the longed-for trip to Europe. Feelings without control were destructive; virtue and manners must be learned, and there is little difference between unloved and untaught.

Few contemporary filmmakers appreciate the necessity of treating religious thought in their adaptations with the paramount importance that nineteenth-century writers like Alcott did in their novels; film, after all, is made for commercial purposes, to attract audiences and to make money, and filmmakers are under no obligation to be wholly authentic (though they would undoubtedly claim a different kind of integrity to their works). Nevertheless, the weakness shared by all of the adaptations of Alcott's *Little Women,* from Cukor's to Armstrong's, is that—despite being handsome period pieces that create seductive but superficial nostalgia and atmosphere through costumes and regional scenery—they ignore the most vital elements of nineteenth-century life, that is, the presentation of that period's values, and not just our own.

Notes

1. An earlier version of this essay appeared as "Filming the Nineteenth Century: *The Secret Garden* and *Little Women*" in *ATQ* 10.4 (Dec. 1996), 273-92.

2. In the recent BBC/A & E production, there are brief moments when Darcy is alone in his world and we see life through his eyes. This subverts Austen's remarkable use of point of view, since after the opening chapters we see the world through Elizabeth's eyes, as we must if we are to share the shock of her realization of her own bias.

3. See in particular the second part of *Anne of Green Gables,* totally rewritten, and *Jane of Lantern Hill,* unrecognizable in its sensationalism.

4. *Little Women* was also remade several times for television—CBS-TV (1950), NBC-TV (1958), CBS-TV (1958), NBC-TV (1969), Series British TV (1970), CAN-TV (1977)—and it was remade yet again as an American made-for-television movie (1978; dir. David Lowell Rich), starring Meredith Baxter Birney, Susan Dey, Ann Dusenberry, Eve Plumb, Robert Young, and William

Shatner. Dorothy McGuire played Marmee, and Greer Garson made her television-movie debut as Aunt March. A short-lived television series, also called *Little Women,* followed; that series ran a mere four episodes, from February 8 until March 8, 1979.

The 1978 television film apparently took some real liberties with Alcott's story. As Carol Gay writes, "Alcott's feminist propensities are dwelled on and emphasized so that Jo, played by Susan Dey, becomes totally liberated; while nursing Laurie back to health, she not only disrobes him but stays all night with him, crawling into bed and lying side by side with him in the morning hours, totally perverting the maternal impulse that Jo exhibits so strongly in the book. Aunt March . . . becomes a militant feminist recounting to Jo a cautionary tale about her own youthful life, implying that the one saving grace to her life was her wisdom in consummating that love before her young man was killed" (31). Producer David Lowell believed that television would give him a chance to depict what earlier versions lacked; he felt he could "do it correctly for the first time" (Lowell, quoted in Gay 32).

5. James Limbacher writes that there was also a British silent film version, which he dates to 1917. Unfortunately, that version is lost, and even references to it are few. Limbacher suggests, however, that it was the basis for at least two subsequent musicals, a British version called "A Girl Named Jo" and an American version called simply "Jo" (Limbacher 121).

6. After reading the book, Cukor admits that he "was startled. It's not sentimental or saccharine. . . . It's full of that admirable New England sternness, about sacrifice and authority" (Cukor, quoted in Gay 32).

7. In fact, Mason and Heerman won an Academy Award for Best Adapted Screenplay for their screenplay of Cukor's 1933 film.

8. LeRoy also portrays with too much opulence the genteel poverty of the Marches and prettifies all of his characters, who are always seen perfectly made-up and costumed.

9. While the Technicolor added interest, the Technicolored rainbow that appears above the March home at the film's end only added to the sugary quality of LeRoy's version.

10. The exception is the child actress Margaret O'Brien, who plays Beth in the 1949 version.

11. Readers who were disappointed that Jo did not marry Laurie might find this version satisfying, since the Professor is far more attractive than the adult Laurie. Anne Hollander, in fact, observed that "Armstrong's movie is the only one to reward Jo's forceful independence with a really sexy, intelligent lover who also won't interfere with her work."

12. Gary Arnold, in his review of the film for the *Washington Times,* notes that Marmee, although "a maternal paragon to rely upon," makes only "fleeting inspirational appearances" (C-14). By contrast, however, Janet Maslin suggests

that Susan Sarandon's character emphasizes the "marm" in Marmee, with "an excess of instructional dialogue that echoes the thinking of Alcott's progressive Concord parents." Maslin also comments on the "occasional feminist mouthful" that Marmee speaks as well as on the "stridency" of her sentiments (C-1). And Rita Kempley observes that the film's "dusting of contemporary feminism" and its "political corrections . . . about suffrage, abolitionism and social work" are left to Marmee, a "bustling matriarch" whose role "seems to draw equally on Grandma Walton and Betty Friedan."

The 1997 version of *Little Men* was not the first adaptation of Alcott's novel. Earlier versions included *Little Men* (1934; dir. Phil Rosen), a Mascot production, and *Little Men* (1940; dir. Norman Z. McLeod), an RKO production. *Little Men* was also remade as a television production (1960; NBC-TV). Adaptations of other Alcott works include *An Old-Fashioned Girl*, made into a film by Eagle Lion (1948; dir. Arthur Dreifuss), and *Inheritance* (Inheritance/Cosgrove Meurer Productions; dir. Bobby Roth), a television film that premiered on American network television early in 1997.

14. Just as the filmmakers have done, many contemporary critics reject or refuse to see the religious belief that informs the world that most nineteenth-century fiction portrays; further, they impose current values and concepts on the texts.

Since it is mostly women critics who write about women authors, they have been, sadly, the most guilty of this kind of distortion. The early pioneering works in the field opened new territory. Plunging enthusiastically into unexplored and exciting areas, many scholars failed to do the kind of thoughtful and exhaustive research that already existed for each canonized male author and therefore their work lacked the kind of information from which valid conclusions are drawn. Finding themselves uncomfortable with the religious climate of most nineteenth-century fiction, they accepted the unfortunate terms "sentimental" or "sentimentality," with their connotations of overdone emotionalism and the irrational, evoking a kind of pitying contempt, to describe behavior or speech governed by religious knowledge or attitudes. Yet the period's strongest definition of women's role, the doctrine of separate spheres, gave women the task of transmitting values to the next generation; given the century's belief in progress, the task was vital, and, indeed, might be read as a kind of empowerment. Certainly it is logical that women's narratives should reflect these ideas. Whether we like it or not, and regardless of personal belief, religion is pervasive and important to the time, and to ignore either its importance or its function is to falsify the text.

15. There are a few exceptions to my general statement; for example, popular novelist Clara Louise Burnham, a Christian Scientist, wrote several of her novels to explain (and perhaps gently sell) her religious belief to readers.

16. Earlier in our century, T. S. Eliot called the result of belief "A condition of complete simplicity/Costing not less than everything" ("Little Gidding," V, 40-41). Like most major religions, Christianity is rigorous and demanding, and its virtues are often at the opposite extreme from the qualities, especially in women, prized by the late twentieth century.

17. Of interest to this discussion is the reaction of contemporary women scholars to the forces that shape nineteenth-century women characters; self-denying virtues seem to be the same qualities that kept women "in their places" and made them powerless and all but invisible outside the home. Just as Harriet Beecher Stowe's Uncle Tom, with his complete submission to his Christian belief, could be (mis)interpreted as subservience to white authority, so the submission of women to the same beliefs can be read as bowing to patriarchal power and the stifling of freedom. The qualities that we applaud in women today would have seemed outrageous in the nineteenth century; in the same way, our own time rejects the standards of one hundred years ago.

Works Cited

Alcott, Louisa May. *Little Men*. Boston: Roberts Brothers, 1871.

——. *Little Women*. Boston: Roberts Brothers, 1870.

——. *An Old-Fashioned Girl*. Boston: Roberts Brothers, 1870.

Arnold, Gary. "*Little Women* Finally Gets a Woman's Touch." (Rev. of 1994 Armstrong version of *Little Women*.) *Washington Times* 21 Dec. 1994: C-14.

De Jong, Mary, guest ed. Special issue on "Religion and Anglo-American Women." *Women's Studies* 19 (1991).

Eliot, T. S. "Little Gidding." In *Four Quartets*. London: Faber & Faber, 1944.

Ellis, Kate. "Life with Marmee: Three Versions." In *The Classic American Novel and the Movies*. Ed. Gerald Peary and Roger Shatzkin. New York: Ungar, 1977. 62-72.

Englund, Sheryl A. "Reading the Author in *Little Women*: A Biography of a Book." *ATQ* 12.3 (Sept. 1998): 199-219.

Gay, Carol. "*Little Women* at the Movies." In *Children's Novels and the Movies*. Ed. Douglas Street. New York: Ungar, 1983. 28-38.

Hollander, Anne. "Portraying *Little Women* through the Ages." *New York Times* 15 Jan. 1995: Sect. H: 11, 21.

Kempley, Rita. "The Gift of *Little Women*." (Rev. of 1994 Armstrong version.) *Washington Post* 21 Dec. 1994: C-1.

Little Women. Brady Productions, 1918. Dir. Harley Knowles. Perf. Lillian Hall, Dorothy Barnard, Florence Flinn, Isabel Lamon, Kate Lester, Conrad Nagel. Silent.

Little Women. RKO, 1933. Dir. George Cukor. Perf. Katherine Hepburn, Frances Dee, Jean Parker, Joan Bennett, Spring Byington, Edna May Oliver, Douglass Montgomery, Paul Lukas. Videocassette.

Little Women. Metro, 1949. Dir. Mervyn LeRoy. Perf. June Allyson, Margaret O'Brien, Elizabeth Taylor, Janet Leigh, Mary Astor, Rossano Brazzi, Peter Lawford. Videocassette.

Little Women. Columbia Pictures, 1994. Dir. Gillian Armstrong. Perf. Winona Ryder, Claire Danes, Trini Alvarado, Kirsten Dunst, Samantha Mathis, Susan Sarandon, Gabriel Byrne, Christian Bale. Videocassette.

Little Women. BBC, 1970. Dir. Paddy Russell. Perf. Angela Down, Jo Rowbottom, Sarah Craze, Janina Faye, Stephanie Bidmead, Stephen Turner, and Frederick Jaegar. CBS-FOX Videocassette.

Louisa May Alcott's "Little Men." Allegro Films/Released by Legacy, 1997. Dir. Rodney Gibbons. Perf. Mariel Hemingway, Chris Sarandon, Ben Cook, Michael Caloz.

Maslin, Janet. "The Gold Standard for Girlhood Across America." (Rev. of 1994 version of *Little Women.*) *New York Times* 21 Dec. 1994: Sect. C: 1.

McCarthy, Todd. Rev. of *Little Women* (1994 Armstrong version). *Variety* 14 Dec. 1994.

Rev. of *Little Women* (1918 Knowles version). *New York Times* 4 Nov. 1918. In *New York Times Film Reviews 1913-1968.* Vol. 1. New York: New York Times & Arno Press, 1970. 45.

Rev. of *Little Women* (1918 Knowles version). *Variety* 15 Nov. 1918. In *Variety Film Reviews 1907-1980.* New York: Garland, 1983.

Rev. of *Little Women* (1933 Cukor version). *New York Times* 17 Nov. 1933. In *New York Times Film Reviews 1913-1968.* Vol. 2. New York: New York Times & Arno Press, 1970.

Rev. of *Little Women* (1933 LeRoy version). *Variety* 21 Nov. 1933. In *Variety Film Reviews 1907-1980.* New York: Garland, 1983.

Rev. of *Little Women* (1949 LeRoy version). *Variety* 23 Nov. 1949. In *Variety Film Reviews 1907-1980.* New York: Garland, 1983.

Rev. of *Little Women* (1949 LeRoy version). *New York Times* 11 March 1949. In *New York Time Film Reviews 1913-1968.* Vol. 2. New York: New York Times & Arno P, 1970. 2317-18.

Tompkins, Jane. *Sensational Designs: The Cultural Work of American Fiction, 1790-1860.* New York: Oxford UP, 1985.

10

LOVE ON THE ALGERIAN SANDS:
REVIVING CIGARETTE IN *UNDER TWO FLAGS*

Victoria Szabo

Under Two Flags (1936) is a film in dialogue with its predecessors. By the time the film was released, the story was already familiar to readers of the novel and to stage and screen audiences. The novel, written by a young Louise de la Ramée ("Ouida"), had its beginnings in 1865 as a serial in the *British Army and Navy Review*. Published in 1867 as a triple-decker, it went into more than sixty editions in the next ten years alone and became a hit in both England and America (Sutherland xviii).[1] The *New York Times,* counting at least eight major dramatic adaptations since 1870, ranked *Under Two Flags* a "hardy perennial" of the stage.[2] Two silent-film versions (Fox Film Corporation, 1916; dir. J. Gordon Edwards, and Universal Pictures, 1922; dir. Tod Browning) complemented the print and stage versions of the story as well and paved the way for the big-budget Hollywood spectacle in 1936, starring Ronald Colman, Claudette Colbert, Victor McLaglen, and Rosalind Russell. (See Figure 28.) With each new popular form, a new *Under Two Flags* made its debut. One did not supersede the other entirely, however; earlier versions coexisted with later ones. After the 1936 film opened, for example, Grossett & Dunlap brought out yet another edition of Ouida's novel, this one featuring pictures of all of the film's stars.

The adaptation-history of *Under Two Flags* complicates the questions of authenticity that often figure into discussions of novel to film adaptations, particularly in the case of nineteenth-century novels, where fidelity to period detail can obstruct meaning. In this case, the "original" of the 1936 film *Under Two Flags* consists not only of Ouida's novel but also of the dramatic and film adaptations that gave the story continued immediacy into the twentieth century. While this expanded idea of the original text is arguably true for any novel that has been adapted for stage or screen, it is particularly true of a novel like *Under Two Flags,* which has never had the aura of an unassailable classic about it. The focus for a proper study of the adaptation of Ouida's novel therefore

Figure 28. The poster for *Under Two Flags* (1936), "starring Ronald Colman and featuring Claudette Colbert, Victor McLaglen, Rosalind Russell, and a cast of 10,000," suggests just how spectacular the production was. © Twentieth-Century Fox

becomes not so much how the details of the novel get transferred from one medium to another but rather how the core narrative is revisited with new accompaniments and contexts and how those changes alter the story's meaning. This is not to say that the details are unimportant in themselves, but rather—and more significantly—that those details help subvert or reinforce a particular "take" on a familiar tale.

In *Novel to Film: An Introduction to the Theory of Adaptation,* Brian MacFarlane outlines a methodology for approaching film adaptations of novels.[3] By articulating the distinctions between what is transferable and what is adaptable in the movement from novel to film, MacFarlane makes a case against "fidelity" criticism and in favor of an "intertextual" understanding of the relationship of film to novel. This type of intertextual approach pays attention to the social and critical context of both works as well as to the inherent differences in the media in order to value both novel and film as discrete, yet interrelated entities. The closeness of a film adaptation to the novel depends on the degree to which the central story and relationships between characters remain intact and on how the defining details translate from one medium to another. Formal differences arise out of the novel's linearity versus film's spatiality, the novel's verbal versus the film's multimedia signifying systems, and the novel's propensity for telling versus film's showing. Since strict fidelity is impossible, MacFarlane suggests, analyzing the processes of transference and transformation is at the heart of adaptation criticism. MacFarlane's methodology offers an ideal vantage point for examining *Under Two Flags,* the mid-Victorian novel, and *Under Two Flags,* the big-budget Hollywood talkie, as extremes of a continuum rather than as two sharply differentiated entities. The novel and the film thus become intertextually related to one another; reading one provides insight into the other.

While preparing for battle, one of the Legionnaires stationed in Algeria in *Under Two Flags* (1936) remarks: "We're all supposed to be trying to forget something, but there's so much noise around here I can't remember what it is I'm supposed to forget!" In this as in many other moments, the film version of Ouida's 1867 novel *Under Two Flags* is unmistakably a product of modernity.[4] The joke, original to the film, is twofold—the soldier has succeeded in forgetting, his ostensible goal for joining the Foreign Legion, yet by forgetting he betrays the core identity of the Legionnaire as represented in popular culture. Like an actor who has forgotten his lines, the bumbling soldier does not quite seem up to the challenge of playing himself. In fact, it is his homely self-consciousness about the fact of his forgetfulness that marks him as modern. No glorious or tragic hero, he is instead an ordinary man in the midst of a romance, a place-holder for the skeptical viewer whose willed credulousness allows the story to do its work once again.

This modern forgetfulness permeates the film adaptation of the novel and provides an implicit commentary on the action similar to that of a narrator. At the same time, the filmmaker's sometimes absurd additions to the story introduce an element of ironic distance to the familiar tale as well as encourage escapist immersion in it, by structuring the viewer as a knowing participant in an escapist fantasy that disavows a political agenda in favor of a personal one. The hero, Private Victor, like the unnamed soldier who succeeded in doing so, joins the Legion to forget his aristocratic past; yet he obviously clamors to be reminded of it at every turn. Cigarette, the camp-follower heroine, forgets her opportunistic loyalty to Victor's commanding officer and subjects herself instead to unrequited love for the lower-ranking hero. The second heroine, the aristocratic Lady Venetia, forgets her class privilege long enough to venture out into the "real" Africa that Victor suggests is just over the next rise. (See Figure 29.) Even Sidi Ben Youssiff, the Arab against whom the Legion fights, forgets momentarily that he is an Arab when he recalls Oxford teas with Victor.

This pervasive motif of forgetfulness also emphasizes the history of the Near East in the popular imagination as it had evolved since the mid-Victorian period. From *Under Two Flags* (1867) and the subsequent stage and film adaptations of Ouida's story to the travel narratives of the 1880s of Ouida's good friend Sir Richard Burton, who prided himself on the ability to "pass" as an Arab and advocated war to secure imperial conquests, from T. E. Lawrence's World War I sympathy with the Arabs in *Seven Pillars of Wisdom* (1926) and the "Lawrence of Arabia" craze to Rudolph Valentino's *The Sheik* (1921) and Christopher Wren's 1924 *Beau Geste* and the film that followed, the desert-hero negotiating the Near East had figured largely in the popular imagination. Whether by joining the Legion or by mingling with the Arabs, "going native" became a synecdoche for finding oneself.[5]

Even for Ouida, the notion specifically of Algeria as a site of personal discovery and transformation was far from new. The forgetful soldier's remark in the film underscores the French Foreign Legion's special appeal and mystique, which began with the first recruitment of the *Chausseurs d'Afrique* in 1831 by King Louis-Phillipe of France. The Légion Étrangére was an army composed of the misfits of many nations, bound together by common fealty to France, whatever their national and class backgrounds. That their histories were sealed lent them an air of mystery and of danger; even the name of their unit suggested their strangeness and alienation from the roles they chose to inhabit. (The

Figure 29. Class inhibitions do not limit the enjoyment that Lady Venetia (Rosalind Russell) feels on a visit to the "real" Africa with her dashing Legionnaire, Victor (Ronald Colman). © Twentieth-Century Fox.

name of Ouida's novel *Under Two Flags* itself implies the conflict between past and present allegiances that lent dramatic interest to the figure of the Legionnaire.)

Ouida was not alone in her examination of issues such as identity. Nineteenth-century popular romance, whether set in distant colonies or in drawing-rooms, helped imagine a world in which identity was circumstantial rather than innate, the product of economics, social structures, location, and self-will. Such fictions tapped into the gender, class, national, and racial questions of identity that had shaken Europe and the United States throughout the wars and reform movements and that continued into the early twentieth century. Domestic fiction explored these issues by telling and retelling, with variations, the marriage plot. Sensation fiction upended convention, illustrating the economic or animalistic motives that lay below the surface of seeming love-relationships, and often highlighted remote settings as an arena in which to pursue these possibilities without an immediate threat to the *status quo*. The adventure novel, coinciding with the late Victorian and Edwardian era of High Imperialism, lent this process of self-determination national and even racial importance. Whether its presence served as a social safety valve or a provocation to disorder, the Legion in particular (like imperial settings in general) figured heavily in popular romance as a site of forgetting and self re-creation.

Like other nineteenth-century romances, which offered ready-made collections of stories to adapt, *Under Two Flags,* a story framed doubly by imperial and domestic concerns, afforded the filmmaker a chance to pick and choose the kind of meaning to assign to the bare outlines of plot. The presence of the "Household" and the "Desert" in Ouida's novel reflected a long-standing connection between the two forms and traded on the symbolic correlation between the domestic as Europe and the domestic as the private sphere of individual relationships.[6] Domestic realism, a genre associated with women, offered an excellent opportunity to show rather than tell, precisely because the story in itself was likely already to be familiar; and indeed repetition of the story was itself of cultural value. The narrative elements of domestic fiction were variations on the middle-class marriage plot, with conventions that would have been obvious to readers and that did not need explication. Focus on these elements derived of a realist aesthetic of exemplary fiction-writing; the didactic impulse was alive and well in Victorian novels by women. Insofar as canonicity for women writers has been granted, it has thus often been for unique ways of telling familiar stories.[7] Adventure fiction, a genre geared toward boys and men, meanwhile gained ground in the late Victorian and Edwardian periods. The genre usually featured an intrepid European explorer triumphing amidst colonial wilds and often proved a didactic counterpart to feminine domestic fiction.

Though its relationship to adventure fiction is more obvious, in its concerns with wealth, status, and appropriate marriages, *Under Two Flags*—the novel—could be also be seen as a more extreme version of novels like *Mansfield Park* or *Jane Eyre,* where an off-stage but influential imperial setting provides an important complement to the action at home. One could imagine a film version of the novel that telescoped the hero's Algerian service much in the manner that film versions of *Jane Eyre* have tended to excise Jane's time with her country cousins. This time "outside" would be immensely useful for advancing the plot and strengthening character, but without in itself affecting the fundamental relationships at the core of the tale. This thematic road-not-taken represents Ouida's specifically Victorian concerns regarding class, marriage, and the relationship of the aristocracy to "the people." Insofar as her novel reunites Bertie/Victor with his best friend, his lady love, and his horse, Algeria might never have happened. Interpreted this way, Bertie/Victor's service in the Foreign Legion becomes simply the proving ground for his masculinity and honor, a necessary antidote to an enervating modern age. This, in fact, seems the approved reading, the one Ouida's narrative appears to encourage.

Such a reading, however, leaves out a key element—the character of Cigarette, and, along with her, most of the positive representations of self-assertive womanhood the novel offers. The 1936 film adaptation, by contrast, highlights this element by working out yet again the relationships among the principal characters in order to make sense of the sacrifice of the story's heroine.

The film, directed by Frank Lloyd, featured the familiar cast of characters: Louis Victor (Colman), the aristocrat-turned Legionnaire who joins up after taking the blame for his brother's crime; Cigarette (Colbert), the camp-follower who loves Victor, saves his life, and dies for him; the aristocratic Lady Venetia (Russell), whom Victor grows to love; Major Doyle (McLaglen), Victor's commander, who in turn loves Cigarette and hates Victor. As in the two earlier silent versions, the relationships among the members of this quartet are essentially stable, the one exception being the addition of a rivalry between Victor and his commander for the affections of Cigarette. Part of the film's drama arises from the fact that Victor's commander keeps sending him out on impossible missions in hopes of getting him out of the way. Yet the commander's motives differ. In Ouida's novel, the commander Chateâuroy hates Victor because Victor is an aristocrat while Chateâuroy is the son of a tradesman. Not until the 1921 silent film version is Chateâuroy's hatred of Victor linked to Cigarette (though in that version Chateâuroy also hates Victor for his breeding).[8] By 1936, however, the transformation is total: Victor's class background becomes relevant only insofar as he is able to charm Lady Venetia; Chateâuroy, now Doyle, hates Victor merely because he has "stolen" Cigarette.

This shift in emphasis completes the process of making Cigarette rather than Victor the center of the story. Correspondingly, the love story among the individual characters takes precedence over the political and social questions that their relationships embody. The increased importance of Cigarette is immediately apparent in the 1936 film reviews, which refer to earlier versions of *Under Two Flags* in terms of the stars who played her in American productions—Blanche Bates (1901) and Margaret Mayo (1904) on stage, Theda Bara (1916) and Priscilla Dean (1922) on film.[9] The *New York Times,* which called Ouida's tale "Cigarette's tragic story of devotion unto death," pointed out that the role of Cigarette had been a star vehicle since Theda Bara, "the silent screen's sinuous siren," had decided she wanted a "non-vampire" role. Sex goddess Priscilla Dean, whom John Sutherland described as lounging "voluptuously in Oriental silks on a divan" in her rendition of Cigarette, was replaced by the "milder" person of Colbert.[10] Colbert herself replaced the histrionic newcomer, French actress Simone Simon, who was originally slated to play Cigarette, bringing to the role her cinematic experience and familiar persona.[11] Though Colbert lacked the "wholehearted 'child of nature' qualities Ouida imagined," she offered a star quality and a dash of tomboy charm. Graham Greene commented on this aspect of her performance, calling her the "passionate but pure cocotte who dies of her wounds, after a mad gallop with windblown fringe and in enchanting trousers to save the company."[12]

Cigarette's centrality in the 1936 film highlights a strand half-submerged in Ouida's fiction—the self-assertive heroine who combines the best of masculine valor and feminine beauty as she moves from domestic to international triumphs. Ostensibly about Bertie Cecil, the English Life Guardsman whose backstory occupies the first volume, the novel *Under Two Flags* oscillates its focus between the suffering Cecil faces as he becomes Louis Victor, a private in the French-Algerian army, and Cigarette's unrequited love for him. That this love is manifested in personal heroism in battle reflects both the respect Cigarette deserves and the impossibility that Victor could ever regard her as a serious love-interest. "He was grateful to her," reports the narrator, observing Victor's ambivalence; "but despite himself, he was cold to her; despite himself, the life which that little hand he held had taken so lightly, made it the hand of a comrade to be grasped in alliance, but never the hand of a mistress to steal to his lips and to lie in his breast" (277).[13] The conflict between admiration and pity for Cigarette is reinforced by the often-repeated description of her as "unsexed" and of the aristocratic Venetia as a more fitting mate for Victor. The ending of the novel, in which Cigarette dies for Victor, who ends up with Venetia, seems to affirm this judgment; yet, again, Venetia does little to recommend herself throughout.

Such thematic dissonance is typical of the "sensation fiction" of the 1860s and 70s, which—controlled by censors in the publishing industry and circulating libraries—often featured a daring second volume and a conventional dénouement. When it appeared, Ouida's novel was considered "sensational," an epithet that was used to describe writers as diverse as Wilkie Collins, Mary Elizabeth Braddon, and Charles Reade. What all of these writers had in common were emphases on incident; on the relationship of identity to circumstance and social structure; and on a "realistic" representation of the extraordinary, whether criminal, exotic, or passionate. The genre of "sensation fiction" had emerged out of stage melodrama, domestic realism, old-time adventure fiction, and newspaper divorce and crime reports; and it was both critically castigated and extremely popular. It passed the moral censors by allowing its transgressions to fall short of all-out intentional misconduct or by punishing severely those transgressors. Ouida's efforts at poetic description and moral debate in the novel reflected her desire to be seen as a serious artist by the public, a position attained by very few women writers in the period. Yet she continued to be drawn to the sensational and the exuberant. As Graham Greene pointed out in the *Spectator*:

How Ouida would have loved the abandon of this picture [the 1936 film adaptation], the 32,000 rounds of ammunition shot off into the Arizona desert, the cast of more than 10,000 . . . the £5000 which insured Miss Claudette Colbert, Mr. Ronald Colman, Mr. Victor McLaglen and Miss Rosalind Russell against camel bites . . . and, in the words of the programme: "a fort 200 feet square, an Arabian oasis with eight fair-sized buildings, and a forest of transplanted date palms, two Arabian cities and a horse market and a smaller fort." The absurdities are for once not Hollywood's. . . .

The architecture of the film, as Greene suggests, approached something of the grandeur and detail of Ouida's own compositions—the same qualities that her critics scorned but her readers loved.

Ouida was also considered "sensational" because, even though she was a woman, she wrote about military men and aristocratic high life, albeit with more flourish than accuracy and with an eye to the hypocrisy below the surface of high society morals. Even her most military novels featured strong critiques of women—perhaps a distancing move, but also one that she carried out in her very public private life.[14] Ouida's desire for personal glory was expressed in association with the men she admired and about whom she wrote. Surrounding herself with military men, adventurers, and aristocrats, she declared "*Je n'écrit pas pour les femmes. J'écrit pour les militaires.*"[15] Yet Ouida's own presentation reflected her ambivalence about the possibility for a woman hero. She did not strive for a masculine appearance; rather, she considered herself an exception to the general feminine rule in that she had beauty, intellect, and noble instincts. Hair down, surrounded by flowers and her beloved dogs, smoking, trailing lace, holding court with a "voice like a carving knife," as one contemporary remarked, Ouida the celebrity loomed as large as her fictional characters in the public imagination. Her biographers have since commented that Ouida strove to live out the lives of her heroes and heroines; after the publication of her novel *Idalia* (1867), for instance, she was frequently referred to by that name. In Ouida's terms, Cigarette could only be a heroine insofar as she was "unsexed"; but being unsexed, she could never achieve the romance she craved. Again, biographers have pointed out how Ouida's unrequited love for various dashing men ultimately led nowhere; the more conventional woman got the hero in the end.

The 1936 film, however, shows a Cigarette who is both womanly and heroic. Consistent with Ouida's notion that by dying for the love of Victor, Cigarette can retain both her femininity and her glory, the film collapses the novel's scene in which Cigarette saves Victor's life in battle with one in which she saves him from a firing squad by flinging herself in the path of a bullet. Venetia's unworthiness of Victor, by contrast, is expressed by implication. Victor is sentenced to death because he dared to defend the honor of a lady's name, in this case Lady Venetia's. His original trip to Algeria is prompted not only by the desire to protect his brother from criminal charges but also by his chivalrous shielding of the name of the flighty Lady Guenevere (from whom we never hear again), who could have provided him an alibi for the night of the crime. Ouida's general misogyny and contempt for her own sex, apparent in the second reason for Victor's flight and masquerade, illustrate why she generally preferred men to women. That Guenevere was unworthy of Victor's loyalty is reflected in the narrator's condemnation of her for not coming forward to save him: "she sacrificed him for her reputation and her jewels; the choice was thoroughly a woman's" (180). Though Venetia is unaware of Victor's sentence, her ignorance contrasts mightily with Cigarette's heroic gallop across Algeria in search of a General's pardon.

Another important difference between the novel and the 1936 film lies in how Algeria is represented and in how Victor is characterized in relation to that setting. Ouida's novel reveals that the Algeria of the 1860s was already developing into the site of sexual experimentation and interracial contact for which it would become famous by the turn of the century.[16] In the period depicted in the novel, however, French colonization had not yet occurred on a wide scale; Algeria was still very much a separate place from Europe, though it bore distinct traces of European influences. In *Under Two Flags,* Ouida introduces Algeria by way of Algiers, which she depicts as a romantic amalgam of East and West:

In the straight white boulevards, as in the winding ancient streets, under the huge barn-like walls of barracks, as beneath the marvellous mosaics of mosques, the strange bizarre conflict of European and Oriental life spread its panorama. Staff-officers, all a-glitter with crosses, galloped past; mules, laden with green maize and driven by lean brown Bedouins, swept past the plate-glass windows of bonbon shops; grave white bearded Sheiks drank *petit verres* in the *guinguettes;* Sapeurs, Chausseurs, Zouaves, cantinières, all the varieties of French military life, mingled with jet-black Soudans, desert kings wrathful and silent, eastern women shrouded in haick and serroual, eagle-eyed Arabs flinging back snow-white burnous, and handling ominously the jewelled hilts of their cangiars. Alcazar chansons rang out from the cafés, while in their midst stood the mosque that had used to resound with the Mueizzin; Bijou-blondine and Belbée La-la and all the sister-heroines of the demi-monde dragged their voluminous Paris-made dresses side by side with Moorish beauties, who only dared show the gleam of their bright black eyes through the yasmak; the *reverbères* were lit in the Place du Gouvernement, and a group fit for the days of Solyman the magnificent sat under the white marble beauty of the Mahometan church. (160)

Yet, while the novel is set in Algeria during the period of French colonization under Napoleon III, the film (according to the opening credits) takes place later, at the turn of the century. This difference of fifty or sixty years is important to the story's representation of the relationship between the West and the East. In accordance with other versions of European imperialism, the goals of France in the earlier part of the nineteenth-century centered more on French rule through native leaders than on outright European control.[17] Napoleon III's assertion that Algeria was "not a French province but an Arab country, a European colony, and a French camp," suggested rule through local powers rather than overt domination. As Patrick Brantlinger, Mary Louise Pratt, and others have noted, however, around the 1880s the terms of European imperialism tended to shift towards intensified colonization and cultural as well as military control.[18] Over time, what had started out as a military effort to facilitate regional economic control took on more explicitly national and racial overtones.

The changing public view of Algeria was significant. While in the 1860s Algeria was considered an exotic blend of East and West, by the turn of the century it was an imperial possession filled with hostile Arabs and ripe for full-scale colonization. This change is depicted in the film's opening scenes, which juxtapose a French flag fluttering in the breeze with the Oriental confusion of the surrounding town. That the important distinction is not between the French and the English but between East and West is reflected in the device that the film uses for translating between the two languages: the camera pans down from the flag to a notice pinned to the wall of the barracks, pauses long enough to reveal that the notice is written in French, blurs, and then refocuses on the same sign in English.

This device is a far cry from Ouida's heavy infusion into her novel of army French, which she used to bolster her claims of authenticity. As Ouida suggests in her introduction to the novel:

This story was originally written for a military periodical. It has been fortunate enough to receive much commendation from military men, and for them it is now specially issued in its present form [as a book]. For the general public it may be as well to add, that where translations are appended to the French phrases, those translations follow the idiomatic and special meaning attached to those expressions in the argot of the Army of Algeria, and not the correct or literal one given to such words or sentences in ordinary grammatical parlance. (2)

Such statements on Ouida's part draw attention to the distinction between French and English, which in turns acts as a springboard for larger issues. In 1867, the idealistic Ouida could portray metropolitan Algeria as a microcosm and the desert as the crucible in which the over-civilized man recognizes the nobility of Napoleonic ideals at the same time that he rediscovers the inherent nobility he shares with the more primitive, but equally worthy, Arabs. In the novel, Victor is highly sympathetic to the Arabs. Upon arriving in Algeria, he decides to fight for the French only after playing a dice game in which, if he wins, he will join the Arabs. Declaring that the Arabs have the right of the conflict, he asserts that they are preferable because they are the "losing side, lords of the soil, that they live free, and have the right of the quarrel" (186). Nonetheless, he abides by the decree of the dice and fights for France.

Later, Victor becomes a hero for preventing an all-out conflict with the Arabs. After his ignoble superior Chateâuroy orders the capture of the most prized maiden of the powerful Arab leader Sidi Ben Youssiff, Victor recognizes the inappropriateness of the action, threatens Chateâuroy with the public exposure of his lowly origins, and returns the woman to the Arabs, thereby averting a war. Afterwards, during his visit with the Arab leader, Victor remarks, "I wish I had come straight to you, Sidi, when I first set foot in Africa" (213). The narrator remarks, "between them was a brotherhood that beat down the antagonism of race, and was stronger than the instinctive hate of the oppressed for all who came under the abhorred standard of the usurpers. He liked the Arabs and they liked him" (215). Sidi then draws an important distinction between the French and Arab soldiers and between all of them and the "Bureaucratie"; he observes that it is the money-grubbing "hell-spawn of civilization" (215) that is really at fault for provoking the conflict between East and West. The narrator confirms the point again later, noting of Victor that the "Semitic, Latin or Teuton race was very much the same to him" and that Victor characterizes the "conflict of the races" as "cant" (244). (Such sentiments alone would have been considered "sensational" during the Indian Mutiny, the Crimean War, and other colonial conflicts, an era during which the wartime horrors helped to solidify nascent notions of the ineffable "otherness" of the Orient in the popular imagination and of the necessity for suppressing the native element in all of the imperial possessions.)

The film picks up on the implicit polarization of East and West by setting the action later in Algerian history, after the end of the Second Empire that Ouida romanticized. The opening credits are presented in a book that is purported to be by Ouida: *Under Two Flags: A Tale of the French Foreign Legion.* (Ouida's original novel was actually subtitled *A Tale of the Household and the Desert.*) Domesticity and foreignness are no longer juxtaposed, as in the literal separation of the action in England and in Algeria that the novel emphasizes; rather the film folds the domestic narrative into the imperial one. Algeria is less a place of individual self-discovery and re-creation than it is one of self-affirmation against hostile forces—it is a backdrop rather than an agent. The description of the setting that the film offers highlights this attitude: "North Africa at the turn of the century—a land of eternal mystery—primitive, barbaric, the camel train its only link with the outer world." After a shot of camels slogging across the desert, Oriental flutes piping in the background, this framing narrative resumes: "Abeshé—French military headquarters in Southern Algeria—the white man's most distant outpost, on the fringe of the vast uncharted desert of Gidi."

Victor's encounter with the Arab chief of the film version reflects this different attitude about Algeria and the Arabs who inhabit it. In the film, Sidi Ben Youssiff is not the pure Arab type that Bertie/Victor admires but instead becomes a striking example of the failure of the civilizing impulse. The film draws upon the interconnections between Arab and European worlds, impossible in Ouida's time but created by French colonization and the movement of Arabs into the metropolis, ultimately only to suggest the limited hope for true boundary-crossing. Rather than being a noble nomad with whom Bertie/Victor feels an ineffable kinship, Sidi Ben Youssiff becomes a former classmate at Oxford whom Victor beguiles into holding off an attack on the French by appealing to his memories of "Professor York's teas" as a talisman of his sincerity. After a struggle to remember their connection, the Arab laughs and remarks: "Oh, but this is amusing, old classmates meeting in the heart of the desert as enemies." Then he adds, "If what you have told me is true I will be indebted to you for the rest of my life. If not, this renewal of an acquaintance I'm afraid shall be . . . short-lived." Serving up some tea, he continues: "Shall we imagine we are again at one of Professor York's teas?" The veneer of civilization becomes a game; the transformation is not lasting. That Victor himself comes intending to deceive his old classmate reflects a lack of faith, albeit justified. Learning that Victor has tricked him, Sidi turns his Oxford experiences back onto him, revealing yet again his true barbarity: "You remember our soccer games? Well, we shall play soccer, on horseback. And you, ho-ho, shall be the ball!"

By transforming Algeria into a site of inevitable conflict rather than of self-exploration, the film closes down another means by which Victor finds himself in the novel. As Joseph A. Boone has pointed out, the cultural transvestitism implied in serving two flags or in assuming native garb extended to gender identity and sexuality as well. By the mid-nineteenth century, the Near East was commonly associated with same-sex activity, particularly between men but also between harem women. (Ouida might well have heard from her friend Richard Burton what he was later to refer to as the Arab "Sotadic Zone," where sex between men was common.) Boone's description of T. E. Lawrence and others assuming Arab drag seems to hark back to Ouida's representation of Victor in the desert: "coupled with a persistent misogyny, this ambiguity issues forth in a complicated modality of homoerotic desire that is expressed sometimes in puritanical asceticism and sublimation, sometimes in sadistic outbreaks of violence, and sometimes in swooning surrender to the desert's harsh beauty" (96-97). Boone goes on to describe how Lawrence linked an erotic ideal of male-male love with a political interest in Arab sovereignty—an issue in which Ouida's Victor also has a stake.

This reading of Ouida's novel is reinforced by the first volume—omitted in the film—in which the hero, known as Bertie Cecil, is described in extraordinarily feminine terms. Part of this representation has to do with the old idea of the soldier as an aristocratic dandy, but Cecil's appearance and relationship with his best friend, "The Seraph," suggest a more overt femininity and homoeroticism. Called "Beauty" by his peers in the Household Guards, Bertie Cecil is said to be the equal of any woman in appearance. His face

had as much delicacy and brilliancy as a woman's; handsome, thoughtful, languid, nonchalant, with a certain latent recklessness under the impassive calm of habit, and a singular softness given to the long, dark, hazel eyes by the unusual length of the lashes over them. His features were exceedingly fair—fair as the fairest girls' . . . his hair was of the softest, silkiest, brightest chestnut; his mouth very beautifully shaped; on the whole with a certain gentle, mournful love-me look that his eyes had with them, it was no wonder that great ladies and gay lionnes alike gave him the palm as the handsomest man in all the Household Regiments—not even excepting the splendid, golden-haired Seraph. (3)

The splendid, golden-haired Seraph, Lord Rockinham, is Bertie/Victor's best friend and the one whom he appears to betray with a forged check (the false shame of which, along with his noble protection of his brother and his mistress, leads him to flee to Algeria). Ouida makes much of the love between the two men, in contrast to Bertie/Victor's ultimately meaningless flirtations with various society women. In fact, in the novel, it is the Seraph's much-younger sister, Venetia, who "looks absurdly like" her brother, who turns out to be the Lady Venetia whom Bertie/Victor re-encounters in Algeria (128)!

This relationship is substantially diminished in the film: Venetia and Victor have had no prior acquaintance at all, and "Seriff" is a much older figure whom Victor knows only casually.[19] The adult Venetia, we learn in the novel, is sexually pure, cold, and endlessly proud; she was wed to a prince who died without being able to consummate the marriage. In the novel, it is difficult to imagine that Bertie/Victor feels much passion for her; theirs seems more a class than a sexual match. But it appears of little matter to Bertie/Victor, whose previous mistresses proved a languid pastime rather than a serious, passionate interest.

The significance of these elements of the novel is reinforced by the film—ironically, however, by the film's omissions rather than by its inclusions or additions. Turn-of-the-century North Africa had become a popular destination for gay and bisexual male writers such as André Gide, Oscar Wilde, and E. M. Forster (Boone 90). Any hint of effeminacy in the film's version of Victor might have conjured up notions of homosexual experimentation; even friendliness with the Arabs might have hinted as much. For a story that is ultimately about heterosexual pairing, such notions become irrelevant at best and damaging at worst. Thus, as it does with his prior relationship with Venetia, the film also omits Victor's relationship with "The Seraph" and his nickname amongst the Legionnaires, "*Bel à faire peur.*"

Just as Victor is masculinized in the film, Cigarette is feminized, further preparing the way for an all-out love story. The novel represents Cigarette as nearly "unsexed" equally by her military valor, her flirtatious self-assertion, and her fiery democratic principles. As Ouida points out in the novel, it is her youth alone that keeps her attractive as a woman:

She was very pretty, audaciously pretty, though her skin was burnt to a bright sunny brown, and her hair was cut as short as a boy's, and her face had not one regular feature in it . . . She was pretty, she was insolent, she was intolerably coquettish, she was mischievous as a marmoset, she would swear if need be like a Zouave, she could fire galloping, she could toss off her brandy or her vermouth like a trooper, she would on occasion clench her little brown hand and deal a blow that the recipient would not covet twice, she was an *enfant de Paris,* and had all its wickedness at her fingers, she would sing you *guinguette* songs till you were suffocated with laughter, and she would dance the cancan at the Salle de Mars with the biggest giant of a Cuirassier there. And yet, with all that, she was not wholly unsexed, with all that she had the delicious fragrance of youth, and had not left a certain feminine grace behind her, though she wore a vivandière's uniform, and had been born in a barrack, and meant to die in a battle; it was the blending of the two that made her piquante, made her a notoriety in her own way; known at pleasure, and equally, in the Army of Africa as "Cigarette," and "L'Amie du Drapeau." (197-98)

Cigarette is truly an amalgam of opposites. After she manfully defends Victor in the novel against the charge that he is effeminate (a trait also associated with his upper-class breeding), she loses her status as a romantic heroine. The novel creates in Cigarette a heroine at once far superior to everyone around her and yet degraded because she has been "unsexed" by her life as a camp-follower and as an adoptee of the Algerian army. Since she is simultaneously a coquette and a soldier, the only future the narrative can project for her beyond her youth is life as a worn-out prostitute. Winning the French cross for valor in battle, she subsequently dies for "Beauty" by taking a bullet meant for him by a firing squad; in so doing, she achieves for herself the best of all possible worlds.

By making her more explicitly feminine, the film simultaneously diminishes Cigarette as a heroine and allows for the real possibility of her union with Victor, the man she loves. Such visual details as her long hair and her civilian dresses go a long way towards negating the boyish charm and personal heroism that in the novel made Bertie/Victor think of her more as a comrade than as a woman, just as Victor's masculinity is fortified by raucous drinking, long battle scenes, and assertive pursuit of Venetia. A man who looks like a woman or a woman who looks like a brown young boy might, after all, suggest the homosexual content that the adaptation represses and not the love story amidst the desert sands that the filmmakers want to create.

As the *New York Times* reviewer noted, the 31-year-old Claudette Colbert could not quite pull off this "child of nature." And yet, the film as it was constructed would have made it nearly impossible for her to do so. Difficult as it is to imagine Colbert dancing a furious can-can, it is more difficult still to imagine her as the Joan of Arc figure whom Ouida portrays. Her feminization, however, has the effect implicitly suggested in Ouida's novel of splitting the female ideal into two distinct forms. In scenes written for the film, Cigarette is introduced as the proprietress of a café where the soldiers relax. She flirts with the men and sings them songs, much as the novel describes. Here, however, she also serves the men and is the paramour of Major Doyle. Her loyalty soon shifts to the more dashing Victor. Yet even her inconstancy makes her more attractive because more believable. After Victor catches her at horse-swindling, the two ride off in a race in which Cigarette must kiss Victor if she loses. When she does lose, Victor suggests she might prefer to kiss the horse instead. She rides off again, furious, and he follows her into the desert, where they tumble to the sand and indulge in several kisses. Upon returning from that adventure, Cigarette is in love, and she plans a romantic dinner for the two of them. Unfortunately, she is set up to be jilted, for Victor has met the aristocratic Lady Venetia, and he pursues her as he pursues his wish to resume his former station in life.

In both novel and film, Cigarette ultimately sacrifices herself for Victor, and in both she seems to die happy. In the film, however, her death is more of an implicit reproach to Victor for not appreciating her. Whereas the novel's dark prognostications make Cigarette's future seem dim and her sacrifice almost a relief, the film's death scene vindicates her both for her love and for her heroism by allowing her to die for France rather than for Victor. In the film, Cigarette, having saved the regiment (though her concern is really mostly for Victor), lies dying in Victor's arms, asking for one more kiss and overcome with happiness that he would cry for her. Her pathetic gratitude touches Victor; they kiss passionately and she dies in bliss.

By granting her this degree of feminine attractiveness and by providing her with some last-minute regard by the hero, the film builds on the implication of the novel that in calling Cigarette "unsexed," both Victor and Venetia judge her too harshly. In the novel, Cigarette's nursing of soldiers and love for the oppressed parallel the much-admired exploits of Florence Nightingale in the Crimea and offer a tentative suggestion for how an adventuresome but still feminine woman could make her way in the world. Though the novel's Victor remains unmoved by Cigarette, the narrative implies criticism of him for it: "He was grateful to her; but despite himself, he was cold to her; despite himself, the life which that little hand he held had taken so lightly, made it the hand of a comrade to be grasped in alliance, but never the hand of a mistress to steal to his lips and to lie in his breast" (277). *Despite himself,* he bows to conventional notions of class and gender. In the film, no such difficult choice has to be made. Cigarette never really marches into battle with the men; when she performs her heroic actions, she is actually on an errand to beg Major Doyle to stop sending Victor to his doom. She only happens to see the soldiers whom she summons as reinforcements for the climactic battle scene in the desert. Though in both novel and film she receives the French Cross, the highest military honor available to a civilian, in the novel she deserves it wholeheartedly, while in the film she gets it only after warring with herself over whether she would rather let Victor die or save him for Venetia. The effect is to diminish her status as an idealist but to make her more sympathetic to the audience as a romantic heroine.

While the novel does not fully treat the relative merits of the two women, the film expands on their relationship. In the novel, Cigarette describes Venetia's limitations in terms that are never directly refuted. When Cigarette dies via the firing squad, she is saving Bertie/Victor's life for a third time (the first time being from an Arab thief, the second in battle). After one of these early episodes, she points out to Victor her superiority to her aristocratic rival. Comparing Venetia to a "silver pheasant," Cigarette remarks, "If I had been like that dainty aristocrat down there—pardieu! It had been worse for you. I should have screamed, and fainted, and left you to be killed, whilst I made a *tableau.* Oh-hé, that is to be 'feminine,' is it not?" (273). Such scenes, however, are always undercut in the novel. In her encounters with the same silver pheasant moments before, Cigarette had become aware of her personal inadequacies. In looking at Venetia she

looked at all the nameless graces of rank with an envy that her sunny, gladsome, generous nature had never before been touched with—with a sudden perception, quick as thought, bitter as gall, wounding and swift and poignant of what this womanhood that he had said she herself had lost, might be in its highest and purest shape. (262)

The coexistence of these two views of Cigarette—or, to put it another way, these two views of womanhood—cannot be expressed adequately in film. "Nameless graces" are difficult to present visually, and the characteristic restraint that marks Venetia's class is hard to credit amidst the Arabian sands. "Courtly negligence, regal grace, fair brilliant loveliness, the delicious serene languor, of a pure aristocrat" (269) replace personality in the novel and lend a certain validity to Cigarette's sense of inferiority, but they convey only a background demeanor in film.

Transformed into much more of a creature of action, the film's Venetia is therefore a worthier alternative to Cigarette. She reassures Victor that she loves him, regardless of rank, and dares to love him despite their social gulf. As he prepares to go to battle, she declares her feelings to him, promising that she will be there when he gets back: "I know nothing of you . . . except your soul. When two people love each other like this . . ." He admits his love but protests. When she asserts that "some day your service will end," he interrupts to tell her that it will never end, that he would exchange his service "for a prison cell." Despite these scare tactics, Venetia remains steadfast in her admiration.

Clambering over a wall to escape into the village, Rosalind Russell is a far cry from the proud aristocrat Ouida describes. In the film, Venetia becomes an adventurer, eager to see the "real" Africa with her Chausseur, who is romantic to her because he is a common soldier rather than despite it. Seeing him at a dull party is "the first exciting thing to happen to me in this whole monotonous country," she pouts. Dared by Victor, the film's Venetia makes trips outward, venturing to see a snake charmer in the Algerian dusk and then riding out on horseback for a rendezvous with Victor in a remote desert monastery. Victor draws her out from one location to the next; egging her on, he asks, "you don't think that was the real Africa, do you?" When she appears in the moonlight on horseback and wearing a see-through veil over her features, they reflect on how the grove is the real Africa and how the monastery situated within it must have a story. Venetia is interested only in hearing the story that Victor refuses to tell. Nonetheless, they kiss. Meanwhile, Cigarette waits in the café, her simple romantic dinner tame but all the more poignant in comparison with the aristocrat's exploits.

Venetia's triumph with Victor closes the first half of the film. Having established its primary relationships, the film then turns to the war that threatens the successful fulfillment of the love match. The camel train of the opening marches through again; the French flag again flutters in the breeze; and orders to march are issued, as they were in the first part of the film. But this time the drill becomes the real thing. A quick shot of Fort Ansera, erected in honor of those massacred by the Arabs in April of 1870, highlights the stakes of the battle. The triumph of the French army here will mean the triumph of Venetia. Already the ending becomes apparent: we learn in a quick exchange between Venetia and her uncle, Lord Seriff—a much older man, and more distant from Venetia than the "Seraph" the Victor of the novel had known in his previous life—that Victor no longer needs the disguise of a Legionnaire. With his guilty brother dead and the truth told, Victor can come forward without shame. Cigarette's cause now structurally hopeless, the film needs to work out the details and to pit Cigarette against Venetia (as in the novel) in a confrontation about Victor.

Victor is "under two flags," the French and the British, but, more importantly, he is torn between two identities, that of the Legionnaire and that of the English aristocrat, Lord Royallieu. In this sense, Victor's conflict is also between democracy and aristocracy, political options that are reflected in the love story at the heart of the novel. The French democrats are personified in Cigarette, die-hard French patriot, while the British aristocrats are represented by Venetia.

In the American film adaptation released in 1936, the argument between the two is largely moot. In the novel, on the other hand, Cigarette barges in on Venetia and proclaims her hatred for the aristocracy (although in the narrative her vehemence stems from her own sense of inferiority in the face of Venetia's high-born grace). Cigarette criticizes Venetia, expanding her invective outward from her own experience to encompass the many:

I speak of the people. Of the toiling, weary, agonized, joyless, hapless multitudes who labour on, and on, and on, ever in darkness, that such as you may bask in sunlight and take your pleasures wrung out of the death-sweat of millions of work-murdered poor! What right have you to have your path strewn with roses, and every pain spared from you; to only lift your voice and say, "Let that be done," to see it done?—to find life one long sweet summer day of gladness and abundance, while they die out in agony by thousands, ague-stricken, famine-stricken, crime-stricken, age-stricken, for want only of one ray of the light of happiness that falls from dawn to dawn like gold upon *your* head? (466)

Venetia's response, that class antagonism does not help and that her "Order" considers these matters as well, does little to answer Cigarette.

Venetia's personal demeanor, however, and Cigarette's own sense serve as a response. Cigarette acknowledges that the man she knows as Victor is of Venetia's class rather than of her own. In the novel, as this exchange suggests, his true identity is never really in doubt. As Cigarette puts it, if he is an aristocrat, "then he must be always, mustn't he? You think too much of your blue blood, you patricians, to fancy it can lose its royalty, whether it run under a King's purple or a Roumi's canvas shirt. Blood tells, they say! Well, perhaps it does. Some say *my* father was a Prince of France—may be!" (271). As Napoleon's bastard child, Cigarette might lay claim to the natural nobility requisite in Victor's mate, though being unsexed by camp life disqualifies her from actual consideration.

In the film, the confrontation takes a very different form. Cigarette must struggle with her jealousy before she can decide whether to save Victor's life only for Venetia to share it. Hence, the terms of the debate are quite different. True identity arises out of present circumstance rather than out of inherited class background. Yet, here, as in the novel, Venetia is unable to answer the criticism Cigarette lobs:

Cigarette: I love him like you never could. He doesn't belong with your kind. He is of the Legion—my kind. Would you follow him into the desert? Would you march with him, nurse him—I've even shot them so that the Arabs could not take them alive!
Venetia: Oh, you poor child! You *do* love him.
Cigarette: Yes, I do love him . . . I can save him. Why should I save him for you?
Venetia: Can you leave him to die? Can you?

Cigarette, of course, cannot, and so she goes off to save him. What is striking here, however, is Cigarette's assertion that Victor's identity, regardless of his background, is as a soldier. Both Cigarette and Victor are of compatible natures, both fearless soldiers of France. The hints that Ouida offers in the novel, via Cigarette, as to Venetia's unsuitability to Victor are more fully realized in this adaptation from the political to the personal. That Cigarette can save him in the film is a testament not only to her riding ability but also to her feminine influence with Major Doyle, Victor's commanding officer. Similarly, the argument between democracy and aristocracy is much less relevant to an American film audience than it would have been to the English aristocrats to whom Ouida addressed her fiction. Represented in the film, however, it would have tipped the balance too heavily in Cigarette's favor, making Venetia look unworthy in comparison, thereby undoing the work of her midnight adventures with Victor.

And yet these additions to Venetia's character make her at best only an acceptable alternative for Cigarette—the tragedy of the film being that Victor realizes too late what he has lost. The film's final scene shows Victor dressed in an elegant white suit, standing next to but a little separate from Venetia, at the military funeral for Cigarette. Venetia clasps his hand, but he remains somewhat apart, visually. This is in keeping with Ouida's ending, insofar as her coda has the two back in England, reflecting on Cigarette's heroism: "When I think of what *her* love was, how worthless looks my own! How little worthy of the fate it finds! What have I done that every joy should become mine, when she—" In its closing, the novel reaffirms Cigarette's military valor. The two recall Cigarette's sacrifice back in Africa, and the novel ends with the inscription on her tombstone: "CIGARETTE, ENFANT DE L'ARMÉE, SOLDAT DE LA FRANCE." The film does the same, but by ending in Algeria rather than England, it highlights the loss rather than the resolution the novel affords. The final scene, of an Arab band watching in the desert, suggests that the battle is not yet won and reaffirms that Cigarette's sacrifice is significant primarily in personal rather than political terms.

Notes

1. John Sutherland's "Introduction" to the Oxford Popular Classics edition of *Under Two Flags* provides a general overview of the novel's production history. See also his original source, Cecilia Phillips, "*Under Two Flags:* The Publishing-History of a Best-Seller," *Publishing History* 3 (1978): 67-69.

2. "Make Way for a Veteran: 'Cigarette,' Timeless Heroine of Ouida's 'Under Two Flags,' Is Back Again," *New York Times* 26 April 1936, Sect. 9: 4.

3. The reference is to Brian McFarlane, *Novel to Film: An Introduction to the Theory of Adaptation* 3-30. This essay takes inspiration from McFarlane's analysis in the chapter "Back, Issues, and a New Agenda," but it does not attempt to recreate McFarlane's structured approach to adaptation.

4. Credit for highlighting this moment in the film as a product of modern sensibilities goes to the *Time* reviewer of the film, 11 May 1936.

5. Sutherland's introduction draws attention to these antecedents and inheritors of the Legion and Arab mystique.

6. In *Rule of Darkness,* Patrick Brantlinger elaborates on this connection: "Imperialism influenced not only the tradition of the adventure tale but the tradition of 'serious' domestic realism as well. Adventure and domesticity, romance and realism, are the seemingly opposite poles of a single system of discourse, the literary equivalents of imperial domination abroad and liberal reform

at home. In the middle of the most serious domestic concerns, often in the most unlikely texts, the Empire may intrude as a shadowy realm of escape, renewal, banishment, or return for characters who for one reason or another need to enter or exit from scenes of domestic conflict. As in Renaissance pastoral, so in the nineteenth-century English novel: a season of imperial adventure in an exotic setting can cure almost any moral disease" (12).

7. See Radway, *Reading the Romance,* for discussion of the twentieth-century romance reader's response to popular fiction.

8. *"Under Two Flags* (1916);" *"Under Two Flags* (1922)." Internet Movie Database: HTTP://US.IMDB.COM. Accessed 2 July 1997.

9. *"Under Two Flags," Time* 11 May 1936: 56.

10. See the first *New York Times* review of the film, "The Legion Marches Again in a Dashing Revival of 'Under Two Flags,' at the Music Hall," *New York Times* 2 May 1936.

11. "Camera in the Desert: Battling Heat and Sand, a Film Company Is Producing 'Under Two Flags,'" *New York Times* 2 Feb. 1936. This article describes some of the monumental effort that went into shooting the film and notes that, in light of all the work, "the feeling occurs with such realism that the picture must be good." Though the background may have ultimately served to forward domestic interests, that background was quite elaborate and provides a strong interest to the film in its own right. The spectacle is part of the filmmaker's point.

12. Graham Greene, Rev. of *Under Two Flags, Spectator* 7 Aug. 1936: 235.

13. All quotations from the novel are taken from Ouida, *Under Two Flags* (1867; rpt. New York: Oxford U P, 1995).

14. Ouida is on record as one of the earliest denouncers of the "New Woman," and, in subsequent decades, argued against suffrage. She often seems to have considered herself the exception to the general feminine rule. For more on her life, see Monica Stirling, *The Fine and the Wicked: The Life and Times of Ouida;* Eileen Bigland, *Ouida: The Passionate Victorian;* Yvonne ffrench, *Ouida: A Study in Ostentation;* and Elizabeth Lee, *Ouida: A Memoir.*

15. This comment is quoted in Yvonne ffrench's biography of Ouida.

16. See Daniel A. Boone, "Vacation Cruises; or, The Homoerotics of Orientalism."

17. "North Africa: The Countries of North Africa: Algeria: History: The 19th Century: French Algeria," *Brittanica Online.* Accessed 19 March 1998.

18. See Brantlinger and/or Pratt.

19. This is the spelling in the film's credits.

Works Consulted

Bigland, Eileen. *Ouida: The Passionate Victorian.* New York: Duell, Sloan, and Pearce, 1951.

Boone, Daniel A. "Vacation Cruises; or, The Homoerotics of Orientalism." *PMLA* 110.1 (1995): 89-107.

Brantlinger, Patrick. *Rule of Darkness: British Literature and Imperialism, 1830-1914.* New York: Cornell UP, 1988.

"Camera in the Desert: Battling Heat and Sand, a Film Company Is Producing 'Under Two Flags.'" *New York Times* 2 Feb. 1936. Sect. 4: 1.

"Foreign Legion." *Brittanica Online.* HTTP://WWW.EB.COM. Accessed 8 July 1997.

ffrench, Yvonne. *Ouida: A Study in Ostentation.* New York: Appleton Century, 1938.

Greene, Graham. Rev. of *Under Two Flags. Spectator* 157 (1936): 235.

Lee, Elizabeth. *Ouida: A Memoir.* New York: Duffield, 1914.

"The Legion Marches Again in a Dashing Revival of 'Under Two Flags,' at the Music Hall." *New York Times* 1 May 1936. Sect. 19: 1.

"Make Way for a Veteran: 'Cigarette,' Timeless Heroine of Ouida's 'Under Two Flags,' Is Back Again." *New York Times* 26 Apr. 1936. Sect. 9: 4.

McFarlane, Brian. *Novel to Film: An Introduction to the Theory of Adaptation.* New York: Oxford UP, 1996.

"North Africa: The Countries of North Africa: Algeria: History: The 19th Century: French Algeria." *Brittanica Online.* Accessed 19 March 1998.

Ouida. *Under Two Flags.* 1867; rpt. New York: Oxford UP, 1995.

Pratt, Mary Louise. *Imperial Eyes: Travel Writing and Transculturation.* New York: Routledge, 1992.

Radway, Janice. *Reading the Romance: Women, Patriarchy, and Popular Literature.* Chapel Hill: U of North Carolina P, 1984.

Rev. of *Under Two Flags. Time* 11 May 1936: 56.

Stirling, Monica. *The Fine and the Wicked: The Life and Times of Ouida.* New York: Coward-McCann, 1958.

Under Two Flags. Dir. J. Gordon Edwards. Screenplay by George Hall. Perf. Herbert Heyes, Theda Bara, Stuart Holmes, Chaire Whitney. Fox Film Corporation, 1916. Silent.

Under Two Flags. Dir. Tod Browning. Screenplay by Tod Browning, Elliott J. Clawson, Edward T. Lowe, Jr. Perf. Norman Kerry, Priscilla Dean, Stuart Holmes, Ethel Grey Terry. Universal Pictures, 1922. Silent.

Under Two Flags. Dir. Frank Lloyd. Screenplay by Walter Ferris and W. P. Lipscomb. Perf. Ronald Colman, Claudette Colbert, Victor McLaglen, Rosalind Russell. Twentieth-Century Fox, 1936.

"*Under Two Flags* (1916)"; "*Under Two Flags* (1922)"; "*Under Two Flags* (1936)." Internet Movie Database: HTTP://US.IMDB.COM. Accessed 2 July 1997.

11

GEORGE ELIOT ON THE AMERICAN SCREEN

George V. Griffith

From her first appearance on the American literary horizon in 1858 to the publication of *Middlemarch* in 1871, George Eliot was hailed as a genius and welcomed for her "humor and pathos," to use an often repeated reviewer's formula. American readers were especially enamored of her homely "Dutch" realism, for its picturesque quality appealed to a pre- and post-Civil War era American affection for an idealized view of rural England. Her first four books (*Scenes of Clerical Life, Adam Bede, The Mill on the Floss, Silas Marner*), two of which were best sellers,[1] filled that need. American readers weary of the idealizing so characteristic of the fiction of the 1850s written by those Hawthorne had denigrated as "that damned mob of scribbling women," yet unaware of their own idealizing view of pastoral England, thought they found in realism an antidote. When it became clear that realism meant an unblinking commitment to a truth radically opposed to any idealization, however, "humor and pathos" was replaced by "melancholy and gloom." A considerable segment of the American audience, initially ignorant of who "George Eliot" was, added to that shifting view of realism misgivings about her religious beliefs and personal life once those became known, making her a threat to right thinking. Eliot's intent was to widen readers' sympathies. As a realist for whom that phrase meant more than quaint local color, she aimed to guide readers to "do without opium and live through all our pain in conscious clear-eyed endurance" (*Letters* 3: 336). Americans wanted, by contrast, what was so poignantly expressed in a question posed by a reviewer for *Scribner's* (Oct. 1874): "Is there not a Saviour for us?" (701). Americans wanted light and hope and moral uplift. The arc of Eliot's American reputation thus rose quickly from 1858, reaching its peak in the early 1870s, then as quickly declining until her death a decade later. After her death, talk about her disappeared, for dismay over her gloom had abated and she was secure in the ranks of the great, inert, no longer the controversial agnostic and glum realist who lived her life in defiance of society's moral codes. Meanwhile at least one of those early novels, *Silas Marner,* had moved into school curricula, less for its realism than for its sentiments.

The world gave birth to the film industry a decade after it buried George Eliot. By the time film had grown from the novelty of putting moving pictures on screen in the 1890s to the conception of itself as a storytelling art a little more than a decade later, Eliot's work was securely buried among other Victorian "classics." For an industry with a voracious appetite for stories, her early work thus provided material that was safe. Furthermore, the picturesque her first readers admired could now be rendered literally. And since in its first few decades film was an entertainment still in search of respectability, Eliot novels from the era of adulation for her perceived piety were good material. Not coincidentally, therefore, *Silas Marner* (1861) was done in one- and two-reel silent films no fewer than six times by 1922, including a one-reel version titled *A Fair Exchange* by D. W. Griffith for American Biograph and another version by the Thomas Edison studio.

Adaptations of the works of George Eliot to the American screen—both what was done and when it was done—follow the general arc of her reputation during her career and illustrate an American retreat from a clear understanding of her realism. With the exception of a 1937 British production of *The Mill on the Floss,* all Eliot adaptations appeared in two eras on the screen. The first coincides with the age of the silents, culminating in the first feature-length film of an Eliot work, *Romola* (1924); the second occurred in the last two decades of the century when four Eliot works were produced for television and broadcast on WGBH's *Masterpiece Theatre.* The silent era films conspicuously omit *Middlemarch* (1872), the watershed book in Eliot's American reception. Her admirers saw it as a triumph of Eliot's art; for her detractors, it was *prima facie* evidence of why regard for her should be severely tempered. *Middlemarch* laid to rest any hope for the reappearance of the charming Eliot of rural English villages, the Eliot whom the audience constructed from the early books.

It is reasonable to argue that *Middlemarch* was never filmed because of its forbidding density and length. Subtitled "A Study in Provincial Life," the book panoramically surveys life in a mid-sized English community at the time of the first Reform Bill (1832), weaving together in several strong plot lines the lives of at least two putative protagonists and a host of minor figures. Yet length alone could not account for its absence, since *Daniel Deronda* (1876), a novel at least as long, was done in 1922. Moreover, technical limitations for film length in the pre-feature-film era made film directors and writers masters of condensation. Griffith's treatment of *Silas Marner* ran eleven minutes. It seems more likely that the absence of *Middlemarch* from the first period of adaptations reveals how cinematic treatments mirror the path of Eliot's reputation. Early film wanted the moral uplift provided by a Victorian sensibility that Eliot's first books illustrated. The later, gloomier, more analytic Eliot, the *Middlemarch*-era Eliot, was both too thoughtful and too dark for entertainment.

Instead of *Middlemarch,* silent age Eliot films drew from the first of her works to appear in America. Among those were "Mr. Gilfil's Love Story," one of the three *Scenes of Clerical Life* (1858), made under the direction of A. V. Bramble in five reels in 1920. The story of a pious local curate's falling in love with a visiting Italian beauty, it has all the pathos and charm of the early Eliot, work which in review Henry James characterized as suffused with the "romance of reality" (James 892). *Adam Bede* (1859), Eliot's next novel, had what American readers wanted—the picturesque English village, the homely details of the unheroic life, an apparently simple piety and high regard for religious sentiments, and a plot more pathetic than tragic. With the right treatment, a cinematic adaptation could transform the plot into the melodrama characteristic of silent films. *Bede* was done in 1918, starring Ivy Close as Hetty, the young dairymaid who takes the life of her newborn after she is exploited by the local squire. Mutual/Thanhauser produced a 1915 five-reel adaptation of *The Mill on the Floss* (1860) under the direction of W. Eugene Moore and starring Mignon Anderson as Maggie. A reviewer for *Moving Picture World* noted that Eliot's novel was "especially well suited to screen interpretation" and praised the adaptation: "We believe that none of the humanity or realism of the story has been lost by its transmission to the screen." Singled out for praise in an age when filmmakers were beginning to move out of studios and onto locations was the flood that washes away Maggie Tulliver at the novel's end: "That portion of the film dealing with the overflow of the river is vividly realistic, and would suggest its having been staged on the scene of some flood disaster" (MacDonald 2198). Realism remained a touchstone for judgment, reflecting both the photographic, documentary origins of film and the audience construction of George Eliot.

That *Silas Marner* was most often adapted to the silent screen is not surprising. A best seller in America when it was published in 1861, it provided the first age of film both a tale of humble family life and, in its theme of the regenerative power of love, a heart-warming piety that also made it attractive for schools looking for books that could be used for earnest didactic purposes. Its plot, moreover, with the secret of an illegitimate child's birth, blackmail, a robbery, a disappearance, and characters arrayed across class lines from the squire to the cottager, had in it ample material for melodrama. Because the story covers thirty years and builds to the climactic discovery of the past, the plot also confronted the cinematic storyteller with a challenge not always met at a time when the grammar of film was still being discovered. Reviews of several *Marners* noted how confusing the story was. The 1922 *Marner,* according to a *Variety* reviewer, was a "disconnected" story that suffered from "the direction and manipulation of the picture's continuity" (2 June 1922). Reviews illustrate the quickly growing demands being made of film as a narrative medium. Of a loosely adapted *Silas Marner* done in 1922 under the title *Are the Children to Blame?,* a writer remarked that "the moral values of this picture are perfect" (*Variety* 8 Dec. 1922) but went on to scold the filmmaker for lapsed continuity. Victorian sentimentality and moralism were no longer sufficient for the audience, which might have shared the view of a writer who characterized the 1922 *Marner* as a "seven reel treat of tiresomeness" whose "sole redeeming power and box office strength will depend on the title of the book, one that probably every school kid in America has read" (*Variety* 2 June 1922).

Five years before the end of the silent era, the 1924 Henry King production of *Romola* became the first feature-length film adapted from a work of George Eliot's. In *Romola* (1863), Eliot's only venture in historical romance to be done in prose fiction, she departed at some risk from the English village settings of the first successful books.[2] Yet the book did well in the United States, more so than in England. "Curiously enough in America it seems to have surpassed *Middlemarch,*" George Henry Lewes mused in a November, 1876 letter to Eliot's publisher, John Blackwood (*Letters* 6: 312). An historical romance, *Romola* provided its American readers an Old-World appeal that reached farther back in history but was otherwise not substantially different from what they admired in the English village novels. Its self-effacing heroine is a Madonna, a model of Victorian ideals of womanliness, and in Tito Melema, readers could recognize a villain who would be at home on the melodramatic stage of David Belasco. In spite of its setting and idealized heroine, however, *Romola* was not evidence of an Eliot flight from realism or from the ideas about human behavior behind it. Eliot's most important realist idea is that human nature is morally mixed, that we are all small selves inclined to see the world in our own terms. From that egoism each of us is capable of growing. In Eliot, unstained virtue and unmitigated villainy are uncommon, as George Levine notes in his study of realism, using Tito Melema as an example:

It is striking how difficult it is to locate in realistic fiction any positive and active evil. The central realist mythology is spelled out in characters like

George Eliot's Tito Melema, whose wickedness is merely a gradual sliding into the consequences of a natural egoism. (27)

The realist text that emerges from this idea is a counter-narrative to the melodramatic story common in Dickens and throughout the Victorian age. It also proved a struggle for 1920s' filmmakers whose realist energies were spent on the look of films' sets, costumes, props—films that were otherwise exercises in melodrama. Director Henry King, moreover, was a protégé of D. W. Griffith, master of film melodrama.

Tito resembles earlier Eliot figures such as Arthur Donnithorne of *Adam Bede* in his initial resistance to acts he knows to be wrong and in his eventual succumbing to the call of ego. He neglects every opportunity to rescue his stepfather Baldassarre from imprisonment, denies his existence when the old man finds him in Florence, and transforms what might have been a story of the reunion of father and son into a story of stalking and eventual death by one's nemesis. In his easy flirtation with Tessa, he does the same, easing into her exploitation and abandonment after she bears his child. Eliot's realist ideology rested on a powerful sense of the awful consequentiality of our acts, of the rigid determination of cause and effect. To comfort our ego we shrink from obligations, but, as she writes of Tito,

our deeds are like children that are born to us; they live and act apart from our own will. Nay, children may be strangled, but deeds never: they have an indestructible life both in and out of our consciousness; and that dreadful vitality of deeds was pressing hard on Tito for the first time. (159)

Eliot's plea for sympathetic moral judgment of the Donnithornes and Titos is a realist moral judgment and shows how readers who welcomed the picturesque in her representational realism missed the moral grounding of realism. As late as *Middlemarch*, readers still wanted "heroes" and "heroines," terms that even the astute Henry James used in reference to Lydgate and Dorothea in *Middlemarch*.

Most of Henry King's choices in the film *Romola* opt for a Hollywood costume epic and melodrama suitable for his times.[3] Tito is a stage villain without the agony of conscience he suffers in the novel and hence without any viewer sympathy. Romola is exploited innocence as it might have appeared in Dickens and routinely appeared in the films of Griffith and others in the 1920s. King invents some characters, deletes others, dramatically alters the plot, oversimplifies the historical events, and in the last title reduces the film to a patronizing platitude about women. Little wonder that one could read in the popular press:

The story of "Romola" is one that throbs with romance, adventure, intrigue and the glamor of the times when men fought for the pleasure of fighting and when women applauded their knights' abilities with the lance and the sword. (*Hudson Dispatch* 9 Feb. 1926)

Casting Lillian Gish in the title role assured both commercial success and a melodramatic treatment. An already established melodramatic heroine in D. W. Griffith films, Gish was wildly popular in the first age of the movie star and fan magazine. She was the old-fashioned girl. Even in the American Jazz Age, she did not bob her hair, roll her stockings, smoke, drink, or use cosmetics. In the film she is all innocence and passivity, emphasized by contrast to her sister Dorothy, who plays Tessa with a contadina girlishness and energy, and by the camera, which composes shots for Gish and holds them so that one might almost be looking at a Renaissance portrait, a Madonna or a Ginevra de Benci. The static pose that emphasizes her loveliness also robs her of any self-determination and highlights the pathos of her victimization, although it confirms the title following her introduction: "The lily maid of Florence, learned of books but of the world untaught." When an orphaned Romola wanders the streets and country alone, King replicates one of the most recurring tropes of Victorian melodramatic treatment of the helpless maiden. And unlike the more activist character in the novel who comforts Tessa and others, Gish's Romola kneels at the foot of the cross on which Savonarola burns at the film's end, with Tessa's child in her arms, a Virgin Mary. She no doubt reminded viewers of her role in a Henry King film of the preceding year, *The White Sister,* in which she had played a nun similarly helpless to shape her destiny.

William Powell's Tito is also a melodramatic, not realist invention. Except for his first scene when viewers see him as a shipwreck victim on the streets of Florence, throughout he is a stage villain, dallying with the heart of a country girl whose ignorance he exploits, lying to Romola and her father about his past and his intentions, stealing and manipulating to assure his rise in Florence's political struggles. Eliot's Tito does the same, but neither easily nor quickly, for he is honestly troubled by conscience. Eliot's narrative pace has the leisure to permit Tito a gradual slide into wrongdoing. In the film he is shot in close-ups that highlight the knowing gleam viewers expect or at medium range, either lurking or casting a worried glance over his shoulder, both cinematic tropes of villainy. He has no more motivation than a villain needs. The film builds a melodramatic tension as Baldassarre vengefully pursues and then unmasks Tito before Romola in a banquet scene, followed by Tito's flight, pursuit, and death.

As though Tito's actions were not sufficient to establish his character, King invents a character (Carlo Bucellini, a family friend and suitor to Romola) whose worried look he cuts to repeatedly in reaction shots to warn the viewer of Tito's menace. Other King inventions include another exposure scene in which Romola, Tessa, and Tito meet, providing the women knowledge of Tito's bigamy; Tessa's death by drowning after she jumps from a window with Tito; and the film's closing scene in which Romola's failed effort to save Savonarola is followed by the "ever-faithful" Carlo's heroic appearance "to comfort Romola" and the platitude of the closing title: "The world will learn its greatest love from women like you, Romola—women who stand at the foot of every Cross—and teach men to be more kind." The inventions enhance the idealizing of Romola and the demonizing of Tito to craft a commercially successful film for the 1920s.

Only the slow pace of the film works against melodrama's frenzy. In part the pace can be explained by a general slowing of films in the twenties, which saw a decreased use of the moving camera and less furious editing as well as technical achievements in lighting, film, and cameras that had the effect, according to one historian of the silent film, of steadily increasing "the virtuosity of the purely pictorial aspect of the film" (Everson 11). But it also comes of King's having been lured, as was Eliot, by the setting. Gish remarked that the film was "too slow-paced" (264) and that it "failed to arouse my enthusiasm for anything but the beauty of its period" (262). King hired an Italian academic, Dr. Guido Biagi, Director of the Laurentian Library in Florence, as a consultant to assure the film's authenticity. King built fifteen Florentine palaces and the cathedral of Florence on a scale nearly as large as the original. These are shot at medium and long range throughout. Gish herself was shot in close-ups in carefully lit static compositions, as though King were photographing Renaissance Madonnas, slowing the speed of the narrative and giving the film a painterly look. (See Figure 30.) The *New York Times* (2 Dec. 1924) reviewer marveled at the settings of the film and mentioned the "many heads in close-ups . . . that resemble paintings by old masters. The gowns worn by Lillian Gish make her look like some wistful beauty of the fifteenth century who had come to life through modern shadows" (13). The wedding banquet scene is composed and lit as though it were *The Last Supper*. Douglas Fairbanks, according to Gish, thought it "the most beautiful picture ever made" (264).

Romola was a great success. It opened at the George M. Cohan Theater in New York and at Grauman's Egyptian Theater in Hollywood in December, 1924. Gish attended its Hollywood premiere. It ran for

Figure 30. To enhance the Madonna-like qualities of her character in *Romola* (1924), Lillian Gish was often shot in carefully lit close-ups. (Courtesy of Museum of Modern Art Stills Archive)

twenty weeks in New York, nudging admissions to a new high of $2.00. *Moving Picture Stories* published *Romola* from the photoplay (10 Mar. 1925), and the New York Public Library reported that demand for Eliot's novel was impossible to meet. Yet Eliot's adaptation to the American movie theater screen ended in spite of the success of *Romola,* the last American feature film of an Eliot novel. The film may have succeeded in preserving Eliot's reputation as a classic writer, but if it did, it did so without confronting the truth about her as a realist. And film had still not dared to tackle *Middlemarch.*

II

Film audiences of the last two decades have been able to enjoy the works of Austen, James, the Brontës, and Hardy in feature-length films; George Eliot readers have had to content themselves with television adaptations of *Silas Marner, Adam Bede, The Mill on the Floss,* and *Middlemarch.* All were joint BBC-TV/WGBH productions for *Masterpiece Theatre,* whose unmistakable birthmark they wear. Although they dramatize the books with a greater thoroughness than any other films have, they illustrate how a process of ignoring or taming Eliot's realist ideology has continued.

As Laurence Jarvik argues in his study of *Masterpiece Theatre,* from its beginnings, that television venture has been shaped by an intricate politics in which such interested players as the Mobil Oil Corporation, the BBC, WGBH, PBS, the Corporation for Public Broadcasting, the British and American governments, and an upper middlebrow audience have all worked to promote their own interests.[4] *Masterpiece Theatre* became "cultural capital," in the words of French theorist Pierre Bourdieu, which could be exchanged for other kinds of capital: public relations for Mobil, continued government funding and profits for the various production and broadcasting entities, political capital for the governments themselves, and, in Bourdieu's terms again, "distinction" not only for those involved in the productions but also for the audience itself.

Masterpiece Theatre productions that have best served all those competing interests have tended to be safe, works whose credentials are established in the word "masterpiece." They dip into a past from whose pains the audience is secure, a past that also acts as anodyne against any present pains. As Jarvik argues, even the format of *Masterpiece Theatre* (the vintage 1950s celebrity host, the commercially uninterrupted presentation, the single sponsor) provides American audiences a nostalgic weekly reminder of such exercises in quality television from the so-called "Golden Age" of TV broadcasting ('50s and '60s) as the *Kraft Mystery Theater* or the *General Electric Theater* (209).

Above all, American audiences get to exercise the same Old-World ache that Eliot's first American readers felt for England, best embodied in the title of Hawthorne's book, *Our Old Home.* From the array of Victorian and Edwardian works adapted to the props in the host's set (Union Jack, monocle, sporting and military prints), *Masterpiece Theatre* provides what Christopher Hitchens calls, in his study of Anglophilia, a "Sunday evening debauch of Englishness" (42). "America wants to see England on the screen," said British director Alexander Korda, whose London Films was a supplier of programs to *Masterpiece Theatre.*[5] *Masterpiece Theatre*'s England has for the most part been an Anglo-Saxon England of Empire, of civility and order, still master of the world, not the declining post-industrial England now inhabited by the multiracial offspring of Empire. It gratifies American audiences with colonial illusions about our British ancestry, much as the British themselves are moved, according to Robert Hewison, by products of "the heritage industry," a phrase he uses to describe all those British efforts to sustain ideas of their own past grandeur in a climate of decline.[6] Timothy Brennan poses a similar argument in his analysis, seeing *Masterpiece Theatre* as an effort "to fuse together the apparently incompatible national myths of England and the United States in order to strengthen imperial attitudes in an era of European and North American decline" (374). *Masterpiece Theatre* strives to give "a nostalgic and tranquilizing quality" (Jarvik 210) to an art that Eliot saw as committed to painful illumination.

Although both *Middlemarch* and *Daniel Deronda* appeared on a list of proposed programs rejected by WGBH as early as 1973 (Jarvik 142), *Masterpiece Theatre* did come to do *Middlemarch,* but not before the early, more pastoral novels were produced. TV treatments at the end of the twentieth century have thus replicated both Victorian America's reception of the novels and the film era's first ventures in Eliot at the beginning of this century. *Silas Marner* appeared first in the 1986-87 *Masterpiece Theatre* season, followed by *Adam Bede* in 1991-92. Both were directed by Giles Foster and had Patsy Kensit in a starring role as the older Eppie and as Hetty; Ben Kingsley played Silas Marner. Although both strive for fidelity to Eliot's texts, *Marner* is more successful, its screenplay by Louis Marks and Giles Foster seldom departing from the novel. Panoramic shots of gentry hunting fox across a hedgerowed English countryside on a misty morning and lingering shots of the squire's stately home and the village church establish the film's *Masterpiece Theatre* credentials without departing from the novel, which was itself an Eliot hymn to English pastoral, replete with a Wordsworthian epigraph. John J. O'Connor, reviewing for the *New York Times* (14 Mar. 1987), applauded: "The production beautifully captures the feel of a small village in the 19th century" (54). Moreover, *Silas Marner,* a moral fable and the least complex of Eliot's novels, is fit both for *Masterpiece*

Theatre treatment and audience ease with its pastoral setting, its hopeful themes of love and redemption, and its ending in a marriage.

With *Adam Bede,* director Giles Foster and screenwriter Maggie Wadey had more novel to accommodate, producing a feature-length film shown in two episodes uncomfortably broken on *Masterpiece Theatre.* Eliot's *Adam Bede* stops at Chapter Seventeen, "In Which the Story Pauses a Little," to afford the narrator space to justify her writing of "more or less ugly, stupid, inconsistent people" (151). Her realist manifesto applauds "the faithful representing of common things" and asks the reader to see in it "the secret of deep human sympathy" (153). Foster and Wadey lavish cinematic affection on the "common things," but in their direction and omissions they misunderstand the novelist's plea for a felt, realist's sympathy. The film is unsympathetic to Hetty, largely because the director opts for film clichés of feminine sensuousness. Whereas Eliot waits until her seventh chapter to introduce Hetty, Foster fills his first scene after the credits with a close-up of Hetty's painted, parted lips, taking in a berry, a shot he later repeats more than once. In tight shots, she is pouty, her eyes and lips heavily made-up, curls cascading to her shoulders. In one scene, she throws a black lace scarf over her bare shoulders and wears a broad-brimmed hat, looking every bit a young woman in a Bonnard painting. Little wonder that Alistaire Cooke, introducing the second segment, describes Captain Donnithorne as "besotted with a pretty dairymaid." "You could say that the Captain seduced Hetty," he goes on, "had she not been so willing." Eliot, though hard on Hetty for her sensuous egoism, sees her as victim as well, caught in a web of circumstances involving the choices Arthur Donnithorne and others make.

Yet the film is easier on the Captain and, in its most significant omission, fails to grapple with Eliot's idea of the corporate consequences of our deeds. Three chapters of the novel are devoted to Donnithorne's coming-of-age feast, in which the old squire's tenants delight, for young Arthur's maturing promises a new age of farm improvements and better living. The festivities emphasize the communal character of Hayslope life. Arthur's fall is not just Hetty's but everyone's, a point made less clear in the film, which omits the feast altogether. Instead, the film opts for personal tragedy and the clichés of made-for-TV romance. When Adam rushes to meet Dinah in the film's closing scene, the film is faithful to the text, but the shot of two lovers rushing towards each other in a wildflower field, heavily overscored with an orchestra rich in violins, resembles those used in perfume ads. Adam and Dinah will wed, as in the novel, and Hetty escapes execution, to be transported to Australia instead, the transportation an invention of the film. Eliot hoped that in our growth from egoism we would suffer and in that suffering we would cultivate sympathy and understanding of the pains of the human condition. It would be an awful result of all our suffering if its only result were "the same self-confident blame, the same light thoughts of human suffering, the same frivolous gossip over blighted lives, the same feeble sense of that Unknown towards which we have sent forth irrepressible cries in our loneliness," she intoned in *Adam Bede* (407). Faithful as it is to a realism of representation, *Masterpiece Theatre* retreats from honest probings of the lonely "Unknown." The film instead cultivates the easy hypocrisy that Eliot condemns, the reveling in a drama of "a blind love, a reckless passion, a careless flirtation, a tragic triangle," as a Mobil ad in the *New York Times* (18 Feb. 1992) puts it, while sustaining the idea that Eliot is a Victorian moralist quick to reward the patient and the pious and to punish the self-indulgent female who would rise above caste and class.

The twenty-third season of *Masterpiece Theatre* in 1993-94 finally brought *Middlemarch* to American audiences in six episodes and brought Eliot an acclaim she had not known since the early 1860s, although now as then for reasons that skirted an honest look at her realism. At one million pounds per episode, it was the most expensive BBC-TV production ever, largely because of the thoroughness of the effort; its location shooting in Stamford, England, which retained enough of the look of the 1830s to make it realistic; and its elaborate props and costumes, which included not simply historically accurate apparel for hundreds but also a steam train and horse-drawn carriages and coaches. To English cultural critic Chris Baldick, the BBC's taking on so serious and weighty a book suggested something more than "the usual tastefully lit crinolines and country houses of literary adaptation" (33); rather, the meaning of the production lies in "the context of attempts by the great institution shaken by high Thatcherism to re-establish their position in national life by the customary means of pageantry and ritual" (34). Such covert meaning is lost on the American audience, which finds its gratifications in the customary high-toned English appeal of *Masterpiece Theatre*.

The film's omissions, as far as characters and incidents of plot are concerned, are few and insignificant, and the only inventions are a few sexual scenes that Victorian conventions would never permit but on which 1990s' television insists. But its chief omission shields American audiences from Eliot's gloomy analysis and foregrounds those nearly Dickensian plot features of the book fit for serial TV. Most audibly absent is the voice of the narrator, which was implicated in reviewers' assessments of the gloomy tone of *Middlemarch*. Professor A. V. Dicey, reviewing *Middlemarch* for the *Nation* (23 & 30 Jan. 1873), was "inclined more than half to curse the day when George Eliot began rather to reflect than to copy" (351). His complaint was echoed in numerous others that detected a growing gloom in the voice of a narrator whose intrusiveness in the earlier books was far less troubling. The book's realism was perfect, according to a reviewer in *Old and New* (Mar. 1873), who was so enamored of the idealized English village that he proposed we could "find that very borough town in England [where] she spent her girlhood and her youth," but he continued, "it's a pity that the story leaves one so sad" (352). A novel should give us "some expression of the hopefulness, of the belief in the existence of something better than what we see," said another reviewer (Perry 439). American readers and magazine essayists did not think the homely world they loved in *Adam Bede* was unconnected to a grand, transcendent one toward which we all could hope to move. Yet it was just that connection which *Middlemarch* seemed to challenge. Reviewing only the first number in its serial publication, a writer in *Appleton's* (Jan. 1872) noted that Eliot's "Prelude," in which she casts Dorothea as a St. Theresa, prefigured that Dorothea was to be a "foundress of nothing" (26) while her less thoughtful sister was to prosper. The "Prelude," which could have been done as a voice-over, perhaps over an opening title sequence, is missing from the film, which permits the narrator's voice to enter only at its conclusion, identified in the credits as "the voice of George Eliot." As a result, Dorothea's frustrated vocation, a damning indictment in 1871, seems a small matter. The BBC *Middlemarch,* which opens with Dr. Lydgate's arrival by coach in Middlemarch and his salute to a steam train ("the future," he says), instead shifts the locus of frustration to Lydgate's troubled marriage and his entanglement in Middlemarch politics and also to the melodramatic Raffles/Bulstrode blackmail plot. The book's pessimistic view of idealism's defeat by the weight of the quotidian is muted by the noisy Dickensian melodrama of Bulstrode's sordid past, his blackmailing by Raffles, and Raffles' suspicious death. In short, the film comes closer than any other to an honest grasp of Eliot's realism in its comprehensiveness, but the absence of the brooding narrator transforms a serious meditation on England's history, women's vocation, and the lofty imponderables into a richly costumed and pleasant panorama of England of yore, which is what viewers turn to *Masterpiece Theatre* to see.

Middlemarch proved successful, if commercialization and press attention are any measure. The United Kingdom was gripped for a time with "Middlemarchmania," as an impressive five and one-half million viewers tuned in weekly and the novel shot to the top of the best seller lists, where it had not been since 1871. In the United States, the WGBH

Educational Foundation, for only the third time, produced an elaborate twenty-four page, full color *Teacher's Guide* that was mailed to educators throughout the country. WGBH also packaged and sold the videotape, and numerous local PBS stations used *Middlemarch* as a fund raiser, offering *Middlemarch* mugs and tee shirts for contributions at a certain level. Random House reissued its edition of the novel. Material from the BBC press kit appeared widely in reviews of the series, and essays about the film, the book, and the author were featured in the *New York Times, New York Review of Books,* and *New Yorker.* Victorianists chatted for months about the production on the electronic newsletter, *VICTORIA,* and an issue of *The George Eliot-George Henry Lewes Newsletter* (Sept. 1994) included a forty-five-page symposium of scholars weighing in on the merits and faults of the film.

Emboldened by the success of *Middlemarch,* the BBC and WGBH brought *The Mill on the Floss* to *Masterpiece Theatre,* which it used to open its season three years later. Though the elegant country house and Constable landscapes meet *Masterpiece Theatre* specifications, the production squeezes the book into a single, two-hour presentation. The most clearly autobiographical of Eliot's books, *The Mill on the Floss* was an exercise in nostalgia, reflected in the leisurely pace of the first half of the book, which develops Maggie's loving relationship with her severe but loving brother Tom. The film races through Maggie's childhood, omitting landmark scenes (Maggie pushing Lucy into the mud, Maggie running away to the Gypsies), important characters (Bob Jakin, one Dodson aunt), and keys to motivation (Maggie's reading Thomas à Kempis) in a fashion uncharacteristic of *Masterpiece Theatre.* These omissions do not distort the book so much as did the 1937 British film production, whose 1930s studio ending had Maggie drown with Philip Waken and Tom marry Lucy. Nevertheless, because screenwriter Hugh Stoddart hurries through the childhood section of the novel, he flees Eliot's sympathetic realist judgment by making possible an easy condemnation of the severity of the Dodsons and of Tom, especially as he represents "Dodsonness." Maggie's childhood seems less joyful. When Maggie and Tom leave Mr. Stelling's after Mr. Tulliver loses his lawsuit, Eliot consciously echoes Milton in a sentence that closed Volume One of the three-volume edition:

They had gone forth into their new life of sorrow, and they would never more see the sunshine undimmed by remembered cares. They had entered the thorny wildness, and the golden gates of their childhood had forever closed behind them. (171)

In the *Masterpiece Theatre* production, little seems Edenic, and all of the humor is missing. The adult Maggie's dilemma, her yearning for a nostalgic return to childhood, would seem puzzling to those unfamiliar with the book were it not that the film rewrites Eliot's realism for our age, casting Maggie as victim in a melodrama. The *New York Times* (10 Oct. 1997) reviewer thought the first half of the film "not the most exciting part" and praised the script because it "cuts through the novel's thicket of philosophy, natural history and sociology" on which "generations of students have gagged" (29). That Eliot voice whose absence the reviewer praises asks us not to condemn anyone in the novel but to "feel" the "oppressive narrowness" of the lives of the Dodsons and Tullivers: "The suffering, whether of martyr or victim, which belongs to every historical advance of mankind, is represented in this way in every town, and by hundreds of obscure hearths" (238-39). This larger vision, as the reviewer's comments make clear, is difficult for *Masterpiece Theatre* to attain.

III

George Eliot's challenge to her readers was more moral than aesthetic, for she was no innovator in narrative technique or design. Rather, she called upon readers to abandon the easy moral judgments of the idealizing story she pilloried in an essay titled "Silly Novels by Lady Novelists." Her realism anchored the reader sometimes uncomfortably in the world of actual moral judgments where there are no heroes and heroines. Absent the transcendent truths provided by both a religious tradition she no longer practiced and an aesthetic tradition that equally falsified, she saw only immanent truths. Her Religion of Humanity was expressed in unrevealed texts urging a sympathetic judgment on all, a judgment her American audience found difficult to achieve, in spite of their being deeply moved by her stories. As a result, they constructed an American Eliot whom they consigned to the great in spite of her growing gloom.

Although no George Eliot novel has been brought to the screen with the same frequency as *Jane Eyre* or *Wuthering Heights* or *The Christmas Story,* the range of her work adapted to film is second perhaps only to Dickens among Victorian novelists. Americans wanted to see Eliot's works on the screen in the early age of film, and after nearly a half-century of decline, they want to again, if only on the less commodious TV screen. But film's origins as lowly entertainment for a mass audience accustomed to melodrama and music hall only augmented the American reluctance to meet her high realist standards. An American Anglophilia, moreover, has further colored perceptions of her work, always insisting that her pastoral landscapes serve as backdrop for pathos, the darker intrusions of the narrative voice notwithstanding. The film medium can tell her stories without her voice; its audience finds film's pictures more valuable than thousands of her words. The result has been that Eliot on the American screen has been the Eliot whom her readers in 1860 always wanted.

Notes

1. According to Mott (307) and Hart (308), both *Adam Bede* and *Silas Marner* were best sellers in the United States.

2. *The Spanish Gypsy,* published in 1868, was a lengthy historical romance done in verse. D. W. Griffith did a one-reel adaptation in 1911 for Biograph.

3. Sweeney and Winston argue that the King film does not completely conform to the pattern of melodrama because it provides Romola a moment in which she challenges the patriarchal order of melodrama.

4. The audience I have called "upper middlebrow" Herbert Gans labels an "upper-middle taste public" whose culture is distributed through "the so-called class media or quality mass media." This group "provides the major audience for public television, network documentaries, and prestigious dramatic television specials" (84). They want content neither too experimental nor too vulgar, each of which characterizes audiences, in Gans's terms, above and below them.

5. "British Films Today and Tomorrow" in *Footnotes to the Film,* ed. Alexander Davy (London: Lovett Dickson, 1938), 167-68.

6. By contrast, LeMahieu argues that the American fascination with television dramatizations of the Edwardian experience from the mid-60s to the mid-80s rests on the audience seeing contemporary problems of class, gender, and nation in the drama of the Edwardian world.

A George Eliot Filmography

1909 *A Fair Exchange* (based on *Silas Marner*)
        Director: D. W. Griffith
        Biograph
        1 reel
        Starring: Mack Sennett

1911 *Silas Marner*
        Director: Theodore Marsten

        The Spanish Gypsy
        Director: D. W. Griffith
        Biograph

1913 *Silas Marner*
      Producer: Thomas Edison
      Director: Charles J. Brabin

1914 *Felix Holt*
      Director: Travers Vale
      Biograph
      2 reel

      Gwendolin (based on *Daniel Deronda*)
      Biograph
      2 reel

1915 *The Mill on the Floss*
      Producer: Mutual/Thanhauser
      Director: W. Eugene Moore
      5 reels
      Starring: Mignon Anderson, George Marlo, Harris Gordon,
          W. Eugene Moore

      Romola
      Producer: Cinès (Italy)

1916 *Silas Marner*
      Producer: Thanhauser
      Director: Ernest C. Warde
      7 reels

1918 *Adam Bede*
      Director: Maurice Elvey
      Starring: Gerald Ames, Ivy Close, Bransby Williams

1920 *Mr. Gilfil's Love Story*
      Director: A. V. Bramble
      5 reels
      Starring: Mary Odette, Henderson Bland, Dora de Winton,
          John Boella

1921 *Daniel Deronda*
      Director: Courtenay Rowden
      Starring: Reginald Fox, Dorothy Fane, Ann Trevor

1922 *Silas Marner*
Producer: Associated Exhibitors
7 reels

Are the Children to Blame? (based on *Silas Marner*)
Producer: Chopin Features
Director: Paul Price
5 reels

1924 *Romola*
Producer: Inspiration Films/MGM
Director: Henry King
12 reels
Starring: Lillian Gish, Dorothy Gish, William H. Powell,
Ronald Colman

1937 *The Mill on the Floss*
Producer: Standard Pictures
Director: Tim Whelan
Starring: James Mason, Geraldine Fitzgerald, Frank Lawton,
Victoria Hopper, Griffith Jones

1985 *Silas Marner*
Producer: Louis Marks; BBC/A & E/WGBH
Director: Giles Foster
Screenplay: Louis Marks and Giles Foster
Starring: Ben Kingsley, Jenny Agutter, Patsy Kensit

1991 *Adam Bede*
Producer: Peter Goodchild; BBC/WGBH
Director: Giles Foster
Screenplay: Maggie Wadey
Starring: Iain Glen, Patsy Kensit, Susannah Harker, James Welby,
Julia McKenzie

1994 *Middlemarch*
Producer: Louis Marks; BBC/WGBH
Director: Anthony Page
Screenplay: Andrew Davies
Starring: Juliet Aubrey, Robert Hardy, Douglas Hodge, Michael
Hordern, Peter Jeffery, Patrick Malahide, Trevyn McDowell,
Rufus Sewell

1994   *A Simple Twist of Fate* (based on *Silas Marner*)
        Director: Gillies MacKinnon
        Screenplay: Steve Martin
        Starring: Steve Martin

1997   *The Mill on the Floss*
        Producer: Brian Eastman; BBC/WGBH
        Director: Graham Theakston
        Screenplay: Hugh Stoddart
        Starring: Emily Watson, James Fain, Ifan Meredith, Bernard Hill

Works Cited

Baldick, Chris. "Central Television." *New Statesman and Society* 7 (14 Jan. 1994): 33-34.

Bourdieu, Pierre. *Distinction: A Social Critique of the Judgement of Taste.* Cambridge, MA: Harvard UP, 1984.

Brennan, Timothy. "Masterpiece Theatre and the Uses of Tradition." *American Media and Mass Culture: Left Perspectives.* Ed. Donald Lazere. Berkeley: U of California P, 1987. 373-83.

Eliot, George. *Adam Bede.* Ed. John Paterson. Boston: Houghton Mifflin, 1968.

——. *The George Eliot Letters.* Ed. Gordon S. Haight. 9 vols. New Haven: Yale UP, 1954-78.

——. *The Mill on the Floss.* Ed. Gordon S. Haight. Boston: Houghton Mifflin, 1961.

——. *Romola.* Everyman's Library. London: Dent, 1968.

Everson, William K. *American Silent Films.* New York: Oxford UP, 1978.

Gans, Herbert J. *Popular Culture and High Culture: An Analysis and Evaluation of Taste.* New York: Basic, 1974.

Gish, Lillian, with Ann Pinchot. *The Movies, Mr. Griffith, and Me.* Englewood Cliffs, NJ: Prentice-Hall, 1969.

Hart, James D. *The Popular Book.* Berkeley: U of California P, 1950.

Hewison, Robert. *The Heritage Industry: Britain in a Climate of Decline.* London: Metheun, 1987.

Hitchens, Christopher. *Blood, Class, and Nostalgia: Anglo-American Ironies.* New York: Farrar, Straus & Giroux, 1990.

James, Henry. Rev. of *Scenes of Clerical Life,* by George Eliot. *Atlantic Monthly* (1858): 890-92.

Jarvik, Laurence. *Masterpiece Theatre and the Politics of Quality.* Lanham, MD: Scarecrow P, 1999.

LeMahieu, D. L. "Imagined Contemporaries: Edwardian Costume Drama." *Historical Journal of Film, Radio and Television* 10 (1990): 243-56.

Levine, George. *The Realistic Imagination: English Fiction from Frankenstein to Lady Chatterley.* Chicago: U of Chicago P, 1981.

MacDonald, Margaret I. " 'The Mill on the Floss.' " *Moving Picture World* 18 Dec. 1915: 2198.

Mott, Frank Luther. *Golden Multitudes: The Story of Best Sellers in the United States.* New York: Macmillan, 1947.

Perry, T. S. Rev. of *Middlemarch. North American Review* 116 (1873): 352-56.

Sweeney, Kevin W. and Elizabeth Winston. "Redirecting Melodrama: Gish, Henry King, and Romola." *Literature/Film Quarterly* 23 (1995): 137-46.

Variety 2 June 1922.

Variety 8 Dec. 1922.

CONTRIBUTORS

Kate Ellis writes poetry and teaches Creative Writing, English Literature, and Women's Studies at Rutgers University. She is the author of *The Contested Castle: Gothic Novels and the Subversion of Domestic Ideology.* Her articles on feminism and film have appeared in *Jump Cut* and in other publications, including *The Classic American Novel and the Movies, American Media and Mass Culture: Left Perspectives,* and *Left Politics and the Literary Profession.*

George Griffith is Professor of English at Chadron State College in Nebraska. He is working on a book on George Eliot and America.

Lin Haire-Sargeant is a novelist, playwright, director, and teacher. Her novel *H.—The Story of Heathcliff's Journey Back to Wuthering Heights,* first published by Simon & Schuster/Pocket Books in 1992, has since been translated into twenty languages and sold worldwide. She is also author of an "Introduction" to the Pocket Books edition of *Wuthering Heights.* Haire-Sargeant is a founding partner of the FireDog Theatre at the Arlington Center for the Arts, which produces new works by area playwrights. She is an Assistant Professor of Literature at the Massachusetts College of Art.

Tom Hoberg is Professor of English at Northeastern Illinois University and acts as Academic Liaison for the Illinois/Indiana Chapter of the Jane Austen Society of North America. He teaches in the areas of Eighteenth and Nineteenth-Century British and American Literature and in Women's Studies. He also has an interest in Arthurian Literature and is a member of the International Arthurian Society.

E. Ann Kaplan is Professor of English at SUNY Stony Brook, where she founded and directs The Humanities Institute. Kaplan has published widely in gender, film/media, and cultural studies as well as in psychoanalysis, postmodernism, and multiculturalism. Her many books include *Women in Film: Both Sides of the Camera; Rocking Around the Clock: Music Television, Postmodernism and Consumer Culture; Motherhood and Representation;* and, most recently, *Looking for the Other: Feminism, Film and the Imperial Gaze.* Her many edited and co-edited collections include *Psychoanalysis and Cinema; Postmodernism and Its Discontents;* and, most recently, *The Politics of Research and Generations: Academic Feminists in Dialogue.* She is currently working on issues to do with aging, trauma, and ethnicity. In addition, a revised and expanded version of *Women in Film Noir* appeared in 1998, and an edited volume of classic essays in feminism and film for Oxford University Press is forthcoming.

Barbara Tepa Lupack, formerly Fulbright Senior Lecturer in American Literature in Poland and in France and Academic Dean at SUNY, has written extensively on American literature, culture, and film. She is author of *Plays of Passion, Games of Chance: Kosinski and His Fiction* and *Insanity in Contemporary American Fiction: Inmates Running the Asylum* and editor of *Take Two: Adapting the Contemporary American Novel to Film* and *Vision/Re-Vision: Adapting Contemporary American Fiction by Women to Film.* Her most recent books include *King Arthur in America* and *Arthurian Literature By Women: An Anthology* (both with Alan Lupack) and *Critical Essays on Jerzy Kosinski.*

Shirley Marchalonis is Professor Emerita of English and Women's Studies at Penn State University and taught at the Berks Campus. She is the author of *The Worlds of Lucy Larcom, 1824-1893* and *College Girls: A Century in Fiction,* and editor of *Patrons and Protégées* and *Critical Essays on Mary Wilkins Freeman.*

Marilyn Roberts is Professor and Chair of English and Fine Arts at Waynesburg College, Pennsylvania. She received her Ph.D. from Columbia University and her M.A. from the University of Newcastle-upon-Tyne. Her publications include articles on drama and on screen adaptations of Shakespeare.

Ronnie Jo Sokol is a special education teacher at Evanston Township High School in Illinois. A life member of the Jane Austen Society of North America (JASNA), she presents slide lectures of her marathon hikes in Jane Austen's footsteps.

Victoria Szabo is Academic Technology Specialist for the Introduction to the Humanities Program at Stanford University. Formerly Instructional Multimedia/Technology Specialist for the Humanities at Grinnell College, she is completing dissertation research on women sensation writers and the Victorian publishing industry; she is interested in the intersections of high art and popular culture as they occur across media and genres.

Martin Tropp is a Professor of English at Babson College in Wellesley, Massachusetts, and the author of two books: *Mary Shelley's Monster: The Story of Frankenstein* and *Images of Fear,* a study of how horror story imagery shaped responses to lived experience from the 1830s to the First World War. He is currently working on a book to help students read and respond in writing to academic texts.